TIBERIUS AND HIS AGE

Tiberius and His Age

MYTH, SEX, LUXURY, AND POWER

EDWARD CHAMPLIN

EDITED BY
ROBERT A. KASTER

PRINCETON UNIVERSITY PRESS
PRINCETON & OXFORD

Published by Princeton University Press
41 William Street, Princeton, New Jersey 08540
99 Banbury Road, Oxford OX2 6JX

press.princeton.edu

Library of Congress Cataloging-in-Publication Data

Names: Champlin, Edward, 1948– author. | Kaster, Robert A., editor.
Title: Tiberius and his age : myth, sex, luxury, and power / Edward Champlin ; edited by Robert A. Kaster.
Description: Princeton ; Oxford : Princeton University Press, [2024] | Includes bibliographical references and index.
Identifiers: LCCN 2023056362 (print) | LCCN 2023056363 (ebook) | ISBN 9780691139241 (hardback) | ISBN 9780691261591 (ebook)
Subjects: LCSH: Tiberius, Emperor of Rome, 42 B.C.-37 A.D. | Emperors—Rome—Biography. | Rome—History—Tiberius, 14–37. | BISAC: HISTORY / Ancient / Rome | BIOGRAPHY & AUTOBIOGRAPHY / Historical
Classification: LCC DG282 .C49 2024 (print) | LCC DG282 (ebook) | DDC 937/.06092—dc23/eng/20240325
LC record available at https://lccn.loc.gov/2023056362
LC ebook record available at https://lccn.loc.gov/2023056363

British Library Cataloging-in-Publication Data is available

Editorial: Rob Tempio and Chloe Coy
Production Editorial: Sara Lerner
Jacket Design: Katie Osborne
Production: Erin Suydam
Publicity: William Pagdatoon
Copyeditor: Lachlan Brooks

Jacket Credit: ZU_09 / iStock

For Linda

CONTENTS

FOREWORD

NOT LONG AFTER HIS landmark *Nero* appeared (Cambridge, MA, 2003), Ted Champlin decided that his next project would have the emperor Tiberius as its focus. In the proposal presented to Princeton University Press late in 2007, he described its general aim in these terms:

> This book is undeniably in some ways a sequel to my *Nero*, in its attempt . . . to understand the familiar, often legendary, actions of its subject by locating them within their cultural context, and in its emphasis on the centrality of myth in Roman life—again, mythic imagery will permeate . . . the entire book.

As the years passed and Ted worked at his subject, seven of the nine chapters in the present book made their way into print, and though the outline of the study that he initially proposed changed in the course of that work, his central aim did not. As he wrote four years ago,

> What makes Tiberius *interesting*? The answer lies in his passion for (and mastery of) subjects like astrology, gastronomy, above all mythology, which, far from being trivial or eccentric, were central to the cultural debates of his day. There is an immense modern bibliography on this cultural context which has gone all but untapped by biographers, not to mention an astonishing variety of lesser-known ancient sources. The tensions and creative interactions between culture, specifically learned culture, and politics, between reclusive scholarship and supreme power, between the passions of Tiberius and his sway over tens of millions of souls, go far to explain not only his baffling personality . . . but also the crucial early development of the public image and attributes of a Roman emperor, . . . the ultimate ancestor of our western concept of an "emperor."

Unhappily, however, as the years passed and Ted worked, his health declined, until it became clear that he would not be able fully to realize the book he had planned. And so, encouraged by Ted and his wife Linda Mahler, and by Rob Tempio, who oversees Ancient World, Philosophy, and Political

Theory for Princeton University Press, I undertook to assemble the writings, published and unpublished, that would approximate his vision.[1]

The first chapter, "Tiberius the Wise," presents a portrait of the Good Emperor to set against the Bad Emperor so familiar from the pages of Tacitus, Suetonius, and Cassius Dio: drawing especially on the "astonishing variety of lesser-known ancient sources" noted just above, the chapter recaptures a Tiberius who assumed, in the popular imagination of his age, the character of a figure—quite literally—from folklore. The next three chapters then shift the focus from folklore to myth. "Tiberius and the Heavenly Twins" treats the public identification of Tiberius and his dead younger brother with the Gemini, Castor and Pollux, a brilliant and complex manipulation of an image that tapped into a reservoir of broad popular support for his family. Moving from public image to self-conception, "The Odyssey of Tiberius Caesar" surveys the evidence for Tiberius' obsession with—his near channeling of—the hero of the *Odyssey*, the great Odysseus, the man of many wiles. Then "The Death of the Phoenix" ranges over solar imagery, fire worship, Zoroastrianism, and the conflagration of the universe to demonstrate that both Tiberius and many of his subjects believed that, somehow, he would be resurrected.

The two chapters that follow—"Sex on Capri" and "Mallonia"—deal with several of the outrages that the emperor allegedly perpetrated in his retreat on Capri and suggest that the tales as they appear in our main historical sources are ultimately the work of a brilliant fantasist who knew and hated Tiberius. These relatively short studies are then followed by three longer portraits of men in Tiberius' orbit: the gourmands Asellius Sabinus and Marcus Apicius—the former also one of the great wits of his age—and the "partner" of Tiberius' labors, Sejanus. Though Sabinus and Apicius appear only briefly in our literary sources, their characters and the places they occupied in the culture of their times are here brilliantly reconstructed from hints, traces, and associations gleaned from a wide array of other sources. And though Sejanus is necessarily prominent in ancient and modern accounts of Tiberius' reign, he emerges here as a more nearly three-dimensional figure than the cutthroat plotter of the Tacitean narrative, a member of the equestrian order perhaps more like Maecenas than most readers have suspected.

Warm thanks are owed to the Press' two referees, Alison Cooley and Carlos Noreña, who not only endorsed the project but understood what Ted was aiming to accomplish; to Werner Eck, for quickly helping me to solve a bibliographical puzzle; to the editors and publishers who gave their permission to include here the essays that originally appeared in their journals; to Rob Tempio and Chloe Coy of Princeton University Press, for their enthusiasm and ever-ready assistance; to Sara Lerner, who oversaw production for the Press, Lachlan Brooks, for her keen copyediting, and Mary Coe, for her rich and lucid index;

to the Magie Fund of Princeton's Department of Classics, for defraying the cost of the indexing; and, above all, to Ted Champlin and Linda Mahler for their encouragement as I began this project and their repeated help along the way. I have edited all the pieces gathered here, the previously published essays more lightly than the unpublished, to eliminate some repetition and to reduce extended quotations of ancient Greek and Latin to the minimum needed, and I have very occasionally added a comment ("Ed. note") in the footnotes. But all the views expressed by Ted, and the arguments through which he advanced them, remain unchanged.

Robert A. Kaster
Kennedy Foundation Professor of Latin, emeritus
Princeton University, October 10, 2023

SUETONIUS' *TIBERIUS* is cited throughout as "Suet.," Tacitus' *Annals* as "Tac.," and Cassius Dio's history as "Dio"; unless otherwise indicated, I use what I take to be the best available English translations of these works, viz.:

Cary, E., trans. 1914–27. *Dio's Roman History*. 9 vols. Cambridge, MA and London.

Hurley, D. W., trans. 2011. *Gaius Suetonius Tranquillus: The Caesars*. Indianapolis, IN.

Woodman, A. J., trans. 2004. *Tacitus: The Annals*. Indianapolis, IN.

Other translations—generally in the Loeb Classical Library—are cited as they are used. The names of other ancient writers and texts are abbreviated according to the conventions used by *OLD* (for Latin), *LSJ* (for Greek), and *OCD* (those not otherwise accounted for, e.g., "Oros."); journal titles are generally abbreviated according to the conventions of *L'Année philologique*.

Other abbreviations used in this book:

AE   *L'année épigraphique: Revue des publications épigraphiques relatives à l'antiquité romaine*. 1888–. Paris.

ATU   H.-J. Uther. 2004. *The Types of International Folktales: A Classification and Bibliography Based on the System of Antti Aarne and Stith Thompson*. FF Communications 284–86. 3 vol. Helsinki.

BGU   Königliche Museen zu Berlin. 1895–. *Aegyptische Urkunden aus den Königlichen Museen zu Berlin*. Berlin.

BNJ   Brill. 2007–. *Brill's Neue Jacoby*. Leiden. (Now accessible as *Jacoby Online*.)

CCAG   Franz Cumont, Franz Boll, et al., eds. 1898–1924. *Catalogus Codicum Astrologorum Graecorum*. 12 vols. Brussels.

CEIPAC   *Centro para el Estudio de la Interdependencia Provincial en la Antigüedad Clásica* (http://ceipac.ub.edu/).

CGL   G. Loewe and G. Goetz, eds. 1888–1923. *Corpus glossariorum Latinorum*. Leipzig.

CIL   *Corpus Inscriptionum Latinarum.* 1862–. 17 vols. Berlin.

EE   Deutsches Archäologisches Institut. 1872–1913. *Ephemeris Epigraphica: Corporis inscriptionum Latinarum supplementum.* 9 vols. Rome and Berlin.

FGE   D. L. Page, ed. 1981. *Further Greek Epigrams.* Cambridge, UK.

FGrH   F. Jacoby, ed. 1923–. *Die Fragmente der griechischen Historiker.* 4 parts. Berlin and Leiden.

Forcellini   E. Forcellini, J. Facciolati, et al. 1896. *Lexicon totius latinitatis J. Facciolati, Aeg. Forcellini et J. Furlanetti seminarii patavini alumnorum cura, opera et studio lucubratum.* Padua.

FPL   E. Courtney, ed. 2003. *The Fragmentary Latin Poets.* 2nd ed. Oxford.

FRHist   T. J. Cornell et al., eds. 2013. *The Fragments of the Roman Historians.* 3 vols. Oxford.

FRP   A. S. Hollis, ed. 2007. *Fragments of Roman Poetry c. 60 BC–AD 20.* Oxford.

I. de Delos   F. Dürrbach et al., eds. 1926–72. *Inscriptions de Délos.* Paris.

IG   *Inscriptiones Graecae.* 1873–. 15 vols. Berlin.

IGI   E. Miranda, ed. 1990–95. *Iscrizioni greche d'Italia.* 2 vols. Naples.

IGRR   R. Cagnat et al., eds. 1901–27. *Inscriptiones Graecae ad res Romanas pertinentes.* 4 vols. Paris.

I. It.   *Inscriptiones Italiae.* 13 vols. Rome 1931–.

IK Ephesos   H. Wankel et al., eds. 1979–. *Die Inschriften von Ephesos.* Inschriften griechischer Städte aus Kleinasien Bd. 11–17. Bonn.

IK Parion   P. Frisch, ed. 1983. *Die Inschriften von Parion.* Inschriften Griechische Städte aus Kleinasien Bd. 25. Bonn.

IK Sestos   J. Krauss, ed. 1980. *Die Inschriften von Sestos und der thrakischen Chersones.* Inschriften griechischer Städte aus Kleinasien Bd. 19. Bonn.

ILCV   E. Diehl, ed. 1925–31. *Inscriptiones Latinae Christianae veteres.* 3 vols. Berlin.

ILMN   I. G. Camodeca, M. Kahlos, and H. Solin, eds. 2000. *Catalogo delle iscrizioni latine del Museo Nazionale di Napoli.* Vol. 1, *Roma e Latium.* Naples.

ILLRP A. Degrassi, ed. 1957–63. *Inscriptiones latinae liberae rei publicae.* 2 vols. Florence.

ILS H. Dessau, ed. 1892–1916. *Inscriptiones Latinae Selectae.* 3 vols. Berlin.

IvO W. Dittenberger and K. Purgold, eds. 1896. *Die Inschriften von Olympia.* Berlin.

Lewis and Short C. T. Lewis and C. Short. 1958. *A Latin Dictionary.* Oxford.

LSJ H. G. Liddell and R. Scott. 1968. *A Greek-English Lexicon.* Revised by H. S. Jones. With a Supplement. Oxford.

LTUR E. M. Steinby, ed. 1993–2000. *Lexicon topographicum urbis Romae.* 6 vols. Rome.

MI Thompson, S. 1955–58. *Motif-Index of Folk-Literature: A Classification of Narrative Elements in Folktales, Ballads, Myths, Fables, Mediaeval Romances, Exempla, Fabliaux, Jest-Books, and Local Legends.* 6 vol. Bloomington, IN.

MRR T. R. S. Broughton. 1951–1986. *Magistrates of the Roman Republic.* Vols. 1–2, New York, 1951; vol. 3 (Supplement), Atlanta, 1986.

OCD S. Hornblower and A. Spawforth, ed. 2012. *Oxford Classical Dictionary.* 4th ed. Oxford.

OLD P. G. W. Glare, ed. 1968–82. *Oxford Latin Dictionary.* Oxford.

Otto A. Otto. 1890. *Die Sprichwörter und sprichwörtlichen Redensarten der Römer.* Leipzig. [Cited by entry-number.]

PIR² E. Groag et al., eds. 1933–. *Prosopographia Imperii Romani saec. I. II. III.* 2nd ed. Berlin.

POxy. B. P. Grenfell, A. S. Hunt., et al., eds. 1898–. *The Oxyrhynchus Papyri.* London.

RE A. F. von Pauly, G. Wissowa, et al, ed. 1894–1963. *Paulys Realencyclopädie der classischen Altertumswissenschaft.* 50 vols. Stuttgart.

RIC C.H.V. Sutherland and R.A.G. Carson, eds. 1984. *The Roman Imperial Coinage.* Vol. 1. Revised ed. London.

RPC A. M. Burnett, M. Amandry, and P. P. Ripollès. 1992–. *Roman Provincial Coinage.* London and Paris.

RTAR *Receuil de Timbres sur Amphores romaines* (https://rtar .univ-amu.fr/rtar/).

SEG   *Supplementum Epigraphicum Graecum*. 1923–. Amsterdam and Leiden.

*SRPF*³   O. Ribbeck, ed. 1897–98. *Scaenicae Romanorum poesis fragmenta*. 2 vols. 3rd ed. Leipzig.

SVF   J. von Arnim, ed. 1903–24. *Stoicorum veterum fragmenta*. 4 vols. Leipzig.

TLL   *Thesaurus Linguae Latinae*. 1900–. Leipzig.

TrGF   B. Snell and R. Kannicht, ed. 1971–2004. *Tragicorum Graecorum Fragmenta*. 5 vols. Göttingen.

PART I

Representation
and Self-Fashioning

1

Tiberius the Wise

THE PARANOIA AND the cruelty of the aged tyrant in his island fortress are stunningly captured in the horrific tale of the fisherman:

> A few days after Tiberius reached Capri, a fisherman found him alone and surprised him with the gift of a large mullet. He was terrified because the man had crept up to him through the rough on the inaccessible back side of the island, and so he ordered the fish scrubbed over his face. When the fisherman was congratulating himself during his punishment because he had not offered the emperor the particularly large crab that he had caught, Tiberius ordered his face lacerated by the crab as well.[1]

Tiberius the Monster. But what kind of monster?

A century later, the emperor Hadrian ("IIis bones be ground to dust!") was on his way to Tiberias in Judaea when he passed an old man planting fig-tree shoots. He mocked him for thus investing in the future, especially when he learned that he was one hundred years old. The man calmly replied that if he was worthy, he would eat the figs; if not, he was working for his children as his ancestors had worked for him. Hadrian told him to let him know if he did eat the figs. In due course the trees produced and the old man set off with a basket of figs to see "the king." Hadrian ordered that he be seated on a chair of gold and that his basket be emptied and filled with denarii, saying to detractors: "His Creator honors him, and shall I not honor him too?" When she heard this, the wife of the old man's neighbor ("a woman of low character") prodded her husband into going with another sack of figs to the palace, in hopes of likewise exchanging them for denarii. But the king ordered this man to stand before the palace gate, where everyone coming in or out was to pelt his face with a fig. When he reproached his wife later that evening, she replied, "Go and tell your mother the gladsome tidings that they were figs and not citrons, or that they were ripe and not hard!"[2]

Some 1,200 years later and much further east, an even more frightening conqueror, Timur (Tamerlane), was preparing to attack the city where dwelt the holy fool, Khoja Nasr-ed-Din Efendi. The Khoja offered himself as ambassador to the emperor and asked his wife which would be the better present to take, figs or quinces. Quinces, she assured him, but, ever dubious of a woman's advice, he filled a basket with figs and hurried off to Timur. Timur had him brought in and ordered his servants to throw the figs at his bald head—and as each one struck him the Khoja called out, "Praised be Allah!" When the emperor asked why, he replied, "I thank Allah that I followed not my wife's advice; for had I, as she counseled me, brought quinces instead of figs, my head must have been broken."[3]

About a hundred years earlier, the tale was told in Italy of a vassal who had brought his lord a basket of figs, knowing that he was fond of them, but unaware that figs were plentiful after a large harvest. Insulted, the lord had his servants strip the man and bind him and throw the figs one after another into his face. When one almost hit him in the eye, he cried out, "May the Lord be praised!" When the signore inquired why, he replied, "Sire, because I had been encouraged to pick peaches instead, and if I had picked them I would be blind by now." Laughing, his lord had him untied and dressed, and rewarded him for the novelty of what he had said.[4]

The tale passed into proverb. The people of Poggibonsi paid an annual tribute of peaches to the court of Tuscany, to be enjoyed by the ladies-in-waiting and the pages. One year, peaches being scarce and expensive, they sent some juicy figs instead. Outraged, the pages dumped the pulpy figs over the ambassadors from Poggibonsi, who recalled, as they ran away, that peaches would have had pits in them, and they cried out, "Luckily they weren't peaches!"[5]

In brief, the story of the fisherman is a dark variant of the comic motif, number J2563, in Stith Thompson's *Motif-Index of Folk Literature* (*MI*), "Thank God they weren't peaches!" Even better, it is a variant not merely of a motif but of a whole tale, number 1689 in Aarne-Thompson-Uther's *The Types of International Folktales* (*ATU*), "Thank God They Weren't Peaches":

> A poor man (fool) plans to bring peaches (beets) to the king (another high-placed person) as a present. His wife persuades him to bring figs (plums, onions) instead. (Because they are not ripe,) the king throws them at the man's head. He is glad (thanks God) that they were not peaches.[6]

ATU lists variants reported in some twenty-two countries, regions, and cultures, spread from Southern and Southeastern Europe through the Near and Middle East, with outliers in North and South America.[7] Obviously details vary considerably, misogynism seems to intrude, and the story may intertwine with others;[8] but the soft fig is ubiquitous and the essential elements are the same: a powerless man presents a powerful one with an edible gift; the powerful man takes offense and punishes the head of the offender with the food itself; whereupon the unfortunate victim unexpectedly gives thanks that the present was not a similar but harder, more damaging edible that he had almost given in its stead. All of which must cast real doubt on the story of Tiberius and the fisherman: it looks as if a hostile source has reached not into history to blacken the princeps, but into folklore. Tiberius the Monster might be a fantasy.[9]

The lens of folklore, if we choose to use it, offers a rather different view of his career. First, some examples wherein his alleged adventures can be seen in a different context:

When the young Tiberius was a student on the island of Rhodes, according to Plutarch's lost biography, a donkey gave off large sparks while it was being groomed, thus predicting his future rule.[10] MI H171, "Animal (object) indicates election of ruler"; particularly, MI H171.3, "Horse indicates election of emperor."

After his accession, "when a funeral was passing by and a jester called aloud to the corpse to let Augustus know that the legacies which he had left to the people were not yet being paid, Tiberius had the man hauled before him, ordered that he be given his due and put to death, and bade him go tell the truth to his father" (Suet. 57.2; cf. Dio 57.14.1, dating the incident to the year 15). A classical scholar rightly drew attention to the similarity between this most unlikely tale and the scene in Book 2 of the Aeneid, where Priam bitterly reproaches the cruel Pyrrhus as no true son of Achilles—Pyrrhus bids Priam go as a messenger to the dead, to tell Achilles of his degenerate son, and kills him.[11] In fact, both are unheroic versions of MI H1252.4, "King sends hero to otherworld to carry message to king's dead father."

Likewise, early in the reign, a slave named Clemens masqueraded as his recently dead master, Agrippa Postumus, the last grandson of Augustus, and stirred up trouble in Italy. Tiberius had him captured by a trick and brought to the Palatine. After torturing him, the princeps asked how he had become Agrippa. Clemens is said to have replied, "The (same) way in which you became Caesar." Tiberius had him executed and the body disposed of (Tac. 2.39–40, cf. Dio 57.16.3–4: all of this supposedly in private). Centuries earlier, when Alexander the Great had asked a prisoner, "Why are you a pirate on the sea?," the man replied, "Why are you a pirate for the whole world?" And, two hundred years after Tiberius, the praetorian prefect Papinian asked the notorious brigand Bulla Felix, "Why did you take to robbing?," only to receive the by-now inevitable, provocative reply, "Why are you prefect?"[12] All three anecdotes are versions of MI U11.2, "He who steals much called king; he who steals little called thief." In each of the three examples here, the notably awkward question is predicated on the answer. In the Tiberian anecdote, we can see how the interchange was grafted onto the supposed interrogation.

Another tale concerns the inventor of unbreakable glass, which appears in various versions. Petronius has him bring it to "Caesar," drop it on purpose, and hammer out the resulting dent. He thinks his fortune is made, but Caesar, after carefully inquiring whether anyone else knows the secret, has the man executed for, if word got out, gold would be worthless. The Elder Pliny was skeptical. "They say" that a method for making glass flexible was invented *Tiberio principe*. Without actually implicating the princeps, he reports that the artisan's workshop was destroyed so as not to devalue copper, silver, and gold, "but the story has for long been more repeated than certain." Much later, Cassius Dio (via Zonaras) relates a quite different version under the year 23. An architect devised a brilliant method for shoring up a large portico that had begun to lean (details are given): his name is unknown because the jealous Tiberius would not let it be entered in the records. The resentful princeps simultaneously rewarded the man and exiled him. The inventor later approached him to beg pardon, purposely dropping a glass cup and miraculously restoring it—for which the princeps had him executed.[13] The tale has been garbled in Dio's transmission, and has surely been influenced by Hadrian's supposedly lethal jealousy of the architect Apollodorus, to weave together two separate stories. It does not appear in *MI* or *ATU* but has been identified as the earliest example of a new motif, "The Impossible Product."[14]

When Tiberius withdrew at the height of power into self-imposed retirement on Rhodes and later on Capri, he allegedly did so in time-honored fashion. Tacitus tells us of Lucilius Longus, "a sharer in all his sadnesses and delights and from among the senators the only companion in his Rhodian withdrawal" (4.15.1), and of the single senator, Cocceius Nerva, learned in the law, and the single knight, Curtius Atticus, who accompanied him to Capri (4.58.1). In fact, however few may have joined him on the initial journeys, he certainly dwelt on those islands surrounded by a large retinue and with many friends and relatives, including senators and equestrians, among his long-term guests.[15] The misleading impression of the single faithful companion following his king into exile reflects not reality but romance, as with *MI* J1634, "To follow the king." Not surprisingly, after naming Nerva and Atticus, Tacitus adds that the rest of his company on Capri "were endowed in liberal studies, mostly Greeks, in whose conversations he might find alleviation": *MI* J146.1, "King prefers educated men as company."

During his final illness, Tiberius suspected that Macro, his praetorian prefect, was currying favor with his likely successor, Gaius Caligula. According to Dio, he commented to Macro, "You do well, indeed, to abandon the setting and hasten to the rising sun." A century and a half later, likewise near death, when a tribune asked him for the watchword, Marcus Aurelius replied to him, "Go to the rising sun, I am already setting." And long before, when the elderly Sulla had opposed the granting of a triumph to the young Pompey, who was not even a senator at the time, Pompey observed to him that more people worship the rising than the setting sun.[16] Although the motif is not to be found in MI, the setting and the rising suns offer a natural metaphor for the passing of power from the old ruler to his young successor, with the focus in all three examples here on the actions and attitudes of their servants and subjects.

And, to return to the fisherman and Tiberius' love of high places, there is the marvelous story of the astrologer and Platonic philosopher Thrasyllus. Our three sources give confusing accounts. According to Tacitus, Tiberius—as he became adept in the art of astrology on Rhodes—would have its practitioners brought to him in his house high on the cliffs, to consult about the future. If he suspected any fraud, he would have a strong freedman throw the offender into the sea on their return journey. Thrasyllus was thus brought to him over the rocks and Tiberius, impressed with the astrologer's knowledge of his future greatness, asked him if he could comment on his own situation. After some calculation, Thrasyllus fell into a panic and cried out that an uncertain and almost final crisis was upon him. Whereupon the princeps embraced him, congratulated him on his knowledge, assured him of his safety, and took him among his most intimate friends.

So Tacitus. Suetonius tells a very different story, placing it just before Tiberius' return from his Rhodian exile. Among different omens of his good fortune, Thrasyllus, one of his learned friends, predicted that the ship coming into view was bringing good news. This at the moment that Tiberius had decided to throw him into the sea, because his prophecies were false and he knew too many secrets. And Dio, in his turn, had both tales. Once in Rhodes, Tiberius was about to push Thrasyllus off the walls, because he was the only one who knew all his thoughts, when he noticed and commented on the astrologer's depressed demeanor, and Thrasyllus replied that he felt some danger loomed over him, whereupon Tiberius valued him even more and spared him. Then, apparently separately, Dio related the story of the ship.[17]

There are significant differences among the three versions, but the bones of the story are clear: in a high place, a seer foresees his own imminent danger at the hands of his master, who spares him at the last moment, impressed by his skill. Although it may not appear so at first glance, this is closely related to MI J2133.8, "Stargazer falls into well," and ATU 1871A, "Star Gazer Falls into Well," and hence is folkloric:

A philosopher (Thales) always looks up in order to observe the stars. He falls into a well. An old woman asks him why he wants to learn about the stars, when he cannot even walk on earth without stumbling.[18]

The missing link here, as A. H. Krappe saw, is the death of Nectanebus in the Alexander Romance (1.14). Nectanebus—magician, astrologer, trickster, and former king of Egypt—was, of course, the real father of Alexander the

Great, unbeknownst to Alexander and his putative father Philip. When the young man asked him about the stars, Nectanebus took him to an out of the way place in the country and showed him the night sky. Alexander led him to a pit and let him fall into it, and when the grievously injured astrologer asked why, Alexander replied: because his teacher concerned himself with the heavens but knew nothing of what happened on earth. Nectanebus exclaimed that no man could avoid his fate: his art had told him that he would be slain by his son, and he explained to the amazed Alexander the complicated tale of how this had come to pass. Grieving, Alexander carried the body back to his mother, and together they raised a great tomb for him. In short, the Nectanebus tale combines the story of the comical Thales, the philosopher so intent on the stars that he falls into a ditch, a wise man unable to see his own fate, and the story of the murderous prince who throws down the astrologer, or means to throw him down, from a height—a wise man who can do nothing to alter his fate, whether he perceives the danger or not.[19] The common elements are the seer who cannot see or cannot avoid his fate, and the danger from falling down while looking up at the stars—which leads us back to Thrasyllus.

Two consistent elements in the stories thus far catch one's attention. First, some of the bad ones, while casting Tiberius in a harsh light, are not intrinsically, or at least in other variants, negative. Where Tiberius is cruel and suspicious, Hadrian recognizes his error and rewards the old man, or the lord laughs and rewards his vassal—and in general, pelting with squashy figs is intended to be comical and humiliating, not lethal. Where Tiberius is merely jealous of the craftsman he executes, the prudent "Caesar" acts in statesman-like manner to save the economy of his empire from collapse. And while Tiberius at first doubts the prophecies of Thrasyllus and fears his knowledge, he comes to recognize his abilities. Indeed, the story of the paranoid princeps has a happy ending: on an objective reading, it would have been dangerous for a wise monarch to let a real seer live, and it is a tribute to his learning and perspicacity that the princeps who preferred to converse with other men of learning saw through charlatans and recognized the genuine article. It is well enough established that one at least of our lost sources, behind Tacitus, Suetonius, and Dio, was violently hostile to Tiberius: we might suspect that the dark cast of stories, which are in other contexts more positive or at least neutral, can be attributed to someone who did not like the princeps, and in some cases they have obviously been tacked on to Tiberian anecdotes.

Second, these tales are all concerned with power, its use, and its abuse: the lord's overhasty reaction to the underling's gift; the omen of future rule; the similarity between rule and banditry; the role of the companions of the king in exile and in daily conversation; above all, the removal of danger through summary violence (the public critic, the pretender to the throne, the thoughtless craftsman, the wise man who knows too many secrets); and the passing of the torch to a successor. Tales of power gravitate naturally to a princeps: the cumulative effect of these monarchical stereotypes must be to cast doubt on the historical truth of any single item.

Three extraordinary stories should be added to this account, anecdotes told of Tiberius Caesar that raise him far above any stereotype. Each one is marvelous; taken together, they make him a figure unique in ancient folklore. *Assem para et accipe auream fabulam, fabulas immo*, as the storyteller says: give me a penny and you will hear a golden tale, or rather tales.

First, there is the haunting story told by Plutarch, in his essay on the decline of oracles. It was related to him by a historian named Philippus, who had in turn heard it from an eyewitness:

> The father of Aemilianus the orator, to whom some of you have listened, was Epitherses, who lived in our town and was my teacher in grammar. He said that once upon a time in making a voyage to Italy he embarked on a ship carrying freight and many passengers. It was already evening when, near the Echinades Islands, the wind dropped, and the ship drifted near Paxi. Almost everybody was awake, and a good many had not finished their after-dinner wine. Suddenly from the island of Paxi was heard the voice of someone loudly calling Thamus, so that all were amazed. Thamus was an Egyptian pilot, not known by name to even many on board. Twice he was called and made no reply, but the third time he answered; and the caller, raising his voice, said, "When you come opposite Palodes, announce that Great Pan is dead." On hearing this, all, said Epitherses, were astounded, and reasoned among themselves whether it were better to carry out the order or to refuse to meddle and let the matter go. Under the circumstances Thamus made up his mind that if there should be a breeze, he would sail past and keep quiet, but with no wind and a smooth sea about the place he would announce what he had heard. So when he came opposite Palodes, and there was neither wind nor wave, Thamus from the stern, looking toward the land, said the words as he had heard them: "Great Pan is dead." Even before he had finished there was a great cry of lamentation, not of one person, but of many, mingled with exclamations of amazement.

The proximity in time of the death of the god Pan to the death of Jesus excited comment in later antiquity, but its significance here lies in the immediate sequel:

As many persons were on the vessel, the story was soon spread abroad in Rome, and Thamus was sent for by Tiberius Caesar. Tiberius became so convinced of the truth of the story that he caused an enquiry and investigation to be made about Pan; and the scholars [*philologoi*], who were numerous at his court, conjectured that he was the son born of Hermes and Penelope.[20]

Plutarch reports the story with a wealth of circumstantial detail and on the basis of irrefutable eyewitness evidence: a character in one of his dialogues reports having heard it from a man who happened to be sailing with Thamus. Nevertheless, the uncanny tale of the wanderer who is ordered by a (supernatural) voice to announce that a superhuman figure has died, and who is then greeted by loud (supernatural) mourning when he does so, is undeniably folkloric, and often vouched for by what folklorists call a FOAF, the Friend of a Friend. Plutarch's tale, beautifully told, is a version of *MI* F442.1, "Mysterious voice announces death of Pan" (cf. B342, "Cat leaves house when report is made of death of one of his companions"), and indeed one version of a folktale type in itself, *ATU* 113A, "Pan is Dead":

A man (dwarf) hears a voice (of a cat) that tells him to announce that a third figure (the god Pan, the king of the cats) is dead. The man does not recognize either the voice or the name of the dead person. When he comes home he tells what happened. When the maid (cat) hears this, she says she has to leave (is now king of the cats), goes away, and never comes back.[21]

The arresting aspect of Plutarch's account is not that a folk motif or tale is applied to Tiberius, but rather that it is a tale told to Tiberius. A supernatural mystery is presented to the princeps, who turns to his wise men for a rational explanation. It is a curiously liminal situation, as if a flesh-and-blood American president were one day confronted with strong evidence that a folk belief turned out to be real—the return of Elvis Presley, for instance. Why the tale should attach itself to the passionately intellectual Tiberius is worth considering. For a start, his obsession with mythology was notorious, and marvels were reported to him (as they were to other rulers): an embassy from Olispo recounted that a triton had been seen in a nearby cave and was heard to play on a conch shell; various monsters, *beluae*, and many Nereids turned up on the coast of the Santones; and the enormous tooth, over a foot long, from the skeleton of a giant hero was brought to the princeps for measurement after an earthquake.[22]

———

Here is the second tale. In his *Jewish Antiquities*, Josephus discussed Tiberius' legendary procrastination in receiving embassies, replacing governors, and conducting trials. When the princeps' friends questioned his slowness, he replied, in the matter of governors, that those who stayed in their provinces for short terms worked hard at extortion from the provincials, but those who remained for a long time grew sated with their profits:

> He told them this fable by way of illustration. Once a man lay wounded, and a swarm of flies hovered about his wounds. A passer-by took pity on his evil plight and, in the belief that he did not raise a hand because he could not, was about to step up and shoo them off. The wounded man, however, begged him to think no more of doing anything about it. At this the man spoke up and asked him why he was not interested in escaping from his wretched condition. "Why," said he, "you would put me in a worse position if you drove them off. For since these flies have already had their fill of blood, they no longer feel such a pressing need to annoy me but are in some measure slack. But if others were to come with a fresh appetite, they would take over my now weakened body and that would be the death of me." He too, he said, for the same reason took the precaution of not dispatching governors continually to the subject-peoples who had been brought to ruin by so many thieves; for the governors would harry them utterly like flies.[23]

The fable told by Tiberius is a classic version of *MI* J215, "Present evil preferred to change for worse," and specifically of J215.1, "Don't drive away the flies." As a tale, it is one of three different forms taken by *ATU* 910L, "Do Not Drive the Insects Away":

> A sick (injured) man covered with sores is bothered by flies. He refuses any help, saying that hungry flies bite twice as hard as full ones.

Another of the three main versions is assigned to Aesop in Aristotle's *Rhetoric* (2.20), and later variants appear across Southern and Central Europe, from Portugal to Bulgaria. But the real Tiberius is not the fictional Aesop. An exhaustive survey of "Fables in Ancient Historiography" produced a striking observation: all known fables related by ancient historians are embedded by them in speeches from a leader to his people or to his friends, usually to dissuade them from a foolish course of action by pointing out the inevitable consequences that only he is wise enough to foresee.[24] The overwhelming majority of these wise leaders are Greeks: Aesopean fables were traditionally the refuge of the downtrodden, often slaves, allowing them to say things they couldn't say openly. But, however such foreigners might act, fables weren't quite the thing for a proud Roman nobleman—the only other secure historical example is a chilling tale attributed to Sulla (App. *BC* 1.101), the blood-drenched dictator of the old Republic, a patrician like Tiberius, who shared several of his cultural interests. Why the princeps Tiberius should relate an Aesopean fable is a question worth considering.

Tiberius the good governor joins Tiberius the curious intellectual as a figure of folkloric interest. A remarkable cluster of popular proverbs about government adheres to him. Soon after taking over sole rule, he told his friends that the empire was a monster, and so beset was he by dangers that he often, we are told, repeated the old maxim that he had a wolf by the ears.[25] (The problem is that you don't know whether to hold on or to let go.) On another famous occasion, when his governors wanted to load the provinces with new taxes, the wise princeps, again the people's champion, famously wrote back to them, in the words of another beloved proverb, that it was the job of a good shepherd to shear his flock, not skin it.[26] As chance would have it, the imperial shepherd had learned about the rapacity of lupine governors from an astute barbarian who had surrendered to him some years before. He asked why the man's newly conquered people had rebelled and fought against the Romans for so long, and the barbarian replied, recalling yet another old proverb, "You Romans are to blame for this; for you send as guardians of your flocks, not dogs or shepherds, but wolves."[27] Sometimes people criticized his actions, not realizing that they were for the common good. To these he replied mildly with another proverb, taken from the most famous half-line in Latin popular drama, *oderint dum metuant*, "Let them hate me so long as they fear me." The melodramatic words of a stage tyrant he cleverly molded into a virtuous new form: *oderint dum probent*, something like: "Let them hate me so long as they approve of my deeds."[28]

———

This is the third golden tale:

> Once Tiberius Caesar on his way to Naples had reached his country seat at Misenum, which, built on the summit of a mountain by the hand of Lucullus, commands a view of the Sicilian sea in front and the Tuscan sea behind. Here one of the high-girt flunkeys, whose shirt of Egyptian linen was drawn smoothly down from his shoulders and embellished with hanging fringes, began, while his master was strolling through the cheerful shrubbery, to sprinkle the scorching earth with a wooden watering-pot, making a display of his function as an attendant upon the emperor; but he was laughed at. Thereafter, by detours well known to himself, he runs ahead into another promenade and proceeds to lay the dust there. Caesar recognizes the fellow and realizes what he is after. "Hey, you!," says the master. Whereupon the fellow, as you might know, bounces up to him, propelled by the thrill of a

sure reward. Then in jesting mood his mighty majesty, the *princeps*, thus spoke: "You haven't done much, and your efforts are labour lost; manumission with me stands at a much higher price."[29]

So Phaedrus in the fifth fable of his second book, with a promythium more pointed than usual: this is a "true story," *vera fabella*, intended to correct the behavior of the flocks of busybodies, *ardaliones*, at Rome. But *vera fabella* is ambiguous: it is also a "true fable," that is, "truly a fable," and it is also *MI* J554, "Intemperance in service." But the point here is that Tiberius is for the third time to be discovered in a highly unusual, if not quite unique, situation: not just that a folkloric theme is applied to him and presented as if it were history, but that soon after his death he has passed over into folklore and become explicitly the subject of a fable, an honor accorded to very few historical figures.[30]

Common to these three extraordinary tales is the striking quality of liminality noticed in the first: in each, Tiberius Caesar is poised between the world of popular belief and the world of historical action, investigating the death of a minor deity, explaining his policy by means of a proverbial fable, rebuking an obnoxious servant within a fable. What binds them together is the supreme virtue of wisdom, or at least shrewdness, and it is not just wisdom in daily life, but precisely that statesmanlike wisdom in the public service that we have already seen in the tale of unbreakable glass and, perhaps, the testing of Thrasyllus: Caesar consults with his wise men to reassure the people on a matter of religion, he explains to his less perceptive friends why he acts in the public interest by prolonging governors, he curbs the antics of a servant in the imperial household. Tiberius the tyrant is a familiar figure from the histories of the period—we are told that when news of his death reached Rome, some ran around crying out, "Tiberius to the Tiber"—but we can now see that the "people" may have enjoyed another quite different image as well: an image of Tiberius the wise king.

———

There is a Bad Tiberius and a Good Tiberius. Tiberius the Monster is all too familiar. Notorious for the cruel persecution and the murders of his nearest kin; notorious for lethal assaults on the aristocracy through the revival of the treason law and the machinations of Sejanus, the all-powerful prefect of his praetorian guard; notorious for the bloodbath after the fall of Sejanus in 31 CE: he was perhaps most infamous for his escape from Rome during the last eleven years of his life, to his massive cliff-top palace on the island of Capri, the so-called Villa of Ino[31] with its sheer drop of one thousand feet to the sea, there to live out his old age in a wild fantasy of scholarship, sadism, and sex. Tiberius is not an attractive figure. This is thanks above all to the attacks of the three Furies of early imperial historiography: Tacitus, Suetonius, and Cassius Dio. In their indelible portrait of the second princeps, he will forever be for us the old monster who hounds to death family, friends, and enemies alike: cold, proud, bitter, gloomy, secretive, duplicitous, savage, depraved.

And yet no modern historian would accept this picture. At a glance, we can see that Suetonius is at his worst in his biography of Tiberius, constantly contradicting himself and repeatedly misunderstanding his sources, whether intentionally or inadvertently; while Tacitus is at his most ambivalent, portraying a man at once noble and vicious, simple and devious. The crucial question is: what were the sources on which Tacitus, Suetonius, and Dio depend? There is staggeringly little evidence, and the nature of these lost sources has been hotly debated, with no conclusion in sight. This is not the place to go into the matter, so let me state a central hypothesis here, leaving discussion for elsewhere. As Eduard Schwartz saw over a century ago, chief among the now lost writers was "an unknown annalist of great talent, probably writing soon after Tiberius' death."[32] This man was extremely well informed about the principate of Tiberius, which he obviously experienced firsthand. I believe that he knew Tiberius well and disliked him intensely.

More specifically, he was intimately familiar with Tiberius' complex character and with his tastes in literature, mythology, and popular culture—in fact, he was rather like Tiberius—and he was able brilliantly to distort and even to fabricate evidence to paint the portrait of a monstrous human being.[33]

As a popular modern biographer of the second princeps asserted long ago, vividly but not inaccurately:

> he has always been, and he remains, the greatest psychological problem in history. He is Hamlet and Lear and Othello rolled into one; and he is more than this. We have a mass of evidence about Tiberius that for nearly nineteen hundred years baffled any attempt to understand him. We can easily construct two men out of the material, both of which are perfectly credible. . . . [34]

This schizophrenia is easily visible in any of our three main sources, and quite understandable. We know that they had access to at least two annalistic histories written within a generation of Tiberius' death, not to mention minor commentaries (including the memoirs of the younger Agrippina, who had good reason to abhor her great-uncle), the *acta senatus* (a major source, as Syme argued, for Tacitus), and even (for Suetonius and Tacitus) the memories of old men. Not all of these were necessarily inimical. But there is also something else, quite different from them. Consider the following three items:

First, our surviving sources offer a cluster of standard charges against the second princeps. According to Suetonius' catalog of Tiberian vices, the floodgates of *maiestas* charges were opened by the denunciation of a man (unnamed) for removing the head of Augustus from a statue and substituting another (unidentified): the senate heard the case, witnesses were examined under torture, and the defendant was condemned. Thereafter it became a capital crime to beat a slave or even to change one's clothes (!) near a statue of Augustus, to carry a ring or a coin with his image on it into a latrine or a brothel, or to express an adverse opinion about any word or deed of his—indeed, a man died for having an honor decreed him by his *colonia* on a day honors had been decreed to Augustus. Thus Suetonius, not in control of his absurd material; in fact, according to Tacitus' fuller and much clearer account, the case of the substituted head (Tiberius for Augustus) actually resulted in the *acquittal* of the defendant (Granius Marcellus) on the charge of *maiestas*.[35] The supposed pollution caused by the contact of a ring or coin bearing the *princeps'* image with latrine or brothel finds an echo in what appears to be a fragment of Dio, to the effect that a noble ex-consul lost his life and his fortune for carrying a coin with the princeps' image on it into a latrine. Tiberius the stage tyrant is made to explain, ploddingly, "With my coin in your bosom you turned aside into foul and noisome places and relieved your bowels" (Dio 68 fr. 2). Again, this appears to be free embroidery of the truth. According to Seneca, an informer had observed a senator reaching for a chamber pot at dinner while wearing a ring with the image of Tiberius Caesar. The informer called on their fellow diners to note that it had been brought near to his private parts and was, as it were, already preparing the accusation, when a quick-thinking slave showed that the ring was on his own hand—he had removed it from his drunken master (*Ben.* 3.26.1–2).

So: an atmosphere of paranoia and persecution. No one today would believe the nonsense retailed by Suetonius and Dio (Tacitus corrects the headless statue story, and Seneca makes no claim that his ring anecdote is representative of any law); the legal basis of the charges is nonexistent; and, most importantly, another tale offers a markedly alternate view of one of the allegations. It was said that, in his travels, the sage Apollonius of Tyana once arrived at the city of Aspendus in Pamphylia in the middle of a famine, which had been caused by powerful men hoarding grain for export. The people blamed their magistrate and wanted to burn him alive, but they held back, giving time for Apollonius to arrive and save the situation. The mob had hesitated because the magistrate clung to statues of the emperor, and images of Tiberius were even more feared and inviolable than the great statue of Zeus at Olympia. It was even said, Philostratus continues in his biography of Apollonius, that a man was held guilty of treason simply for striking his own slave when the slave was carrying a silver drachma with the princeps' image on it.[36] That is, a Greek novel of the third century preserves an echo of the same fanciful tales but, as often in the folkloric versions of charges leveled against Tiberius, the view of him is *positive*. As a protector of the persecuted high and low, the godlike *princeps* was unmatched, for not only did his great statues provide sanctuary surer than that of Zeus himself, his smallest image on a coin was not an instrument for oppression but a talisman against it.

Second, there are the stunning judgments of Tiberius offered within ten or fifteen years of his death by a man who had little reason to love him:

> He held sway over land and sea for twenty-three years without allowing any spark of war to smoulder in Greek or barbarian lands, and he gave peace and the blessings of peace to the end of his life with ungrudging bounty of hand and heart. Was he inferior on birth [to Gaius Caligula]? No, he was of the noblest ancestry on both sides. Was he inferior in education? Who among those who reached the height of their powers in his time surpassed him in wisdom or learning? Was he inferior in age? What other king enjoyed a happier old age? Why, even when still young he was called "the elder" because of his diffidence about quick-wittedness.

and

> Tiberius detested childish jokes; he had been inclined to seriousness and austerity since childhood.

and

> Tiberius was a man of profound common-sense and the cleverest of all his contemporaries at knowing a person's secret intentions, and he surpassed them as much in sagacity as in rank.[37]

This admiration comes from Philo of Alexandria, a scholar whose estimate of another man's learning is not to be taken lightly. It has been asserted that Philo writes like this to make the contrast with Caligula, but there was nothing to be gained by it, and he could just as easily have condemned Tiberius for paving the way for his successor. More to the point: how could he possibly have published this sort of panegyric so soon after the death of Tiberius if it were patently absurd?

And third, there is the arresting glimpse of Tiberius in, of all places, the *Apology* of the pugnacious Christian polemicist, Tertullian (5.2):

> It was in the age of Tiberius, then, that the Christian name went out into the world, and he referred to the Senate the news which he had received from Syria Palestine, which had revealed the truth of his [Christ's] divinity;

he did this exercising his prerogative in giving it his endorsement. The Senate had not approved beforehand and rejected it. Caesar held to his opinion and threatened danger to accusers of Christians.

Again, the context is one of piety.

The stories of Philostratus and Tertullian, and the opinions of Philo, join the golden tales passed on by Plutarch, Josephus, and Phaedrus. All six authors record material not found elsewhere, and all but Josephus stand outside the historiographical tradition (Philo and Phaedrus were contemporaries of Tiberius, Josephus and Plutarch born soon after his death). What their vignettes combine to offer us is a consistent sketch of a good monarch, marked by his now familiar twin virtues, wisdom and piety. Along with his learning, Philo praises his wisdom, his commonsense and, twice, his shrewdness, the ability to see farther than others into affairs and the hearts of men, and to act appropriately: this accords with what we have already seen, his ability to distinguish true men of learning from false, to see the virtue in retaining governors (all were bad shepherds, as he well knew, but the older ones were less harmful), to discern the fatal effects of a marvelous new invention, to find the rational (and comforting) explanation for the death of a deity, to see through the falseness of a servant. And allied with this vision is a religious authority, reflected in his judgment of Pan, or the power of his statues greater than that of Zeus' image at Olympia.

Tiberius' interest and skill in religious matters is well attested in our mainstream sources, but it is the outsiders who bear powerful witness to the princeps' piety. Just as Tertullian offers us the protector of the Christians against the senate, so Philo offers us the protector of the Jews against his own governor, Pontius Pilate (*Leg.* 304–5): when Pilate set up gilded shields in Herod's palace and the Jews sent a complaint to Rome,

> what words, what threats Tiberius uttered against Pilate when he read it! It would be superfluous to describe his anger, although he was not easily moved to anger, since his reaction speaks for itself. For immediately, without even waiting until the next day, he wrote to Pilate, reproaching and rebuking him a thousand times for his new-fangled audacity and telling him to remove the shields at once.

And perhaps most revealing of this imperial piety is the story of the giant's bones in yet another historiographical outsider, Phlegon. An embassy brought Tiberius an enormous tooth and offered to deliver the rest of the bones. Wishing to know the size of the dead hero but feeling it a sacrilege (*anosia*) to disturb the body, he had a geometor estimate the size of the body from the tooth, and then sent the tooth back. A brilliant example of the combination of punctilious piety and extraordinary shrewdness that is so Tiberian, signalled by a typical consultation of his wise men by the learned princeps on an intellectual problem with political consequences: "He summoned a certain geometor, Pulcher by name, a man of some renown whom he respected for the man's skill."[38]

Imperial wisdom and imperial piety are not mere abstract attributes but potent weapons for the public good. They make Tiberius the champion of the people against oppression by his own governors (repeatedly), by the senate, and by private citizens. This is not to say that the historical Tiberius was or was not a good princeps—although there is indeed a great deal of evidence in the mainstream tradition to show his public concern for good government and the *pax deorum*, his modesty and restraint, above all his *providentia* for the empire (a major slogan), his constant vigilance.[39] Good man or bad, there was a potent *image* of him, all but forgotten now, as the good old ruler, wise and clever, pious and just, an image rooted in folklore, fable, and anecdote. Strange as it may seem, no Roman emperor comes near to matching him.

———

There is a curious balance between the beginning of Tiberius' sole rule and its end, as they are presented by Suetonius. For two years after taking over the empire, the princeps did not set foot outside the gates of the city (*pedem porta non extulit*); thereafter he went no further than the neighboring towns (*propinqua oppida*), and then but rarely and for a few days only. However, after the deaths of his sons Germanicus and Drusus (in 19 CE and 23 CE, respectively), he sought retirement in Campania, and he never returned to Rome for the rest of his life, although twice he came very near.[40] The years of not leaving are strikingly true: we can place the princeps outside the city only twice in his first twelve years, once in 16 CE with the dedication of suburban temples in the *Horti Caesaris* and at Bovillae (that is, just around the end of the two-years-within-the-gates period), and once in 21 CE with a long visit to Campania, allegedly in contemplation of retiring there.[41] But his not returning for his last eleven years is strikingly untrue, or rather deeply misleading. Indeed, Tacitus writes of a princeps not secluded on Capri but spending "his extreme old age nearby [Rome] in the countryside or on the shore, often encamping at the walls of the City" (under the year 26), "on frequent detours encircling and dodging his fatherland" (under 33), while we know that Tiberius came up to the very outskirts of the city not merely twice, as Suetonius would have it, but in each of his last six years, after the fall of Sejanus.[42] That is to say, the reign has been neatly bifurcated between "Rome only" for its first half and "not Rome" for its second: the former somewhat, the latter considerably exaggerated for effect, by Suetonius or (more likely) his source. And in each half, Tiberius, we are told, acquired an appropriate nickname.

In his account of the princeps' time in Rome, before the account of his final departure to Campania with which it is balanced, Suetonius describes Tiberius' repeated and elaborate preparations for a visit to the provinces and the armies, various logistics arranged, vows undertaken for his safe return. Eventually, people joked about the matter, calling him Callipides, who was known (as the biographer glosses helpfully) from the Greek proverb, for his running and not getting even a foot forward.[43] Who Callipus (the proper form) may have been is unknown, but the original image has survived elsewhere, and it is referred to by Cicero in a letter to Atticus.[44] The point here is that the new princeps Tiberius was compared to a proverbial figure, bringing him again into the realm of folklore, and it should be noted that the nickname, while mocking, is not necessarily unfavorable; indeed, it might be affectionate.

Which brings us back to Capri and the fictitious fisherman in the latter half of Tiberius' reign. Unregarded by classicists, it has long been clear that the anecdote was an exceedingly hostile version of a standard and humorous folk tale about figs, known from very widespread (if later) sources elsewhere. The raw material for this attack can be found in two places.

First, the fish. Had the fisherman been literate and familiar with the *acta diurna* published in the capital, he might have known better than to present a *grandis mullus* to this particular princeps. For some years earlier, a *mullus ingentis formae* had been sent to Tiberius Caesar, who ordered it to be sold at the market (in Rome). "Unless I am mistaken, friends," he said, "either Apicius or P. Octavius will buy it." And sure enough, one of the two epicures, Octavius, bought the four-and-a-half-pound mullet for five thousand sesterces.[45] That is to say, the horrific fisherman story at Capri is surely a doublet—princeps rejects large mullet—inspired by an incident set at Rome, real or fictitious. It is a hostile counterpart to a tale that actually presented Tiberius in favorable fashion as shrewd, witty, and moderate.

At the same time, the creator of the Tiberian fisherman has been inspired by one of the best-known folktales in the world, *ATU* 736A, "The Ring of Polycrates":

> When King Amasis learns about the military success of Polycrates he advises him not to provoke the jealousy of the gods. As sign of his humility he should throw away the thing he likes most. Thereupon Polycrates throws his most precious ring into the sea. Some days later a fish is given to him in which the ring is found.

Of the many accounts and references in ancient authors, Herodotus offers the classic version.[46] A few days after Polycrates, the tyrant of Samos, had solemnly thrown his ring into the sea, a fisherman caught an enormous fish and decided to present it to him. On being granted an audience, the fisherman explained that he had decided not to sell such a treasure in the market but to bring it as gift truly worthy of Polycrates and his rule. Pleased as much with the compliment as with the gift, Polycrates invited the man to dine with him. It was while preparing the fish that the cooks found the ring in its stomach. Realizing that Polycrates is doomed, Amasis, the king of Egypt, renounces his friendship so as not to be saddened by his imminent end. What has this to do with Tiberius?

Again, the creator of the horrific story of Tiberius and the fisherman has given us an adaptation of another tale, but here he cleverly inverts it. In both, a fisherman honors his ruler with a fish of marvelous size. Polycrates accepts it with pleasure and grace, and disaster ensues for him, in the form of crucifixion by a treacherous Persian satrap. But Tiberius rejects the fish with fear and brutality, and disaster follows not for him but for the donor. The moral of the story is that Tiberius died in full possession of his power, a luckier and a wiser Polycrates who had outwitted fate to the end.

It would not be surprising if this comparison with a figure of legend occurred to the contemporaries of Tiberius, friends or foes. Like Polycrates, Tiberius was a conqueror in war and a patron of the arts who surrounded himself with the leading Greek intellectuals, and he was rumored to be a monster of vice. Like Polycrates, "tyrant of the islands and the shores," Tiberius had a notorious penchant for islands, basing himself for seven years on Rhodes and eleven on Capri, earning in his last years a new nickname: he was now *nesiarchos*, Lord of the Island.[47] And as it happens, he actually *had* the ring of Polycrates. But the princeps of Rome had learned from the fabled unhappy end of the tyrant of Samos. He kept the ring safe and not much valued in the Temple of Concord, which he had vowed in 7 BCE to restore, and which he had long ago dedicated in his own name and that of his dead brother Drusus, on January 16, 10 CE.[48] This retention and neutralizing of the ring of fate irresistibly recalls the last scene in *Raiders of the Lost Ark*. In the realm of folklore, Tiberius was, indeed, *sagacissimus senex*, an extremely shrewd old man.[49]

2

Tiberius and the Heavenly Twins

IN MARCH OF THE YEAR 37, old, ill, and alarmed by a portent, Tiberius
Caesar moved south from Rome to the Bay of Naples. Eager though he was to
return to his refuge on Capri, declining health and foul weather detained him
at his villa at Misenum. "A few days before he died," says Suetonius, "the tower
of the Pharus collapsed in an earthquake on Capri."[1] From his bedroom at
Misenum, the dying princeps could surely see the great lighthouse far across
the bay, on the eastern heights of the island. Was he aware that its flame
had been extinguished? That may have signalled the end of a story that he had
begun to write forty-five years before, at the death of his beloved brother.

The story was inspired by two men who became gods, Castor and Pollux.
Originally Kastor and Polydeukes, the immensely popular twins of Greek
myth were also commonly known as the Dioskouroi, Zeus' boys, or the Tyn-
daridai, the sons of their earthly father Tyndaros. The reports of their parentage and birth are complex and contradictory.[2] In some strands, they and their
sister, Helen of Troy, were all three the children of Leda and Tyndaros, the
King of Sparta; in others, they were the offspring of Leda and Zeus, who had
visited the queen in the form of a swan, and they may or may not have been
hatched from an egg or eggs. But, most importantly, at some point, it became
established that Polydeukes was, or was potentially, immortal, while Kastor
was born to die: possibly because they had different fathers, Zeus and Tyndaros. Each brother had a special talent recognized as early as Homer, for in the
Iliad their sister Helen calls them Kastor, breaker of horses, and the strong
boxer, Polydeukes (Il. 3.237). The twins were renowned as heroes in two great
expeditions, the Calydonian boar hunt and the voyage of the Argo, as well as
in a few adventures of their own, but they are best remembered for what happened after their death. Kastor was cut down in a brawl. As he lay dying, Polydeukes prayed to Zeus that he be allowed to die with his brother. Zeus offered
him a choice: either to live forever himself with the gods on Olympus, or to
share Kastor's fate, alternating with him one day under the earth and one day
on Olympus. Polydeukes chose the latter. How this alternation was effected is

a matter of ancient debate, essentially over whether the brothers were together in each place for a day or actually exchanged places with each other. But invariably, in literature and in history, they appear after death as divinities together, and they represent the very incarnation of brotherly love.

Polydeukes' choice was decisive. Early on, the brothers became the savior gods, *soteres*, the averters of evil, *alexikakoi*. Like Herakles, these divinized mortals were great helpers of their fellow man, with two areas of special concern. They were famed as the protectors of sailors especially, and of all travelers by sea: in one version of their story, Zeus placed them among the stars as the Gemini, the heavenly twins, and Poseidon rewarded their brotherly love with command of the winds, whereby they became the saviors of shipwrecked mariners. They also developed an inclination to appear and bring or announce victory in battle, the most famous instance in Greek history being the Spartan defeat of Athens at the sea battle of Aegospotami in 405 BCE. On that occasion, they materialized as two stars, but normally by land you could recognize them by a handful of particular human attributes: they turned up at critical moments as a pair of beautiful young men mounted on white horses, bearing spears in their hands and wearing on their heads the distinctive *pilleus*, the half-egg-shaped hat or helmet, often crowned by a star.

Their cult spread from Sparta throughout Greece, and eventually to Sicily and Southern Italy in the west, from where it early established itself in Latium around Rome. Some fifty years ago, a bronze tablet was excavated at a temple in the territory of Lavinium that bore the dedication in archaic Latin: *Castorei Podlouqueique qurois*, "to Castor and Pollux, the kuroi."[3] The dating of the tablet to the late sixth century BCE accords marvelously with the dramatic entrance of the Dioscuri into Roman history, at the Battle of Lake Regillus, traditionally assigned to 499 or 496 BCE. According to the common version of this story, at the height of a battle between the Romans and their Latin neighbors, the dictator Aulus Postumius vowed a temple to Castor and Pollux if they would come to his aid. They did, and the Romans won. Later that same day, two tall and handsome young men, battle-weary and in military gear, appeared at Rome, to wash and water their horses in Lacus Iuturnae, the Pool of Juturna, at the eastern end of the Forum, near the Temple of Vesta. They announced the victory to passersby before disappearing, and the next day news arrived from the dictator, reporting the details and the divine intervention.[4] Their temple, usually called the Temple of Castor, was erected in the Southeastern corner of the Forum, next to the Pool of Juturna, and it was dedicated by the dictator's son in 484 BCE. So went the standard (but not necessarily correct) version of the arrival of the heavenly twins in Rome.

Castor and Pollux reappeared in the Forum to announce victories at other crucial moments in Roman history—after the great battles of Pydna

(168 BCE), Vercellae (101 BCE), and Pharsalus (48 BCE)—and their temple became one of the focal points of the community by the time of the Late Republic, a meeting place for the Senate within, a speakers' platform and voting area without, a center for debate and riot. Above all, as warriors on horseback, the brothers became patrons of the Roman knights who, every year on July 15, the anniversary of the battle, celebrated a great equestrian parade, the *transvectio equitum*. Up to five thousand of them, wearing olive crowns and dressed in purple robes with scarlet stripes, attended the annual sacrifice at the Temple of Mars out on the Via Appia and then rode in procession through the city and the Forum to pass by the Temple of Castor on their way to the capitol. The temple was also a hub of activity in daily life, a sort of bank and repository of weights and measures, surrounded by various enterprises: cobblers, moneylenders, a cloakmaker, and slave-dealers are attested, and there were certainly taverns nearby.[5] Some twenty-nine shops were actually built into the podium beneath the temple, one of which was a combination barbershop, beauty salon, gaming parlor, pharmacy, and dentist's office, where dozens of extracted teeth were excavated in the 1980s, along with what may be tongue depressors and probes, not to mention coins, gaming pieces, jars for unguents, drinking glasses, and cups.[6] If the scores of oaths in Roman comedy are any guide to life in the streets—"Ecastor!" or "Mecastor!," and even more "Edepol!," meaning "By Castor!" and "By Pollux!"—the twin gods who presided over this bustle were casually called upon by everyone everywhere. In sum: Castor and Pollux were deeply embedded in the Roman consciousness; they conjured up specific vivid images; and they were very popular indeed.

According to tradition, their ancient temple was dedicated on January 27, 484 BCE. It was restored sometime in the second century; reconstructed in 117 BCE by the triumphing general L. Caecilius Metellus Delmaticus; repaired to some extent in 74 BCE by the notorious praetor Gaius Verres; and then rebuilt by Tiberius Caesar and dedicated by him on January 27, 6 CE, in his own name and that of his brother Drusus, who had died in the autumn of 9 BCE.[7] Tiberius, in fact, completely replaced the five-hundred-year-old Temple of Castor in the heart of Rome with a new building dedicated to the immortal twins by two brothers, one by now the coruler with, and son and heir apparent of, the princeps Augustus, the other dead now more than thirteen years. This association of Tiberius and Drusus with Castor and Pollux at the heart of Rome was a brilliant political statement, emotive, even provocative.[8]

The story begins with the death of Castor, breaker of horses. From 12 to 9 BCE, the two young brothers had conducted brutal campaigns of conquest in the North, Tiberius in the Balkans, Drusus in Germany. Drusus penetrated with fire and sword as far the Elbe, but he withdrew, discouraged, it was later said, by a woman of superhuman stature who predicted his imminent end. He died at the age of thirty, sometime late in 9 BCE. Among the grim omens—wolves howling in the camp, the wailing of unseen women, shooting stars—one stands out: two young men were seen riding through the middle of the entrenchments. The uncanny appearance of two horsemen in a military camp could suggest only one thing to Romans: a visitation by the heavenly twins. Yet here, for the first time in history, they did not anticipate or report a victory, they warned of disaster.

The true magnitude of the ensuing calamity might not at first glance be obvious. Later authors are unanimous in reporting simply that Drusus died in camp of "some illness," *morbus*, *nosos*,[9] but a markedly different account was offered by Drusus' contemporary, Livy, who was actually composing his history of Rome when the young general died. His version survives only in a brief and contorted summary of Book 142, five sentences long: Drusus carried the war against the German tribes across the Rhine, but "he died of a broken leg, caused by his horse falling upon it, on the thirtieth day after it happened." Perhaps we can reconcile death from a broken leg with death from "some disease"—gangrene following on a fracture, say—but the unique detail of the broken leg is striking. Livy, in fact, chose to conclude his enormous history with the death and funeral of Drusus in 9 BCE, followed, apparently, by a brief mention of the legendary destruction of the entire army of Quinctilius Varus in Germany in 9 CE, some seventeen years later. His point was surely that the death of Drusus was disastrous indeed for Roman history: the young man would have conquered Germany, as contemporaries lamented, and the tremendous Varian disaster, *clades Variana*, with its loss of three legionary eagles and between fifteen thousand and twenty thousand men, would never have happened.[10] It was that important for the history of Rome.

Some three or four decades later, when Tiberius was long established as princeps, Valerius Maximus offered a dramatic narrative of his brother's death:

> It has been our fortune to behold a pair of brothers once the glory of the Claudian clan, now also of the Julian. Our Princeps and parent (*sc.* Tiberius) had so great a love implanted in his heart for his brother Drusus that when at Ticinum, where he had come as victor over enemies to embrace his parents, he learned that in Germany Drusus' life hung in the balance from a grievous and dangerous sickness, he at once dashed off in a panic. How swift and headlong his journey, snatched as it were in a single breath, is evident from the fact that after crossing the Alps and the Rhine, traveling day and night and changing horses at intervals, he covered at a full stretch two hundred miles through a barbarous country recently conquered, with his guide Antabagius as his sole companion. . . . Drusus too . . . at the very moment that separates life from death ordered his legions with their

ensigns to go meet his brother, so that he be saluted as Imperator. . . . To these I for my part know that no example of kindred affection can suitably be added save Castor and Pollux.[11]

Tiberius' frantic dash to his brother's bedside, from Northwest Italy to Germany across the Rhine, became the stuff of legend. The drama has two acts. First, the headlong race north, recounted by Livy (now lost) and retold by others, and the dying Drusus' struggle to show his brother the honors befitting a victorious general, the last fraternal kiss and embrace, the ritual closing of the eyes.[12] Then, act 2: funereal deliberation. The German tribes cease fighting, as a sign of respect. Tiberius brings the corpse to Rome, walking ahead of it all the way. For the first stage, in enemy territory, from the summer camp to their winter quarters, probably at Mainz, the body was borne by the young general's centurions and tribunes; thence it was carried by the leading men of each town and city passed by the cortege. Augustus and Livia joined it at Ticinum, and from there they proceeded to Rome, where Drusus was eulogized extravagantly, buried with elaborate ceremony in the vast family tomb of Augustus, and showered with honors. Among the latter was the award of the name "Germanicus," signifying the conqueror of Germany, which was also to be borne by his two small sons.[13]

Drusus' posthumous fame as Drusus Germanicus was enormous and enduring, his family the keepers of the flame. His young widow was routinely identified for decades, in literature, inscriptions, and papyri, as "Antonia Drusi," Antonia the wife of Drusus: she survived him by almost forty-five years and never remarried. Their elder son (born in 15 BCE) was known, after his adoption by his uncle Tiberius in 4 CE, as Germanicus Julius Caesar, and became the darling of the Roman people. His younger brother, the future princeps Claudius (born in 10 BCE), is regularly named on inscriptions as Tiberius Claudius Nero Germanicus, son of Drusus Germanicus. Claudius' predecessor and his successor as princeps, Gaius and Nero, were routinely identified as the grandson and great-grandson of Drusus. But the architect of his memory seems to have been their matriarch, Livia, later Julia Augusta, who is named on inscriptions as mother of Drusus Germanicus decades after his death.[14] Seneca, writing not too long after her demise in 29 CE, assures us that, "She never ceased from proclaiming the name of her dear Drusus. She had him pictured everywhere, in private and in public places, and it was her greatest pleasure to talk about him and listen to the talk of others—she lived with his memory."[15]

Memory is never neutral, and Drusus was important to the dynasty, as Claudians supplanted Julians: contemporary writers competed in elaborate posthumous praise of his virtues. For Valerius Maximus, Drusus Germanicus was "the particular glory of the Claudian family, his country's rare ornament, and, best of all, one who by the grandeur of his achievements, in the perspective of his years, marvelously matched the Augusti, his stepfather and his brother, the two divine eyes of the commonwealth." For Velleius Paterculus, Drusus Claudius the brother of (Tiberius) Nero was "a young man endowed with as many great qualities as man's nature is capable of receiving or application developing. It would be hard to say whether his talents were the better adapted to a military career or the duties of civil life; at any rate, the charm and the sweetness of his character are said to have been inimitable, and also his modest attitude of equality toward his friends. As for his personal beauty, it was second only to that of his brother." For Seneca (who imagines Claudius referring to his father as Drusus Germanicus), he "would have made a great Princeps, and had already shown himself a great leader. For he had penetrated far into Germany, and had planted the Roman standards in a region where it was scarcely known that any Romans existed."[16]

Others explicitly invoked Drusus as their muse. A now anonymous poet addressed his ponderous *Consolation* to Livia on the loss of her son, praising in 474 lines not only these two but every member of the dynasty whom he could recall. And sometime in the late 40s CE, while serving in Germany, Pliny the Elder was inspired in a dream by an image of Drusus, *Drusi Neronis effigies*, "who had conquered widely in Germany and died there" to write a history of all of Rome's German Wars. The image commended his memory to Pliny and begged the writer to save him from the injustice of oblivion. Oblivion was not a likely prospect under the rule of Drusus' son Claudius, but the posthumous injunction was a neat way for a scholarly officer to win the attention of his princeps.[17]

"Drusus Germanicus" accordingly figured prominently on public monuments and their inscriptions, most memorably in the record of elaborate posthumous honors decreed by the senate in 20 CE to his elder son Germanicus, himself untimely dead in 19 CE. These included a triumphal arch in the Circus Flaminius, surmounted by a statue of Germanicus Caesar standing in a chariot and flanked by statues of family members, of which the first named was "Drusus Germanicus, his natural father and brother of Tiberius Caesar"; another arch near Drusus' cenotaph on the Rhine; and, set up in the portico of the Temple of Apollo on the Palatine, among the portraits of other distinguished men, two busts "of Germanicus Caesar and of Drusus Germanicus, his natural father and the brother of Ti. Caesar Augustus."[18] In so emphatically displaying the long-gone Drusus, not only did the senate have its eye on the dynasty, but both senate and dynasty also had their eyes on the public. *Drusi magna apud populum Romanum memoria*, "the memory of Drusus among the Roman people was considerable," as Tacitus wrote about events that unfolded in 14 CE, over two decades after the man's death, and Dio confirms that a few years earlier, in 6 CE, during a time of urban disorder, the people had been comforted by a mark of honor to the memory of Drusus, who was a popular figure.[19]

Not only is memory never neutral but, another truism, it is contentious. Discord had arisen immediately. The soldiers wanted to burn Drusus' corpse in his armour, but "his brother against their will snatched away the sacred body," according to the *Consolation to Livia*, while Seneca has Claudius praise Tiberius for maintaining discipline and restoring the old-fashioned way of mourning at a time when the army "was not only disconsolate but distraught, and claimed the body of the loved Drusus for itself." In fact, a compromise was reached, as his troops were allowed spontaneously to erect a cenotaph on the banks of the Rhine, around which soldiers would run on an anniversary day each year. The soldiers' love for Drusus surely contributed to their idolatry of his elder son, Germanicus Caesar, and it even transferred to his younger son. After the murder of Caligula, the praetorian who discovered Claudius hiding in the palace called out to his companions, "Here's a Germanicus: let's carry him off and make him emperor!"[20]

Drusus' "great memory" among the people of the city of Rome was an even more serious matter, for as Tacitus goes on to explain, "it was believed that, if he had been in charge of affairs, he would have given them back their freedom." Suetonius agrees: Drusus did not hide his intention to restore the old Republic whenever he should be able to, and he even wrote a letter to his brother in which he talked about forcing Augustus to restore liberty.[21] The reality of these plans of Drusus is dubious and not too important—they do have the ring of propaganda manufactured in factional struggles over the following decades. The significant element is their role in his posthumous popularity. Suetonius is indignant at another use to which they were put: some authors had dared to assert that Augustus was suspicious of Drusus, that he recalled him from his province, and that, when Drusus was slow to respond, Augustus had him removed by poison. Impossible, says Suetonius, offering four proofs of the princeps' great affection for his stepson: he always named the young man coheir with his own sons, as he once announced in the senate; in his funeral laudation before the people, he solemnly called upon the gods to make his Caesars (that is, his sons Gaius and Lucius) like Drusus, and to give himself as honorable a death as they had given Drusus; he wrote a verse eulogy for him and had it inscribed on the tomb; and he composed a memorial of his life in prose. But what do these actions prove? Three of the four displays of affection were certainly posthumous; the fourth, the assertion about his will in the senate, might well be too; and a fifth, omitted by Suetonius, certainly was—that is, the composition of the inscription for the statue of Drusus that the princeps added to the galleries of Roman heroes that lined his new Augustan Forum.[22] Whatever affection he may have felt for his stepson in life, he made a great public show of that love when the man was dead.

Augustus' expropriation of the popular memory of his stepson was outrageous. Orchestrating the posthumous memorials, he delivered a lachrymose eulogy in the Circus Flaminius that quite overshadowed the words of Drusus' brother Tiberius, spoken earlier in the Forum. This was part of a creative outburst by the stricken princeps, along with the verse epitaph, the prose memorial, the honorific inscription on the statue base.[23] But he went much farther than mere association: he essentially adopted the dead Drusus into his family. At the funeral, the corpse was surrounded by the busts not only of his Claudian ancestors but of the Julii, to whom Drusus was not related. He was buried not in the family tomb of the Nerones, but in Augustus' great Mausoleum, the tomb of the Julii, *tumulus Iuliorum*: as the anonymous poet put it, somewhat obtusely, Drusus would not join in burial his forefathers of old. And among the statues of Roman heroes that lined the Forum Augusti, that of Drusus stood not with the great men on one side of the square but with the Julian family on the other. For Ovid, the brothers were from the clan of the gods (that is, Julians, not Claudians), while Valerius Maximus called them the fraternal pair, formerly the glory of the Claudian clan, now also that of the Julian.[24]

Drusus' funeral, his burial, his memorial: all Julian. What did the man's brother, Tiberius Claudius Nero—later Tiberius Julius Caesar—make of all this? His reaction, when it came, was Tiberian in its subtlety and deliberation.

———

To reconstruct it, we must first consider three brief notices offered by Cassius Dio in what is our only narrative account of the reign of Augustus. After the funeral, Tiberius was dispatched back to Germany to renew the campaign. His success there was rewarded with the acclamation as Imperator for a second time and the promise of a triumph when he returned to take up his second consulship in January of 7 BCE.

Tiberius, on the first day of the year in which he was consul with Gnaeus Calpurnius Piso, convened the senate in the Portico of Octavia, because it was outside the pomerium. After assigning to himself the duty of repairing the Temple of Concord, in order that he might inscribe upon it his own name and that of Drusus, he celebrated his triumph, and in company with his mother dedicated the so-called Livian shrine.[25]

Thus, the year began with a strong display of family unity. In the past, Tiberius' real military accomplishments had not earned him a triumph. By contrast, in 8 BCE he had been occupied with the grimly inglorious task of pacifying the frontier in the wake of his brother's death, and he had won no notable victory. Yet now he was awarded his triumph. He had also been consul a mere seven years earlier: triumph and second consulship in 7 BCE thus recognized him as the bulwark of the regime. Since he could not cross the sacred boundary of the city before the celebration, he summoned the senate to meet him not in the senate house but a few hundred meters away, outside the pomerium, in the Porticus Octaviae, next to the Theater of Marcellus in the Campus Martius. Augustus had built this large and lavish portico, which enclosed several public buildings, from the spoils of his campaigns in Dalmatia in the 30s BCE, and he had dedicated it in the name of his sister, Octavia. Tiberius' choice of setting for the senate was thus a gracious bow to the princeps and the Dalmatian triumph that he had celebrated in 29 BCE, and the gesture was neatly balanced by his subsequent dedication, immediately after his own triumph, of the equally lavish Porticus Liviae over on the Esquiline Hill, together with his mother, Livia, the wife of the princeps.

Fitting nicely within this display of dynastic concord came the announcement that he would restore the great temple dedicated to Concordia at the Northwestern end of the Forum. But Dio's account prompts questions. Why choose a structure freighted with uncomfortably Republican associations, one that commemorated the bloody conclusion of a period of violent discord, the suppression of Gaius Gracchus and his followers in 121 BCE? What "restoration" did the temple need, and why did Tiberius in fact then completely rebuild it? Most curiously, what does Dio mean when he gives as Tiberius' motive for repairing Concord the arresting "so that he might inscribe upon it his own name and that of Drusus"?

The following year, his role as champion, if not heir, of the regime was confirmed by the grant of the tribunician power, but that was soon followed by his retirement to Rhodes. En route, Dio tells us in an aside, Tiberius forced the people of the island of Paros to sell him the statue of their beloved goddess Hestia, the Roman Vesta, "so that it might be set up in the temple of Concord."[26] In time, he came back to Rome as a private citizen, in 2 CE, but then, after the deaths of Lucius in 2 CE and Gaius Caesar in 4 CE, he returned to center stage as the second man of the empire: he was adopted by Augustus, he received the tribunician power again, and he was dispatched for more hard fighting in Germany, returning to Rome each winter. There, on January 27, 6 CE, he at last dedicated the great temple in the Forum in his own name and that of Drusus—but, to our confusion, it is the wrong temple.

In 6 CE, as Dio briefly records, Tiberius dedicated "the Temple of the Dioscuri, upon which he inscribed not only his own name—calling himself Claudianus instead of Claudius, because of his adoption into the family of Augustus—but also that of Drusus." Not the Temple of Concord, but the Temple of Castor and Pollux. It was to be another four years before the Temple of Concord was dedicated at last, on January 16, 10 CE, the anniversary of the day on which Augustus had received the name "Augustus." Thus Dio, again very briefly: "The Temple of Concord was dedicated by Tiberius, and both his name and that of Drusus, his dead brother, were inscribed upon it."[27] The Forum now shone with not one but two gleaming and very new versions of its largest temples, overflowing with carefully selected old master paintings and sculptures, all allegedly paid for by the triumphal spoils of two brothers, one of whom had returned from virtual exile less than eight years before, while the other had been dead for seventeen years.[28] In short, Tiberius Caesar took immense care to erect two enormous public shrines in the heart of Rome— marble-clad, bursting with artworks—that explicitly, in their dedicatory inscriptions, and implicitly, in the deities whom they honored, immortalized his relationship with his brother.

The gaps and curiosities in this extraordinary sequence raise questions that cannot be answered. We do not know when Tiberius vowed to rebuild the Temple of Castor. We may deduce from the sequence of the two dedications, Castor in 6 CE and Concord in 10 CE, that he promised the former sometime before he promised the latter in January of 7 BCE; or we might at least assume that he vowed Castor before sailing into retirement in the latter half of 6 BCE; but we do not know.[29] More importantly, we do not know why these two temples needed repair. The standard repertory of Roman topography suggests that Concord "was destroyed either by a fire or by the lightning that struck the Capitoline and other areas in Rome in 9 BCE," while Castor "was probably devastated in the fire of 14 or 9 BCE," but there is no evidence whatesoever, literary or archaeological, for either assumption. Moreover, the argument from silence is strongly against them: the damage to other monuments is recorded, so how could two of the greatest temples in Rome possibly be ignored?[30] Whatever their state of disrepair—each was little more than a century old, and both had been worked on in the intervening years—the essential point is that Tiberius did not repair or restore them: he replaced them, on a larger scale. And the only motive we are given, in the case of Concord and again from Dio, is that he wanted to inscribe his own and Drusus' name on it.

The place to start is with what mattered so much to Tiberius: the dedicatory inscriptions naming the two brothers on the architrave of each temple. Concord's dedication is completely lost, but exiguous fragments of that on the Temple of Castor have survived and they have recently been the subject of meticulous analysis and hypothetical restoration by Géza Alföldy, first published in 1992 and enshrined now in his monumental 1996 edition of the inscriptions of the emperors and their families from the city of Rome. His reconstruction of the text reads as follows:

On the left side of the frieze:

> [Ti(berius)] C[aesar Augusti f(ilius) Divi n(epos) Claudianus],
> [co(n)]s(ul) [iter(um), imp(erator) ter, tribunic(ia) pot(estate) VII,
>   pontif(ex)],

On the right side:

> [Nero Claudius Ti(beri) f(ilius) Drusus Germa]ni[cus],
> [Augusti privignus, co(n)s(ul), i]imp(erator) [iter(um)], au[gur],

And beneath these, in larger letters, running the entire length of the architrave:

> [aedem Pollucis e]t C[asto]r[is incendio consumptam de manubiis
>   r]ef(ecerunt).[31]

That is, Alföldy suggests that the names and titles of the two dedicators will have appeared in shallow twin columns, side by side: "Tiberius Caesar, son of Augustus, grandson of the god (Julius), Claudianus, consul twice, imperator three times, in the seventh year of his tribunician power, pontifex," and "Nero Claudius, son of Tiberius, Drusus Germanicus, stepson of Augustus, consul, imperator twice, augur." And along the bottom, in a third line, the dedication concludes "rebuilt with their spoils the Temple of Pollux and Castor when it had been destroyed by fire."

Alföldy's reconstruction is brilliant, based on encyclopedic knowledge of Roman—and especially Augustan— epigraphic language and conventions, and on minute attention to the size, shape, and position of both the surviving letters and the fragmentary stones on which they are inscribed. Most of what he suggests looks right, in the light of convention and close parallels, and it is argued with clarity and in great detail.[32] But it is also bold, almost preposterous, since the original dedication is all but nonexistent: the proposed reconstruction of its text runs to some 180 letters, of which a mere thirteen actually survive in whole or in part, on six scattered fragments. Moreover, serious doubts have recently been expressed, carefully but briefly, by Siri Sande, one of the excavators and principal publishers of the temple and its finds.[33] Not least of these doubts are her agnosticism about the relationship of four of the six fragments to the temple, two of which may be too shallow for a structure of its size, and her belief that one of the two undoubted fragments has been wrongly located in Alföldy's reconstruction. But equally serious doubts can be raised in turn about Sande's objections, not least that her proposed single-line text for the dedicatory inscription is impossible.[34] The epigrapher and the archaeologist look at the world with very different eyes, and the amateur stands at an impasse.

Much of Alföldy's proposed text must be right, that is, a major monument of Augustan Rome is inconceivable without the details of the nomenclature and titles of the dedicators in some form as he presents them, whatever the physical layout of the texts may have been. On the other hand, anything suggested by an epigrapher within square brackets must be taken exempli gratia. Within this beckoning void, an elastic variety of standard contractions may be called upon to fit the space available, precise numbers may give a false sense of security, and the longer the connected prose, the less accurate the proposal is likely to be—thus here, for reasons presented earlier, the words *incendio consumptam* seem more than hazardous. Rather than accept the text of *CIL* VI.40339 as right or wrong, however, let us proceed on the assumption that it is good to think with. This is above all because of Alföldy's sharp-eyed observation and incorporation of known details the significance of which has gone unremarked. It must then be understood that nothing that follows here—nothing—depends on his reconstruction of the dedicatory inscription on Tiberius' temple: rather, his reconstruction reflects otherwise attested fact for three remarkable novelties. In its pristine condition, this was one of the largest known dedicatory inscriptions in the Roman world. It ran to over twenty-seven meters and the letters in the bottom row were over half a meter high. Emblazoned across the facade of a major and popular temple at the very heart of the capital, it was meant to be seen.

First, on it, Tiberius named himself Claudianus, so Dio tells us. We must believe him on this, for he took pointed care to note both the name and the reason for it. And, of course, the inscription was there for all to read in his day, so any doubter could stroll down to the Forum to check it in person. It must have read Claudianus.

For the first forty-four years of his life, Tiberius had been known as Tiberius Claudius Nero, the son of Tiberius. After his formal adoption by the princeps on June 26, 4 CE, his legal name for the rest of his days was Tiberius Julius Caesar, the son of Augustus. Invariably in literature and normally on inscriptions, the family name Julius was omitted, and he was known by the austere and imposing abbreviation, Tiberius Caesar. After the death of his adoptive father in 14 CE, he might even be known as Tiberius (or, sometimes, Tiberius Julius) Caesar Augustus. When adopted at Rome under the Republic, an adoptee took on the full name of his new father, but it was a common custom to retain a form of the original family name as an extra surname (cognomen or agnomen): thus, a Lucius Aemilius Paullus adopted by a Publius Cornelius Scipio becomes Publius Cornelius Scipio Aemilianus, known to all as Scipio Aemilianus; indeed, Tiberius' own grandfather, Livia's father, was a Claudius Pulcher adopted by a Livius Drusus, hence Marcus Livius Drusus Claudianus. But never, anywhere, in hundreds of Latin and Greek texts, literary, epigraphical, and papyrological, by himself or by anyone else, is Tiberius Caesar ever called Claudianus—only here.

The Roman Forum was the very center of Roman history, and what Augustus had done with it over his decades in power well represents the heart of his program, that is, he preserved and restored it as a living museum of Rome's glorious past while inserting himself everywhere as the culmination of that glory.[35] He restored various emotive antiques, the Pool of Juturna itself, next to Castor and Pollux, the Black Stone outside the senate house, the little shrine to Venus of the Sewers, all reminiscent of Rome's earliest days. But pious restoration was always put to use. The obscure Temple of Janus near the senate house was transformed into the locus of a major ceremonial, the forgotten ritual of closing its bronze doors when the Roman world was at peace: Augustus, the prince of peace, closed them three times, once more than in all previous history. On a huge triumphal arch at the eastern end of the Forum, he listed all of the winners of triumphs and all of the consuls in Rome's glorious history: the arch was topped with a statue of Augustus, the winner of more triumphs and holder of more consulships than any previous Roman.

Indeed, he converted the old political center of Rome into a monument to himself and his family, for wherever you turned the prospect was dominated by Augustus. The Forum was, so to speak, Julianized. At the Southeastern end, facing the capitol, stood the new temple to the Divine Julius, flanked by the triumphal arch of Augustus and a triumphal arch dedicated posthumously to his adopted son Gaius Caesar. Along the two sides of the Forum stood Rome's two largest administrative buildings, Julius Caesar's Basilica Julia, completely rebuilt after a fire and renamed for Augustus' sons, Gaius and Lucius Caesar, and the Basilica Paulli, now masked by a new portico and likewise named after the two young Caesars. At the Northwestern end of the Forum stood the Rostra, adorned with the prows of ships captured over the centuries, which now acquired a golden statue of Augustus on horseback and the prows of ships captured at his victory at Actium. The Curia, the regular meeting place of the senate, burned down after Caesar's death, was now the Julian Curia, with Augustus' name prominent on the facade. Inside was a statue of Victory, commemorating his victories in the civil wars and the golden Shield listing his four cardinal virtues. The Forum as reconceived by Augustus was not a crude monument to his own achievements; it intertwined his own glory with the glories of the Roman past.

The reconstruction and dedication of the Temple of Castor marks a new stage. It too was a shrewd blend of the old and the new for, again, a completely new building replaced and yet continued a Republican structure. More precisely, it heralded the arrival of its builder in a suitably ambivalent way. At first glance, it fits the standard Augustan practice: a new Caesar, Tiberius, emerges for the first time on the monuments of the city, and the name of Augustus surely appears on his inscription as father and stepfather of the dedicators.[36]

Yet the simple word "Claudianus" shifts the balance forever, breaching the Julian monopoly of the Forum. It undercuts the adoption of Tiberius to emphasize his old natural family, an emphasis implicit in the whole structure, dedicated by two loving Claudian brothers to two loving brother gods.[37]

Before Tiberius, Augustus had adopted his two grandsons. Yet in no surviving text, literary or documentary, is there any hint of the names with which Gaius and Lucius Caesar were born, the sons of Marcus Vipsanius Agrippa; that is, nowhere is either called Vipsanianus, or (since Agrippa had dropped the "Vipsanius") Agrippa or Agrippianus. Augustus himself had been born Gaius Octavius and had taken at the age of eighteen the name of his great-uncle, through a dubious "testamentary adoption," to become Gaius Julius Caesar and, although known briefly as Octavian—Cicero seems to be the only contemporary to call him by that name—on no public document does he ever bear the adoptive cognomen Octavianus. That is, Augustus systematically suppressed the memory of former family ties within the pseudo-Julian family he had created and imposed on the Forum. However, by January of 6 CE, he was sixty-eight years old and slowing down. Tiberius' unique addition of the adoptive Claudianus to his own name on one of Rome's central monuments in 6 CE emphatically marks the shift in power that had begun in 4 CE. In fact, it was not unique. Although the cognomen appears only here in our sources, it surely recurred once, in 10 CE, when the same two loving brothers erected, at the other end of the Forum and dominating it, a similarly new-old temple from the same spoils and dedicated it to a similarly fraternal ideal, Concord. The Claudians had arrived.[38]

There is a second anomaly in the dedicatory inscription from the Temple of Castor, one that verges on the bizarre—indeed, we might take it for a joke, if a joke is conceivable set out in gilt letters half a meter high, towering over the facade of a grand public monument.

Suetonius tells us that, from his German spoils, Tiberius "also dedicated the Temple of Concord as well as that of Pollux and Castor in his own and his brother's name."[39] Pollux and Castor: not Castor and Pollux. Again, as with Dio above, we cannot doubt Suetonius: his manuscripts betray no sign of trouble, and again, any contemporary reader in Rome who had forgotten the monumental text could revisit it in the Forum.[40]

The history of the temple's name is complex, not to say confusing. Under the Republic and Augustus, for Latin authors and inscriptions it was invariably called *aedes* or *templum Castoris*, the Temple of Castor, not the Temple of Castor and Pollux. Even the Romans thought this noteworthy. In 65 BCE, so the well-known anecdote ran, the curule aediles Julius Caesar and Marcus Bibulus produced games with public funds, but Caesar alone won all the popular goodwill. Bibulus then ruefully remarked that what had happened to Pollux happened to him, for just as the temple set up in the Forum to the twin brothers was called Castor's alone, so his own and Caesar's munificence was said to be Caesar's alone.[41] This anomaly can be explained by the assumption that the original fifth-century temple was dedicated to Castor alone—despite the much later legend of the Battle of Lake Regillus, and despite his being joined at a later date by Pollux in the temple (probably at its reconstruction in 117 BCE), and for reasons unknown.[42] The phenomenon of separate cults to one or other of the brothers is adequately attested in the Greek world, so the original anomaly is eminently plausible in the early fifth century BCE, but designation as the Temple of Castor alone, even after he had been joined there at some stage by his brother, continues well into the principate—again in both literature and epigraphy—and it is apparently peculiar to Rome. Under the principate, it was also sometimes called the Temple of Castor and Pollux. But, even then, Castor might still subsume Pollux, as their shrine was occasionally called the Temple of the Castors, *aedes Castorum*, an arresting term, again peculiar to the cult at Rome, that the Romans never explained.[43]

This subordination of Pollux to Castor seems to reflect the way that people thought of the heavenly twins. Overwhelmingly, to the Romans as to us, they are "Castor and Pollux": scores of literary references attest to this order, with the conjunctions "et" or "ac," or in lists of gods without conjunction. Instances of "Pollux and Castor" are exceedingly rare. Before Tiberius, they had appeared thus only twice in Propertius and Ovid, and after him that order soon disappears.[44] In short, whatever rare exceptions there might be, to the Romans of the Republic and early principate, the twins were Castor and Pollux and their temple was inevitably, for centuries, the Temple of Castor: whatever poetic variations there might be, to solemnly proclaim the popular Temple of Castor as the Temple of Pollux and Castor was contrary to a degree. The only plausible explanation for this contrarian order is that the comparison was not general, of pair with pair, but specific: Tiberius was proclaiming himself as Pollux the immortal and Drusus as Castor, the dead twin—a comparison rendered all the more pathetic, or ironic, in that it equated Castor, the mortal tamer of horses, with Drusus, who in one version of his end died because of a fall from his horse. The Temple of Pollux and Castor cries out for attention.

This leads to the third and strangest anomaly of all in its dedicatory inscription, one so obvious that it is invariably overlooked. As reconstructed, the text probably informed the world that, "They rebuilt with their spoils the Temple of Pollux and Castor." As everyone agrees, E and F were the last two letters of the text, since the fragment on which they are preserved fit into the right-hand end of the architrave, diminishing before the end, and they must represent the verb [r]ef(ecerunt), "they [that is, the two dedicators just named] rebuilt."

A good parallel lies in the dedicatory inscription repeated over each gate of the southern Italian town of Saepinum:

> Ti. Claudius Ti. f. Nero pont. cos. II, [imp. I]I trib. potest. V / Nero Claudius Ti. f. Drusus Germ[anicus] augur cos. imp. II / murum portas turris d. s. p. f. c.;

or, with standard abbreviations expanded,

> Tiberius Claudius, son of Tiberius, Nero, pontifex, twice consul, twice imperator, in the fifth year of his tribunician power, (and) Nero Claudius, son of Tiberius, Drusus Germanicus, augur, consul, imperator twice, took care that the wall, gates, and towers be built with their own money.

This unique text is dated by the iteration of Tiberius' tribunician power precisely to the year between late June 2 BCE and late June 1 BCE, roughly six or seven years before the dedication of Pollux and Castor in Rome, and roughly six or seven years after Drusus' death.[45] The final "c," for *curaverunt*, confirms the *refecerunt* at Rome. That is, the Saepinum inscription and the enormous inscription at Rome both boldly proclaimed a grand fantasy, something that everyone knew to be untrue. Drusus did not pay for anything "from his own purse," as proclaimed at Saepinum, or "out of the proceeds from his military spoils": Drusus was dead. There is nothing like it in Roman history. Occasionally, a dedication might be made posthumously, by relatives or friends of the dedicator, but never is his death, like that of Drusus, simply ignored.[46]

The rededication of the Temple of Castor to Pollux and Castor shows two complementary sides of Tiberius the notorious mythologist: the erudite and the practical. As an ardent lover of myth, he knew the story of the Dioscuri, their joint life of constant warfare (beyond the violent adventures of the Calydonian boar hunt and the quest for the Golden Fleece, the brothers were invariably at war, raiding, harrying, liberating, laying waste). He knew of their immortal love for each other, the violent death of one, the grand sacrifice of the other to resurrect him. He also knew that amid the wildly varying accounts of the brothers' paternity and maternity, and that of their sister Helen, the one constant was that Pollux / Polydeukes was the son of the god Jupiter / Zeus (perhaps just as Tiberius was now the son of Augustus). And as an ardent lover of the obscure detail, he knew that Pollux was the elder brother.[47] With his new Temple, he did precisely what Pollux had done for Castor: he made his dead young brother immortal.

At the same time, Tiberius knew as well as anyone the practical value of the myths of the heavenly twins to a Roman statesman, the savior gods, benefactors of mankind, talismans of victory, beloved at Rome for five centuries, patrons of the knights, casually invoked by the people every day. The death of

Drusus was a stroke of luck, his resurrection a stroke of genius. Whether he was so popular during his lifetime, whether he and his brother were so close, cannot be known. What is well attested is Augustus' much-vaunted love for his younger stepson, however posthumous, and his elaborate commemoration of his virtues. These played straight into Tiberius' hand, since the princeps could hardly object to the public exhibition of fraternal piety by his own loyal son. How he played that hand—the jolting intrusion of the name "Claudianus," the arresting inversion of Pollux and Castor, the reminder of the lost conquest of Germany in the spoils of Drusus "Germanicus," the insistence that Drusus was not really dead—in short, the whole great display of the heavenly twins, presents Tiberius the myth-maker as he crafts an original symbolic complex, a Claudian complex, from a popular ancient monument and a wildly popular dead hero. His notorious addiction to mythology mattered: he mastered Augustus at his own game.

———

The gaps in Cassius Dio's account leave the chronological sequence unclear. When did Tiberius first conceive of the Claudians as Castor and Pollux? And more importantly, what happened to that conception after the erection of the two temples?

As to the first, there seems to be a piece of relevant evidence, a brief inscription from the theater of Caesarea, the capital of the province of Judaea, discovered almost fifty years ago. As recently restored, again by Géza Alföldy, it can be read as follows:

[Nauti]s Tiberieum
[—Po]ntius Pilatus
[praef]ectus Iudae[a]e
[ref]e[cit]

How to understand this? As might be imagined, the epigraphic appearance of Pontius Pilate, the prefect of Judaea from 26 to 36 CE, has stimulated an enormous bibliography.[48] Controversy has engulfed the first line: what was the lost first word represented by the surviving "s," and what was the "Tiberieum" restored by Pilate?

Alföldy drew attention to two passages in Josephus, in which the historian wrote of King Herod's construction of his shining new city of Caesarea, built and named to honor Caesar Augustus. Its crowning glory was the great harbor (hence Maritima) that Josephus describes twice at admiring length. Part of this harbor's enormous breakwater was surmounted by a stone wall: "From this wall arose, at intervals, massive towers, the loftiest and most magnificent of which was called Drusion after the step-son of Caesar," to which is added, in his other version of the same account, "he died young."[49] The loftiest tower should correspond, as the archaeologists have recognized, to a structure the remains of which lie at the end of the Southern breakwater of the harbor (now under water), and which presumably served as a lighthouse. Alföldy argued forcefully that this Drous(e)ion, in Latin "Druseum," must have had a pendant, on the Northern breakwater—the "Tiberieum" of the Pilate inscription. He then drew attention to Josephus' remark that Herod dedicated this safe haven to the sailors there, *tois ploizomenois*, which gives us the correct restoration of the word lost at the beginning of the Pilate inscription: [*nauti*]*s*, the Latin equivalent, which neatly fills the space available. Hence the inscription is to be read: "Pontius Pilatus, prefect of Judaea, restored the Tiberieum for the sailors." Not only is this elegant, but it must be correct.[50]

More speculative is the corollary, again drawn by Alföldy, that Drusus and Tiberius were being compared by King Herod, as the author of the *Consolation to Livia* would compare them, with the "harmonious stars," the brothers Castor and Pollux, in their role as the protectors of sailors at sea: the lighthouses, named after the two Claudian brothers, beckoned mariners with their starry light into the safe haven. Werner Eck subsequently pointed out that the great lighthouse at Alexandria is said to have been dedicated "to the Savior Gods on behalf of the sailors." That is to say, in his ambitious new harbor works at Caesarea, Herod consciously recalled the dedication of the Pharos, the lighthouse par excellence of antiquity, to Kastor and Polydeuces, the savers of sailors in distress.[51]

The association of Tiberius and Drusus with the heavenly twins is attractive indeed and would lead to a reasonable date. There is no hint that Tiberius and Drusus were in any way compared with Pollux and Castor before the death of Drusus—indeed, the death of a brother ought to be the precipitating event. Drusus died in 9 BCE, King Herod in 4 BCE: these would give us the terminal dates for the conception.[52] As Dio tells us, Tiberius announced his intention to build the Temple of Concord on January 1, 7 BCE, in his own and his brother's name. Again, Dio does not inform us when the Temple of the "Dioscuri" was vowed, but it too was dedicated in the name of the Claudian brothers, while Suetonius likewise links the temples as dedicated in the brothers' names and as paid for by their *manubiae*. And we can see that both temples proclaim aspects of concord. There is no proof then, and the silence of Dio is problematic, but it seems most likely that the Temples of Concordia and Pollux et Castor were conceived as a pair, and the glorious idea of comparing himself and his brother to the twin gods came to Tiberius in the year 8 BCE, very soon after Drusus died.[53] Among the grim portents of his death was the appearance of the two superhuman youths riding through his camp in

Germany: Castor and Pollux, come not to announce victory but, horrify-ingly, to take the young man away. Did Tiberius the mythographer exploit, perhaps even invent, this tale?

The notion is speculative, dependent on the dedication of the Pharos of Alexandria to the Dioskouroi, but the evidence for that is uncertain, and then on the hypothetical Tiberian and Drusian lighthouses at Caesarea Maritima.[54] The later development and significance of Tiberius' heavenly twins is much clearer. What came of it all, and what was the power of their myth at Rome?

As we might expect, loyal contemporaries celebrated the connection of Castor and Pollux with the Claudian brothers. In his *Fasti*, under January 27, Ovid wrote of the new shrine: "The sixth day before the next Kalends a temple was dedicated to Ledaean gods. Brothers from a family of gods founded it for the brother gods near Juturna's pool." Similarly, the author of the *Consolation to Livia* writes:

> Add too the Ledaean brethren, concordant stars, and the temples conspic-uous in the Roman forum. . . . Yet—woe is me!—Drusus will never see his bounty nor read his name upon the temple's front. Often will Nero weeping humbly say: "Why brotherless, alas!, do I approach the brother gods?"

The two poets were writing within a decade or so of the dedication of the temple, while not much later Valerius Maximus would make the comparison with Castor and Pollux explicit in prose.[55] But there is much more here than the flattery of courtiers and literary men. With Castor and Pollux, Ti-berius, the reserved and sardonic patrician who detested crowds, continues to reveal the shrewd politician, associating himself and his family with the popular heavenly twins through his equally popular dead brother.[56]

The connection had an impact on the turbulent political situation at Rome in 6 CE. In that year, Augustus faced great public upheaval, touched off by an unpopular tax he had imposed to fund his new military treasury, and exacer-bated by a severe grain shortage and widespread fires. "This lasted," Dio tells us,

> until the scarcity of grain was at an end and gladiatorial games in honor of Drusus were given by Germanicus Caesar and Tiberius Claudius Nero, his sons. For this mark of honor to the memory of Drusus comforted the people, and also the dedication by Tiberius of the Temple of the Dioscuri, upon which he inscribed not only his own name—calling himself Claudia-nus instead of Claudius, because of his adoption into the family of Augustus—but also that of Drusus.[57]

The gladiatorial games are juxtaposed by Dio with the dedication of the temple, and we should assume that the two were part of one celebration: why else hold memorial games thirteen years after the death of the man honored?

Not only did they serve to remind the people of their lost hero, but they also presented his sons and heirs, both called Germanicus in his honor, and they underscored the closeness of Tiberius and Drusus, for Tiberius had adopted his elder nephew, Germanicus, now nineteen and quaestor designate, on the same day that he himself had been adopted by Augustus. In the midst of turmoil, the people were comforted.

When Tiberius was adopted by Augustus in 4 CE, he brought with him two sons, the adopted Germanicus and his own Drusus: almost the same age, from then on the two new brothers were known as Germanicus Caesar and Drusus Caesar. Ovid took the hint. The poet who had linked Tiberius and Drusus with the refounding of the Temple of the twin gods in the Forum, shifted the association to the next generation. Writing from exile in far off Tomis during Augustus' final years, he referred to Germanicus and Drusus as "your grandsons, the young stars." Later, he was more explicit in his imagined recreation of Tiberius' triumph over the Pannonians and Dalmatians, which was celebrated on October 23, 12 BCE: as Tiberius proceeded, "his dutiful offspring [Germanicus and Drusus Caesar], along with you [the poet's friends, Messalla and Cotta Messallinus], accompanied him, worthy of their parent and of the names given to them, similar to those brothers, occupants of the nearby temple [that is, Pollux and Castor] whom the Divine Julius observes from his lofty shrine."[58]

Germanicus died in 19 CE, but in 20 CE by a happy chance twin sons were born to Drusus Caesar and his wife Livilla, the sister of Germanicus: Tiberius Julius Caesar and Germanicus Julius Caesar. The normally taciturn Tiberius was so overcome with joy that he could not restrain himself from boasting to the senate that never before had any Roman of such rank been blessed with twin sons. In 23 CE, the mint at Rome issued some remarkable coins, depicting the heads of two little boys facing each other set atop crossed cornucopias, with a caduceus in between, both symbols of good luck.[59] The hint was taken up in the Greek-speaking provinces. Coins at Cyrene and Corinth portray the brothers, the latter as "the twin Caesars." An alert citizen at Salamis, in Cyprus, proclaimed himself "Priest of Tiberius for life and of the twin sons of Drusus Caesar, Tiberius and Germanicus Caesar." Best of all, a private cult was likewise established in Ephesus, dedicated to "the new Dioscuri, the sons of Drusus Caesar."[60] Hopes were dashed all too soon when, to his grandfather's grief, the younger twin died some time in 23 CE, the same year as his father Drusus. Curiously, his surviving brother came to be known informally as Tiberius Gemellus, Tiberius the Twin, a reminder of what might have been.[61]

The evidence for the association of the heavenly twins with the emerging Claudian dynasty is sparse but clear, and there is one overlooked tale that brilliantly illustrates just how deeply meaningful it was for the people of Rome.

In his *Natural History*, Pliny tells a marvelous story. Talking birds are the subject, and, when he he comes to the raven, he writes:

> Let us also remember the favor in which ravens are held, as is attested not only by the Roman people's sense of propriety but by their actual indignation. During the principate of Tiberius, a young bird, from a brood hatched on top of the Temple of the Castores, flew down to a shoemaker's shop nearby, where it was welcome to the owner of the workshop because of religious considerations. It soon learned how to talk, and every morning it flew to the Rostra facing the Forum and greeted Tiberius by name, then Germanicus and Drusus Caesar, and, after that, the people of Rome as they passed by; finally, it returned to the shop. The raven was remarkable in that it performed this duty faithfully for several years.
>
> The tenant of the shoemaker's shop next door killed the bird, either out of rivalry or in a sudden fit of anger, as he claimed, because his shoes had been stained by its droppings. This aroused such dismay among the plebs that the man was first driven out of the district and subsequently done away with, while the bird's funeral was celebrated with enormous ceremony. The draped bier was carried on the shoulders of two Ethiopians, preceded by a flutist and with garlands of all kinds along the way to the pyre, which had been constructed on the right-hand side of the Appian Way at the second milestone on what is called Rediculus' Plain.[62]

The emotional intensity of the people is astonishing. As the tale would have it, the killer is ostracized and, indeed, murdered. A bird is honored with elaborate obsequies, complete with flutist, flowers, appropriately dark pallbearers, procession, and cremation—all this in an age when many of the mourners might expect no funeral for themselves. Much more is at stake than the loss of a favorite popular performer, which would soon have died in the course of nature. The physical setting in the heart of Rome is key. The bird is accepted as a guest by the cobbler out of piety, *religione commendatus*, before ever it begins to speak: it has come, after all, from Castor and Pollux. And, when it does quickly learn to talk, it does not perform in the shop. It flies rather to the other end of the Forum to address the world from, of all places, the Speakers' Platform—sensation!—and there, directly in front of the Temple of Concord, the messenger from the gods loyally salutes the dynasty

But the uncanny aspect of the incident is this. After deploring the whole affair, Pliny gives us a precise date for it: *hoc gestum M. Servilio C. Cestio cos. a.d. kal. V Apriles*, the raven's funeral took place on March 28, 35 CE. Now Germanicus Caesar had departed from Rome as long ago as 17 CE, and he had died in Antioch on October 10, 19 CE. Drusus Caesar died at Rome on September 14, 23 CE. Tiberius himself left the capital in 26 CE and never set foot within the pomerium again. That is, for several years, *plures annos*, the raven saluted two long dead princes and a long absent princeps. In 6 CE, the people had been consoled in their affliction by the games and the temple that honored Drusus, their fallen hero. Now, three decades later, they honored the talisman of his departed family and his gods, and (whether true or not) they drove out and murdered its destroyer. Their devotion in life and death is amazing: with it, we catch a glimpse into a world we have lost, but one that Tiberius understood.[63]

Suetonius records three omens predicting Tiberius' death two years later. The first was a straightforward prophetic dream on his last birthday, November 16, 36 CE: he had brought a famed statue of Apollo from Syracuse to set up in the library of a new temple of the divine Augustus, and the statue had warned him in the dream that it would not be dedicated by him. The second was the collapse of the lighthouse in an earthquake on Capri a few days before he died, March 16, 37 CE. And the third was the curious behavior of a brazier at Misenum, with no date specified but surely in his last days there (Suet. 74): "At Misenum the ashes from the glowing coals and embers which had been brought in to warm his dining-room, after they had died out and been for a long time cold, suddenly blazed up in the early evening and glowed without cessation until late at night."

As to the second of these portents, Suetonius' Latin reads *turris phari*, with "pharus" being taken to mean lighthouse, referring to *the* lighthouse, the famous Pharos at Alexandria.[64] In his recent exhaustive study of the ruins of Tiberius' villa on Capri, Clemens Krause has argued that it was indeed modeled on the famous lighthouse of Alexandria, but there is a surprise. The Pharus of Tiberius is not to be identified, as it commonly is, with the remains of the rather small, so-called "Torre del Faro" near the modern entrance to the site, if only because the massive villa itself, lying directly to the North, would have blocked a large segment of its light from the Bay of Naples. Rather, the Pharus should be seen as a much, much larger structure that dominated the far end of the great *ambulatio* to the northwest of the villa. Its ruins are meager, but calculating from the impressive dimensions of the rectangular base of this so-called "Loggia della Marina"—assuming a length of forty-nine meters for the outer walls, which appear to have been over four meters thick—Krause offers the striking deduction that the multistory structure, far from being a mere model or small-scale replica, rivaled in height and dimensions the great Pharos of Alexandria itself. That is, it would have towered some three hundred feet above the cliff top, which itself loomed just over one thousand feet above the sea. To judge from the extent of its platform and the thickness of its foundation walls, the structure must have been enormous, dwarfing even the massive villa. If not the Pharus of Tiberius, it is very difficult indeed to imagine just what else it might have been.[65]

Like their great model at Alexandria, ancient lighthouses signalled harbors, havens for sailors, more often than dangerous coastlines. Tiberius' Pharus, perched high on a sheer and soaring cliff really did neither: rather, it drew attention to itself and the fabulous, multistory palace of the supposed recluse who lived in its shadow. An enormous lighthouse of little practical importance, perhaps three hundred feet high and visible from afar, erected on his private estate by a princeps who shunned extravagance, should be something more than a general symbol of imperial benevolence. Like the dedicatory inscription on his temples at Rome, it demanded attention. If it did bear a special meaning to him and the world, how better to remember the Savior Gods whose kindly symbol the Pharos was, the heavenly models for the brothers Claudius?

The evidence for that symbol is, admittedly, slim. There is no doubt of the role of the Dioskouroi as the great saviors of sailors in peril. And, intimately connected with this, there is also no doubt of the twins' close identification with what is now known as St. Elmo's Fire. That is, in the midst of storms at sea, they appeared with their twin stars (which are repeatedly described as flames) to play harmlessly and reassuringly about the masts of ships in danger and to calm the threatening seas.[66] Was the security of their heavenly fire around the masts at sea extended to that offered to mariners by the flame on high in a lighthouse? That seems plausible but, against all the references to St. Elmo's Fire reassuring seafarers in storms at sea, there is only one reference to a lighthouse beckoning them to a safe haven. That is precisely Lucian's version of the dedicatory inscription on the Pharos of Alexandria: "Sostratos, the son of Dexiphanes, the Cnidian, dedicated this to the Saviour Gods on behalf of those who sail the seas." Doubts have been expressed about its reliability: Lucian lived half a millennium after the Pharos was dedicated; Strabo appears to give a different version of the text; other "savior gods" have been proposed, perhaps all of the sea gods, perhaps the reigning Ptolemies. But against this, it can be urged that Lucian saw what he saw—indeed, reported it in a work on how to write history; Strabo's version does not contradict his; and there is overwhelming evidence that "Theoi Soteres" without further definition would evoke the divine twins before any other divinities.[67]

Lucian's text is offered in support of his contention that history ought to be written not for the present generation but for eternity, and as such, it concludes the tale of the inscription on the Pharos, which recorded the name of the king in plaster and was intended to fall off over time to reveal that of Sostratus in stone beneath. The fable is unlikely, but what of the text? Hundreds of Lucian's readers had seen the inscription, including some of the most learned men in the world, and it was there for all to observe: how or why would he get it wrong? Indeed, he draws our attention to the physical text visible in his own day, in commenting on Sostratus' aim: "In this way not even he was looking to the immediate present or his own brief lifetime, but forward to our time and to eternity, as long as the tower stands and his skill survives."[68]

If we are then justified in accepting that Lucian's text of the inscription on the great Pharos in his day is accurate, and that the Savior Gods are who they should be, Kastor and Polydeukes, it maps neatly onto the only known near life-size replica of the lighthouse, the enormous Pharus on Capri for almost two centuries, the construction of a princeps known for his close personal identification with Castor and Pollux.[69] The collapse of the latter structure would, indeed, be an especially fitting portent of the imminent end of the surviving brother.

Its personal significance to Tiberius is signalled by the flaring up of the ashes over at Misenum. The tale of that phenomenon must have been inspired by a Claudian family tradition, as recorded by Suetonius in his biography of the princeps (19): "Although he left very little to fortune and chance, he entered battles with considerably greater confidence whenever it happened that, as he was working at night, his lamp suddenly and without human agency died down and went out; trusting, as he used to say, to an omen in which he had great confidence, since both he and his ancestors had found it trustworthy in all of their campaigns." The two portents are clearly opposites: if the lamp dying out without human intervention is an omen of success for a Claudian, the brazier reviving without human intervention should foretell disaster.[70] This small flame at Misenum is then intimately connected with the history of the second princeps. So too, we may now suspect, was the great flame of his lighthouse on Capri. When both were extinguished, the surviving brother departed and brought to an end his new tale of the heavenly twins.

Appendix: Gaius Caesar, Lucius Caesar, and the Dioscuri

In an excellent paper on "The Dioscuri and Ruler Ideology," B. Poulsen argued "that Augustus had already set the precedent of using Castor and Pollux as deities for the propagation of heirs in connection with Gajus and Lucius," and that he "had planned a rededication of the temple of Castor in connection with Gajus and Lucius." These conclusions are in danger of becoming orthodoxy, but what is the evidence for them?[71]

1) As *principes iuventutis*, Gaius and Lucius supposedly led the revived *transvectio equitum*, the parade of the knights past the Temple of Castor and Pollux every July 15, dressed like the two gods. This is fantasy. Gaius and Lucius headed the parade not as *principes iuventutis* but as *seviri turmae* (D 55.9.9), that is each led but *one* of the *six* squadrons of knights. More generally, there is no evidence that the twins were ever considered leaders

of the parade, or that the *principes iuventutis* were thought to represent them as such. And *all* participants wore the same dress according to Dionysius (cf. Valerius Maximus 2.2.9a), and *all* of them rode white horses. Moreover, if Lucius gained the honors of the *principatus iuventutis* and the sevirate in 2 BCE—as is standardly assumed, but the date may be 4 BCE (Swan 2004, 88–91 on all of this)—and if Gaius left for the East in 1 BCE, it would follow that, at most, they were able to join in one parade together (Lucius died in 2 BCE). Indeed, if, as C. B. Rose has argued forcefully (2005, 45), Gaius left in May of 2 BCE, they did not ride together at all. That might, of course, be ignored in public images, but it is very awkward. Moreover, the brothers are simply *not* portrayed on coins with any of the attributes of the divine twins.

2) Augustus had two paintings of Alexander the Great by Apelles installed in his Forum, one showing Alexander with Victory and the Dioscuri (Plin. *NH* 35.93–94). As Alexander was Augustus, the two young Caesars were the Dioscuri, so the argument goes. Wishful thinking.

3) There are "several" provincial examples of "these parallels" with the twins. In fact, only three are presented, one of which is very dubious and one of which is not relevant. (3a) First is a Cypriot inscription, from Salamis, *IG* III.997, reread by T. B. Mitford in 1947 (whence *AE* 1950.7) and 1974 (T. B. Mitford, "A Note from Salamis," in D. W. Bradeen, M. F. McGregor, eds., *ΦΟΡΟΣ* [1974], 110–16) as the bottom layer of a palimpsest, in the last instance supposedly naming Gaius and Lucius as "twin sons" and Augustus as Zeus Caesar, but the reading is most suspect and the interpretation both error-ridden and unconvincing. (3b) A coin from Tarraco in Spain calls Gaius and Lucius twin Caesars, Caesares Gemin(i), *RPC* I.211. (3c) An inscription from Ephesus honors Trajan's doctor, T. Statilius Crito as (among other things) priest of Anaktores, of King Alexander, and of Gaius and Lucius, in that order, in the early second century: *IK Ephesos* III.719. What this tells us about the plans of Augustus over a century earlier is unclear, whether (the) Anaktores must be the Dioskouroi is by no means demonstrated, and there is no obvious connection between them and Gaius and Lucius in the text. Even if these three texts were all unproblematic, there is no explicit or clearly implicit reference to the Dioscuri in them, and such random items can hardly reflect any broadcast imperial policy.

That is all there is, and from this, Poulsen deduces that Augustus intended to rededicate the Temple of Castor to his grandsons, with the Claudians as his fallback choices. Despite this assurance, there is no sign that Augustus ever had any particular interest in the temple or its gods, and, in all, the public documents concerning Gaius and Lucius—some of them recording elaborate honors at length: the *Tabula Hebana* and the *Tabula Siarensis*, and the funerary decrees from Pisa, *ILS* 139, 140—there is no sign of any association with Castor and Pollux. Indeed, the statues of the two young men later used in processions were apparently stored, as that of Germanicus would be, in the Temple of Concord, not that of the Castores (*Tab. Siar.* frag. b, col. 3, lines 8–11).

A pair of statues found at Corinth (not adduced by Poulsen et al.) *may* show the young men as Castor and Pollux: however, not only does this pair fail to tell us anyting about Augustus' policy at Rome, but these two statues—alone among forty-one such representations of one of the supposed "twins"—offer a clear example (along with their non-representation as the Dioskouroi on coins) of the dog not barking in the night. The standard work on their portraiture is properly circumspect.[72]

Finally, it should be noted that powerful arguments were presented not long ago for the view that Tiberius' retirement to Rhodes in 6 BCE caused, rather than was caused by, Augustus' promotion of Gaius and Lucius as his heirs.[73] That is to say, any putative alignment of the two Caesars with the heavenly twins would have come after that of Tiberius and Drusus.

The association with Castor and Pollux is made explicitly in our sources not with the Caesares but with the Claudii, first Tiberius and Drusus, then Tiberius' twin grandsons. The conclusion should be that it was invented by Tiberius the mythographer and has nothing to do with Augustus and his Julian sons.

3

The Odyssey of Tiberius Caesar

Tell me, Muse, of the man of many ways, who was driven
far journeys, after he had sacked Troy's sacred citadel.
Many were they whose cities he saw, whose minds he learned of,
many the pains he suffered in his spirit on the wide sea,
struggling for his own life and the homecoming of his companions.
Even so he could not save his companions, hard though
he strove to. They were destroyed by their own wild recklessness,
fools, who devoured the oxen of the Sun God Hyperion,
and he took away the day of their homecoming.[1]

WHAT DID IT mean to live in a world alive with myth?

After the War at Troy came the great wanderings, the Greek heroes trying to return to their homes, the Trojans to find a new homeland. Greatest of all were the adventures of Odysseus as related in Books 9–12 of Homer's *Odyssey*, and embellished by the works of countless other authors and artists. Blown off course, Odysseus and his fleet sail into a world of folklore and magic, dangerous but thrilling, a world outside of normal time and space, a universe of witches, monsters, ghosts, and enchantments, of marvels like lotus and moly. Yet, it is also a journey to the furthest frontiers of the real world, and from the time of Homer onward an enormous lore grew up about Odysseus' itinerary and the many places visited by him and his crew. By common consent, his adventures unfolded in the west, far beyond Ithaca. Indeed, many of the heroes of the War at Troy, both Greeks and Trojans, made their way to Italy and settled there, mainly on or near the eastern, Adriatic coast. Some of the Trojans also won through to Sicily. But "the west coast of Italy on the other hand, so far as the Achaean heroes are concerned, is almost the exclusive preserve of Odysseus, who, unlike his contemporaries, does not in normal tradition settle and die on Italian soil, but returns home."[2] Once past the straits of Scylla and Charybdis, between Italy and Sicily, the wanderer had made landfall and he left many many memories as he

passed up along the coast. This western, Tyrrhenian shore of Italy was reserved
for the greatest of heroes. Heracles had travelled everywhere on foot in the previous generation. Aeneas would sail by soon after Odysseus, stopping in many of
the same places. And a thousand years later, the princeps Tiberius would likewise follow in the wake of the king of Ithaca.

The prime evidence for his journey lies in over seven thousand marble fragments discovered by chance in 1957 in a seaside cavern that was part of a great
villa complex on the coast at Sperlonga, 120 kilometers south of Rome.[3] From
some of these fragments four monumental sculptural groups have been reconstituted with immense care and dazzling ingenuity. Everything—everything—
about these reconstructions is controversial: the chronology of the pieces and
of their installation, their forms, origins, influences, relationships, meanings.
And the stakes are high, for, together with the Laöcoon, which came from the
same Rhodian workshop, they stand, it has been said, "at the heart of the debate
about originality in Roman art." Are they early imperial replicas, in marble, of
monumental groups created in bronze in the high Hellenistic age, perhaps in
the decades between 180 and 140 BCE? Or, rather, are they virtuosic translations into monumental marble, produced during the late Republic, of small
paintings or sculptures created in the third century? Or some version of either
of these possibilities? Or something else again? The bibliography is bewildering, passions run high in the scholarly "war of Sperlonga," and debate is ham-
pered by the lack of publication both of the site and of the many other works
of art, not to mention the thousands of fragments, found there.[4] But only two
questions are relevant here. What, broadly speaking, was being depicted in the
four major sculptures? And—regardless of their previous forms and histories
and antecedents, as a group or as individual pieces—who was responsible for
their being gathered and displayed at Sperlonga?

As painstakingly reconstructed, the four principal groups were set facing
outward in a large cavern, thirty meters deep, that opens directly onto the
sea—partly submerged in seawater, with man-made benches, walkways, and
wall niches inside—and in one of the two inner recesses within that cavern,
twelve and twenty-five meters deep, respectively, that branch off in the rear to
left and right. Rising dramatically out of the great round pool in the center of
the grotto was the horrifying attack of the enormous sea monster Scylla, almost four meters high, on Odysseus' ship and crew. Scylla, terribly beautiful,
towers above the stern of the ship, from which she has torn the rudder. Her
lower body is all tentacles that trap, and savage dogs that tear and devour, five
of the hero's companions, as he watches, armed, tense, and helpless, and his
steersman is dragged by the monster to his fate. Further within, on the rocky
floor of the narrower chamber to the right, a second enormous and equally
spectacular group depicted Odysseus and his men blinding Polyphemus in his

cave. The drunken giant lies sprawled back on a rock, naked and exposed, at least five meters long. One of Odysseus' companions holds a wineskin and watches as two others drive the stake, sharpened and red-hot from the fire, upward, and the hero guides it into the giant's single eye.

Farther out, two smaller pairs of statues stood on platforms flanking the entrance walls of the cave, and thus framing the Scylla and the Polyphemus groups within. Both recall earlier events at Troy. On the right, a treacherous Odysseus is about to attack his companion Diomedes from behind: this captures a story, not in the *Iliad*, in which the two Greek heroes steal the talismanic image of Athena, the Palladium, from the Trojans, and Odysseus decides to claim all the glory for himself. And on the left side of the entrance stood a version of the so-called Pasquino group, the subject of which continues to be hotly debated. Known in other copies, and especially from the famed "talking statue" Pasquino in Rome, this also presented two warriors, one of them holding the limp body of the other, his dead comrade. The figures have been variously identified as Menelaus with the body of Patroclus, Ajax with the body of Achilles, or Odysseus with Achilles (all scenes from the Trojan War), and even Aeneas with Lausus, the son of Mezentius (from the *Aeneid*). The arguments are complex and often highly technical, but only one seems decisive, at least where Sperlonga is concerned. Three of the four carefully sited groups indisputably depict scenes from the adventures of Odysseus. How could the fourth conceivably not?

The four groups at Sperlonga were all copies of the highest quality, replicas or versions of originals created in the third or second centuries BCE. The original "Pasquino" may well indeed have represented other heroes when it was created—Menelaus or Ajax—but that need not have worried the collector who acquired the pieces and carefully arranged their display in the grotto at Sperlonga: indeed, it is commonly agreed that they were created or adapted for this particular setting. The "Pasquino" is almost entirely lost, so we do not know how it may have varied from its exemplar, but just as literary artists were free to manipulate versions of a myth, so a sculptor could deviate from his pattern, adapting it to a new subject, especially at the prompting of his patron. In the standard version of events at Troy, Ajax recovered the body of the fallen Achilles, but a variant account did indeed assign that glory to Odysseus.[5] In short, if the pair did not represent Odysseus and the dead Achilles originally, they will have been transmuted into those heroes for the context of the Sperlonga cave.[6]

Who commissioned these stunning Odyssean tableaux and their mise-en-scène? Surely the princeps Tiberius, as the great majority of scholars would agree, with more or less hesitation. There is no proof, but the circumstantial evidence is overwhelming.

In 26 CE, Tiberius and Sejanus were dining in a natural grotto at a villa named "Spelunca" (The Cave), between (as Tacitus puts it) the gulf of Amyclae and the hills of Fundi. Rocks at the entrance fell in, servants were crushed to death, and rescuers found the praetorian prefect crouched over the body of the princeps, shielding him from the stones—from that time his reputation for fidelity was assured. Suetonius, in his account of the same incident, refers to the praetorium, or imperial villa, near Tarracina, called Spelunca, and adds that many banqueters and servants met their deaths.[7] We can thus locate Tiberius at a villa that he owned at Sperlonga (a later form of Spelunca), and the ruins are indeed set near the water's edge precisely between the ancient gulf of Amyclae and the hills of Fundi (modern Fondi, about fifteen kilometers away by road), and down the coast from Tarracina (modern Terracina, about twenty kilometers away). And we can place Tiberius in a grotto there with a triclinium, just what we have on the ground. At the same time—whenever, and for whatever purposes, the Odyssean sculptures may have been created or replicated—there is no chronological objection to their being set up in their grotto during the period of Tiberius' ascendancy between 4 and 26 CE, or indeed much earlier.[8]

We can be pretty sure how he came to be there. Spelunca was part of the territory of Fundi, a flourishing town set inland on the Via Appia and dominating the fertile Caecuban plain. It is well known that Tiberius' maternal grandmother, Alfidia, was a native of Fundi: her father was a member of the local aristocracy. Moreover, a Claudian ancestor of Tiberius was almost certainly patron of the town more than a century earlier, and Tiberius himself was even thought by some ancient authors (erroneously but with good reason) to have been born at Fundi. Thus, he had deep roots in the area, which (it must be noted) had no known ties with his stepfather Augustus. It is a fair conjecture then that he inherited the future praetorium from his grandmother Alfidia, but when she died is unknown.[9]

In 20 BCE, at the age of twenty-one, Tiberius had left Rome for the east, as head of the expedition sent to restore the king of Armenia and to recover standards lost by earlier generations to the Parthians in battle, a diplomatic mission of great importance to Augustus, presented as a symbolic victory. On the return journey, besides the obligatory visit to Troy, cradle of the Roman race, he had stopped at the island of Rhodes, then a shining center of Greek intellectual life, and he had fallen in love with its charm and its climate, pausing to study with the rhetor Theodorus of Gadara.[10] Fourteen years later, he chose Rhodes as the site of his premature retirement. He immersed himself then in the world-famous cultural life of the island, strolling unaccompanied through the gymnasium, conversing with the professors and assiduously attending their lectures, and he met one of the great influences on his life,

Thrasyllus, the leading intellectual of the age, who would nourish his passion for astrology and became his close companion for four decades.[11] And during his years of retirement there, from 6 BCE to 2 CE, if not earlier, he appears to have developed a strong Rhodian aesthetic.

The rudder of Odysseus' ship in the Scylla group at Sperlonga proudly bears the names of three sculptors in a Greek inscription: "The Rhodians Athanodoros son of Hagesandros and Hagesandros son of Paionios and Polydorus son of Polydorus made (this)." The discovery of these names in 1957 caused great excitement, for they are the same men recorded by Pliny the Elder as the supreme craftsmen from Rhodes who made the Laocoön, named (in Latin) as "Agesander and Polydorus and Athenodorus." In Pliny's day, in the 70s CE, the Laocoön group stood "in the house of the emperor Titus," and in 1506 it was discovered, apparently still *in situ*, in the area of the Baths of Trajan in Rome. Now the find spot presumably lay within the boundaries of the Horti Maecenatis, the Gardens of Maecenas, who had bequeathed them to his great friend Augustus in 8 BCE, and it was in those gardens in the inner suburb of Rome that Tiberius had settled when he returned from Rhodes as a private citizen in 2 CE.[12] Moreover, the signature of one of the sculptors, "Athanodorus son of Hagesandros of Rhodes made (it)," also appeared on a now-lost statue base discovered in Tiberius' large imperial villa at Castiglione on Capri, 250 meters above the sea. And again on yet another now-lost base apparently from the great imperial villa at Antium.[13] That is, a pattern emerges: works from a single Rhodian workshop have turned up in four great early imperial villas, three of them at the seaside (Antium, Sperlonga, Capri), the fourth (the Gardens of Maecenas, to be counted as a suburban villa rather than an urban house) imitating the decorative and architectural programs associated with maritime villas, including an artificial nymphaeum. The particular taste of a wealthy imperial connoisseur emerges as well. Who but Tiberius?[14]

The physical context of the sculptures at Sperlonga is as arresting as their quality, in the conscious and elaborate integration of art with landscape. Statue bases imitate natural rock, artificial niches and grottoes are added to real ones, a sculpted ship set in a pool with rocks represents a real ship sailing by cliffs on the sea. Forty years ago, Hans Lauter argued that such a conception of "Landschaftskunst," the marriage of art and its contextual landscape, was specifically Rhodian in origin. He drew examples from around the island of Rhodes but concentrated on the large second-century BCE park in Rhodini, a suburb of the modern city of Rhodes and still a place for retreat and refreshment with a delightful stream running through it. The ancient park included a complex system of caves with cool places to sit, lookouts, architectural enhancements of the landscape, appropriate flora, running water in channels both natural and artificial, and, above all, artworks of different sizes displayed in niches and on bases. Lauter concluded that the artistic ensemble of cavern and artworks at Sperlonga—"architecturally organized nature"—finds its closest and indeed unique parallel and antecedent in the sculptural grottoes and landscape of the "Rhodian park." In fact, it is difficult to find any other programmatic precedent for the sculptural grotto, and it coincides neatly with the origin of the sculptors and with Tiberius' affection for the island.[15]

It might yet be objected that other aristocratic villa owners with similar interests could be found along the coast of Latium, for the contemporary Strabo remarks of this very expanse, between Tarracina and Caieta, that "there are wide-open caverns of immense size at this place, which have been occupied by large and very costly residences." In fact, the remains of very few villas have turned up along this stretch of the coast, and no other nymphaea or enhanced grottoes have been detected.[16] There are simply no other possible sites that fit the location described by Tacitus and Suetonius; indeed, it is hard to imagine Tiberius or anyone calling his villa The Cave if it were but one of many in the area. More importantly, no other site between Antium to the north and Baiae / Misenum to the south rivals Sperlonga even remotely, for the Odyssean grotto was but a part of a massive villa whose grounds and buildings stretched for hundreds of meters along the seashore, and probably around a cape and up into the hills, replete with pavilions, dining rooms, and walkways, all linking substantial residential complexes.

Moreover, phantom alternative locations aside, the sculptures found at Sperlonga are stunningly distinctive. No other private display is even remotely comparable in size—the only valid comparison is with monumental works of art displayed in public at Rome—and the groups are, whatever individual flaws they may have, masterworks: the patron who commissioned their creation and installation commanded immense resources.[17] Yet, for all their startling size and quality, the cavern that presents them is an intensely *private* setting for a connoisseur, part of an enormous villa complex perched between mountains and sea, with no near neighbors. It was not on the way to anywhere, for the Via Appia curved inland from Tarracina on the coast to the west, only rejoining it at Formiae to the east.[18] And the immense display in this private retreat has one other unique feature: it has been observed that the exhibition of Odyssean groups with Polyphemus and Scylla became a marker in the definition of imperial space; that is, the two groups at Spelunca are referred to and played upon in later grottoes at Baiae under Claudius, in Nero's Golden House in Rome, at Domitian's Alban villa, and at Hadrian's Tivoli—all imperial villas—and *only* in imperial grottoes. Hence, that we should conclude, "It is in their display of a Polyphemus and / or a Scylla group, then, that they declare their relationship with the original imperial grotto at Sperlonga, and distinguish themselves as imperial."[19]

Since it is important for what follows, and since there have always been and will be doubters, the case for Tiberius as the owner of the grotto and sculptures at Sperlonga must be summed up. Tiberius Caesar possessed an imperial villa (praetorium) with dining grotto, the ancient descriptions of whose physical location (Amyclae, Fundi, Tarracina) and name (Spelunca) precisely match what is on the ground—there are no alternative sites anywhere in the region—and (unlike Augustus) he had close ancestral ties with the place, the home of his maternal grandmother. Tiberius early developed a taste for the intellectual life and amenities of the island of Rhodes, a taste reflected in a collector's enthusiasm for the works of one Rhodian workshop; in a connoisseur's interest in the sculptural grotto; in a recluse's love for privacy; and in a student's happy memories of the island. Moreover, familiarity with the Sperlonga sculptures has cost modern observers our sense of wonder: magnificent trees tend to obscure a unique forest. These works are of stupendous size. They are masterpieces. They are displayed in a stunning setting. Yet they lay hidden in a cavern on a remote private estate, a Xanadu or San Simeon, where no one but guests and servants could have seen them, and their display was consciously recalled (Polyphemus, Scylla, and the setting) by later imperial villas. In brief, this is as close as we will get to proof, short of an inscription naming him, that the Sperlonga villa, and its astonishing display of Odyssean sculpture, belonged to the princeps Tiberius.[20]

What did this display mean to its owner? One cultural phenomenon, well studied in the last few decades, offers both context and insight: the romantically resonant "landscape of allusion."

Along with conquest, the Romans acquired wealth and culture, and a constantly developing self-perception. One mirror that broadly reflects that self-perception is offered by their engagement with and redefinition of the vast and amorphous corpus of Greek mythology, an engagement amply attested in painting and sculpture, in poetry and drama, indeed in all areas of Roman culture. Nourished on tales familiar since childhood, wealthy Roman officers, officials, merchants, and eventually tourists returned from abroad with vivid memories of the thousands of places where gods and heroes had lived their adventures—the footprint of Hercules here! the chains of Andromeda there!—and they carried with them, or had sent to them, or had reproduced, works of art and craft, sculpture, painting, jewelry, and tableware that represented the great moments of those adventures.

The next stage of this cultural imperialism is more creative—that is, reformulation of the old and foreign tales in a familiar and appropriate setting at home. Gardens, groves, and grottoes, actual or painted, were the favorite locations for these visualizations, which were expressed above all in sculptural and even living tableaux: watch Orpheus or Actaeon attacked in a realistic "wild" setting, glimpse nymphs and satyrs disporting on the lawn or in caves, stroll and converse in the company of famed philosophers. Bettina Bergmann, who has done more than anyone to familiarize us with this phenomenon of active engagement with Greek myth, captures the atmosphere in the late Republic and early Principate, when

> the Romans went to the actual places of myth, heard about them in recitations of new poems, saw them performed as plays or skits against convincing scenery, walked past them as sculptural tableaux in parks, or sat beside them on their own or their neighbors' painted walls or gardens. In each case, the attraction lay in the variation, like an actor's improvisation, and the pleasure in the degree to which a traveler, listener, or viewer could "enter" the fantasy and participate in its reenactment.[21]

Let us then approach the grotto at Spelunca, to observe the observers. Just breaking the surface of the pool outside is an outdoor dining area, a sort of triclinium on a small rectangular platform in the water, roughly eight meters by seven meters.[22] It faced directly into the cavern so that diners might enjoy the sculptural tableaux. The theatricality of the ensemble is underscored, and the effect of a theater enhanced, by seats carved into the rock at the entrance on either side. In starkly cheerful contrast to the horrific scenes displayed within, the end of the dining platform that faced the cave held a square water basin, on three edges of which perched laughing young satyrs, poised to scoop water onto the guests, while a slightly larger Eros sat pouring water from a pot into the basin. Thus, audience and action, seats and stage, were clearly demarcated and diners had a choice as to the extent to which they wished to enter the reenactment. With Odysseus, they could walk the plains of Troy, clamber around the cave of the Cyclops, even row to the straits of Scylla. Or, as at a theater, they could sit snugly on their island with the bridges to the mainland withdrawn, separated from the horrors they viewed, reassured by the smiling satyrs and Eros before them, savoring the dramatic effects of the setting sun as it poured directly from the west into the cave, and soothed always by the sound of the sea around them.[23]

Basic to all modern interpretation of the cavern is the assumption, surely correct, that the sculptural complex presented a program that was meant to be read as a whole and interpreted according to taste. Each group was to be contemplated not just in itself but in relation to the others, each scene was part of a larger play. A first glance would show the ancient guest that the sculptures had been artfully balanced in their physical setting. The two large tableaux with several figures, off the vertical axis in the center, catch Odysseus and his followers in mortal struggle with monsters on his voyage. Framing these, by contrast, are the smaller, two-figure groups: Odysseus paired with another great

hero, alive or dead, not on the sea with monsters but back on the human battlefield of Troy, at critical moments in the siege. The monumental, multi-figured
Scylla and Polyphemus groups depict moments of wildly baroque horror at
the height of the action; the smaller two-man groups capture a tense hiatus
in the middle of action. The smaller groups, closer to the viewer, present an
earlier, Iliadic phase of the hero's life, framing and leading into the larger and
later Odyssean adventures.

More precisely, the different groups can be read as displaying various and
contrasting familiar aspects of the character of Odysseus, both in themselves
and in relation to each other, as A. F. Stewart observed thirty-five years ago, in
an essay that remains the best introduction to the meaning of Sperlonga. Thus,
we see the hero's sense of duty to Achilles, his innate trickery with Diomedes,
his valor with Scylla, his clever resourcefulness with Polyphemus. The two
groups on the left (Achilles and Scylla) stress his bravery, those on the right
(Diomedes and Polyphemus) his deviousness—and the two incidents on
the left occur in daytime, those on the right, appropriately, in the dark. "Each
group was also positioned in the cave in a location appropriate to where the
action it depicted originally occurred: the two scenes on the plain of Troy on
the flat incurving rim of the basin at the front, the Scylla group in the centre
of the pool, and the blinding of Polyphemus in the gloom of the long cavern
at the rear—eerily illuminated, we may imagine, by the flickering light of
torches on feast-nights. This is sculpture at its most sophisticated, a *tour de
force* commissioned or procured for the mansion of a connoisseur."[24]

Yet for all the painstaking reconstructions and brilliant readings of the individual groups and of the overall program of the grotto, however controversial, there is a startling omission, one that will strike even the most casual
observer of both the site and its ground plan: the program is seriously unbalanced. That is, the elaborate care with which the figures were arranged
surely demands that they must originally have included a *fifth* group. The two
pairs of warriors flank the cavern's entrance to right and left; Scylla rises in the
middle; Polyphemus is blinded in the smaller cave to the right rear; but there
seems to be nothing in the smaller cave to the left rear, nothing corresponding
to Polyphemus: it is empty, and so the whole complex is thrown off balance,
massively weighted to the right. However it has long been known that this
second cave to the rear must have displayed its own group, for in it are to be
found the remnants of a large rectangular cement base that measured roughly
6.5 by 2.65 meters, and an inspired guess even once identified what that group
might have represented, but it is only within the last fifteen years that exiguous
fragments from it have been identified, by B. Andreae.[25]

According to his interpretation, at least three figures were involved: one was
Odysseus, with cloak thrown back over his shoulder; the second was another

hero, naked and strong, striding from right to left; and the third was a man standing on tiptoe with his heel raised, none other than Philoctetes, the wounded archer. This hero, a companion of Heracles and the inheritor of his bow and arrows, was one of the Greek leaders in the expedition to Troy. En route, he had been bitten by a snake near a shrine (different gods are implicated in different versions of the tale). The wound ulcerated, inflicting unbearable pain on Philoctetes and emitting a stench too horrible for others to bear. The hero was abandoned to his fate on the island of Lemnos, and the Greeks sailed on to ten years of warfare. An oracle proclaimed that Troy could not be taken without the bow and arrows of Heracles and perhaps, in some versions, not without their owner too, Philoctetes himself. A deputation was then sent from the army to bring the archer and his weapons to Troy: a scene from that fateful embassy was depicted in marble in the cavern at Sperlonga.

Again, the wily Odysseus is central. He had been the one who had originally advised the abandonment of Philoctetes, or he was, at the least, in some versions, deeply implicated in that decision. But, more importantly, he was the leader of the expedition sent to bring the man to Troy. In one account, he and Diomedes persuade the wounded archer to forget the past and to join them in sacking Troy, but in others he must practice deceit. He wins possession of the bow, the abandoned man's sole means of support, and forces Philoctetes to come with them.[26] Philoctetes then sails to Troy, is cured of his wound, and slays Paris in a duel. The group at Sperlonga presumably depicted a dramatic moment in Odysseus' deception of Philoctetes, with the third figure representing his companion Diomedes or (as in Sophocles) Neoptolemus, the young son of Achilles.

The recovery of this fifth group, however hypothetical, underscores the contingency of any interpretation of the whole complex, the fragility of conclusions based on a fraction of the known fragments, the danger of mistaking a part for the whole. Nevertheless, the resulting sculptural quincunx would be particularly satisfying, if only for its sense of balance and proportion among the five groups. A neat symmetry might now also be perceived along transverse axes, between the small groups at the entrance and their opposite numbers at the rear. In the right front and left rear, we would have Odysseus and a companion hero poised at a moment of dramatic tension as the fate of Troy hangs on an Odyssean trick. And if the companion in the rear was indeed Neoptolemus (the figure seems to Andreae to be that of a young man, so less likely to be the mature Diomedes), there is the added irony that the heroes in both scenes are or soon will be in conflict, and the trick will fail. In striking contrast, the scenes at left front and right rear would be more immediately active and heroic, Odysseus in actual conflict, his success dependent on the limp body over which he stands (Achilles, Polyphemus). And again, the two scenes might be undercut by irony: the blinding of Polyphemus and Odysseus' subsequent boasting will lead to the wrath of Poseidon, the Cyclops' father, and thus to all of the hero's later woes; while the saving of Achilles' body will lead to the disaster of the adjudication of his armor—and, perhaps a deeper irony, that rescue may not have been Odysseus' in the first place.

Be that as it may, the three major sculptural groups—Philoctetes (?), Polyphemus, Scylla—would display three complementary aspects of Odysseus the hero in conflict with, respectively, a civilized man, a wild brute, and a monster of nature. With the first opponent, he employs guile alone; with the second, a combination of guile and force; with the third, he is helpless in the face of overwhelming violence, which his intelligence can only mitigate by choosing the lesser of two evils, Scylla rather than Charybdis. What unites his three very different adversaries is that each of them lives alone, withdrawn from human society: Philoctetes unwillingly, a man reduced to living by himself; Polyphemus the ultimate wild man, a member of a race without institutions, individuals who care for no one else; and Scylla, the beautiful girl who has been turned by a jealous rival into a monster of nature.[27] And, as everyone knew, the three lonely Odyssean antagonists, now reanimated in three large caverns at Spelunca, each lived in a cave.

Of all the natural features in a landscape of allusion, sophisticated Romans cherished a special love for caves.[28] So common around the Mediterranean, caves represented an antithesis to human civilization and, like gardens, were portals into another world. Caves were places of solemn cultic significance: Zeus after all had been born in a cave, Demeter had retired to one in a time of global crisis, and, on a lower plane, nymphaea, grotto-shrines to the nymphs, dotted the seashore and the countryside. At the same time, caves were terrible places, the lairs of monsters, the sites of abnormal, antisocial activity (sexual transgression in particular), and potential entrances to the underworld. But paradoxically, they were also places of delight, refreshment, and comfort, shelter from the elements and refuge from the summer's heat, scenes of bucolic relaxation, the haunts of nymphs and amorous satyrs. A nymphaeum, a cave of the nymphs, came to signify a place of amenity rather than one of cult, with no more religious significance than the Museum, the home of the Muses. To conjure up the complex allusions implicit in caves, the Roman connoisseur used artifice to tame, even to improve upon, nature, just as he did with his gardens. Hence, in the grotto at Spelunca we find traces of ancient embellishment everywhere: ornate and multicolored stuccoes, marbles, mosaics; enhancement of the natural stone with limestone, cement, and seashells; and especially, the shining colors of the paint on the sculptures themselves. Hence too, probably, the addition of transitory stage elements that are lost to us, not just lighting effects but decorations, music, costumes, even the performances of human actors. In short, a grand and crowded theater, presenting what has rightly been called an Odyssey in marble.[29]

Beyond the proscenium of this theatrical grotto, the diners caught arresting glimpses of an even more elaborate mythical landscape. As noted above, immediately to the left of the entrance is the bow of another ship carved from the rock and sailing out in a direction opposite to that of the stern in the Scylla group. This, a mosaic inscription informs us, was none other than the Argo, the vessel of Jason and the Argonauts, which had passed through many of the same dangers as Odysseus and his comrades.[30] Affixed directly to the cliff face above the entrance to the cavern there hovered a statue of Ganymede as he was snatched up to heaven by the eagle to serve as Zeus' cupbearer and lover—Ganymede, the Trojan prince, clad in Eastern dress and appropriately carved from Phrygian marble, the most beautiful of mortals and, because of the jealousy of Hera, the most distant cause of the Trojan War.[31] And to the right—whether visible to the diners is not known—carved from similarly exotic marble and likewise affixed to the cliff of the headland, the princess Andromeda hung in her chains, awaiting just as she had done so long ago the arrival of the sea monster to devour her, and the unexpected advent of Perseus on winged feet to turn the monster to stone with the head of Medusa.[32] The positions of the Argo, Ganymede, and Andromeda can be ascertained, but they are only three among scores of other works associated with the villa and its grounds whose original placement is unknown.[33] With the immensely elaborate statuary and apparatus within the cavern and on the dining-room island before it, and the complex associations of the other myths surrounding it, we catch sight of a very crowded landscape indeed, a compendium of classical myth dominated by the adventures of Odysseus.[34]

And if we draw back even further from the artifices of the cave and its surroundings, and look around us, we realize that the natural landscape itself is a map of allusions. Another phenomenon comes into play here, likewise much studied in the last few decades: the equally romantic "places of memory."[35] The concept is an elastic one, encompassing all of those media that aid in the creation of a shared identity for a society or a social group, the focuses of collective or cultural memory, ranging from sites and monuments to artistic and literary works. Particularly resonant was a sense of place, the recognition that great events had transpired at a particular locale, connecting the present with the past, explaining to us who we are, and presenting examples for us to follow in the future. At Rome, this sense of place was numinous; there was nowhere in the city that was not full of religion and the gods, as Livy has Camillus say in a speech in which he argues that to abandon the city to an enemy was unthinkable. Physical memories of gods and heroes thronged the classical landscapes through which they had passed, and were shown with pride to visitors.[36] Inevitably a lore grew up over the centuries and spanning the continents, about the travels of the heroes around the world—Hercules, Odysseus, Aeneas especially, but hundreds of others as well—the purpose being to explain the history of a place or a people, and to tie it to the history of others. Such lore might be impossibly complex and contradictory. No matter: a standard narrative usually evolves, and one could always choose the material that appealed, to create a narrative of one's own.

Diners at Spelunca had but to turn around to see, looming dramatically behind them on the western horizon, about thirty kilometers across the sea, Mons Circeius, modern Monte Circeo, which had very early been identified by the Greeks with Aeaea, the island home of Circe the enchantress. Only ten kilometers to their right lay the town of Formiae, the home of the Laestrygones. As everyone knew, Odysseus had sailed from the Laestrygones to Circe—that is to say, right past The Cave, Spelunca. Circe's Mountain is central to its story. Strabo, Tiberius' contemporary, offers a valuable sketch of

> Circaeum, a mountain which has the form of an island, because it is surrounded by sea and marshes. They further say that Circaeum is a place that abounds in roots—perhaps because they associate it with the myth about Circe. It has a little city and a temple of Circe and an altar of Athene, and people there show you a sort of bowl which, they say, belonged to Odysseus.[37]

Other sources confirm the long-standing existence of a local cult to the goddess Circe, and tourists were shown not only the bowl of Odysseus, but the myrtle-clad tumulus raised by the hero to his companion Elpenor, who had fallen to his death from the roof of Circe's palace after a bout of heavy drinking.[38] After releasing his men from their animal enchantment, our hero stayed a year on the island of the goddess, feasting with his crew on endless supplies of meat and wine (hence the bowl left behind, hence the death of Elpenor), while he shared her bed. From this offshore union of king and goddess sprang sons who colonized the mainland, according to various ancient stories. Many different names and relationships were elaborated, and connections with the Etruscans to the north and with the Ausones of Campania to the south, but the sons and in some cases grandsons of Odysseus and Circe settled mainly in neighboring Latium, where one of them became the eponymous ancestor of the Latins, and where they founded Praeneste and Tusculum in the hills above Rome, Ardea and Antium up the coast, and (in no fewer than five different versions) Rome itself.[39]

One son, Telegonus (the "far-born"), future founder of Tusculum, stayed with his mother Circe and became the hero of his own epic, the *Telegoneia*, composed in the middle of the sixth century BCE by a Eugammon of Cyrene. Searching for his father in Ithaca, he mistakenly kills him, thus fulfilling a prophecy that Odysseus would be slain by his son. He brings the body back to Aeaea, along with his stepmother Penelope and his stepbrother Telemachus. There, bizarrely, Telegonus marries Penelope (to produce "Italus"), and Telemachus marries *his* stepmother Circe (to produce "Latinus"). Matters get complicated in various versions, but apparently the immortal Circe bestows immortality on the other three of this strange Odyssean quartet of stepmothers married to stepsons, and packs two or all three of them off to the Isles of the Blessed. But Odysseus himself she either inters or, in one late version, brings back to life to keep for herself. Either way, it is clear that Odysseus ended up on Mons Circeius.[40] That is, from his final home on Circe's mountain to the west, close by across the water, the hero Odysseus watched the master of the villa at Spelunca, even as Tiberius, the master of the villa, watched his hero Odysseus in the cave: a place reverberating with memory indeed.[41]

The palace at Sperlonga, in short, was the very heart of an early imperial reimagining of the tale of Odysseus on a grand scale.

Reminiscences of Odysseus and his companions could be discovered in every corner of Italy, and his descendants colonized Latium and other regions, but places of real memory—places that the hero had actually visited—are restricted to two well-defined areas on the western coast of the peninsula.[42] One we have just visited, the region known as Latium Adiectum on the Gulf of Gaeta, running from Circe and Circeii in the north down past the villa at Spelunca to Formiae and the Laestrygones, and reaching perhaps to Sinuessa on the southern boundary.[43] The other was the coast of Campania, where it runs around the shore of the Bay of Naples and down to its southern approaches. Here, the memories of Odysseus crowd in again, clustered in the north around the golden Bay of Baiae, and in the south around the Cape of Surrentum.

In the north, one tradition had the hero land on Pithecusa, the modern Ischia, the large island off the northwestern end of the great bay. Opposite Pithecusa on the mainland lay Misenum, the base of the Roman fleet on the western coast of Italy, and site of the imperial villa where Tiberius died: it was named after Odysseus' companion Misenus.[44] Just to its east sat Baiae on its small gulf, the pleasure capital of Italy, named after Odysseus' steersman Baius. It too was the site of an imperial villa where relics of Tiberius' childhood were still on display a century after his death. Very near that palace (as it was later called) an artificial grotto was carved into the seaside rock and outfitted as a nymphaeum with a pool of water, a complex with sophisticated system of jets and fountains, and a triclinium for dining, adorned with statues of gods and with the imperial family displayed in niches along the walls. Set in the apse at the inner end of the nymphaeum, a large statuary group showed Odysseus offering wine (water actually flowed from his cup and the wineskin) to Polyphemus, just before he blinds him. As scholars agree, this is a clear reference to the cave at Spelunca, probably dating to the early years of the reign of Claudius, Tiberius' nephew, and like Spelunca it was set in the midst of an Odyssean landscape.[45]

This region lay under Calypso's spell. Inland, just beyond Baiae, was Lake Avernus, traditionally the portal into the realm of Hades and the site of one of Odysseus' greatest adventures: its area was, according to one tantalizing tradition, dedicated to Calypso—not surprisingly, for the island where the nymph had lived with Odysseus, and the setting for stories about her, lay in the sea just off the shore of the neighboring port city of Puteoli.[46] It was from here, presumably, that Auson, one of their sons, pushed inland to give his name to the nearby area of Campania (loosely defined) that included the cities of Cales and Beneventum: Ausonia, a name that then spread famously to define all of Italy.[47]

To the south, by contrast, the coast running around the Bay of Naples and beyond was—in the phrase coined by Norman Douglas—"Siren Land," dominated by the imperial island of Capri. East of Baiae and about thirty-five kilometers due north of Capri, across the Bay, lay Parthenope, otherwise Naples, named after one of the three sirens. Some sixty-five kilometers to the southeast of Capri was the island of Leucosia, her sister, off the cape of Poseidon, between Paestum (Greek Poseidonia) and Velia (Elea). Closer to Capri, less than fifteen kilometers down the coast of the mainland, one sailed in the wake of Odysseus past the actual Islands of the Sirens, the Sirenes or Sirenussae (modern Li Galli), while somewhere on the Sorrentine peninsula opposite Capri, on what some called the Cape of the Sirenussae, there stood an ancient temple dedicated to all three sirens. But best of all, the heart of Siren Land was dominated by a sanctuary built and dedicated by a grateful Odysseus to his patroness Athena on the very tip of the Sorrentine cape: the Athenaeum, the modern Punta della Campanella.[48]

What of Capri itself, Tiberius' base for the last eleven years of his life? We undoubtedly glimpse the expected landscape of mythological allusion on his private island refuge: Augustus proudly displayed there the bones of giants and the armor of heroes, and Tiberius is said to have peopled its caves and rocky hollows, *antra et cavas rupes*, with little Pans and nymphs.[49] It is more difficult to make a direct connection between the tastes of the second princeps and the material remains on Capreae than is the case for Spelunca. Yet imagination is not to be dismissed, for, after Tiberius' death and the departure of Gaius for Rome in 37 CE, his island remained a private and inaccessible imperial estate, and no later princeps is on record as visiting it, let alone residing there. That is to say, its ruins and the surviving fragments and artworks look to be something of a time capsule from the early principate.[50]

Capri is particularly famous for its seaside caves, and several traces of human artifice inevitably put us in mind of Spelunca. Two somewhat isolated grottoes, the Arsenale, near the Marina Piccola, on the south coast of the island, and Matermania on the east coast, were certainly transformed into caves of the nymphs and preserve remains of elaborate decoration and furniture, in the former for dining, in the latter for cult.[51] Better, in 1964 and 1975, four badly corroded marble statues, along with other fragments, emerged from the waters of the Blue Grotto itself. These have been reconstructed as a version of a marine *thiasos*, an assembly of sea gods, a sculptural grouping popular with the Roman patrons of Greek artists. Here the company includes at least three fish-tailed tritons, originally affixed to the cavern wall and positioned to rise dramatically out of the water. Some of them probably blew on conch shells as they celebrated the fourth figure, a bearded Poseidon, the god of the sea. The grotto itself is presumed to have been connected with the villa at Gradola, up the cliff nearby to the east, or even with the huge villa of Damecuta that dominated the northwest headland of the island.[52] And yet another great villa, on the height of Castiglione, 250 meters above the sea, with panoramic views to the south, enjoyed two grottoes below it, both developed, the larger of which held niches for statues and was certainly the nymphaeum for the residence above. That villa of course boasted of a small bronze copy of a statue signed by Athanodorus son of Hagesandros, one of the three sculptors of the Laocoön and of the Sperlonga Scylla group.[53] The combination of glorious cliff top maritime villas with lavishly decorated seaside grottoes suggests a certain taste at work.

Greatest by far of all the imperial properties on Capri was the villa on the northeastern corner of the island, the massive remains of which loom on their vertiginous cliff some 334 meters, just over a thousand feet, straight above the sea. Again, no inscription names the owner, but it is universally and rightly assumed that this was Tiberius' main residence and retreat on the island. The ruins have always been identified with, and must be, the so-called Villa of Jupiter mentioned by Suetonius as the refuge from which the apprehensive princeps directed the destruction of Sejanus and its bloody aftermath. Inaccessible by sea and by land approachable only up a long, steep, and controllable slope, the enormous ruins match the descriptions left by our ancient sources: *Tiberi principis arx*, the citadel of Tiberius Caesar; *altissima rupes*, the loftiest crag, from which he anxiously watched for signals of Sejanus' fate at Rome; *angusta rupes*, the narrow crag upon which he perched with his crowd of astrologers.[54] And, appropriately for the home of the First Citizen of the empire, the villa, perhaps seven stories tall, has recently been claimed as the first true palace in the Roman West.[55] No maritime grotto alive with heroes or tritons or nymphs can be associated with this palace—the sea is too far below, the cliff too sheer to allow any access—but on its top story there was probably a grand semicircular dining room, oriented due east, with stunning panoramic views of the island, the entire Bay of Naples, and the Amalfi coast stretching away to the south. Every time that Tiberius dined there with his guests, quizzing them perhaps about the finer points of mythology, he and they could gaze around at the panoramic Odyssean landscape to the north, the east, and the south, and directly over at the Temple of Athena, erected by Odysseus on the heights of the Sorrentine cape, a scant five kilometers across the strait.

The palace itself poses a mythological conundrum for—despite near universal acceptance—the name "Villa of Jupiter" is a phantom. Historians, archaeologists, and translators acknowledge that there is a problem but, after careful discussion, almost everyone accepts that name, which is found only in Suetonius' biography of Tiberius. Yet Maximilian Ihm, who produced the standard edition of *The Lives of the Caesars*, was adamant: Suetonius wrote not "Villa Jovis" but "Villa Ionis," the "Villa of Io."[56]

Suetonius' narration of Tiberius' assault on Sejanus in 31 CE is a tour de force, compact and suspenseful. As the plot unfolds in Rome, Tiberius nervously awaits events on the towering crag on Capri. Contingency plans are in place: if there is a rising in the capital, the imprisoned grandson of the princeps is to be released and put in charge there, while ships lie ready to whisk Tiberius away to the legions. He spends his time watching from the cliff for signals that he has ordered to inform him immediately each step of the way:

But even after Sejanus' conspiracy had been crushed, he was in no way more secure or confident, and for the next nine months, he did not leave his deep seclusion in the "villa that is called Jupiter's" (*villa quae vocatur Iovis*).[57]

Suetonius then goes on at length and in confusing fashion to describe Tiberius' anguish during the bloodbath after the death of Sejanus, but the climax of his tale is surely this vivid image of the princeps in the "villa that is called Jupiter's." How appropriate that the master of the world should be so removed, so far from the blood in the streets of Rome, high above human affairs, brooding in a villa named after the greatest of Roman gods.[58]

But it was not called the Villa of Jupiter. The manuscript tradition clearly preserves IONIS (the genitive of Io) from the archetype, not IOVIS (the genitive of Jupiter). Ihm reported: "Ionis" was the reading in all but one of the manuscripts that he consulted for his text, including the oldest and best of them, the Memmianus; the one exception known to him (along with some much more recent manuscripts) was the Laurentianus; all of the close relatives of the Laurentianus nevertheless preserve the archetype's "Ionis" against its "Iovis"; and the Laurentianus frequently transposes the letters "v" and "n" elsewhere.[59] In short, Suetonius, our only source for the name, seems to tell us that the great palace was called the Villa of Io.

Why? Ihm thought that we just couldn't know and that there was room for the play of fantasy: the name might, for example, derive from a work of art that depicted the myth of Io, a painting perhaps, one especially beloved by Tiberius. But to postulate that the First Citizen named a huge palace after a single, unattested, and otherwise unsuspected work of art is fanciful in the extreme. Granted, Tiberius may not himself have been responsible for naming the villa (as Ihm noted), but—whoever chose it—surely the name must have had some significance for him or for Augustus. It is very hard to see how Io, a victim of Jupiter's love—a woman whose story amounts to being first imprisoned and then forced to wander the earth in the form of a cow—could have such a special, inexplicable, and otherwise unreported resonance for the first men in Rome that one of them, let alone any third party, would name a palace after her.[60] What is worse, Io was commonly identified in the Greco-Roman world with the Egyptian goddess Isis.[61] Isis was always a figure of great suspicion to Roman authorities, her cult at Rome often incurring their official displeasure, and in 19 CE, deeply upset by a bizarre criminal incident at her temple, Tiberius allegedly crucified her priests, razed her temple, and had the goddess' image thrown into the Tiber.[62] His subsequent retirement to the Villa of Io on Capri might seem too ironic even for Tiberius.

Emendation of Suetonius' text may indeed be in order. Perhaps it ought to read IOVIS after all, but in that case, we should be sure that the name was not chosen by Augustus or Tiberius: although they might be portrayed by artists as Jupiter, it is hard to conceive of either man acting as the ruler of the gods in this fashion. Or perhaps IUNONIS, as conjectured by Heinsius,[63] after Juno, the wife of the ruler of the gods, which seems inexplicable and most unlikely. Or perhaps we should accept IONIS as transmitted, but translate it differently, as the genitive singular not of Io (feminine) but of Ion (masculine), making it the "Villa of Ion" and recalling the son of Apollo who was king of Athens and the protagonist of a play by Euripides.[64] But Ion has no mythical resonance. And that, generally, is the trouble with Ion, Io, Jove, and Juno: none of them seems to be relevant to Capri or significant to Tiberius, the lover of myth. But there is another figure from mythology, one who *is* both relevant and significant, and whose name has been proposed, in an easy emendation. Could the "Villa IONIS" of the manuscript have been in reality the "Villa INONIS," the Villa of Ino?[65]

Ino conjures up a web of stories and ritual, but the essence of her tale is this. She was the daughter of Cadmus of Thebes. Her sister, Semele, seduced by Zeus himself, had borne the new god Dionysus. Hera, Zeus' wife, took her revenge on the family: she drove Athamas, the husband of Ino, mad. He slew their son Learchus and would have slain Ino, his wife, and their other son Melicertes, had not the young Dionysus temporarily blinded him. Ino leapt with Melicertes from a cliff into the sea near Corinth and drowned, but Zeus took pity on her and changed them both into gods: she became Leucothea, the White Goddess, and he became Palaemon, and the Isthmian Games were founded in their honor.

Ino plays a special role in the *Odyssey*. After his fabulous adventures on the return from Troy—the Lotus-Eaters, the Cyclops, the Land of the Dead, the Sirens, Scylla and Charybdis (twice), and so forth—Odysseus, the last survivor of all his crew, is washed up on the shores of Ogygia, the island of the nymph Calypso. There he languishes in the goddess' power for seven years, until Athena persuades Zeus to set him free, and Zeus sends Hermes with his command to Calypso. Odysseus builds a raft and sets out with directions home from Calypso, but his enemy Poseidon conjures up a terrible storm. Odysseus prepares to die, but then

> The daughter of Kadmos, sweet-stepping Ino called Leukothea,
> saw him. She had once been one who spoke as a mortal,
> but now in the gulfs of the sea she holds degree as a goddess.
>   (*Od.* 5.333–35)

Ino takes pity on Odysseus, and in the form of a seagull urges him to strip himself of his clothes and abandon his raft. Entrusting himself to her immortal veil, he is to swim to the land of the Phaeacians and there, with face averted, he must return the veil to the sea. The ever-suspicious Odysseus, not knowing who the benevolent deity may be, decides nevertheless to obey. His raft is destroyed, and, after several harrowing escapes, he washes up at Scheria, the island of the Phaeacians, where he dutifully returns the veil. The mysterious, unmotivated intervention of the unknown goddess into his story is rich in implications, and Ino / Leucothea has generated considerable scholarly attention.[66] However we interpret the incident, it is clearly of fundamental importance in Odysseus' journey home: Ino brings about the end of his adventures in the world of fantasy and his reentry into the world of daily life, through the liminal realm of the Phaeacians, whence he will be magically transported to Ithaca. Odysseus was deeply in her debt: she saved his life and brought him home.

Ino, Leucothea, the White Goddess, has moreover a connection with the Siren Land. Her cult is attested in Naples, city of the siren Parthenope to the north. In his *Natural History*, Pliny the Elder lists the offshore islands of Italy, working his way southward down around the Bay of Naples and arriving at "next, about eight miles from Surrentum, Capreae, renowned for the citadel of the *princeps* Tiberius, about 11 miles in circumference, (and then) Leucothea." So, the White Goddess had an island somewhere in the vicinity of the *arx Tiberii*—but without further comment, Pliny veers off to sea from Leucothea, over to Sardinia, returning to the mainland only much further south, at Paestum.[67] Where was the mysterious island of the White Goddess, east of Capri? No one seems to know.[68]

Let us assume that the princeps could see the island of the goddess from his palace, and then consider where the palace was set: *imminet aequoribus scopulus*, the cliff hangs over the sea.[69] Tiberius was notoriously sardonic. "The Villa of Ino," one might almost say "Ino's Leap," would be a grimly appropriate nickname for a dwelling set so high above her waters. And yet Tiberius was also a romantic. Ino had fallen as an innocent and unhappy queen, but she had risen again as a happy immortal. As a goddess, she would save the one hero worth saving, Odysseus, and for that she deserved every honor.

To recapitulate the story thus far. The complexity and grandiosity of the display in the grotto at Sperlonga allows us to infer a patron intensely fascinated, to put it mildly, with the hero Odysseus, and a cumulative but circumstantial argument demands that we identify that patron with Tiberius Caesar. The Tiberian implications can then be mapped, again circumstantially, onto the two essentially Odyssean regions of the western coast of Italy, Latium Adiectum and the Bay of Naples, each harboring a magnificent refuge for the princeps. His inferred fascination with the King of Ithaca, it is argued, was the obsession of a powerful man who was a recluse, a romantic, and a connoisseur. What might it all mean?

The answer was supplied thirty-five years ago by A. F. Stewart in his now classic paper on the finds at Sperlonga, referred to earlier. Stewart offered complex and compelling arguments for "two mutually supporting, but nevertheless independent, possibilities: that as far as their setting, arrangement and treatment of subject-matter are concerned, these sculptures fit in fairly well with what one might look for in grandiose mythological compositions of the early Julio-Claudian period, though the blend of pedantry and horror in decoration meant for the dining-room indicates an owner of somewhat unusual interests; and that the literary and artistic tastes of Tiberius, together with his known predilections in dinner-table entertainment, were such as to furnish a suitable climate in which sculpture of this kind, erudite, academic and monstrous, could have flourished" (1977, 86).

In a coda to his essay, Stewart asked "why Odysseus, above all the Greek heroes, should have been chosen as the subject for the Sperlonga sculptures," and he suggested two converging explanations. One was that the western coast of Italy had long been filled with memories of Odysseus. As we have seen, the mapping is precise, with two private retreats of Tiberius centrally located, secluded but dominating, in two clearly defined coastal regions of Latium Adiectum and Campania, the most Odyssean areas in all of Italy. Stewart's other proposed explanation for the Odyssean theme of the Sperlonga sculptures was that the character of the hero displays a "curious similarity in some respects to that of the emperor" Tiberius—suggesting, that is, a very personal interest—and in this regard he shrewdly recalled the notorious questions with which Tiberius, addicted to mythology, notoriously tested his entourage of grammarians.[70]

Let us begin with those *grammatici*. Suetonius is our main source here. In his exhausting catalog of the vices of the princeps, he assures us that, although Tiberius took great pleasure in his *Graeculi*, he was not kind to them. For example, he was accustomed to posing questions to them from his daily reading. One of them, the grammarian Seleucus, inquired of his servants what authors he was reading and when, so that he might arrive prepared. Tiberius removed him from his company and later drove him to suicide, or so it is alleged.[71] Suetonius returns to the matter later in the biography, in his discussion of the literary tastes and studies of his subject. So fond was Tiberius of the three poets Euphorion, Rhianus, and Parthenius, that not only did he compose Greek poems in imitation of them, but he dedicated the writings and the busts of all three in the public libraries of Rome, among those of the foremost ancient authors. As with his daily reading, this passion was duly noted by learned men, *eruditi*, and many of them responded as, in Suetonius' awkward phrasing, they competed to publish a lot of works about these authors for him. And, as an expert in mythology, Tiberius loved to test his *grammatici* with such questions as: "Who was Hecuba's mother? What was Achilles' name among the maidens? What did the Sirens sing?"—"though puzzling Questions, not beyond all conjecture."[72]

The key to these questions was first offered by Stewart: "All three may be referred, in one way or another, to Odysseus and his doings." That is: "Hecuba failed to denounce him when she discovered him in Helen's bedroom, and on the fall of Troy became his slave; it was he who discovered Achilles 'among the maidens' at the court of Lycomedes; and as for the songs of the Sirens, there was only one man who could have enlightened Tiberius as to these."[73] Moreover, as it happens, yet another question, allegedly posed by the princeps in all seriousness, concerned the much-debated parentage of the god Pan. The numerous scholars, *philologoi*, summoned by Tiberius agreed that Pan was the son of the god Hermes and of the mortal Penelope, the long-suffering wife of Odysseus.[74] "Perhaps then," Stewart concludes, "we may be forgiven for imagining that he found the character of the wily Odysseus thought-provoking, and, privately, maybe even congenial."

Indeed, there are further hints of this personal attraction to Odysseus, from two unexpected sources, again oblique but arresting.

Learned men churned out works for him on Euphorion and Rhianus and Parthenius, all (to us) idiosyncratic Hellenistic poets of exceptional learning, ingenuity, and obscurity. A passing notice in Diogenes Laertius tells of yet another grammarian, Apollonides of Nicaea, who dedicated to Tiberius Caesar yet another commentary, not on the poems of his three favorites, but on the *Silloi* ("Mockeries") of yet another Hellenistic poet, Timon of Phlius. Timon was an older contemporary of the Tiberian favorites Rhianus and Euphorion, and, like them, a devout Homerist, but this immensely sophisticated satiric poet and sceptic philosopher enjoyed a talent much more congenial to modern tastes.[75] In the three books of the *Silloi*, he mercilessly derided the battles of the various philosophical schools in Homeric terms, vividly pinning down the doctrines and the personalities of the warring philosophers with a memorable sharpness that would appeal to a man of Tiberius' mordant disposition. The work is now lost, but its extensive remains suggest that "Homeric terms" is a pallidly inadequate description of the *Silloi*, for it has been estimated that almost 80 percent of the 133 surviving fragments have a Homeric resonance in one or more of three senses: parody of Homeric formulae; parody of epic language in general; and parody of whole passages and larger units (battles, the catalog of ships, Odysseus' visit to the underworld, the view from the walls of Troy).[76]

Even more to Tiberian taste, much of the poem was cast in the form of an Odyssean *nekuia*, the trip to the underworld where Timon encountered the bickering shades of great thinkers, just as Odysseus had met the heroes in Hades in Book 11 of the *Odyssey*. And most importantly, the hero of Timon's poem was apparently the one philosopher who came in for nothing but praise: his master, the original sceptic, Pyrrho of Elis. In one fragment, the poet says of him that "no other mortal man beside could stand up against Pyrrho," lifting a half-line from Homer: "Then no other mortal man beside could stand up against Odysseus."[77] Tiberius must have known and would surely have been delighted by the poem's combination of biting satire, brilliant Homeric parody, and a markedly Odyssean hero. A good commentary on such a work would be a shrewd appeal for the favor of the princeps.[78]

Our second source of Odyssean illumination comes from a much higher authority than Tiberius' grammarians. At some time during the last decade of his life, Augustus had charmingly expressed his esteem for Tiberius in a letter dispatched to his adopted son and colleague, far off at war in the north, that is, between 4 and 13 CE. He wrote that whenever any matter arose that required careful consideration, or whenever he was upset by something, then, by heaven, he missed Tiberius terribly, and a particular Homeric verse came to mind:

> Were he to go with me, both of us could come back from the blazing
> of fire itself, since his mind is best at devices.

Everyone knew the context of this sentiment from the *Iliad*, the scene in which Diomedes of the great war cry chooses a single warrior from all the Greek army to join him in a nighttime raid on the Trojan camp:

If indeed you tell me myself to pick my companion,
how then could I forget Odysseus the godlike, he whose
heart and proud spirit are beyond all others forward
in all hard endeavors, and Pallas Athene loves him.[79]

The quotation aptly encapsulates Odysseus' unique combination of military virtues, that is, cunning intelligence and fierce courage, thought and action. Could there be a more authoritative recognition of the avatar of Tiberius, who was now the chosen companion of Augustus himself?

The Odyssey in marble at Sperlonga, the immersion in numinously Odyssean landscapes, the preoccupation with Odysseus apparently remarked upon by ambitious Greek intellectuals: despite the accumulation of suggestive detail, the case for Tiberius identifying himself with, or as, Odysseus remains circumstantial. Only once can we catch a glimpse of him, in old age, briefly assuming the mantle of the Greek hero, yet even that is uncertain.[80] But if the identification is plausible, the fact that we cannot prove it is itself suggestive. What is striking here is the marked contrast with the very public identification by Tiberius the mythomane of himself as one of the heavenly twins, Castor and Pollux, and his public manipulation of their potent myth at Rome.[81] His Odysseus is rather a *private* passion, appropriate to the inaccessible house on the cliffs of Rhodes, the remote Xanadu at Sperlonga, and then, for years on end, the great palaces and playgrounds of Capri, the private island to which no one came without his permission. For relaxation, Tiberius preferred the company of two groups of men. One was a small number of true friends, men like himself of high rank, whether patricians or new men, equals with whom he could relax unreservedly. The other was a rather larger circle of intellectuals, mostly Greeks, "whose conversation he found relaxing" and "whom he especially enjoyed," although the relationship was always tense and competitive—in the end, Odysseus himself could not save his companions from their folly.[82] It is here, in his private life, that the fascination with Odysseus would be indulged. Whether the general public knew of it or not was something Tiberius would not care about.

Hence, we will never know whether the "curious similarity" of the characters of princeps and hero proceeded from fascination to identification. But again, Stewart summed up the case admirably, without forcing a conclusion on the reader:

Certainly Tiberius, like Odysseus, "cherished dissimulation"; his intellect was penetrating, his caution excessive, his anger quick, his harshness proverbial, and his pride in his own achievements, especially military ones, enormous. . . . Close to some extent, then, in temperament and close also in fortune: Tiberius, too, had spent a great deal of his life (up to his fifty-first

year) abroad; he had had his time of campaigning in the field, and his
time in exile (eight years to be precise), enduring multiple humiliations
before attaining what was due to him. Of course, none of this is in any sense
conclusive.[83]

As Ronald Syme wrote about Tiberius' excursions in old age, "What then
resided in the devious mind of Ti. Caesar, no biographer could tell, or anybody
else."[84] Nevertheless, let us speculate, not about the presentation of an image,
but about the possibilities of self-identification with, indeed immersion in, the
character of a legendary hero.

After the war at Troy came the great wanderings, and greatest of all were the
adventures of Odysseus. In his day, Tiberius had fought and wandered more
than anyone. He had seen real warfare as a teenager in the Spanish campaigns
of Augustus in the 20s BCE and as a young general in Rhaetia in 15 BCE. And
then relentlessly, as a mature commander in chief in the north with hard fighting, often on a massive scale, for six years, 12–7 BCE, and for another ten long
years, from 4 through to 13 CE. He was setting off on yet another campaign in
Illyricum in 14 CE when called back by the death of Augustus. Exhausted, he
never left Italy again. Indeed, he had wandered through most of the world—
Italy north and south, Sicily, Spain, Gaul, Germany, Rhaetia, Pannonia, Dalmatia, Macedonia, Achaia, Thrace, Asia, Syria, and Armenia—and some of
those regions he had explored thoroughly. But even when he confined himself
to Italy, his wanderings did not cease.

Two of them attract attention precisely because his motives in each case
baffled his contemporaries, and there is no modern consensus about them. Let
us assume that Tiberius was fascinated by, and deeply knowledgeable about,
not just mythology in general, but Odysseus in particular; that he was attracted
to the personality of a hero who was secretive, intelligent, and proud, a recluse
who was also a leader of men; and that he could appreciate the parallels between two lives of war and travel, his own and Odysseus', lived by leaders who
longed for the peace and quiet of home. The mythical Odysseus may provide
some insight into the character of the historical Tiberius.

First, in the summer of 6 BCE, with little warning and against the vigorous
opposition of his mother and stepfather / father-in-law, Tiberius sailed away
into self-imposed retirement on Rhodes. Intense speculation ancient and
modern as to his motives has generated much heat but little light. The reasons
suggested then were many: growing dislike of his wife, Julia; or the hope that
his absence might increase his authority; or anger at not being adopted by
Augustus; or retirement in favor or fear of Julia's growing sons, Augustus' sons
by adoption; or the love of learning; or simple exhaustion after his labors.[85]

Be that as it may, in his absence, Julia fell—spectacularly. Late in 2 BCE, she was accused of liaisons with many lovers and was banished to the island of Pandateria (later, in 3 CE, she was transferred to Rhegium, on the mainland) by Augustus, who was devastated by his daughter's adulteries. He rebuffed Tiberius' subsequent applications to return home from Rhodes but, after Julia's two elder sons—his sons by adoption—died, he was forced to rely again on his stepson, who had finally come home in 2 CE, to resume his place as the second man in Rome in 4 CE. Augustus disinherited Julia and forbade her burial in his mausoleum. Soon after his death in 14 CE, she died of starvation, allegedly with Tiberius' acquiescence.

Tiberius had remained on the island of Rhodes for seven long years, the last four of them unwillingly. Seven years was just the length of time that Odysseus languished on Calypso's island, an unwilling guest pining for home. Odysseus was released by Zeus, Tiberius summoned home by Augustus.[86] What might a dedicated Odyssean make of these dramatic events?

While her husband was detained abroad, Julia was unfaithful, allegedly committing adultery with five noblemen, not to mention other senators and knights. When the debauchery, or conspiracy, was unmasked, one of the ringleaders killed himself and the others were sent into exile by Augustus. At least one of them was executed soon after Tiberius succeeded as First Citizen in 14 CE.[87] Not a good comparison with Odysseus' heroic revenge on the suitors of his long-suffering wife.

But there was of course a long, post-Homeric tradition of the *unfaithful* Penelope, which Tiberius, the lover of recondite lore and literature, surely knew.[88] One version, already old in the time of Herodotus and much repeated by later authors, claimed that she had borne the god Pan to Hermes, but others would have her seduced by one or other of her noble suitors to produce Pan, while one extreme variant has her give birth to him after enjoying intercourse with "all" of the suitors (hence the god's name). Remarkably, Tiberius subscribed, later if not sooner, to the version that made an adulteress of Penelope. When news reached him of the death of the god Pan, and he was inclined to believe it, his learned men conjectured (in Plutarch's words) that Pan was the son of Hermes and Penelope. This was hardly a novel theory, since the story had been widespread for centuries.[89] Would Tiberius' *philologoi* have dared to impugn the chastity of Odysseus' wife if they knew that the First Citizen would resent it? The story of the exiled prince, longing to come home, turning his back on immortality and eternal youth for the love of his wife, even as she enjoys adultery with noble suitors: that would be a very attractive self-image to a disappointed romantic like Tiberius, or to any grammarian disposed to curry favor with him.

Then there is also the singular behavior in the last six years of his life. After the disastrous rock fall at Spelunca in 26 CE, Tiberius retreated south to

Campania but, tiring of the crowds there, removed the next year to Capri. The last eleven years of his life divide into two remarkably distinct periods, defined geographically. For several years, from 26 to the summer of 32 CE, he did not stir from Capri and the adjacent mainland. Those same years saw Sejanus edging toward supreme power at Rome, his precipitous fall, and its bloody aftermath. For nine months after the death of his colleague, Tiberius watched events from the island, and then came an astonishing change: from 32 until his death in 37 CE, the princeps divided his time between Capri and Rome.

Suetonius asserts that, after he removed to Capri in 26 CE, he attempted only twice to return to Rome, once in 32, getting as close as his gardens near the Naumachia across the Tiber, and once in 37, advancing to the seventh milestone on the Appian Way. But the biographer omits at least four other occasions when he came up, for every year after the fall of Sejanus, the princeps in fact journeyed to the immediate outskirts of his capital.[90] Suetonius' omissions may be intentional and pointed, not ignorant, for technically Tiberius did not enter the city limit of the *pomerium*, always preferring to remain in the suburb, and the value of the word "attempted" (*conatus*) is uncertain.[91] As with the retirement to Rhodes, the mysterious motives of the First Citizen for what his nephew Claudius would later call his *apsentia pertinax* again excited speculation. Suetonius variously suggests that the reason was simply unknown; or that he feared the people or the aristocracy; or that he was alarmed at a portent. Or, perhaps more likely, is the report of Tacitus that the stars had warned him not to return. Portent or stars, both clearly indicated that he would die if he returned to the city.[92]

Tacitus contributes two astonishing glimpses of the elderly princeps, not secluded in his palace on Capri at all, but wandering restlessly in the vicinity of Rome. In his account of the year 26 CE, the historian claims that, after leaving it for the last time, "he passed his extreme old age nearby in the countryside or on the shore, often encamping at the walls of the City." And seven years later, in 33, after giving only vague reasons for his absence, Tiberius had the senate decree for him a military escort whenever he should enter the senate house, "but," comments Tacitus, "he never once approached even the roofs of the city, still less the public council, on frequent detours encircling and dodging his fatherland."[93]

These strange peregrinations, encamping, encircling, dodging, near but never quite reaching home, might again remind us of the voyages of Odysseus, the man who strove for so many years to come home without actually getting there. And although Odysseus did eventually return to his kingdom, many different and often conflicting tales tell how he set off on his travels yet again; indeed a bewildering number of exploits are woven into the tradition that the hero who tried so hard to get home could not stay there.[94] He left Ithaca for many reasons: in the restless search for adventure; or to atone for the deaths of the noble suitors; or in disgust at the adultery of his wife; or, most commonly, in apprehension of the prophesy given him by the incomparable seer Teiresias, which proved to be true, that his son would kill him. Wanderlust, guilt, revulsion, but most of all, fear of a death foretold. Warned by his hero, perhaps Tiberius knew better than to go home at all.

Or perhaps he was already there. Capri was a Greek island. Greek was spoken there and Greek customs were followed. Augustus had treasured the arms of Greek heroes there, he had composed Greek verses on the island, and he would have his Roman companions wear Greek dress; the hellenophile Tiberius succeeded him with his company of Greekling intellectuals. Capri was the private property of the princeps, and Sejanus would infamously dismiss Tiberius as the master of the island, its "nesiarch." Now, Tiberius and every literate person knew that his predecessor as ruler on Capri in the age of Odysseus had been King Telon, husband of the Campanian nymph Sebethis and father by her of the aggressive prince Oebalus, who would conquer much of the adjacent mainland of Campania and then proceed to join Turnus in his fight against the Trojan invader Aeneas. But Oebalus' father, King Telon, was old, and stayed on his island kingdom.

The people of Capri were the Teleboi. They hailed from Acarnania, in northwestern Greece, and were famed for their skill as sailors and pirates. Indeed, Teleboas, their eponymous founder and the presumed ancestor of King Telon, was the son of Poseidon, god of the sea. The Teleboi were thus particularly associated with islands off the coast of Acarnania: the Echinades, immediately adjacent to the southwest; Taphos and its sister islets further north, next to Leucas; and the large Cephallenia, further to the southwest, beyond which lies the open Ionian Sea. These islands of the Teleboi form a large semicircle in the sea. Nestled within their embrace, close up against Cephallenia, lies one other island: Ithaca, the fabled realm and homeland of Odysseus. The evidence is complex, often contradictory, but for each of them—for the Echinades, for Taphos, for Cephallenia, indeed for the Acarnanian coast itself—traditions held that they had all once belonged to the kingdom of Ithaca. Perhaps, then, in retiring to his Greek refuge, the Teleboan island of Capri, Tiberius came as close as he ever wanted to be to home.

4

The Death of the Phoenix

IN 27 CE, two horrific disasters struck Rome in quick succession. First, a temporary amphitheater in the suburban town of Fidenae collapsed, killing and injuring tens of thousands of people. Immediately thereafter, an extraordinarily violent fire devastated the Caelian Hill in Rome. Tiberius reacted with speed and generosity. He had left Rome the previous year on a private journey to Campania, ordering in an edict that no one should disturb his peace and quiet there. Even then, he was obliged to fend off crowds of well-wishers, so he retired in 27 CE to the even deeper seclusion of Capri. Yet when his suffering people called out for him, he returned to the mainland and allowed everyone to approach him. The senate passed appropriate remedial measures, the aristocracy welcomed their stricken fellow citizens with open houses and medical care. Then, "when the Caelian Hill was destroyed by fire," Tiberius won great popularity with massive, spontaneous munificence. Details are lacking. Where was he? Campania? Rome? What precisely did he do? The great historian Tacitus is at his worst. He obscurely insinuates that the collapse of the amphitheater was Tiberius' fault; he ignores his emergence from Capri and his public availability; he lapses into antiquarian detail about the name "Caelian" Hill (the senate had proposed that it now be changed to "Augustan"); and he pointedly undercuts the good deeds of both the aristocracy and the princeps by juxtaposing with them the wave of prosecutions that engulfed everyone. The great biographer Suetonius separates the two calamities, amphitheater and fire, to suggest that, after retiring again to Capri, Tiberius henceforth simply abandoned the government, and that after the fire he compensated (only) some of the landlords of apartment buildings, an action of which he was so proud that he ordered the name of the Caelian be changed to Augustan (no mention of the senate's initiative in the matter).[1]

Central here is Tacitus' account of how the senate reacted to Tiberius' generosity after the great fire. Leading senators thanked him and a decree was proposed to the following extraordinary effect:

That the Caelian Hill shall hereafter be known as "Augustan," since, with everything ablaze all around, only a likeness of Tiberius, located in the house of the senator Junius, survived the violence intact. The same thing once happened to Claudia Quinta, and her statue, having twice escaped the fury of fires, was consecrated by our ancestors in the shrine of the Mother of the Gods. The Claudii are sacred and acceptable to the divinities, and there is an obligation to augment the holiness of a place in which the gods have displayed such honor to the Princeps.[2]

Claudii, not Julii: but Tiberius had not been a Claudius for over twenty years, since his adoption by Augustus in 4 CE.

Almost seven decades before the miracle on the Caelian, his mother Livia and his father Tiberius Nero had been buffeted by the chaos of civil war (Suet. 6.3):

After being taken all over Sicily and Achaia, he [Tiberius] became an official ward of the Spartans because they were clients of the Claudians. His life came into danger when the family was leaving there at night; flames suddenly broke out on all sides of the forest and enveloped the whole company and part of Livia's clothing and her hair caught fire.

That is to say, in 40 BCE, the infant Tiberius and his parents (both Claudii) had narrowly escaped a spontaneous and uncannily ferocious fire.

Four decades later, on the day before he learned, in 2 CE, that he would be recalled by Augustus from his long, self-imposed exile on Rhodes, his tunic was seen (*visa est*) to catch fire while he was changing his clothes.[3] Indeed, sometime in the following ten years, between 4 and 13 CE, Augustus wrote to Tiberius, who was off fighting far away,

If something comes up that requires careful thought or if something makes me angry, then, by Jupiter, I need my dear Tiberius badly, and this Homeric verse comes to mind:

If this man follows me, then even through the blazing flames
May we both come home; for he has understanding and is wise.[4]

As it happens, this echoes Horace's description of the young Tiberius' victory over the Raeti in 15 BCE, wherein he, "the elder Nero," harasses the enemy troops unharmed and spurs his spirited steed *medios per ignes*, through the midst of the fires.[5]

"The Claudii are sacred and acceptable to the divinities." The favor of heaven was displayed in an invulnerability to flame, both a mark of sanctity and a family trait. Tacitus attributed the Caelian fire to chance, but the people of Rome knew better, the same people who idolized the deeds and the memory of Tiberius' brother Drusus and of his nephew and adopted son Germanicus.[6] Now, in 27 CE, the princeps—not Tiberius Julius Caesar but another "Claudian sacred and acceptable to the divinities"—was far away. "People were maintaining that it was a fatal year and that the Princeps' counsel of absence had been undertaken with unfavorable omens." That is, it could be argued, the people knew that he was their talisman and they wanted him back.[7]

There is much more here than the simple if astonishing immunity to fire. The miraculous burning of his tunic on Rhodes was for Suetonius but one omen of Tiberius' bright prospects. Another occurred years earlier, in 20 BCE, when the future princeps embarked on his first independent campaign. Altars had been set up by the victorious legions of Antony and Caesar (the future Augustus), after their victories at Philippi in Macedonia: they burst spontaneously into flames when the twenty-one-year-old Tiberius passed by with his army.[8] Another omen of future rule, recorded by Plutarch, presumably in his now-lost "Life of Tiberius," was the donkey that gave off sparks while the young Tiberius studied oratory in Rhodes later that same year. Spontaneous yet harmless combustion is a universal sign of future greatness for the human object of the flames, but Tiberius is unique in that the three incidents recorded of him are three more than those recorded of any other Roman princeps.[9]

Equally uncanny and likewise unique, Tiberius did not *need* fire. According to another Claudian family tradition that is surely related to the family's immunity from flames:

> Although he left little to luck and chance, he was nonetheless more confident entering battle whenever it happened that when he was working into the night, his light suddenly wavered and died with no one putting it out. He trusted, as he said, in this sign that had proved astonishingly reliable in every test of leadership for himself and for his ancestors.[10]

A sign sent to the ancestors, those same Claudii who were sacred and acceptable to the divinities, and a reliable one both for them and for him.

Suetonius cites Tiberius himself for this family tradition, but there is a sequel of which the princeps may have been unaware. The context of the dying flame in Suetonius is explicitly military; hence, it is unlikely that Tiberius experienced the family omen of the light going out after 13 CE, the last year in which he took the field. Flash forward to his death a quarter of a century later:

> A few days before he died. . . . At Misenum ashes from the burned wood and bits of charcoal that had been brought in to heat the dining room but had already died out and were long cold suddenly burst into flame at dusk and cast a steady light far into the night. (Suet. 74)

This marvel was surely connected in the minds of observers with the Claudian tradition of a lamp going out the night before success. It too happens at night, and since the object here is a brazier, not a lamp, the phrasing is significant: not that it burned or it heated, but that it shone, it cast light. The dying flame of a lamp had been a good omen. This is its reverse: the living flame predicts his death.

But there is another mark of his independence from fire while he lived. Dio notes a curious trait in passing: Tiberius was dim-sighted in the daytime but saw best in the dark. Suetonius adds arresting detail: "His eyes were unusually large and, strange to say, had the power of seeing even at night and in the dark, but only for a short time when first opened after sleep; presently they grew dim-sighted again." Pliny is yet more dramatic in his *Natural History*: "They say that it was in Tiberius' nature—something reported of no other man born of mortal parents—that when he awoke at night he could take in everything as if in a bright light, for a little while, until gradually the darkness closed over him." Pliny's expression is portentous: no other ordinary human being, that is, not of divine parentage, had this gift. A century or two later, in his *Outlines of Pyrrhonism*, the skeptic philosopher Sextus Empiricus—a sober scholar not prone to trivia or sensation—asserts simply in passing that, "Tiberius Caesar saw in the dark."[11]

———

Tiberius and others were aware of his special relationship with fire, but what did it mean to them? Superficially, there is the standard flattery comparing a king or dynast with the sun. An echo of that might be found in an epigram of the poet Crinagoras, which begins, "Sunrise and Sunset mark the world's limits, and the deeds of Nero have passed through both boundaries of the earth" (*Anth. Plan.* 61). And there was later to be Tiberius' notorious retirement to Rhodes, the very island of the sun, although no one seems to make much of the connection.[12] More importantly, Tiberius himself pointedly compared himself with the sun, not once or twice but three times, all in connection with his own death.

First, in an anecdote related by Dio and Tacitus about his last illness in 37 CE, the aged princeps rebukes the prefect of his guard: Macro is abandoning the setting for the rising sun.[13] The new sun here is Tiberius' grandson by adoption, Gaius Caesar, soon to be notorious as Caligula. The metaphor describes a failing ruler and his impatient successor: it was supposedly adapted earlier by Pompey, in speaking of the older Sulla, and later by Marcus Aurelius, in speaking of his son Commodus.[14] The aphorism gains point when Tacitus, after reporting it of Tiberius, goes on in the same sentence to add, "and, when

Gaius Caesar in a chance conversation was deriding Lucius Sulla, he predicted to him that he would have all of Sulla's vices and none of his virtues"—thus bringing us back to Sulla, the earlier setting sun.

Second, forty-two years earlier, Tiberius had used the same metaphor in a similar situation, to explain his abrupt retreat from Rome into private life on Rhodes, in 6 BCE. The historian Velleius Paterculus, a contemporary and fervent admirer, is confident: Tiberius requested from Augustus a leave of absence from his labors but purposely concealed the true reason for his decision. In fact, it arose from a marvelous, indescribable sense of duty and family obligation:

> the reasons . . . for which were revealed later when Gaius had already assumed the *toga virilis* [5 BCE] and when Lucius' coming of age was likewise recognized [2 BCE], namely that his brilliance should not stand in the way of the careers of rising young men.

Ne fulgor suus orientium iuvenum obstaret initiis: scholars today agree that this statement reflects the official version, but what should be noted is the phrasing.[15] *Fulgor* is of course an attribute of the sun, but the expression *orientes iuvenes*, "rising young men" is deceptive. While it seems naturally appropriate to the situation, its use here is, in fact, unique: suns rise everywhere in literature; sons only once, and then in a solar context.[16] The neat and sardonic balance of *fulgor* and *orientium* should be Tiberius' own adaptation of an old adage, one of his favorite habits. Here it is not simply the setting and the rising suns, but a sun that sets prematurely and voluntarily, and not one but two rising suns to whom men would transfer their allegiance.

A third remarkable anecdote told by Suetonius concerns Tiberius' insight into Caligula's savage nature, *ferum ingenium* (*Cal.* 11):

> The extremely shrewd old man had so clearly perceived it that he several times declared that Gaius lived for his own [i.e., Tiberius'] and everyone else's destruction, and that he was rearing a viper for the Roman people and a Phaethon for the world.[17]

Recorded here in a single awkward sentence are two predictions by Tiberius about universal disaster, one about Gaius, one about himself. They are, in fact, contradictory. In the first, Gaius lives while Tiberius and everyone else are destroyed (*exitio suo omniumque vivere*). But the second (*se. . . . Phaethontem orbi terarrum educare*) should lead to a quite different outcome. Phaethon was the son of the Sun who recklessly attempted to drive his father's chariot, an impossibility that led inevitably to fiery catastrophe for the whole world and to his own fortunate death. Then of course the Sun took over the reins again. Caligula being Phaethon, Tiberius should (yet again) be the Sun. The point of the myth for both Tiberius and his audience was that Phaethon takes charge, proves a disaster for mankind, Zeus destroys him with a thunderbolt, and the Sun takes control again.[18]

Tiberius had a deep interest in a world in flames. The evidence is scattered and evocative, if somewhat confusing. First, Dio, recounting the events of 33 CE, makes the unpersuasive allegation that Tiberius suspected that his young grandson Tiberius Gemellus was not actually the son of his son Drusus, and that he would be murdered by Gaius anyway. Also, in full monster mode, he hoped that if Gaius were his successor, his own misdeeds would be overshadowed and what remained of the senate might be destroyed after his death:

> He is said to have uttered frequently that old sentiment: "When I am dead, let fire o'erwhelm the earth." Often, also, he used to declare Priam fortunate, because he involved both his country and his throne in his own utter ruin.[19]

Suetonius closely follows the same source as Dio. If his adviser Thrasyllus had not dissuaded him, and had death not then prevented him, it is thought (*creditur*) that Tiberius would have killed many more, not sparing even his grandsons. Gaius he held in suspicion and he rejected Tiberius Gemellus as conceived in adultery: "And he might have done it, for he repeatedly called Priam lucky to have survived all his family."

Again, as with Dio: many deaths, and the grandsons Gaius and Tiberius Gemellus, and Priam; but absent from Suetonius is the fire-after-death quotation.

Next, two Neronian echoes of the allegations about Tiberius. Dio introduces his account of the great fire of 64 CE with the following (62.16.1):

> After this Nero set his heart on accomplishing what had doubtless always been his desire, namely to make an end of the whole city and realm during his lifetime. At all events, he, like others before him, used to call Priam wonderfully fortunate in that he had seen his country and his throne destroyed together.

Fire and the living Priam are thus linked again, but there is no sign here of the potential joy in surviving one's family. Yet, next to Dio, we must set Suetonius on the fire of 64. He too is certain, like Dio, that Nero was the arsonist, and he introduces his account with the following (*Nero* 38.1):

> But Nero spared neither the people of his native city nor its walls. Someone quoted him this line in the course of a conversation: "When I am dead, let the earth be consumed by fire." "On the contrary," said Nero, "while I am alive." And he made it happen.

That is, no sign of the living Priam, but again fire after death.

In short: fragmented, but when combined and put into a single context, the two Neronian anecdotes (based probably on a single, now-lost source) offer a doublet of the Tiberian tale (based certainly on an earlier, single, now-lost source). At the heart of the matter: Priam's death in the flames of Troy is linked with the fiery destruction of the universe.

Next, almost ten years before the fire of 64, Seneca had published his treatise *On Clemency*, addressed to Nero. Seneca warns his young pupil that

> many great-seeming but abhorrent utterances have made their way among men and become renowned by being on everyone's lips, like the saying "Let them hate, provided they fear," and a Greek verse like it, spoken by a character who says, "After I am dead, may the earth be confounded by fire," and other things of this sort. Somehow or other human wits have more successfully expressed forceful and passionate sentiments when the subject matter is monstrous and hateful.[20]

Both of the hateful quotations that Seneca so deprecates are associated with Tiberius, and the suspicion might arise that our now-lost source for Nero's actions ten years later had Seneca in mind when he came to recycle the Tiberian anecdote.[21] Be that as it may, Seneca raises, in different ways, two fundamental questions.

First, who is the speaker who looked forward to a world in flames after his death? Seneca's "Let them hate, provided they fear" offers a clue. The notorious sentiment was originally uttered by Atreus, King of Mycenae, in Accius' play *Atreus*, a model for tyrants, and it was deprecated as such by Seneca in his warning to the young monarch Nero. It seems probable, then, that the other sentiment, about the post-mortem fire, from a now lost tragedy retelling a Greek myth, was also expressed by a king. The prime candidate must be the figure juxtaposed in Dio with the quotation: Priam, the last king of Troy. He himself predicts his fate in Book 22 of the Iliad, when he appeals to Hector not to fight Achilles. If Hector falls, Priam will see his family destroyed, sons killed, daughters and daughters-in-law dragged into slavery, children murdered, and Priam, last of all, slain by a spear and eaten by his own dogs—all of which comes true. The old king outlives his family, and his country, dying by the hand of Neoptolemus, son of Achilles, sacrificed on the altar of Zeus the Guardian, as the Greeks devastate the city. In the *Aeneid*, Vergil paints the horrific scene that would be familiar to every literate Roman:

> he dragged him to the very altar stone,
> with Priam shuddering and slipping in
> the blood that streamed from his own son. And Pyrrhus
>   [= Neoptolemus]

with his left hand clutched tight the hair of Priam;
his right hand drew his glistening blade, and then
he buried it hilt-high in the king's side.
This was the end of Priam's destinies,
the close that fell to him by fate: to see
his Troy in flames and Pergama laid low.[22]

Tiberius had a real fondness for applying learned quotations from Greek drama to contemporary situations. If Priam is indeed the original speaker of the dramatic line, Tiberius' own savage reinterpretation of Priam's dying words, or that of our lost source, suggests all sorts of possibilities.

Ἐμοῦ θανόντος γαῖα μιχθήτω πυρί: when Priam, or the unknown tragic hero, cried out the notorious line, what did he mean? The answer may not be obvious. The three modern translations from the three different sources cited above offer three different but similar versions of the verb, μιχθήτω or μειχθήτω: "When I am dead, let fire o'erwhelm the earth," or "let the earth be consumed by fire," or "may the earth be confounded by fire." That is presumably how Tiberius' critics understood the words, as a curse upon mankind, or as a cry of utter despair. But if the princeps did indeed quote the line, is that what he or indeed the unknown tragic playwright intended? The verb μ(ε)ίγνυμι means "to mix." The standard classical Greek dictionary gives a range of senses for its passive form, as follows: 1) to be mixed up with, mingled among, to hold [social] intercourse with, live with; to be mixed or compounded; 2) to be brought into contact with, come to; 3) mix in fight; 4) have [sexual] intercourse with. Nowhere in the dictionary do we see being overwhelmed, or being consumed by, or being confounded by.[23] The closest thing to a hostile sense is the notion of mixing in battle, which is rare, and these citations all come from the *Iliad* and the *Odyssey*. "Confounded by" is the nearest to the actual meaning. However, it should be not "confounded by" but "confounded *with*." This leads us in a quite different direction.

———

The era of Tiberius saw a spectacular historical coincidence that no one noticed at the time: not one, not two, but three immortal beings died in the eastern half of the Roman Empire. They sprang from different cultures (Jewish, Greek, and Syrian) and the manner of their deaths varied (execution, unknown—natural?—causes, suicide), but the three mortal immortals shared two attributes. Each of them came back to life in a most remarkable fashion. And Tiberius Caesar was caught up in all of their stories.

The last chronologically to die and return under the principate of Tiberius was the phoenix. The event is reported by three sources. First, Tacitus' account of Tiberius' last years is dominated by the gruesome parade of prosecutions and deaths at Rome. But the historian leads off the year 34 CE with a long and startling excursus (6.28.1–6):

> With Paulus Fabius and L. Vitellius as consuls, at the conclusion of a centuries-long cycle the phoenix bird came to Egypt and provided the most learned of both natives and Greeks with material for considerable discussion of the wonder. The points on which they agree, and the more numerous matters which are disputed but nevertheless not inappropriate to acknowledge, make a pleasing subject for presentation.
>
> The creature is sacred to the Sun, and those who have depicted its shape concur that in its beak and the distinctiveness of its wings it is different from every other bird. But various alternatives are transmitted on the number of years. The most common is a period of 500, but there are those who assert that the interval is 1,461 and that it was first during Sesosis' rule [2nd millennium BCE], and afterwards during Amasis' [570–526 BCE] and then Ptolemy's (the third of the Macedonians to reign [246–221 BCE]), that the earlier fowl flew into the community whose name is Heliopolis [the City of the Sun], with a considerable escort of other birds wondering at the new face.
>
> Now antiquity is of course a dark age; but between Ptolemy and Tiberius there were less than 250 years. Hence some have believed this present phoenix to be false and not from the land of the Arabs and that it performed none of the feats which ancient memory has affirmed.
>
> With the number of its years completed and when death is approaching, it builds a nest in its own land and pours on it a generative force, from which its issue springs; and the first concern of the latter as an adult is burying its father—not randomly but, after lifting up a weight of myrrh and testing it on a long journey, then, when it is equal to the burden and equal to the expedition, it takes up its father's body and carries it all the way to the altar of the Sun and sacrifices it in flames.
>
> These matters are uncertain and exaggerated by fantasy; but that that particular bird is sometimes observed in Egypt is not disputed.
>
> But at Rome the slaughter was constant.

This passage is unique in Tacitus. Whenever he digresses from his brilliantly structured annalistic narrative—to discuss law, say, or luxury, or astrology—the digression is always apt to, and comments on, the subject and theme of the main text. But the story of the phoenix is not connected in any way with the surrounding narrative, it is there simply because it pleases his fancy to consider the matter, *promere libet*. Indeed, it is a nonevent: he really doubts that it happened at all, but he wants to tell us the legend of the fabulous bird anyway. He does not explain why.

The same incident is treated with similar skepticism by the Elder Pliny in his vast *Natural History*. He begins his tenth book, on the nature of birds, with this:

The Ethiopians and the Indians report birds extremely variegated in color and defying description, and above all the renowned phoenix of Arabia— I hardly know whether legend or not—the only one in the whole world and almost never seen. It is said to be of the magnitude of an eagle, with a flash of gold around its neck, otherwise purple all over, with rose-colored feathers adorning the tail, tufts on the throat, and a feathered helmet gracing its head.

The first Roman to discuss it, and that most carefully, was Manilius, the senator renowned for immense learning, although he had no teacher: no one alive had seen it feeding; in Arabia it is sacred to the Sun; it lives 540 years; when growing old it constructs a nest with shoots of cinnamon and frankincense, fills it with scents, and expires upon it. Afterwards, first a sort of larva is born from its bones and marrow, then this becomes a young bird whose first act is to render proper funeral rites to its predecessor and to carry the whole nest down to the City of the Sun near Panchaia, and to deposit it on the altar there.

Manilius furthermore reports that the revolution of the Great Year co-incides with the life of this bird, and that the same signs of the seasons and the stars return; that this begins about noon on the day on which the Sun enters the sign of Aries; and that it was the 215th year of this revolution when he was writing, when Publius Licinius and Gnaeus Cornelius were consuls [97 BCE]. Cornelius Valerianus reports that a phoenix flew down into Egypt when Quintus Plautius and Sextus Papinius were consuls [36 CE]. And it was brought to the city during the censorship of the Prin-ceps Claudius in the 800th year of the city [47 CE], and displayed in the comitium, as is shown in the public records, although nobody would doubt that this bird was fraudulent.[24]

And finally, Cassius Dio glances briefly at the last sighting (58.26.5–27.1):

In the consulship of Sextus Papinius and Quintus Plautius [36 CE], the Tiber inundated a large part of the city so that people went about in boats; and a much larger region in the vicinity of the Circus and the Aventine was devastated by fire. To the sufferers from the latter disaster Tiberius contributed a hundred million sesterces. And if Egyptian affairs touch Roman interests at all, it may be mentioned that the phoenix was seen that year.

This is all curious and a bit confused. For Tacitus, the nonevent leads off his account of the year 34 CE, yet Pliny and Dio both explicitly date the appearance to 36 CE. In their narrative accounts of Tiberius, Tacitus and Dio clearly rely on the same now-lost narrative history or histories, and, in fact, their coverage of events in the last years of the princeps is extremely thin. Nevertheless, there are other chronological discrepancies between their reports of the 30s, not only on this matter. Moreover, Pliny, encyclopedist but not here an historian, cites as his authority for the year 36 a writer who was also not a historian, but one who agrees with Dio's source as to the date of 36. And it should be noted that Pliny was an actual contemporary of the incident, twelve or thirteen years old in 36 CE, and twenty-three or twenty-four when the false phoenix was brought to Rome in 47 CE, though on the latter occasion he was serving in Germany (PIR^2 P 493). It looks as if the accepted date was 36, and that Tacitus has deliberately transferred it to 34, but there can be no certainty.[25]

None of our three authors was a great believer in the phoenix. Tacitus and Pliny give strikingly similar accounts of the bird: its Arabian origin, its physical uniqueness, its longevity and the cycle of years, the building of its fragrant nest, its death, the generation of the new bird, its flight with the corpse to Heliopolis, the cremation there on the altar of the Sun, the fraudulent contemporary bird. The similarity is all the more striking because there were competing versions of the tale and meaning of the phoenix, in both outline and detail. Indeed, the verbal echoes between our two authors suggest that Tacitus has abandoned his narrative source altogether, and not just its dating, to follow Pliny and his source(s).[26] Yet, since Dio also mentions the incident briefly, it is almost certain that the authority common to him and Tacitus recorded it likewise. Why then this learned but completely irrelevant, not to mention misdated, excursus in Tacitus? He does not explain, but Dio does.

After recording the floods and the fire at Rome, and the reported reappearance of the phoenix, "if Egyptian matters have anything to do with the Romans," Dio concludes the year 36 CE with: "All these were thought to foreshadow the death of Tiberius." He adds somewhat awkwardly that "Thrasyllus, indeed, did die at this very time, and [Tiberius] died in the following spring, in the consulship of Gnaeus Proculus and Pontius Nigrinus [37 CE]." Thrasyllus was the intimate friend of Tiberius for forty years, and a master astrologer. Dio goes on to reveal why he reports the man's death here: Thrasyllus had cleverly deceived Tiberius into halting the grim sequence of executions at Rome in the long aftermath to the fall of Sejanus. He forecast the day and time of his own imminent death, but deliberately persuaded Tiberius that he would live another ten years. An astrological writer indeed confirms that Thrasyllus had discovered a method of predicting the length of a life.[27] Since his calculation about his own death proved to be precisely accurate, Tiberius was supposedly convinced that the second prediction, promising him another decade, would also prove correct, so he was in no hurry to condemn his enemies. Dio introduces Thrasyllus' trick immediately and abruptly after his noncommittal aside about the phoenix, and, in fact, he has left out something important.

A late but reliable anonymous fragment closely resembles yet is independent of Dio's text. It provides the missing link:

> When the phoenix appeared in Egypt, Thrasyllus said that Tiberius' death was clearly predicted, but he kept it from him. Indeed, he reckoned another ten years of life for him so that, hoping to do what he wanted to thereafter, he would be less intent [ῥαθυμότερος] on bloodshed and plunder.[28]

That is, according to this version, the phoenix was not, as Dio leads us to believe, merely one of three commonly observed portents of Tiberius' imminent death. Thrasyllus himself had made the connection.

The intimate friend of the princeps was not just an astrologer. Thrasyllus was the most learned man of his era, *multarum artium scientiam professus*, a polymath who wrote important works on subjects ranging from natural history to philosophy to music to astrology.[29] Indeed he was the master astrologer of the age, and Tiberius' only trusted teacher in the art. But did he in fact calculate that the appearance of the phoenix portended the death of Tiberius? Perhaps not. How could he have kept the prediction quiet, only for it to emerge after he and the princeps were dead? To whom might he have spoken the words? Who passed them on, and when? Moreover, the aura of legend clings to him, as we shall see. His four-decade-long relationship with Tiberius begins and ends with striking symmetry, with a trick: a stunning astrological prediction, in the seclusion of an island, under a cloud of imminent death. But, true or not, it is more important that Thrasyllus was *believed* to have said it. He knew how to predict when a life would end, and he proved it by dying when he said he would. Probably an Egyptian himself, he would know about dying phoenixes, and he would believe that Egyptian matters did indeed have something to do with the Romans. If Thrasyllus said it, it must have been true. But the crucial part is that the phoenix would come back.

The tale of the phoenix is both simple and complex. The fabulous bird is unique, the only one in the world. It lives a very long life in seclusion, and just before or just after its death it reappears in the world of men. By dying, it obtains new life, reincarnated as its own successor. Cremated, whether dead or alive, it is above all the bird of the Sun.[30]

Two main and interrelated versions of its life can be traced over the centuries. In both, the old bird feels that death is near and it gathers aromatics, especially cinnamon, which is flammable. Then the sequence diverges. In one tradition, it dies on a nest constructed from the aromatics. A new phoenix is generated from the decaying body, usually appearing first in a larval stage. When it becomes a bird, it leaves immediately for Heliopolis in Egypt, the City of the Sun, with the remains of its parent, wrapped either in the fragrant nest or in a ball of myrrh. This it places on the altar of the Sun there, to be burned. By contrast, in a somewhat more widespread version, the elderly phoenix sings a prayer to the Sun, then burns itself alive, on the nest built of aromatics. The fire is spontaneous, ignited by the Sun (less often by the phoenix itself), and in many authors the bird has flown from its native land to immolate itself at Heliopolis. The new phoenix arises from the ashes.

Despite the claims of Egyptian antiquity, the phoenix is Near Eastern and, more importantly, the essential elements of its tale are the relatively late creation of Hellenistic learning in the last three centuries BCE. A mass of details accreted around these elements, in scores of authors, across a vast expanse of Europe and Asia, and over centuries. According to taste and purposes, the bird returns to Egypt for dedication, alive or dead, to the Sun at Heliopolis, but its actual dwelling place is unknown; or it may be in Arabia, or India, or Ethiopia, or Assyria, or the Isles of the Blessed, or Elysium. There it may live for five hundred or a thousand years (the most popular lifespans), or one year or 654 or 1,461, up to 7,006 years, or over 972 human generations, again as needed. It may symbolize perfect happiness, or the soul, or personal reincarnation, or the passing of one age of mankind to be replaced by another. But essential to all of the variety is a single element: immortality.

How might the phoenix be associated, by himself or by others, with Tiberius Caesar?[31]

1) The phoenix is, first of all, the king of birds (*rex avium, avis regia*), it flies with royal grace (*regali decore*). When it makes its rare appearance at Heliopolis, it is accompanied by innumerable birds of all kinds (*innumerae comitantur aves*). It is both royal and military (*rex* and *dux*), escorted by a cohort of birds (*alituum cohors*), a huge army of them (*exercitus ingens*), whose endemic conflicts are happily suspended by a general treaty (*commune foedus*). And when their leader is reborn and returns to its home far away, it is again escorted by the pious avian followers.[32] The bird is, as we are constantly reminded, unique—in short, a bird without peer (*avis sine pare*).[33] There is only one such bird in our world, and it outranks everyone. All of this is obviously applicable to Tiberius Iulius Caesar Augustus, monarch and general, unique and without equal in the Roman world.

2) The appearance of the phoenix is appropriately, stunningly, unique. It is very large: only the eagle is comparable in size and shape. Its eyes shine

with an unearthly light, and its head is often surmounted by a nimbus of rays.[34] But, above all, it is noted for its blaze of colors. Descriptions vary as to which parts of its body are which colors, but there is uniformity as to the main three: shining gold, glowing scarlet, and imperial purple, all appropriately fiery.[35]

Like the phoenix, Tiberius was known for his enormous eyes, and if they did not flash fire, as did the phoenix's, he was at least the only human born of mortal parents who could see in the dark.[36]

Moreover, for the last thirteen years of his life, there existed only one man on earth who had celebrated the massive victory parade and ritual of a Roman triumph: Tiberius Caesar, who had starred in the spectacle twice, in 7 BCE and in 12 CE.[37] The costume worn by triumphant generals might vary, but the standard elements recur, all recalling the appearance of the great statue of Jupiter on the Capitoline: a *tunica palmata*, that is, a tunic embroidered with the palms of victory (in gold?) and a broad purple stripe; over that, a *toga picta*, a purple toga embroidered with gold stars; and held above the general's head, a heavy crown of gold shining with precious stones.[38] There were no set rules, there was constant striving both to emulate and to outdo one's predecessors, and there were variations on route, ritual, and costume, but the color palette is fixed: "For Romans, triumphal costume certainly conjured up an image in purple and gold."[39] It is also absolutely clear that, in imitation of Jupiter Capitolinus, the commander was expected to daub his face and body with a paint compounded of minium, or cinnabar, a mineral that could vary in tint from bright orange-red to scarlet.[40] That is, Tiberius alone of living men had appeared before tens of thousands of his fellow citizens as recently as 12 CE, decked out in the palette of the phoenix: gold, purple, and scarlet.[41]

3) The marvelous phoenix lives out its life in an earthly paradise, *loca sancta*. Again, the location varies, generally far away to the east; or far to the west, on the Isles of the Blest; or in Elysium. Its nest is remote and isolated, and the phoenix dwells there alone: when it returns home from its regeneration, it will lose its escort of birds in the ether. In his poem *Phoenix*, Lactantius (1–30) offers the fullest description of the paradise in which it lives, a description echoed in other sources. We are shown a large open plain that lies high above our highest mountains. On it is the Grove of the Sun, *Solis Nemus*, its foliage eternally green, impervious to flame and flood. Indeed, all the woes of humanity are excluded: illness, old age, death; fear, crime, greed; anger, madness, grief; poverty, care, hunger. The weather is serene: no storms, no wind, no frost, no clouds, no rain. At the center of the grove lies the clear, gentle Fountain of Life (*quem vivum nomine dicunt*), with its sweet waters that overflow once a month to irrigate the grove of

trees that bear eternal fruit. Here the bird bathes each morning before dawn, then flies to the top of a tree and greets the Sun with song. It serves in this paradise for a thousand years as the priest or priestess of the grove (the bird is asexual), the attendant of Phoebus.

Tiberius too dwelt in a remote paradise. Tacitus offers a classic ethnographic description of his retreat on Capri that could well describe that of the phoenix far away. To ensure peace, Caesar hid himself away on the island: there, the solitude he craved was guaranteed by the lack of harbors. The climate was of course ideal, the winters mild, protected from gales by mountains, the summers delightful, fanned by breezes from the west. He looked out over the most beautiful of bays, the Bay of Naples, and in his palace on the citadel of the island, he was perched in a very high place indeed. Suetonius similarly remarks that Tiberius especially delighted in the fact that Capri might be approached by only one small beach, being otherwise walled off by immense cliffs and deep sea: after relieving the disaster of the amphitheater at Fidenae, "he returned to the island and completely neglected his duty to the state." But withdrawal was of course an impossible dream for the princeps of Rome. Plutarch captured the essence: Tiberius' island should have been peaceful and free of storms, but the cares of empire poured in.[42]

4) Life in paradise is summed up by the word *felicitas*. More than simple happiness, for the Romans, felicity was also the good luck that brought happiness, and this good fortune is due both to the favor of the gods and to one's own virtue.[43] Eternal felicity is certainly the mood and symbol of life in Elysium and on the Blessed Islands, both suggested as locations for the remote home of the phoenix.[44] Indeed, the bird is the very embodiment of felicity. In the first line of his *Phoenix*, Lactantius introduces the *locus felix* in which it dwells, while toward the end, the sexless bird is *felix* because it need not cultivate the bonds of love. Claudian likewise congratulates it: "O happy bird, *felix*, heir to yourself!"[45] Much earlier, the first-century poet Statius had provided a grandiloquent mock eulogy of the dead parrot of his friend Atedius Melior that plays throughout, obliquely but unambiguously, on the familiar image of the phoenix, leading up to a revelatory last line. The parrot is sent "not without glory" to the shades, cremated with Eastern aromatics, but since he is not wearied by old age, he will actually mount the perfumed flames a happier phoenix (*phoenix felicior*) than the actual phoenix burdened by old age.[46] In Pompeii, a splendid painting adorns the wall of a first-century tavern, the so-called Caupona of Euxinus, probably as the sign of the inn, displaying a phoenix in all its golden glory. Underneath the bird are the words *Phoenix felix et tu*, "the happy phoenix and you." Perhaps

something like: "This is the Inn of the Happy Phoenix, and you will be happy here too."[47]

Whatever cares may have invaded his paradise on Capri, the image of Tiberius was one of extraordinary felicity. That bundle of happiness, good fortune, and divine favor was indeed a very Roman *virtus*, the particular reward of victorious generals, *felicitas imperatoria*. Sulla had even taken the name Felix, Caesar and Augustus had enjoyed felicity but made little of it, and emperors from Galba onward would claim it for themselves (*Felicitas Augusti*) and for the age in which they lived (*felicitas saeculi, felicitas temporum*)—but Tiberius was special.[48]

There are two arresting items of evidence. One is a sword with elaborately decorated scabbard that was excavated in the mid-nineteenth century at Mainz, the home of Rome's greatest military base on the Rhine frontier.[49] A bronze plaque attached to the scabbard shows a seated man surrounded by three standing figures, all eyes fixed on him. The winged goddess Victory floats just above the ground to the right, bearing a spear and a shield with the words *Vic(toria) Aug(usti)* written on it. To the rear stands the bearded god, Mars the Avenger, armed with helmet, breastplate, spear, and shield. And from the left, a young man in the dress of a general offers a small statue of a winged Victory, herself extending a wreath, to the seated figure. This older man sits in Jovian seminudity at the scene's center, his bare chest facing the viewer but head and right arm turned to welcome the younger man and to receive the Victory. A shield leans against his throne, inscribed with the words *Felic/itas/ Tibe/ri*. This striking scene must represent the culmination of the successful campaign led by the young Germanicus in 16 CE to recover the standards lost in the disaster of Varus in 9 CE: vengeance now exacted and Victory proclaimed, thanks to the felicity of Tiberius.[50]

The other item is a brief notice in Suetonius that underlines his special virtue (Suet. 5):

> Some think that Tiberius was born at Fundi, following a flimsy guess because his maternal grandmother was born at Fundi and because an image of Felicity was afterwards set up there officially by a decree of the senate.

Suetonius rejects the conjecture—Tiberius was born in Rome—but there is no doubt that his grandmother was a native of Fundi, an ancestral Tiberius Claudius was probably a patron of Fundi in the second century BCE, and Tiberius' enormous villa at Sperlonga stood a few miles away from the town, within whose territory it lay.[51] If he had a hometown, Fundi was it, as the senate recognized. No other princeps, however felicitous, received any such pointed honor.

Contemporary writers delight in the theme. For Velleius Paterculus, Tiberius as *dux* enjoys a marvelous (*mira*) felicity, and indeed he passed it on: a German enemy who made a special trip to meet the general remarked, "Today I have seen the gods, and I have not hoped for or enjoyed a happier day, *diem feliciorem*, in my life." As Tiberius shares his felicity with others, Valerius Maximus explains the origins of the happy life (*vita felix*) that we now enjoy under the best of leaders (*optimo principe*). To the learned Philo of Alexandria, the learned Tiberius was as noteworthy for his felicity (εὐτυχία) as for his intelligence.[52]

5) Last, *Phoebi memoranda satelles*: the phoenix has a unique relationship with the Sun both in life and in death. Again, it lives in the Grove of the Sun, where it praises the Sun every day, it accompanies the Sun on its daily journey through the heavens, and in the end, it is immolated on the altar at the City of the Sun. Its eyes flash with their own light, its nimbus is solar rays, it blazes with gold and scarlet and purple, it even feeds on the heat of the Sun.[53] Two solar elements are central here.

Over its immensely long life, the phoenix was invulnerable to fire. Thus, Lactantius on the far-off, blessed (*felix*) land in which it dwells: "When the heavens blazed with the fires of Phaethon, that place was immune to the flames." Or Claudian, addressing his blessed (*felix*) subject directly at the very end of his poem: "You know what year it was that burned with the wanderings [or errors] of Phaethon: no disaster destroyed you, the sole survivor [*solus superstes*] when the earth was overthrown. The Fates do not spin out the cruel threads for you and do not have the power to harm you."[54]

Even better, the "Apocalypse of Baruch," dateable sometime within the first two centuries CE, shows us the fiery chariot of the Sun, preceded by a bird as large as nine mountains. Baruch asks the angel, who is revealing the mysteries of God to him, what this bird might be. It is the Guardian of the World (ὁ φύλαξ τῆς οἰκουμένης). Why? "This bird accompanies the sun and spreading its wings absorbs its fire-shaped rays. For if it did not absorb them, none of the race of men would survive, nor anything else that lives, so God appointed this bird." Regardless of the Jewish and Christian form and content of the work, this strikingly un-Judaeo-Christian vision of phoenix and solar chariot undoubtedly reflects earlier Hellenistic thinking.[55] That is: in life not only was the phoenix itself immune to the perils of the universe, but it actively protected mankind every day, a sort of anti-Phaethon.

The second essential solar element is the phoenix's death and rebirth. Two details should be noted. First, it was commonly believed that the bird knew when it was going to die, either intuitively or because weakened by old age: as Claudian puts it, the light of its eyes fades and its nimbus grows faint.[56] Second, a remarkable motif runs through several of our sources: "It is evident that there must have been a tradition according to which the phoenix took new life on a high place—a rock, a mountain, a hill, or a tower, which must be no more than a variant of the others."[57] In 37 CE, Tiberius surely knew that he was going to die, and he struggled to return to his palace on Capri one thousand feet above the sea.

When the great bird dies and is burned, or burns and then dies, it is reborn. But it is more than an eternal being, more than a symbol of eternal life: the Guardian of the World promises new life to mankind. Lactantius assures us that when its time is almost up, it leaves its home on its final journey, so that it may restore the age that is slipping away.[58] The Latin is ambiguous here: *ut reparet lapsum spatiis vergentibus aevum.* This can indeed mean the phoenix's old age, rather awkwardly, but there is no doubt that it also refers more grandly to restoring the age of mankind.

Periodic rebirth through fire roots the phoenix deeply into two widespread beliefs that originated in Greek philosophy. One is the conception of the Great Year, derived variously from Plato and Aristotle, not to mention Berossus.[59] That is the cosmic event that recurs every 12,954 years, when the moon, the sun, and the planets return to the same position relative to the fixed stars or, alternatively, to the same sign of the zodiac as obtained at the beginning of time itself. The *Magnus Annus* is marked by the destruction of the world in flood and fire, followed by its regeneration.

Overlapping with this is the concept of *ecpyrosis*, cosmic conflagration, going back to the pre-Socratic philosophers but most closely identified with the Stoics, especially Chrysippus. The earth is periodically dissolved in fire and recreated.[60] The common element in the Great Year and the Stoic conflagration is the destruction of the world and mankind in flames, but with the assurance of their recreation. The comforting symbol of the phoenix, the bird reborn in flames, fits well with this conjunction, and its appearance could even be taken to mark the joyous beginning of a new Golden Age.[61]

———

Fire was sacred to the ancient Persians. It was not worshipped as such—they had a full pantheon—but it was the central element of their cultic practices and an icon of the divine. Persian priests were the magi. And the founding prophet of their religion was Zarathustra, known to the Greeks as Zoroaster. Western understanding of the real Zarathustra and real Zoroastrianism, of the history and doctrines of the faith, was limited and confused, but Greek and

Roman interpretation of Zoroaster and his "alien wisdom" was spectacular.[62] It was common knowledge that he had lived five or six thousand years ago, that he had invented astrology—did his name not mean "Star-Worshipper" (Diog. Laert. 1.8)?—and that he was the world's first magician.

The Persians say that Zoroaster, because of a passion for wisdom and justice,

> deserted his fellows and dwelt by himself on a certain mountain; and they say that thereupon the mountain caught fire, a mighty flame descending from the sky above, and that it burned unceasingly. So then the king and the most distinguished of his Persians drew near for the purpose of praying to the god; and Zoroaster came forth from the fire unscathed, and showing himself gracious toward them, bade them to be of good cheer and to offer certain sacrifices in recognition of the god's having come to that place.

So Dio Chrysostom (36.40), the earliest source to indicate that the prophet was immune to fire.

Later Persian writings transmit details from his earliest childhood. Prescient demons and wizards had attacked the infant with extreme violence, trying to crush or twist off his head, to stab him, to trample him with oxen or horses, all failures. All mundane as well, but then there is the truly fabulous:

> One of their attempts concerns a huge fire into which Zarathustra is thrown. No harm comes to him from the fire, however, and he is saved.[63]

The centrality of fire to the magi, and our hero's immunity to it from infancy, suggest a rare sympathy between the prophet Zoroaster and the princeps Tiberius. Indeed, Western legend had it that, in the end, Zoroaster died by lightning or flame from heaven, despite his immunity to fire. Tiberius was terrified of lightning, but the paradox of dying by flame after a lifetime of immunity might have its attraction if, like the phoenix, one emerged from the ashes.[64] The two heroes certainly shared common interests. A mass of pseudepigrapha was attributed to the magus Zoroaster, nothing to do with a real man and his religion, all concocted in the world of Hellenistic learning and divided by modern scholarship into three categories.[65] First, many works on astrology, a science to which, as Suetonius puts it, Tiberius was addicted. Second, works on botany. Tiberius displayed a striking interest in and deep knowledge of fruits and vegetables.[66] And third, works on precious stones. Nothing in the mainstream record betrays any concern by Tiberius for the subject, but a widely circulated text known as Damigeron-Evax, *De Lapidibus*, does. Originally in Greek, surviving today in Latin, it begins with a brief letter from Evax, King of Arabia, to Tiberius Imperator, thanking him for the splendid gifts that he had deigned to send him through his centurion Lucinius Fronto, and sending him in return "whatever there is on earth about all the stones of remedies."[67] Astrology, plants, and stones: the three disciplines overlap in many respects, and astrology plays a key role in the other two (indeed, Damigeron was a well-known magician, his name associated with that of Zoroaster). All three imply deep learning in arcana and special mastery of nature and supernature.

We can see a number of Tiberius' traits in a different light when viewed through a Zoroastrian lens. He seems to have become something of a vegetarian: the highest class of magi abstained from meat. He was criticized for not mourning the deaths of his close relatives sufficiently: the attitude of a stoic and patrician Roman indeed, but mourning was also frowned upon by Zoroastrian texts and strongly prohibited by some. Tiberius retreated to study in Rhodes; Zoroaster withdrew from the world in search of wisdom and justice.[68] More broadly, and fundamentally, learned Westerners—Nigidius Figulus and Dio Chrysostom—imposed on the magi the Stoic concept of the *ecpyrosis*, that is, recurrent conflagration and regeneration of the universe, often tied to the Great Year. As we have seen, *ecpyrosis* and rebirth were of interest to Tiberius and his contemporaries.

Central here are two Persian concepts of the divine, especially as understood by Westerners. One was the supreme importance of fire, which, as already noted, was absolutely central to Persian cult as being the essence of the divine world. Fire was sacred in the ancient tradition, to which the followers of Zoroaster added the formal institution of the fire temple. They also added a tradition of sacrificing in high places.[69] Above all, sacred fire must be eternal, undying, unquenched—that is, carefully tended. And a fundamental corollary to this was the strong link between eternal flame and the survival and success of the Persian monarchy. Ever since their first king received fire from heaven, the royal life was bound up with fire. A special royal fire was said to be kindled from the well-protected eternal flames for each new monarch, and it was carefully extinguished when that king died. After his funeral, the process was repeated.[70] The peculiar death and resurrection of the phoenix is strongly reminiscent of the process of Persian royal renewal.

Miraculous fires commonly predict the future greatness of kings and heroes, yet one particular manifestation seems to be unique to Tiberius: the victory altars at Philippi that burst into flame as the young man passed by, en route to the East. But there was a tradition, observed and recorded by Pausanias, that altars in two cities in Cappadocia likewise flared up spontaneously when magi chanted magic words over them.[71] Be that as it may, Tiberius' special relationship with fire ended with his life. He too had a personal flame, kept eternally alight at his palace on Capri: the lighthouse known as the

Pharus, towering perhaps three hundred feet and set on a great height a thousand feet above the sea. Dying, he struggled back toward Capri. A few days before his death, his lighthouse collapsed in an earthquake, and its fire was extinguished.

The other striking Persian conception of the divine is a central notion to Zoroastrians, the *khwarnah* (also rendered as *x˅arənah* and *farnah*). This was "a magic force or power of luminous and fiery nature," a brilliant, glorious, undying flame, "a vital creative force"—Zoroaster's fire came from heaven at the moment of his birth. "As both a guarantee and a sign of success, [*khwarnah*] quickly took on the meaning of '(good) fortune,' through which those who possessed it were able to fulfill their specific function or missions." The Achaemenid kings had already enjoyed a "luminous charisma" special to the dynasty, along with their personal undying fires. In Hellenistic times (we are told) this "hereditary dynastic charisma" was particularly intertwined with the *tyche basileos*, the *fortuna regia* of their successors, the kings of Syria, Cappadocia, Pontus, and Commagene, and its light and fire are represented iconographically by images of the favored king or hero surrounded by or emitting flames.[72] Thus the *khwarnah* accompanied the luckiest of them, a potent mixture of divine favor and royal charisma. Greek and Roman authors translate it as *tyche, doxa, daimon,* and *fortuna,* and indeed recognize that the quality was worshipped as a deity, like their own Tyche or Fortuna. Which leads us back to the remarkable Felicity of Tiberius, that rare and precise compound of luck, virtue, and divine favor.

Khwarnah extended to resurrection. An Avestan text from the time of the Achaemenids assured believers of the prospect of eternal life, incorruptible, indestructible, when the dead rose again.[73] The Zoroastrian concept of resurrection was certainly familiar, however they understood it, to Hellenistic intellectuals from the age of Alexander onward. In his *Philippica*, Theopompus wrote that "according to the Magi men will live in a future life and be immortal, and that the world will endure through their invocations. This is again confirmed by Eudemus of Rhodes" (Diog. Laert. 1.9).

So much of Tiberius' peculiar image can be mapped onto and explained by a special interest in the Persian Zoroaster: the simple uniqueness of our hero, his special relationship with and immunity from fire, his withdrawal from the world in the pursuit of wisdom, his arcane but practical, deep, almost magical erudition, his unique personal felicity. Why not also a belief in personal resurrection? From far-off Sogdiana comes a fragmentary and elusive trickster tale, "a most peculiar story," according to its learned editor, "which despite prolonged study remains rather nebulous," and indeed is little known. It seems that clever Persian thieves have tricked a "Caesar" into believing that he is dead. As he lies in his coffin in his lamp-lit tomb, one of the thieves dons a diadem and dresses in royal robes. "Hey, hey, Caesar, awake, awake! Fear not, I am your *Farn!*"—that is, his guardian spirit, the incarnation of his *farnah*. What follows appears to be knockabout farce, as the thief persuades the grateful resurrected Caesar that he will fly him through the air in his coffin.[74]

———

Much of this evidence for an alternative Tiberian thought-world is fragmentary, obscure, eccentric, sometimes contradictory. Yet the many threads can be woven into a complex image, one shared by both Tiberius and at least some of his subjects. Three central strands should be emphasized.

First, there is Tiberius' very special relationship with fire, amply attested and indeed unique: his ability to pass unharmed *medios per ignes*. His rule was predicted by flame, he himself was a Sun, and he welcomed the prospect of the world's ending in flames.

Second is the promise of return. The reappearance in his day of the phoenix is crucial. The fiery bird is an overwhelming symbol of the First Citizen in the 30s CE: unique, regal, wrapped in symbolic colors, dwelling in a lofty and remote earthly paradise, in perfect felicity, the close companion of the Sun, impervious to its flame. And the passing of the *rara avis* duly marked the passing of kings. But the phoenix, its return potentially signalling the end and the beginning of the Great Year, was also assured of rebirth, even if the world was destroyed by flames and it was *sola superstes*.

Third are the Eastern roots of the image. Tiberius' self-portrait was deeply influenced by familiarity with Persian Zoroastrianism, as filtered through Hellenistic erudition: its fundamental concerns are with fire, invulnerability, royal felicity, and ultimately *ecpyrosis* and resurrection. As a young man, Tiberius certainly came into contact with Zoroastrians and their religion during his expedition to the East, through Cappadocia and into Armenia, and he was not the first Roman aristocrat to be deeply learned, a master astrologer, and perhaps even a magus.[75]

That Tiberius Caesar was indeed a practicing Zoroastrian is confirmed by a unique artifact. Published some fifty years ago, its significance has evaded notice. The facts are these.

The object is an exquisite chalcedony intaglio, greyish and slightly yellow toward the center, an oval, convex on both sides and some thirty-three by twenty-five millimeters. Deeply cut into it is a portrait head of Tiberius in left profile and crowned with a wreath of myrtle. By universal consent, it is a masterpiece from the golden age of Greco-Roman gem-cutting.[76] Its creator has been identified as the Augustan master Dioscurides; the Tiberian portrait is that of a young man, perhaps in his thirties; and the myrtle wreath gives us a precise date. Myrtle was the reward and symbol for an *ovatio*, and the thirty-two-year-old Tiberius celebrated an *ovatio* in 9 BCE for his military success in Pannonia. On January 1, 7 BCE, he celebrated a triumph in honor of his success in Germany. Thereafter, he must have been portrayed wearing triumphal laurel. Our intaglio must therefore have been cut between myrtle and laurel, in either 9 or 8 BCE.[77]

The gem was first published in 1968 by the distinguished archaeologist Henri Seyrig, who wrote that a travelling friend reported that the object had been "on the market" in Tehran, where he was told that it had been found "in Elam"—that is, in the area also known as Susiana, in the west and southwest of ancient Iran, deep within the ancient Parthian / Persian Empire.[78] An inscription has been deeply and carefully cut around the oval edge of the gem, neatly framing the bust of Tiberius. It is in Middle Persian and dated by experts to the third or fourth century, in the early Sassanian period. It reads to the following effect: "O Mihrag, son of Frahad, behold the luminous paradise."[79] The name is significant, to be rendered in Western terms as Mithra, son of Phraates. Mithra is, of course, universal and meaningful. Phraates indicates that the owner was of Parthian, not Persian descent, Phraates indeed being the name of several Parthian kings, including two contemporaries of Tiberius. What follows is "a typically Zoroastrian religious formula, an invitation to admire the luminous splendor of paradise." That is to say, Mihrag is assured that the soul of one who has lived a good life will pass into the infinite light of the sun, for "paradise is luminous, fragrant, spacious, full of every blessing and goodness."

The piece has two physical peculiarities. A hole has been drilled into it, centered at the base of Tiberius' neck, and presumably meant for some sort of pin or screw: the piece was meant to be displayed, perhaps worn. And the inscription has been incised in reverse—that is to say, the gem was converted for use as a seal.[80]

If ever there were a case where image and text join to make an object, Mihrag's gem is it. We have a masterpiece of Hellenistic gem-cutting that portrays a Roman princeps as a military victor. His face has been drawn with an eye of extraordinary size, consonant with a canonical presentation of Hellenistic royalty, and of Julius Caesar and Augustus, to mark "Jovian omnipresence, profound intelligence, and a fine knowledge of men."[81] Two or three centuries later, the gem was the priceless possession of a Parthian of highest rank—we may well suspect a member of the Arsacid family—who carefully transmuted it into a testimonial for his Zoroastrian conviction of eternal life. If we believe that there is otherwise strong evidence to indicate that Tiberius was a Zoroastrian, the next step is inevitable: his convictions were known and his reputation treasured in the East for centuries after his death. Not a saint perhaps, but surely a magus.[82]

All of which leads to the conclusion that, in an Age of Return—in an age when many of his subjects believed that Pan had returned, that Jesus had returned, that the Phoenix had returned—Tiberius Caesar *acted* as if he too would return, whether resurrected alone or with the human race. What he and others really believed is beyond conjecture, but Dio assures us that he frequently repeated the old line, "When I am dead, may earth be mingled with fire," words perhaps first spoken by Priam, King of Troy, as his city and his life ended in flames. When Tiberius recalled the line he well knew, as did his learned audience, what followed. There is a second line to the quotation that commentators ancient and modern ignore, but that Tiberius and his companions would appreciate:

> When I am dead may earth be mingled with fire.
> It matters not to me, for with me all is well.[83]

PART II
Sex and the Sources

5

Sex on Capri

TIBERIUS CAESAR DEVISED unspeakable debaucheries on the island of Capri during the last ten years of his life.* Two paragraphs in Tacitus and Suetonius provide the details. First, Tacitus:

> Cn. Domitius et Camillus Scribonianus consulatum inierant, cum Caesar tramisso quod Capreas et Surrentum interfuit freto Campaniam praelegebat, ambiguus an urbem intraret, seu, quia contra destinaverat, speciem venturi simulans. Et saepe in propinqua degressus, aditis iuxta Tiberim hortis, saxa rursum et solitudinem maris repetiit pudore scelerum et libidinum quibus adeo indomitis exarserat ut more regio pubem ingenuam stupris pollueret. Nec formam tantum et decora corpora set in his modestiam pueritiam, in aliis imagines maiorum incitamentum cupidinis habebat. Tuncque primum ignota antea vocabula reperta sunt sellariorum et spintriarum ex foeditate loci et multiplici patientia; praepositique servi qui conquirerent pertraherent, dona in promptos, minas adversum abnuentis, et si retinerent propinquus aut parens, vim raptus suaque ipsi velut in captos exercebant.[1]

This is rendered into English as follows by A. J. Woodman:

Cn. Domitius and Camillus Scribonianus had embarked on the consulship when Caesar, having crossed the strait which washes between Capri and Surrentum was skirting Campania, in two minds whether to go into the City—or, because he had already decided otherwise, simulating a scene of impending arrival. And, having landed often in the neighborhood and approached the gardens by the Tiber, he retreated again to his rocks and the solitude of the sea, in shame at the crimes and unbridled lusts with which he was so inflamed that, in the manner of a king he polluted freeborn youngsters in illicit sex. Nor was it only good looks and becoming bodies but in some cases boyish modesty and in others the images of their ancestors which acted as the incitement of his desire. And that was the first time that the previously unknown designations of "sellarii" and "spintriae" were devised, respectively from the foulness of their place and their multifarious passivity. And the slaves who were charged with the searching and bringing resorted to gifts for the ready, threats against the reluctant and, if a relative or parent held them back, violent seizure and personal gratification, as though their victims were captives.

Compare Suetonius on the same subject:[2]

Secessu vero Caprensi etiam sellaria excogitavit, sedem arcanarum libidinum, in quam undique conquisiti puellarum et exoletorum greges monstrosique concubitus repertores, quos spintrias appellabat, triplici serie conexi, in vicem incestarent coram ipso, ut aspectu deficientis libidines excitaret. Cubicula pluri-fariam disposita tabellis ac sigillis lascivissimarum picturarum et figurarum adornavit librisque Elephantidis instruxit, ne cui in opera edenda exemplar impe[t]ratae schemae deesset. In silvis quoque ac nemoribus passim Venerios locos commentus est prost[r]antisque per antra et cavas rupes ex utriusque sexus pube Paniscorum et Nympharum habitu, quae palam iam et vulgo nomine in-sulae abutentes Caprineum dictitabant.

This was rendered into English in 1998 by D. W. Hurley in her revision of the 1913 Loeb translation of J. C. Rolfe, which had left the passage in Latin:

On retiring to Capri he devised "holey places" as a site for his secret orgies; there select teams of girls and male prostitutes, inventors of deviant inter-course and dubbed analists, copulated before him in triple unions to excite his flagging passions. Its many bedrooms he furnished with the most salacious paintings and sculptures and stocked with the books of Elephantis, in case any performer should need an illustration of a prescribed position. Then in Capri's woods and groves he contrived a number of spots for sex where boys and girls got up as Pans and nymphs solicited outside grottoes and sheltered recesses; people openly called this "the old goat's garden," pun-ning on the island's name.[3]

Over the centuries, two previously unknown words, *sellarii* (or *sellaria*) and *spintriae*, coined it would seem by Tiberius himself, have provoked thrills of horror and forbidden delight. What do they mean?

Let us start with good modern translations of Tacitus' *sellariorum et spin-triarum ex foeditate loci et multiplici patientia.* A. J. Woodman leaves the two neologisms untranslated but remarks in a footnote, "The former term is de-rived from *sellarium* = 'privy' (see Suetonius, *Tiberius* 43. 1 "in his Capri retreat he even devised *sellaria* as the place for his arcane lusts"); the latter term is connected with the Greek word for catamite." As to that, P. Wuilleumier in his 1975 Budé of Tacitus (apparently following H. Ailloud in his 1931 Budé

Suetonius) notes, as do many others, that *spintria* seems to come from the Greek σφίγκτης = *cinaedus* (i.e., catamite).

Compare the clear version of J. C. Yardley (Oxford World's Classics, 2008) likewise leaving the words in Latin, but understanding them somewhat more definitely: "Then two previously unknown terms were invented: *sellarii* and *spintriae*, named respectively from the foul locations where they operated and their wide range of pathic sexual activities." His note to the passage glosses, "*Sellarii* are men who haunt latrines (see Suetonius, *Tib.* 43); *spintriae* are young male prostitutes."[4]

Even more sharply defined, R. Martin, in his edition of *Annals* 5 and 6 (2001): "And then were invented the hitherto unknown terms of 'stoolmen' and 'squeezers,' derived from the foulness of the place and the multiple submissiveness." His understanding of these precise terms is presented with his customary clarity: "From *sella*, a seat or stool, comes *sellarium*, a latrine; hence *sellarii* are male prostitutes who ply their trade there. The clue to *spintriae* is the phrase *multiplici patientia*, since *patientia* in a sexual context signifies the act of the passive partner (*pathicus*) in a sexual act."

And then, at a slight angle, there is Suetonius' version: not *sellarii* (people), but *sellaria* (places), where the *spintriae* perform. Hurley's brilliantly suggestive "holey places" captures both the sense of "latrine" and its associated vice, as she duly annotates: "*Sellarium*, 'a place for seats,' was a latrine. Tiberius used it to suggest anal intercourse." But older translations are content with the more sedate and equally possible "couches."[5] And Robert Graves' Penguin version (1957, revised by J. B. Rives in 2007) is satisfied with the vague "a private playhouse," while C. Edwards' Oxford World Classics text of 2000 offers the similarly imprecise "a suite which was to be the location for his secret pleasures" for *sellaria . . . sedem arcanarum libidinum*.

No such reticence restrains the translations of Suetonian *spintriae*: "analists" (Hurley); "spintrian perverts" (Graves / Rives on *Cal.* 16.1); "tight-bums" (Edwards); "sphincters"; "male prostitutes"; "the derivation from σφιγκτήρ indicates anal sex"; "a particular group of sodomites associated with Tiberius in his retreat on Capreae."[6]

In short, we seem to have a consensus that the *sellaria* of Tiberius are latrines, that *sellarii* are men who hang around them for immoral purposes, and that *spintriae* are male prostitutes.

————

Let us start with the first two words. *Sellaria* and *sellarii* are unquestionably derived from *sella*, something you sit on: a chair; a seat; a bench. The *Oxford Latin Dictionary* offers a total of four instances of our two words: the entry for *sellarium*, "privy," cites Pliny, *NH* 34.84 and 36.111, and Suetonius, *Tiberius* 43; while that for *sellarius*, "a type of male prostitute (cf. prec.)," cites Tacitus, *Annales* 6.1.[7] How these definitions are reached is a mystery. Three questions occur. What is the relevance of privies or latrines? What does foulness, as in *foeditas loci*, signify? And how many entities are we dealing with?

The first is baffling: whyever latrines? To judge from the rubrics in the *OLD*, a *sella* is a seat, stool, or chair, whence derive the more specific meanings of a magistrate's chair of office, a sedan chair, and a commode. But the leap from that last, special, and not especially common meaning of *sella* to the assumption that a *sellarium* was a latrine full of such *sellae* is pure fancy: sometimes a sitting room is just a sitting room. Regardless of the depravity that unfolded in the place, there is no hint of any lavatorial significance in our two passages in Suetonius and Tacitus. The other two citations of the word both come from Pliny, and both appear in condemnations of Nero's Golden House. In the first, *NH* 34.84, Pliny deplores the emperor's looting of great works of art in Greece and depositing his spoils in the *sellaria* of the Golden House (*in sellariis domus aureae disposita*). In the second citation, 36.111, he reflects on the contrast between the enormous mansions of Caligula and Nero and the modest dwellings of the heroes of the old Republic, whose whole estates took up less space than the *sellaria* of those houses (*minorem modum optinuere quam sellaria istorum*)! Now *sellae* might indeed mean seats in a latrine (Mart. 12.77.9), and the assumption that *sellaria* therefore signify a latrine might be supported by the *foeditas loci* in Tacitus, but that is not at all necessary, and no parallel can be cited. In Pliny, *sellaria* should to the unjaundiced eye mean, neutrally, "sitting rooms," places with seats, which is just how the Loeb translators take it, and Lewis and Short before them, and Forcellini before them.[8]

But, above all, we must reject the fixation on male prostitutes. Implicit in this, explicit in Martin's formulation in 2001, is the assumption that latrines were where male prostitutes plied their trade. But—whatever practices may exist today—there is no ancient evidence for this. The authoritative modern study has laid out the facts: Roman cruising grounds were the baths (above all), brothels—of course—wharves, and theaters.[9] Latrines are a modern fantasy.

If not (or not necessarily) privies, what then, secondly, of the "foulness of the place" that evoked the name *sellaria*? "Foulness" may suggest a range of associations beyond mere scatology, and there is an obvious answer, for *sellaria* lead us not to seats in latrines, but to prostitution. One of the commonest modes of solicitation at Rome was to sit on a chair, *sella*, outside of the place of business, be it brothel, inn, or rented room. Juvenal has a prostitute perched on an *alta . . . sella* (3.136)—indeed, his late, antique scholiast calls her a *sellaria*.[10] That is to say, the connotation of *sellaria*, and the foulness of the place, is not the foulness of latrines and cruising males—let alone of some hypothetical act of sodomy on lavatory seats, or anywhere else—but rather one of advertisement, of show, of displaying oneself on a stool provocatively, in front of one's professional bedroom, for the purpose of prostitution.

Thirdly, there is the crucial matter of numbers. Juvenal's scholiast aside, there are no more than four references in ancient literature to *sellaria / sellarii*: but are there even that many? Both instances of *sellaria* in Pliny refer to a single place or area, somewhere within Nero's Golden House (let us omit Caligula for the moment)—nowhere else in Rome or its vast empire (Capri aside). That is to say, the two references are, in essence, one.

Our two other authorities, Tacitus and Suetonius on Capri, pose a related problem, but in different fashion. No one would doubt that Tacitus and Suetonius shared, and their texts are pervaded by, at least two major sources, now lost. That they are dependent on a single hostile authority for Tiberius' misdeeds on Capri is signalled in these passages by the pairing of *sellarii / sellaria* and *spintriae*; by Tacitus' *conquirent* and Suetonius' *conquisiti*; by the echo between Tacitus' *multiplici patientia* and Suetonius' *triplici serie connexi*; by Tiberius' being attracted by various visual *incitament(a) cupidinis* in Tacitus and his watching *ut . . . libidines excitaret* in Suetonius; and by the prominence in both authors of *pubem / pube*.[11] But there is a curious double vision at play here. Tacitus reports only two new words, *ignota antea vocabula reperta sunt sellariorum et spintriarum*. Suetonius likewise reports only two words, *sellaria excogitavit. . . . sprintrias appellabat*. Yet somehow, three words have crept into our dictionaries: *sellarii, sellaria*, and *spintriae*. It is possible that the common source used all three, and that our two surviving authors each chose to report only two of them, just not the same two. But let us wield a tiny Occam's razor and assume that the lost source recorded only *two* neologisms. The discrepancy should then lie not in variant ancient versions but in a simple modern misunderstanding: Tacitus' *sellariorum* ought to be the genitive plural, not of the otherwise hapax legomenon *sellarii*, but of the neuter *sellaria* otherwise attested in Suetonius and Pliny.[12] In other words, the two references in Tacitus and Suetonius are, essentially, one.

Two lexicographical revisions follow from all of this.

First, *sellarium* with the meaning of "latrine" or "privy" should be deleted from the dictionary, as both unattested and unwarranted. Rather than this general meaning in the unparalleled singular, we should see in the occurrences of the plural noun precise references to two specific *places*, and two only, one of them situated somewhere within an imperial palace at Rome (Nero's, and perhaps Caligula's), the other in an imperial palace on Capri (Tiberius'). Let us go further. Suetonius glosses *sellaria* in the singular, *sedem . . . in quam*, while Tacitus refers to a singular *locus* (*foedus*). Should we then understand, not rooms called *sellaria*, but a suite of rooms (Suetonius' *cubicula*) known collectively as the *Sellaria*, "The Place of Seats" (or "Benches")—in short: "The Brothel"?

That would illuminate what follows immediately in Suetonius' account, young Pans and nymphs offering themselves (*prostantis*) in the woods and groves in an area known as the *Caprineum*, The Shrine of the Goat. That is to say, by reading *Sellaria* as a proper noun, we see that the paragraph forms a unity in Suetonius' mind: for debauchery on Capri, you had the luxury of two venues, one indoors, one outdoors, offering notably similar pleasures. Both presented not only the private act of prostitution but the public act of solicitation that preceded it: to attract their clients, prostitutes sat (*sedere*) on chairs (*sellae*) outside their place of business or they stood there in front (*prostare*)—precisely what we have here with *sellaria* and *prostantis*.[13]

Once invented by Tiberius on Capri, the *Sellaria* (we might surmise) was copied at Rome by Gaius Caligula. Pliny gives the name without details, but Suetonius appears to supply the details without the name in his account of one of the young princeps' schemes for making money: "He opened a brothel [*lupanar*] on the Palatine, setting apart a number of rooms and furnishing them to suit the grandeur of the place, where matrons and freeborn youths should stand exposed [*starent*]."[14] It is not otherwise recorded but only too likely that Nero too had a brothel in his Golden House, for he certainly had a penchant for similar tableaux, in which prostitution in mock brothels and taverns played a central part, around the Lake of Agrippa in the Campus Martius, in the Naumachia of Augustus across the Tiber, and indeed along the riverbanks down to the sea: why not then in a *Sellaria* in his palace? With his disgrace and death, the *Sellaria*, the elaborate mock brothel of the Claudian emperors, disappears.[15]

Second, the word *sellarius*, meaning male prostitute, is also to be deleted from the dictionary, as likewise unattested and unwarranted. Its absence will help to dispel misunderstanding about the notorious *spintriae*.

Soon after the death of the old princeps, his successor expelled the *spintrias monstrosarum libidinum* from Rome—how they got there is a question, for their occupation is inextricably part of the legend of Capri—and he was barely dissuaded from drowning them in the sea (Suet. *Cal.* 16.1; cf. *HA Alex.* 34.4). The story does come in a package of his virtuous deeds from the early days of the reign, but it still seems a bit rich from a Caligula: if *he* disapproved of the *spintriae*, they must have been very bad indeed. Who were they and what monstrous things did they do?

The *OLD*, confident and discreet, offers: "spintria, -ae, *m.* [cf Gk. σφίγκτης] A type of male prostitute," citing Petronius 113.11, as well as the Tacitus and the two Suetonius passages noted above, and Suetonius' *Life of Vitellius* 3.2.[16] Lewis and Short are startlingly forthright: "[From σφιγκτήρ, the contractile muscle of the anus], a male prostitute." The derivation of the term from the Greek seemed obvious to the lexicographers, hence the connotation of anal intercourse. *LSJ* notes an obscure fragment of Cratinus preserved by Photius where Greek σφίγκτης means pederast, and it is glossed as κίναιδος in Hesychius, the only two references cited for the word. Thus, we have in English Martin's "squeezers," Woodman's "catamites," Hurley's "analists." But the derivation of the word from the anal sphincter is highly dubious, the emphasis on intercourse between males especially misleading, the notion of male prostitutes another imported modern fantasy.

We know more about how the word was created than what it actually means. J. André traced the development in Latin of Greek feminine agent nouns with the suffix "-tria": *citharistria, psaltria,* and *sambucistria* are the oldest, followed by *poetria; crotalistria* (and *spintria*); *hierophantria, lyristria, pharmaceutria; sophistria, tympanistria;* and, the latest additions, *ascetria* and *monastria.* As André observed, all are *female* professionals, and we can see that their Latin borrowings (*spintriae* aside) represent three occupational groupings: musical, literary, and religious.[17] J. N. Adams has added the crucial item: at *Satyricon* 37.6, Petronius offers *lupatria*—prostitute—where the Greek suffix is attached to a Latin root, here the common slang term for prostitute, *lupa,* she-wolf.[18] As Adams elucidated, "It is to be presumed that among bilingual speakers of Latin the normal Greek process of derivation was forgotten once the suffix *-tria* had acquired an association with female purveyors of sex (cf. λαικάστρια). Therefore, the suffix could be applied to a Latin base (even one which was nonverbal) provided that the semantic field was appropriate." Hence the sexual terms *lupatria* and *spintria.* In a note, Adams observed that the origin of *spintria* was not straightforward: "It designates someone engaged in an act of copulation involving three participants. The word is masculine in Suetonius, but may originally have been coined as a feminine (since one female can participate in such an act). It may have been generalised to include all three members of the sexual chain, passing into the generalising masculine in the process."[19]

This introduces two fundamental and (as will emerge) related points. One is that the root of *spintria,* like that of *lupatria,* is Latin, not Greek. The other is that the word may have begun (indeed, surely did begin) as a feminine coinage.

The well-attested common Greek word σφιγκτήρ and the obscure σφίγκτης / cinaedus, related though they may be, are misleading. The *spintria's* immediate antecedent should be the Latin *spinter,* bracelet or armlet, something that encircles and binds the arm, known to Plautus and defined by Festus (448–49 L.) as a kind of armlet that women used to wear in the old days on their upper left arm.[20] *Spinter* surely offers a better key to the meaning of *spintria*: at first sight, a *spintria* should simply be a woman who provided the same service for a client, binding and compressing not his arm but his penis, be it orally, vaginally, or anally.[21] In the dynamics of Roman sex, such activities would count as *patientia*, playing the submissive or womanly role, which is the word Tacitus uses to explain *spintria*. A precise definition would thus be "bracelet worker," analogous to *lupatria* as "she-wolf worker," another bilingual hybrid slang term for female sex workers.[22]

What then of the *spintria* as "male prostitute"? Despite the confident definition in our dictionaries, there is no evidence that the *sprintriae* were exclusively male—that is, that their ranks did not include *both* females and effeminate males.

Start with Suetonius 43.1. Again: *Etiam sellaria excogitavit, sedem arcanarum libidinum, in quam undique conquisiti puellarum et exoletorum greges monstrosique concubitus repertores, quos spintrias appellabat, triplici serie conexi, in vicem incestarent coram ipso, ut aspectu deficientis libidines excitaret.* Inelegantly and without punctuation: "He even invented the *Sellaria* a place for secret lusts in which sought out from everywhere gangs of girls and of mature catamites and devisers of monstrous coupling whom he called *spintriae* joined together in triple chains that they might defile each other before him so that he might arouse his declining lusts by the sight."[23]

How the components of this sentence fit together is not at all clear. Specifically, how are the participles *conquisiti* and *conexi* related to the two nouns *greges* and *repertores*? If *conquisiti* refers only to the *greges*, *conexi* must refer only to the *repertores*, thus shaping a chiastic pair: *conquisiti . . . greges* and *repertores . . . conexi*. But if that were the case, then *repertores* would be awkwardly isolated from the phrase *in quam*, which is closely tied to *conquisiti*: that is, the *repertores* would be left outside the *sedem arcanarum libidinum*. Therefore, the two participles must refer rather to both nouns, the *greges* (comprising *puellae* and *exoleti*) and the *repertores* are both *conquisiti* and *conexi*, and the *spintriae* are both male and female.[24]

The few other attestations of the word *spintria(e)* offer no clear indication of its gender. If we look closely at Tacitus, he gives no sure clue as to the sex of Tiberius' victims (which is how he presents them), merely emphasizing their youth, *pueritia*. Nor does Suetonius in the *Caligula* passage noted above. Nor is the alleged attachment of the scurrilous cognomen "Spintria" to Vitellius, after his debauched boyhood on Capri, any indication, since a female nickname (if that is what it is) could always be applied abusively to a male.[25] And the passage in Petronius is, despite speculation, a fragment without context.[26]

Two further arguments may be brought to support the contention that *spintriae* were boys and girls together. One concerns the norms in sexual encounters with more than one partner.[27] First, in ancient times, the number of participants in group sexual encounters was three or four, no more (and of course no fewer).[28] That is to say, there seems to be no example of ancient art depicting more than four people involved in a single sexual encounter (as distinct from simultaneous but discrete acts), and only one such occurrence in literature, in Martial, who dismisses such *Veneris novae figurae* as not real but the novel and overheated imaginings of a filthy poet.[29] And second, the sexes were mixed—that is, both men and women were involved when there were more than two partners. Again, there seems to be no depiction of purely homosexual group sex (in the sense of all male or all female) in Greco-Roman art, and there are only two references to it in literature, the one just referred to (a bad poet's hitherto unknown fantasies), the other in Seneca's lurid denunciation of the unutterably depraved Hostius Quadra, who is depicted in the same passage as indulging in sex with men and women together, and with two and three partners indifferently.[30]

Which leads to the second argument in favor of mixed sport, that is, consideration of the alleged tastes of Tiberius Caesar. Just as he did not transgress the norm of three or four performers, *triplici serie conexi*, so it should be noted that he was not much interested in men as sexual objects: apart from one dubious anecdote in Suetonius, about an alleged double rape (44.2), there is no sign of homosexual desire in the princeps—his tastes are represented as inclined in quite other directions (after, of course, more than six decades of domestic normality). Why then would he want an all-male troupe of prostitutes? And most puzzling, of what use would the notorious books of Elephantis be to such an all-male troupe? All that we know about them indicates that her works were concerned only with heterosexual intercourse.[31]

In sum, *spintria* as "male prostitute" is to be deleted from the lexicon as unwarranted and misleading. That definition is inferred solely from an assumed but unattested connection with the binding sphincter muscle, and hence with anal intercourse between males, and belief in it is confirmed by the supposed but unwarranted association with the fictitious *sellarii* here, and compounded by the misunderstanding, here as elsewhere, of *exoleti* as male prostitutes.[32] Rather, *spintriae* were "bracelet workers," the term indicating female sex workers. Their ranks surely included both females and males so passive, or bisexual, as to be called female sex workers. They performed in groups, and the *spintria* was or could be multiply submissive (*multiplici patientia*) in a tableau of three or four; that is, she or he was penetrated, acted as a "bracelet," two or three ways simultaneously.

A proper translation of Suetonius' *Tiberius* (43.1) should thus read (to rephrase Hurley): "On retiring to Capri, he devised the *Sellaria* as a site for his secret orgies: there select teams of girls and mature catamites, along with inventors of deviant intercourse, [all of] whom he dubbed 'bracelet workers,' copulated before him in triple unions to excite his flagging passions."

———

Spintriae, sellarii, and *exoleti* as male prostitutes are all modern fantasies—indeed, it is most unlikely that the *sellarii* ever existed—and they impede proper understanding of the curious practices on Capri. The frisson elicited by their being *male* prostitutes (men or boys who submitted to men for money, willingly or not) deflects attention from their being *prostitutes* at all. They were not, and therein lies the paradox of the *spintriae.*

Tacitus and Suetonius, and their lost source, are clear. According to Tacitus, the performers were young (*pubem, pueritiam;* cf. *parens*) and good-looking (*forma, decora corpora*), some were modest (*modestiam, abnuentis*), some nobly born (*imagines maiorum*), some actually eager (*promptos*): no hint of professionals—these are freeborn targets of a tyrant's lusts. Suetonius confirms that they were young (*puellae, pube*) and of both sexes (*puellae* and *exoleti;* cf. *utriusque sexus*), but he says nothing about their being professional (or unwilling). The only alleged *spintria* who is named, Aulus Vitellius, offers a perfect example of the type, for he was indeed young (born in 15 CE), an amateur, free, highly born, and apparently eager: "He spent his boyhood and early youth at Capreae among Tiberius' prostitutes (*inter Tiberiana scorta*), being branded for all time with the nickname Spintria (*perpetuo Spintriae cognomine notatus*) and suspected of having been the beginning and cause of his father's advancements in rank at the expense of his own chastity (*corporis gratia*)."[33] But Vitellius was *not* a prostitute, far from it. Whoever the *Tiberiana scorta* may have been—and the phrase should convey Suetonian disapproval more than precise definition—our only evidence suggests that the *spintriae* were well-born youths of both sexes, objects of an old man's fantasies and of their parents' fear or ambition.

But Tiberius *treated* them as prostitutes, adding insult to injury, degradation to sexual abuse, for both of his neologisms were coinages from the language of prostitution: *Sellaria* suggesting a brothel, *spintriae* sex workers. Most significantly, Suetonius presents the princeps not as a participant in, but as a voyeur of, their acts, *ut aspectu deficientis libidines excitaret.* And if we read Tacitus closely, although he sketches a vivid portrait of the lustful tyrant, he does not actually accuse Tiberius of having physical contact with his victims. Good looks, modesty, and noble ancestors were the incitement to his lust, *incitamentum cupidinis. Pubem ingenuam stupris pollueret*: he polluted freeborn youngsters in illicit sex. But this awful picture is something of a trompe l'oeil, for we are not told that he vented his own *cupido* on the noble youths, nor that he polluted them with his own *stupra*, let alone that he might have participated himself in their *multiplex patientia*. The emphasis on his watching, on scopophilia, was surely in the lost source, transmitted by Suetonius and veiled by Tacitus. With the language of prostitution coined by Tiberius, we move beyond voyeurism into theater.

The *cubicula* on Capri were stocked with the most obscene artworks, both painting and sculpture, and the illustrated sex manual of Elephantis, to provide examples if need be. This need for blueprints, as it were, strongly suggests that, whatever outrage the group couplings may have aroused, novelty was not its cause. If the performers were at a loss, when they inspected the artworks around them, perhaps even paused to look something up in the library, they did so to discover *exemplar imperatae schemae*, an example of the posture that had been ordered.[34] That is, if Suetonius is to be believed, the performers were treated neither as creative artists nor as professional sex workers: they were more like actors in a pornographic film, doing what they were directed to do.

The performative nature of these activities suggests that we should locate Tiberius' activities not only in the history of Roman sexual customs but in the broader cultural interests of his day. Three practices might be evoked.

First is the passion for what has been called, romantically but accurately, "the landscape of allusion." In a form of cultural imperialism, well-to-do Romans recreated other times and places, real and fictional, in their own environment, reforming landscapes and erecting buildings, stocking them with original works of art and craft or with reproductions, and then relaxing in their fantasy worlds. Of many examples, Cicero's villa at Tusculum and Hadrian's near Tibur come to mind, the former with its Lyceum and Academy, the latter with its elaborate reimaginings of those Athenian sites appropriate to cogitation—the Lyceum, the Academy, the Stoa Poikilē—along with Egyptian Canopus, the Vale of Tempe in Thessaly, even the underworld. Capri, as the private refuge of the Caesars was just the sort of place where we might expect to find such recreations. Augustus set the tone, naming a nearby islet *Apragopolis*, the City of Leisure. The twelve imperial villas on the island, all certainly stocked with works of art, were given elaborate names, though what those were is not quite clear. Tiberius is forever associated with the greatest of them, the so-called Villa Jovis, the Villa of Jupiter,[35] which included on its grounds an enormous replica of the great Lighthouse of Alexandria, the *Pharos*, and a place called, probably, The Butchery, *Carnificina*. Into such a landscape the mock-brothel, the *Sellaria*, and the mock-shrine, the *Caprineum*, fit comfortably, stage-sets, as we have seen, ostentatiously devoted to depravity.[36]

Within this physical context, second, we should consider the Roman love for elaborate mythological tableaux vivants with costumes and role-playing, a pleasure particularly associated with dinner parties: the image of Victory crowning Metellus Pius at the magnificent banquet of Urbinius; the singing Orpheus and his wild beasts at the silvan banquet of Hortensius; the merman Glaucus dancing—reed-crowned, fish-tailed, painted blue—at the banquet of Antony and Cleopatra; Octavian as Apollo presiding over the feast of the twelve gods; Bacchus and his Bacchantes celebrating the vintage at the house of Silius, the "husband" of Messalina; Ajax gone mad at the banquet of Trimalchio.[37] Or, on Capri, young Pans and nymphs disporting in their native woods and groves outside of welcoming caves and hollows. The actors in such entertainments need not be professional entertainers or servants, for Glaucus and Bacchus were played by senators, Apollo by the future Augustus himself—and the Pans and nymphs by free and even nobly born boys and girls.

And close to this, third, a very special kind of role-playing, with deliberate status reversal: the temporary establishment of private brothels staffed by respectable Roman matrons. As we have seen, Caligula and Nero would later relish these mock brothels and taverns, but the grand example for such elaborately transgressive performances had been provided long before, by the *flagitiosum convivium* staged at his home by a *tribunicius viator* in 52 BCE, attended not only by tribunes of the plebs but by the consul Metellus Scipio himself: on that occasion the host had set to prostitution two noble ladies, Mucia and Fulvia, and a noble youth named Saturninus, *probrosae patientiae corpora.* How far this role-playing actually went is not clear, and it may well be that such occasions were less orgies and more risqué costume parties, but the no less notorious feast of the twelve Olympians hosted by Octavian certainly gave rise to rumors about "new adulteries," and the *vindemia* of Messalina and Silius was a true bacchanal.[38] It is in this context that the *Sellaria* of Caligula at Rome and the tableaux of Nero at Rome and elsewhere are probably to be set: the latter repeatedly emphasized high-class ladies performing in temporary brothels, while the former, with its highly decorated *cellae*, staffed by matrons and freeborn youths who stood (*starent*) to offer themselves, is strikingly reminiscent of the *Sellaria* and *Caprineum* on Capri.[39]

Sexual liberation, costumes, role-playing, exotic locales, privacy. Capri was a very special place of retreat, for there a Roman could cast off the constraints not just of public but even of private life, both *negotium* and *otium*, and indulge in pure idleness, *desidia.* In his last days, Augustus had distributed Roman togas and Greek pallia to his entourage on the island, and he had decreed that the Romans should wear Greek dress and speak Greek, while Greeks did the reverse.[40] Suetonius tells us that Tiberius summoned the eighteen-year-old Gaius Caligula to Capri in 31 CE, presumably as he prepared his coup against

Sejanus. Gaius was able to retain his inhuman composure there despite the swirl of plots around him and the disasters befalling his near relatives. Yet, as his biographer explains, "even at the time he could not control his natural cruelty and viciousness (*naturam ... saevam atque probrosam*), but he was a most eager witness of the tortures and executions of those who suffered punishment." And then the really interesting part: "At night he indulged in dissipations and adulteries (*ganeas atque adulteria*), disguised in a wig and a long robe (*capillamento celatus et veste longa*), and he was passionately devoted to the theatrical arts of dancing and singing, in which Tiberius very willingly indulged him, in the hope that through these his savage nature might be softened (*mansuefieri posset ferum eius ingenium*)."[41] Has Suetonius, as he often did, quite misunderstood the substance of what he transmits? Sexual liberation and sex as performance, theatrical costume and singing and dancing, sanctioned by the princeps as educational. Tacitus reports that some at least of the actors in Tiberius' sellarian scenarios were ready participants; and, most curiously, Suetonius says nothing about the intimidation reported by Tacitus, when he really should have condemned it. Behind the staged horror of the "dark pleasures" of Tiberius Caesar in the Neverland of Capri, might we suspect that some of the actors involved were perhaps relaxing—in precedented, if not at all respectable, Roman ways—perhaps even enjoying themselves? There may not be a lot more to say about Tiberius' interest in sex, but his passion for the theater is another matter.

6

Mallonia

IN THE SECLUSION OF CAPRI, Tiberius transformed himself into a monster of depravity. Words almost fail Suetonius when he comes to describe the debauchery on the island: "He burned with still greater and fouler infamy, hardly right to be discussed or listened to or even believed."[1]

Nonetheless, the biographer bravely continues his catalog of corruption. It culminates with the horrific "Tale of Mallonia":

> *Feminarum quoque, et quidem illustrium, capitibus quanto opere solitus sit inludere, evidentissime apparuit Malloniae cuiusdam exitu, quam perductam nec quicquam amplius pati constantissime recusantem delatoribus obiecit ac ne ream quidem interpellare desiit, ecquid paeniteret; donec ea relicto iudicio domum se abripuit ferroque transegit, obscaenitate[m] oris hirsuto atque olido seni clare exprobrata. Unde mora in Atellanico exhodio proximis ludis adsensu maximo excepta percrebruit, hircum vetulum capreis naturam ligurire.*

Just how much he was in the habit of insulting the heads of women as well, and highborn ones at that, could be seen very clearly in the death of a certain Mallonia, whom, when she was delivered to him and most resolutely refused to endure anything more, he threw to the informers. And even when she was on trial, he did not stop interrupting her, whether she was sorry, until, having left the court, she tore herself home and ran herself through with a sword, after loudly reproaching the shaggy and foul-smelling old man with the obscenity of his mouth. Hence a saying in the Atellan farce at the next games that met with great approval and circulated widely: "The little old he-goat licks the private parts of she-goats."[2]

Suetonius' *Lives of the Caesars* runs to 334 pages in Maximilian Ihm's edition. In all of its riotous exuberance, there is no anecdote more bizarre. Indeed, with Mallonia as our Alice, we tumble into Wonderland.

Let us read the tale again three times.

———

When first reconsidered, its meaning dissolves in a chaos of incongruity, implausibility, and incomprehension. Tiberius was accustomed to taking pleasure in being fellated by women: the technical term is *irrumatio*, whether served by a man or a woman. His indulgence in that particular vice, fellatio by women (for which this passage is the only evidence), is supposed to be made extremely obvious (how so, is not apparent) by one example, that is, the death of a noblewoman who is otherwise unknown to history. She is brought to him and she is thrown to prosecutors when she refuses to suffer anything more. The act itself is omitted. What more would she not suffer? More *irrumatio*? Or some other, worse assault? The nature of the act and its sequel is worth defining, as will be seen in a moment. More disquieting at this point is the Latin: as transmitted in most manuscripts, printed in the standard text, and ignored by translators, it reads *nec . . . recusantem*, which means at first glance that she did *not* refuse to endure anything more.[3]

The tale rushes on, as he throws her to the *delatores*. Even when she is on trial, he does not cease to interrupt proceedings. The Latin is elided. Tiberius' question is not quite attached syntactically to the preceding clause, for the sentence reads literally "and he did not cease to interrupt her even when she was a defendant, whether she were sorry." One might easily infer a verb of speaking ("[asking] whether"), but to understand this as a direct question, as some translations do—"are you sorry?"—seems unnecessarily melodramatic from all that we know of Tiberius' devious character and of Roman trials. It might better be taken to suggest that he was sending her signals to reconsider her position, but without an explicit verb, the meaning must remain uncertain.[4] That he did not stop interrupting her even when she was a defendant is awkward as well, for, although sense can be wrung from the Latin—her resolution might reflect his repeated interjections—on the surface, the text suggests that he had been interrupting her on some previous occasion. Again, the Latin is confused and confusing.

But the trial itself is baffling. This is clearly a formal tribunal (*iudicium*), with prosecutors (*delatores*) and a defendant (*rea*)—that is, the court should be one of the standing criminal courts with juries (*quaestiones perpetuae*). Tiberius here plays a role for which he was well known, sitting as a self-appointed assessor to the magistrate and freely intervening in the interests of justice.[5] But again, in the rush we are not told what the actual charge against Mallonia was, nor do we know the date or the place of the affair. This is a formal trial with prosecutors, and Mallonia runs home to denounce her persecutor. The scene should be set in Rome. But the context demands that the tale unfold on Tiberius' private property of Capri, for Suetonius recounts it in his catalog of vices indulged on the island. And persuasive for Capri as the setting is the fact that the alleged popular reaction to the tragedy surely depends on a spectacular geographical pun. The line so rightly appreciated by the audience means "the little old he-goat licks the private parts of she-goats," but it also means "the little old he-goat licks private parts on Capri"[6]—a pun that demands that we situate Mallonia on the island.

This creates a chronological impasse. Tiberius departed from the city of Rome in 26 CE, never to return, and he retired into his life of vice on Capri the following year. Nowhere is it alleged by any source that he indulged in sexual enormities during his years in Rome, and there is no evidence for his participating in trials on Capri or elsewhere afterward; indeed, the criminal trial of a Roman citizen could not be held anywhere but at Rome.[7] The choice is stark—prosecution in Rome before 26 CE, debauchery on Capri thereafter—but the two should not overlap. The affair floats out of time and space.

Our story rushes to its conclusion. Mallonia tears herself home from the courtroom, procures a convenient sword, attracts an audience for her parting words, and runs herself through after denouncing Tiberius in no uncertain terms.[8] Implicitly but emphatically she compares the old man to a goat, shaggy and smelly, and one who uses his mouth for obscene purposes.[9] But confusion is complete when we contemplate the magnificent punch line. We might be concerned that yet again we must ignore or emend the standard text to make sense of it: the word translated as "saying" is *mora*, meaning "delay" or "lapse of time," which is nonsense.[10] Be that as it may, soon after Mallonia has denounced the obscenity of the mouth of the shaggy, smelly, old goat of Capri ("Goat Island"), the perfect pun is pronounced to an appreciative public: the old goat licks the private parts of female goats, or he licks private parts on Goat Island. Unquestionably, Tiberius is here presented as enjoying *cunnilinctio*, an act that in Roman terms would be submissive and degrading for him. But the whole point of the Mallonia anecdote is that it is the supreme example of his cruelly forcing women to *fellate* him. The two activities are, both physically and in the estimate of society, exact opposites. We have indeed fallen into Wonderland.[11]

———

Nevertheless, on a second rereading of the text, behind this fog of confusion, we can discern a sophisticated intelligence at work (not that of Suetonius, but his source's)[12] with a coherent story to tell. This is particularly striking in the vigorous verb forms, rich and sometimes subtle, which whirl us through the tale.

Tiberius enjoyed insulting the heads of women, *feminarum capitibus in-ludere*. *Inludere* is aggressive, "to make sport of," "to mock," "to fool." It also has the precise and not uncommon meaning of "to use for sexual pleasure," as every reader of Suetonius knew. When a *caput* is involved, the verb means to enforce fellatio, *irrumatio*, an aggressive act, as here. The closest parallel commonly cited is likewise Suetonian, from the life of Julius Caesar. Caesar could not refrain from boasting in the senate about how he had outmaneuvered his enemies to win his Gallic command: "I got exactly what I desired despite the moans and groans of my reluctant rivals: from now on I will be mounting the heads of all of them" (*insultaturum se omnium capitibus*). Here "insult" takes on its full vigour of "leaping upon," and the "moans and groans" (*invitis et gementibus*) represent involuntary submission. That is, his boast can be read as simple crowing over a political victory, but it is expressed in coarsely sexual terms. Moreover, a second wordplay is evident from the context of both the Tiberian and the Caesarian anecdotes. *Caput* commonly signifies not only "head" but "legal status," "legal personality," hence the emphasis on highborn women and senatorial rivals. The two men are portrayed as trampling on civic rights: Caesar gleeful in his metaphor of lust and groaning victims; Tiberius grimly physical.[13]

Mallonia is delivered to Tiberius, *perductam*. Again, within the general meaning of *perducere*, to bring someone or something somewhere, there is the more precise denotation of "to convey a woman to a man's bed (as a pimp)," a sense again familiar to Suetonius' readers and derived from a standard use of the basic *ducere* to signify engaging in paid intercourse.[14] *Ducere* and *perducere* are also commonly used to describe the bringing of a defendant to a trial.

Mallonia most resolutely refuses anything more, *recusantem*. Tiberius throws her to the informers, *obiecit*. The verb *obicere* is startlingly vivid, commonly used to describe the action of throwing living creatures, animal or human, as food to wild beasts, to be torn to shreds, munched, devoured.[15]

He does not stop interrupting her at the trial, *ne ream quidem interpellare desiit*, to discover whether she is sorry, *ecquid paeniteret*. Yet again, what stands out here is the wordplay of the verbs. *Interpellare*, to interrupt, also has a precise meaning: to accost, to solicit a woman. Tiberius, the well-known dissimulator, brazenly seeks her favors while pretending to ask if Mallonia repents whatever crime she may be accused of.[16]

She leaves the trial and hurries home, *domum se abripuit*. *Abripere* is yet another strikingly dramatic verb, and the construction—snatching, dragging, tearing oneself home—is unique.[17]

She loudly reproaches her persecutor, *clare exprobrata*, and runs herself through with a convenient sword, *se ferro transegit*. Again, vividly expressed, although suicide by transfixing oneself with a sword is commonplace in Latin.[18]

The saying derived from an Atellan farce then circulates widely (*percrebruit*): "The little old he-goat licks the private parts of she-goats" (*naturam ligurire*). Again, a precise and colorful verb, meaning "to lick," and yet again it and its derivatives can be employed, as here, to convey an obscene oral act, whether *fellatio* or *cunnilinctio*.[19] And, among its broad and universal meanings, the noun *natura* also has the precise denotation of private parts, especially female.[20]

But, much more commonly, the verb *ligurire* and its compounds and derivatives signify not just the basic action of licking but the concept of licking up, licking clean, of consuming avidly, both food and (metaphorically) money, property, inheritances. Perhaps, then, we could read *natura* in a broader sense. Might *naturam ligurire* also suggest that Tiberius devours the essence of his victims, their nature, their humanity? That would neatly recall, in ring composition, the *capitibus inludere*, insulting the heads of women, with which the Mallonia affair is introduced—sexual assault conceived also as an attack on human rights. While *natura* can admittedly stretch to "human nature" in Latin, it does not quite have the essential meaning of "humanity." But it does in its Greek counterpart, φύσις, and, as we shall see, there is a Greek twist to the tale of Mallonia.[21]

The portrait of a tyrant emerges from this second rereading of these few lines, both directly and by implication from the tumult of the tale they convey. Tyrants trample on the rights of their subjects, tyrants notoriously abuse the system of justice. Tyrants are notorious sexual predators. Tyrants notoriously eat their people and drink their blood. That is, political oppression is here interwoven with sexual abuse and aggressive consumption (wild animals, oral sex), all of it sketched swiftly, in ten lines and a rush of wordplays. Never mind that it makes no sense as a story or as an illustration of Tiberian vice. It coheres as a ferocious attack on tyranny.

Mallonia inevitably recalls the two legendary female victims of tyrannical injustice in Roman history. The first is Lucretia, the chaste wife of a cousin of Tarquin the Proud, the last king of Rome. Raped by Tarquin's son, she summons her relatives, denounces the attack, plunges a dagger into her heart—and the monarchy is soon overthrown.

The second avatar is Verginia, the freeborn daughter of a Roman centurion, in the time when Rome was ruled by the decemvirs. The wicked decemvir Appius Claudius lusts after the girl and has one of his clients drag her into his court, claiming her as his slave. Her father, frustrated in his attempts to assert her free birth, stabs her to death before the crowd—and the decemvirate soon collapses. Verginia is particularly apposite to Mallonia and Tiberius, in that her civic status, her *caput*, is at issue, and the court trying her case is presided over by the very villain who wishes to assault her. And he, the infamous Appius Claudius, was a direct ancestor of Tiberius Caesar.[22]

The legends of Lucretia and Verginia both lead from rape or intended rape by a tyrant to the stabbing martyrdom of his female victim before witnesses— and then to the overthrow of the corrupt regime itself. If the death of Mallonia is indeed meant to recall the deaths of Lucretia by suicide and of Verginia after a sham trial and the subsequent fall of tyrants, she surely embodies the political sentiments of the narrator from whom Suetonius has derived her story.

———

A third review of that story may help here. Let us read it backward.

The line from the Atellan farce is too good to be true. At first glance, it works. The pun on she-goats and the island of Capri is brilliant, innocent on the rough surface but drawing attention to its other meaning. Roman audiences were avid connoisseurs of the meaningful double entendre spoken at the games, dramatic lines lifted from their theatrical context, whether deliberately or by accident, and applied to real life. Yet some might have questioned how apposite this line really was. Mallonia's gibes about shaggy hair and foul smell find no clear echo in any description of the balding and health-conscious Tiberius, and certainly not in his public image, while "little old he-goat" is not particularly apt to a tall and fastidious patrician: it is all rather forced, tailored to fit the spectacular goatish pun of the Atellana. Again, structurally, the Atellan line closing the anecdote is too neat a match for its opening, each with its word-play on a sexual act representing the abuse of a tyrant. And again, the sexual act pilloried in the line is simply not the act of which the tyrant stands accused by Mallonia. The suspicion must arise that the verse—composed by an unknown author and recited at nameless games that were celebrated at an unknown date and an unknown place—is an artistic invention, created for the anecdote.

Goats and oral sex make for a striking, in fact a unique, combination, found nowhere else in the art or literature of antiquity. Goats—hairy and smelly and lustful—do not indulge in *cunnilinctio*. But old men—hairy and smelly and lustful, and compared with goats—might. The general trope appears in Plautus' *Mercator*:

ieiunitatis plenus, anima foetida,
senex hircosus tu osculere mulierem?
utine adveniens vomitum excutias mulieri?

On an empty stomach, with stinking breath, you goaty old man would kiss a woman? In order to make her throw up when you approach her?[23]

Horace and Catullus and Martial and others write not of goats but of men with goatish characteristics. Oral sex is a natural extension. "The little old he-goat licks the private parts of she-goats" is heir to a long literary tradition, and the supposed gibe at the games is a notably sophisticated addition: Atellan farces were emphatically Oscan in origin and subject matter, and the Oscans were famed for their delight in oral sex.[24]

The line is set up by, depends upon, the preceding tale of Mallonia. Who then was she?

The one fact that we are told about her is that she was well-born, *illustris*, yet her name is distinctly unpromising. This is its only appearance in classical literature, and no Mallonius or Mallonia occurs in the epigraphy of the East, or of North Africa, or of the northwestern provinces of Europe. Indeed, they do not occur in Greek at all. In their rare appearances on Latin inscriptions, they reveal a provincial and a distinctly Celtic flavor, found in Spain, in three of the Gallic provinces, and in Liguria. Moreover, in Liguria and in the rest of Italy they suggest a freedman character.[25] The only distinguished members of the family are local decurions at Cumae late in the third century and a polyonymous senator from Vienne in Narbonensis, whose nomenclature is uncertain and who on any calculation lived much later than Tiberius, probably in the second century.[26] The family was not *illustris* under Tiberius. A distinguished Mallonia at Rome in the 20s or 30s CE is improbable in the extreme.

In fact, "Mallonia" too is a pun, created for the occasion, yet another word-play in a passage packed to overflowing with them. Here it is bilingual, based on Greek μαλλός, "a tuft of wool." Mallonia is revealed as a Woolly Female. Who better than a nanny goat to complain about the unwanted sexual advances of a hirsute, malodorous billy goat? She stoutly refuses to suffer anything more from the tyrant. How better for her to express this than in Greek, on the Greek island of Capri: *nec quicquam amplius pati,* οὐδὲν μᾶλλον?[27]

The lady vanishes.

The tale of Mallonia is a fabrication from first to last, a stunningly elaborate fraud.[28] Who invented this angry, witty, extravagant fiction? That question is left for another occasion.

PART III

In the Emperor's Orbit

7

Asellius Sabinus

CULTURE, WIT, AND POWER IN
THE GOLDEN AGE OF GASTRONOMY

VARIEGATED BY ORIGIN, habits, and style, the declaimers formed a noisy menagerie. For some, declamation became a way of life, not a training for the law courts, where a paladin of the schools might fail miserably. It also furnished social betterment, and the chance of notoriety and promotion. Of the performers registered by Seneca, the majority are small town careerists, with few senators or sons of senators. Many of them were crude and brutal in style and argument.[1]

In his *Controversiae*, the Elder Seneca vividly recalled scores of declaimers whose *sententiae*, good and bad, he remembered so well. He seldom failed to criticize even the best of them, often acerbically. Yet, there was one in whom he openly delighted, Sabinus, *urbanissimus homo*, "the most urbane of men" (*C.* 9.4.17), and, "the most charming wit (*venustissimus . . . scurra*) among the rhetors" (*S.* 2.12). His only censure of the man, leveled twice, was that he could not resist a joke.[2]

Seneca does not ascribe *urbanitas* lightly—indeed he does not award the quality to any other declaimer at all—but Sabinus reminds him of it no fewer than three times (*urbanissimus, urbanitate, urbanas res*). *Urbanitas* is elegance, sophistication, refinement—in a word urbanity, civilization, the very antithesis of the rustic and the foreign—and it is frequently expressed through wit. It routinely conveys an attitude of superiority, even of arrogance. An urbane joke is more often than not exclusive, an in-joke: indeed it is often an insult, a zinger. But in Seneca's friend, *urbanitas* is combined with *venustas*, charm. The man was a jester but his jokes were charming and they usually did not sting.[3]

He first appears in a long and curious digression very late in the *Controversiae*, at 9.4.17–21.[4] We are listening to the elderly Seneca as he dictates rapidly, quoting and misquoting from memory. His thoughts tumble out; his Latin is often awkward, frequently obscure, and notably repetitious. A literal translation might look like this:[5]

(17) I remember this *controversia* being declaimed well also by Asilius Sabinus. "Describe," he said, "describe the slaying of the tyrant and your being escorted from the citadel with enormous glory. O you parricide, if you do not understand, even after the tyrannicide, how much more honorably your brother died than you slew." What I did not approve was that he tried to speak wittily in a serious context. But he was a most urbane man, as I have often told you, so that whatever was lacking to him in eloquence he made up for in urbanity.

(18) I remember that when Vallius Syriacus, a fluent man, was prosecuting and seemed likely to undergo a charge of bringing a false accusation, he [Sabinus] appeared with a sad visage around the spectators at the trial, and whenever he ran into Syriacus (who was moving about) he would inquire what his hopes were. Then after the trial, when Syriacus thanked him because he had shown such concern for him, "By Hercules," he said, "I was afraid that we would have one more rhetor." And once, brought as a witness, when he was asked whether he had received [. . .] sesterces from the other side, he said that he had received them. Did he have them? He said he did not know. Then when asked whether he had a charge of bringing a false accuation, "You," he said, "are familiar with my carelessness: I do not know whether I have it, but I know that I received it." And against Domitius, a man of most noble birth who during his consulship had built baths overlooking the Sacred Way and then had begun to go around the rhetors and declaim, "I," he said, "knew that you would do this, and I said to your mother when she complained of your laziness: [in Greek] first swimming, then letters."

(19) I cannot pass by two of his urbane actions. He had accompanied the proconsul Occius Flamma to the province of Crete. The Greeks began to demand in the theater that Sabinus should undertake the highest magistracy. Now it is the custom for the magistrates of the Cretans to let their beard and hair grow. Sabinus got up and imposed silence with a gesture. Then he said, "I have twice undertaken this magistracy in Rome." For he had twice pleaded a case as a defendant. The Greeks did not understand, but they blessed Caesar and requested that Sabinus also undertake that office a third time. (20) Afterward the entire cohort of companions then offended them. They were attacked in the temple by the whole crowd, which demanded that Sabinus should go to Rome with Turdus (he was among the most infamous and hated men). When Turdus promised to go, so that he might get out of there, Sabinus imposed silence and said, "I am

not about to go to Caesar with a tidbit." Afterward it was brought up against Sabinus when he was pleading his case. I remember the man spoke fluently when he had been brought from prison into the senate to ask that he might receive his daily rations. Then he said, complaining of hunger, "I do not seek anything burdensome from you, but that you decide that I either die or live." He also said this, "Do not, I say, listen haughtily to a man of many sorrows: often he who could have pitied begs for pity."

(21) And when he declared that there were wealthy Sejanians in the jail, "Though a man," he said, "not yet sentenced, I beg parricides for bread that I might live." Although he had moved men by a speech both pitiful and fluent, he returned nevertheless to witticisms. He begged to be transferred to the Stone-Quarries, "Not," he said, "that the name Stone-Quarries (*Lautumiae*) might deceive any of you, for the thing is far from sumptuous (*lauta*)." I have related this both that you might come to know the man himself to some extent, and that you might understand how difficult it was to escape from his own nature. How could it be got from him not to jest in declamations, one who used to jest amid his troubles and dangers? Who cannot realize that he should not have jested in those circumstamces? Who can believe he was able to do it?

His Name

Seneca remembers that the *controversia* under consideration was well declaimed by "Asilius Sabinus." He is but one of sixteen or seventeen declaimers recalled as having treated this particular theme, some of them quoted on it as many as four times. Most of them are major and recurring figures in the *Controversiae*, but this is Sabinus' sole appearance in the work. After reciting two brief sentences from his declamation, Seneca deprecates his inability to resist a joke—but he then recalls five of the man's jests, none of them relevant to declamation. And then he also recalls three moving passages from an actual speech of appeal delivered by Sabinus to the senate when he was imprisoned on a capital charge. Serious, but equally irrelevant to this declamation, they are rounded off by a fourth extract from the speech, to demonstrate that the joker just could not desist from joking.

"Sabinus Asilius" turns up once in Seneca's *Suasoriae* (2.12), again with a joke, and again remembered with affection, as "the most charming wit among the rhetors." This raises a small problem. The name "Asilius Sabinus" in the long *Controversiae* passage just quoted above (9.4.17) is a sensible nineteenth-century emendation, now universally accepted, of a clearly corrupt text, and it is derived from "Sabinus Asilius" in the *Suasoriae*. What the manuscripts of the *Controversiae* in fact offer in 9.4.17 is not "Asilius" but "Tullius" or "Iulius" as the *nomen gentilicium*.[6] Whether Seneca refers to the same man in both works remains to be determined. The point here is that "Asilius" is in fact attested only once as his nomen in Seneca's writings (in the *Suasoriae*), not twice.

That observation is relevant to a brief notice in Suetonius' *Tiberius* (42.2). The princeps awarded 200,000 sesterces to an "Asellius Sabinus" for a dialogue in which he had introduced a contest among a mushroom, a figpecker, an oyster, and a thrush: "Asellius," not "Asilius."

Our problem is compounded by the passing mention in another author of a witty criticism leveled by an "Asellius" at the delivery of another orator who happens also to figure prominently in Seneca's *Controversiae*. That is, we have a jest in a rhetorical setting such as one might find in the *Controversiae*, but it is attributed to "Asellius," not "Asilius." Our authority here is none other than Seneca's son—one of the addressees of the *Controversiae*—in his *Letters to Lucilius* (40.9).

And then there is a remark, in a letter addressed by the elderly Augustus to his granddaughter Agrippina, which is cited by Suetonius in his *Life of Gaius* (8.4). In the fragment quoted by the biographer, Augustus informs her that he is sending her son to her. The infant Gaius will travel in the care of Talarius and "Asillius": not "Asilius" or "Asellius," but "Asillius."

Are we dealing with one, two, or three men, and what name or names should we expect? The standard works of reference are remarkably noncommittal.[7] Nevertheless, this should be one man and he should be called Asellius Sabinus. The case for that supposition is worth setting out.

That Seneca's "Sabinus Asilius" and his emended "[Asilius] Sabinus" are one and the same man should be accepted prima facie, as everyone would agree. He is described in the two passages in strikingly complimentary and complementary terms—*urbanissimus homo* (*C.* 9.4.18), *venustissimus scurra* (*S.* 2.12); indeed, behind the repeated praise lies rare and real affection. Much of the passage in the *Controversiae* presents jokes quite irrelevant to Sabinus' eloquence; in the short record in the *Suasoriae*, he is called a jokester.

What is the joke in the latter work? The *suasoria* to be treated—that is, the supposed debate over a famous historical event—was one beloved of declaimers: "The Three Hundred Spartans sent against Xerxes deliberate whether they too should retreat following the flight of the contingents of three hundred sent from all over Greece." Seneca records and comments on no fewer than thirty-five contributions, solemn, forceful, epigrammatic, arguments pro and con, expressions fine or ridiculous. Asilius' contribution is a delightful relief. Another declaimer had very elegantly quoted in Greek an alleged recommendation by King Leonidas to the three hundred, something like: "Take breakfast: you will dine in Hades." Asilius repeated the dramatic words and commented, "I would have accepted for breakfast, but declined for dinner." His remark is fresh, witty, ironic, but its form is more important than its content. The Leonidean *sententia* that evoked it was an epigram by a contemporary Greek declaimer Dorion, but Dorion spoke "not in this *suasoria* but on this theme" (*in hac materia*). Seneca much admired it as *disertissima*, and misremembered the version of it in Herodotus, Dorion's source. But when Sabinus Asilius quotes the remark, he says what *he* would have done in the situation. He could not possibly have intruded himself into a declamation. Thus the joke aligns itself with those in the *Controversiae*: it has nothing to do with the theme at hand.[8] Its very irrelevance—Seneca's simple fascination with the man—is yet further hint that the Sabini in his two works were indeed one man.

Next, the "Asellius Sabinus" who was rewarded by Tiberius for the dialogue "in which he introduced a contest among a mushroom, a figpecker, an oyster, and a thrush"). He was surely the same as Seneca's "Sabinus Asilius." Seneca tells us that his man served on the staff of the proconsul of Crete and Cyrene, Occius Flamma, along with the infamous and hated, but otherwise unknown, Turdus. When trouble arose, he refused to return to Caesar with a tidbit (*mattea*). *Turdi*, thrushes, were *matteae*, delicacies passed around among the guests at a banquet before or after the main courses, and the *turdus* was in Martial's opinion the prime *mattea* among birds. Hence Sabinus' contemptuous dismissal of his disreputable colleague, The Thrush.[9] But Sabinus actually *did* go to Caesar with a *mattea*: precisely with a dialogue presenting a *turdus* in competition with three other *matteae*. In short, Seneca presents us with Sabinus Asilius + Caesar + Turdus, Suetonius with Asellius Sabinus + Tiberius (Caesar) plus *turdus*. It would take a steely resolve to deny that Seneca's irrepressibly witty friend "Sabinus Asilius" and the author of a jeu d'esprit attributed by Suetonius to "Asellius Sabinus" were one and the same man.

By the same logic, he must also be the "Asellius" in the *Letter* of the younger Seneca, whose anecdote maps neatly onto those related by his father. At issue is the hesitant oratorical style of P. Vinicius, who searched excruciatingly for words (*titubat*). The acerbic Varius Geminus remarked of him, "I don't know how you [plural] call that fellow eloquent: he can't string three words together." More succinctly, "When it was asked how Vinicius spoke, Asellius said: 'Long-drawn-out (*tractim*)'" (*Ep.* 40.9). This passage could have been lifted verbatim from the *Controversiae*: Varius' penchant for pugnacious criticism was familiar, and indeed both he and Vinicius are prominent and successful senatorial performers in the *Controversiae*.[10] And yet again: we have a bon mot from Asellius; it appears in an oratorical context; and there is no sign that it was elicited by a declamation.

Finally, there is the outlier, "Asillius" in the letter of Augustus to Agrippina. The excerpt begins thus, literally: "That Talarius and Asillius might bring the boy Gaius on May the 13th, if the gods wish it, I arranged with them yesterday."[11]

Agrippina was travelling to join her husband Germanicus in Germany, but her location is unknown, perhaps already en route, much more likely still in or near Rome. Wherever Augustus may have been, in Rome, or near Rome, or in Campania, the likeliest scenario is not that Talarius and Asillius would travel all the way to Germany, but that they would simply deliver ("bring") the child to Agrippina before she set out. Be that as it may, there is a curious aspect to this small errand. No such name as "Talarius" can be found in the literature or inscriptions, Greek or Latin, of classical antiquity. It should be another joke, not a name but a nickname, one familiar to Augustus and to his granddaughter.

It might recall the *talaria*, the winged sandals of Mercury the messenger god, appropriate to conducting a traveller. But his sandals are rare in Latin and never found in the context of escorting, indeed "bringing" the child might elicit the unfortunate connotation of Mercury the psychopomp.

More attractive would be a play on the *ludus talarius*. This was a louche dance performed by men in long tunics that reached down to their ankles (*tali*). They gamboled to the jangle of cymbals and castanets, an effeminate exhibition and morally suspect. Cicero enthusiastically smears Verres with the *talarius*, then the followers of Catiline, and then social scum of all ranks in general.[12] Indeed, Augustus may have sown trouble for the future: the only other known aficionado of the disreputable art is that very Gaius who would be escorted by "Talarius." As the adult Caligula, he once without warning summoned three apprehensive ex-consuls in the middle of the night, only to startle them by leaping out to the sound of flutes and castanets, to dance about in a cloak and a *tunica talaris* (Suet. *Gaius* 54.2). Perhaps Talarius designated a man with a similar passion for dancing in womanly fashion, The Talarian. It is a witty summation of a character, and one not unexpected in the company of Asellius / Asillius, perhaps even coined by him.

In short, " Asellius," "Asilius," and (combining bits of both) "Asillius" should be a single person, and further aspects and advantages of the amalgamation will emerge below. Whether the variety of spellings is to be ascribed to scribal vagaries or to orthographic variations, Seneca's jesting friend should be "Asellius Sabinus."[13]

His Dates

He first appears in the spring of 14 CE, as an adult, in the letter of Augustus, which was written a few months before the princeps died (Suet. *Gaius* 8.4): May 13 is in the near future, and Augustus was to die on August 19 of that year. Otherwise, Sabinus' life is essentially identified with the era of Tiberius. The year in which he accompanied Occius Flamma in Crete is unknown—there are large gaps in the fasti of Crete and Cyrene—but it is generally agreed (on no firm evidence) that the "Caesar" in whose time Flamma served as governor should be Tiberius.[14] Declaimers with whom Asellius may have interacted can also be dated generally to the same period: P. Vinicius (consul 2 CE, alive in 25); Q. Varius Geminus (praetor, proconsul, and twice legate of the Divine Augustus, hence alive after 14 CE); Vallius Syriacus (executed in 30 CE). But one of them yields a precise date, the consul Domitius.

It is rightly assumed that the *nobilissimus vir* must be Cn. Domitius Aheno-barbus, who served as *consul ordinarius* throughout the year 32 CE.[15] This gives us a valuable fix on the overwhelming cataclysm of the era, the abrupt and horrifying downfall of Sejanus in October of 31 CE and the bloody reprisals against his followers. When Sabinus himself lay in jail awaiting trial he claimed that he had to beg for bread from fellow prisoners, the "rich Sejanians" whom he described as "parricides"—parricide being the standard term of demoniza-tion for enemies of the Father of His Country. That is to say, the tribulations of Asellius Sabinus were *not* connected with the collapse of Sejanus. In the Domitius anecdote, we find him comfortably cracking a joke with aristocratic friends months after the prefect's fall, and in a plea for sympathy, he would later take pains to distinguish himself from, and to denigrate, the Seianiani. Tacitus tells us explicitly that in 33 CE Tiberius executed everyone then in prison ac-cused of association with Sejanus.[16] That should assign Sabinus' incarceration with them to (at the least) a period from 32 to 33 CE, on charges unknown. When and how he may have left prison is unknown.

Seneca probably gathered his rhetorical memories in the latter years of Ti-berius, after 34 CE, in his old age, and he himself died no later than 40 CE. He writes of Sabinus in the past tense (*erat*): whatever the cause, the man was surely dead by the time of Tiberius' own demise in 37 or within a few months of it.

His Life

Who was Asellius Sabinus, where did he come from, what did he do? The clear-est item of evidence is Seneca's description of him as *venustissimus inter rhetores scurra*. That must mean that he was a rhetor himself for, as far as we can see, Seneca seems to use the word strictly to describe professional teachers of rhe-toric. By the days of the late Republic, the profession embraced men from a wide range of social and ethnic backgrounds, often freedmen and foreigners, but also native Italians and even local gentry. Most memorably, by the end of the Republic or in the very early years of Augustus, a Rubellius Blandus from Tibur may have been the first Roman knight to work as a rhetor (*C. 2 pr. 5*). (In fact "primus" is a modern editorial insertion into the text, which may not be necessary—but he certainly was not the last.) Blandus clearly came from a wealthy background; his senatorial son married a patrician Sergia; his grandson was the first consul in his family, and in 33 CE he married Julia, the granddaughter of Tiberius himself. Tacitus deplores the grandson's grandfather as a knight (6.27.1) but, curiously, ignores his professional employment. No member of the senate ever could or did teach professionally, but that leaves an immense range of possible backgrounds for our hero.

Seneca cannot resist recounting two of his "urbanities," *urbanas res*, displayed before crowds in Crete and capped by the witticisms about the greatest magistracy and about the tidbit. The two episodes are neatly balanced. In each, Sabinus interacts with a mob, one excited, the other angry. Each unfolds in a central public gathering place, a theater and a temple. Each time he silences the mob, each time he makes a jest. Yet, neatly fashioned though they are and stripped of detail, these anecdotes raise more questions than they answer. We are not told where this all happened, although the Cretan capital of Gortyn is likely. Nor do we know who Caesar was, although Tiberius is probable. *Urbanas res* here should describe the whole episode, actions as well as words, not just verbal wit but deportment as well, the oratorical gesture for silence, the assured handling of a crowd. For his own purposes Seneca may make punchlines out of what were passing remarks.

More puzzling, the jokes are unintelligible. As to the first, reacting to the offer of the magistracy, even with verbal emphasis (*this* magistracy) and gesture (pointing to the hair and beard of a local notable), who would understand it without an explanation, or even with one? And how does appearing unkempt in court at Rome as a *reus*—for that is the point of his joke—transfer into performing a *magistratus*? Is there some pun we cannot perceive? Seneca adds, not surprisingly, *Graeci non intellexerunt*, and we can sympathize.

As to the second jest, in what language did Sabinus address an angry Greek mob? Surely not in Latin.[17] Surely in Greek, but it makes no sense in Greek: the offensive man's name was Turdus, on which the Latin pun is based, not Strouthos, or whatever the Greek equivalent might be. Perhaps the joke was an aside in Latin, but why then did Sabinus impose silence to make it (or did he drop it into an already existing silence)? And when we are told that the Turdus remark was brought up against him at trial, does Seneca mean a trial involving the disturbance on Crete, or another? What were the charges? How could this joke possibly be held against him? Again, Seneca's sons knew the outcome, but we are in the dark.

The gloom deepens. What was the *maximus magistratus* pressed upon him by the enthusiastic Greeks in the theater? Orth thought that this should be the Cretarchy, that is, the office that would be in charge (in later times at least) of both the imperial cult in the province and the provincial assembly. But this raises yet more questions. Who were "the Greeks" here? Cretans in general (not to mention Cyreneans), or local citizens (perhaps Gortynians)? If the latter, they may have wanted him to hold municipal office (a not uncommon honor for visiting dignitaries). Regardless, what did they understand by him holding the "greatest office" twice in Rome? Not the Cretarchy, of course. Surely not the consulship or the prefecture of the city of Rome, both very senior senatorial offices, and Sabinus was not a senator, let alone a senior senator. Offices in Caesar's gift, so they think (*bene precati Caesari petebant*), but if this is news to the Greeks, they were apparently quite ignorant of the career of a man to whom they were offering their highest magistracy. And what honor could they possibly think they were bestowing upon him for the third time? We do not know.

The one gleam of light is the aura projected by Sabinus, the air of aristocratic assurance. The entourage of a proconsul in a minor senatorial province is a deceptively modest employment.[18] Sabinus was a man who could silence a mob with a gesture, not once but twice. He could gossip with a consul's mother and chaff the noble consul himself. He could criticize the style of the sharp-tongued P. Vinicius, consul ordinarius, seasoned general, and tremendous admirer of Ovid. Seneca observed of this Vinicius not that he was hesitant but that he was very precise, *exactissimus*—that is, he neither said anything that was absurd (*res ineptas*) nor did he tolerate it in others. Sabinus summed up this formidable figure's manner of speaking, in a single bon mot, as *tractim*, long-drawn out: the mot juste, witty but not wounding, neither subservient nor truculent.[19] Sabinus could also affect nonchalance about his own concerns: he admitted receiving a sum of money from the other party in a lawsuit, but had no idea whether he still had it, then could joke in court about his *neglegentia*.[20] And he could mock his own profession, as when he suggested that an orator, if ruined by a lawsuit, would have to fall back on teaching rhetoric.

Another echo of the manner can be heard in his speech before the senate, pleading for his daily bread (9.4.20): "Do not, I say, listen haughtily to a man of many sorrows (*superbe audire hominem calamitosum*): often he who could have pitied begs for pity (*saepe qui misereri potuit misericordiam rogat*)." *Qui misereri potuit* might hint at some former position or attitude of authority. Be that as it may, the humor that Seneca so deplored was on display yet again, tangentially. Otto Ribbeck thought that the second clause was a line quoted from a now-lost *fabula palliata*.[21] But, to render it metrically sound, he had to emend the words spoken by the self-styled *homo calamitosus* substantially: *Saepe qui misereri potuit, rogitat misericordiam*. In fact, the line is not a quotation from a *palliata* but a clever nod to a lower form of comedy. Sabinus has a mime in mind, but one written by a master of the art, Publilius Syrus (243): *Homo qui in homine calamitoso est misericors meminit sui*. If we had any context for it, what character spoke it, and in what play—we might be able to gauge the wit and appropriateness, but we do not, and another witticism eludes us.

Sabinus knew the princeps Augustus personally and was entrusted by him with a private mission. He was rewarded by Augustus' stepson and adopted son Tiberius in princely fashion for what must have been a brief and witty composition. And he knew and joked with the mother of Cn. Domitius Ahenobarbus in 32 CE, the year of his consulship. This grande dame was none other than Augustus' niece, known as Antonia Maior, born in 39 BCE, the elder daughter of Octavia and Mark Antony. Overshadowed by her younger sister, Antonia Minor (a powerful character, sister-in-law, and close confidante of Tiberius), the elder Antonia shows us a hint of personality only in Seneca's brief anecdote.[22] Widowed in 25 CE, she would live to see her son married in 28 CE to Tiberius' granddaughter, and she was in her early seventies when Ahenobarbus served as consul.

Sabinus' easy familiarity with the *domus Caesarum* is striking. Augustus' relaxed note to his granddaughter about escorting the toddler Gaius suggests friendship rather than service, and Sabinus' relationship with Antonia is extraordinary. His chat with an elderly woman has nothing to do with public schoolroom, lecture hall, or court of law. He has been visiting and gossiping with her, and he is confident enough teasingly to pass on Antonia's private grumbling about her son's laziness to the son himself, the consul of Rome. His witticism is in Greek, playing upon a proverb best known from a passage in Plato's *Laws*. The *Suda* explains it succinctly: "To know neither swimming nor letters refers to the entirely ignorant, for among the Athenians swimming and letters were taught from early childhood."[23] A favorite of ancient paroemiographers and philosophical commentators, this proverbial Greek definition of ignorance was certainly familiar to educated Romans: Licinius Mucianus, three times consul, would use it in his stinging attacks on self-proclaimed Stoic philosophers (Dio 66.13.1a), and "Augustus himself taught his grandsons both letters and swimming, and many other fundamentals" (Suet. *Aug.* 64.3). In short, the fortuitous combination of baths and declamation in 32 CE sparks a clever bon mot from Asellius Sabinus recalling a Greek proverb. It is charming and complimentary: Antonia's son, the consul, is identified as neither ignorant nor lazy. Indeed it speaks volumes about the common culture of the Roman elite.

There is more. Both of his "urbanities" in Crete invoke Caesar. When he jokes that he has performed the magistracy twice at Rome, the Greeks take him literally and automatically praise Caesar: whether they understand him or not, they know of or assume his connection with, and patronage by, the princeps himself. When Sabinus jokes contemptuously that he will not go with a tidbit to Caesar, what does he mean? If this were a question of prosecuting some or all of a proconsul's *comites*, proceedings must have begun in the senate. Why was he going to Caesar? We do not know, but the two anecdotes suggest yet again an exceptional relationship, both past and future, with the current princeps.

A family of Asellii flourished in the Roman senate in the last days of the Roman Republic, duly certified by a legendary ancestor, M. Asellius, supposed tribune of the plebs in 422 BCE. The evidence is exceptionally elusive, but the generally accepted prosopographical conclusions are as sound as such things can be.[24] Briefly, M. Asellius M.f. Maec(ia) witnessed a *senatus consultum* in April, 44 BCE, soon after the death of Julius Caesar; and a praetor Asellius is credited with introducing baby storks into Roman cuisine. This gourmand (on whom more later, pp. 146–47) is most likely one of the following: L. Asellius, praetor before ca. 92 BCE; L. Asellius, praetor 33 BCE; or Asellius praetor suffect 33 BCE. If so, he is probably one of the last two, who were father and son, and much closer in date to the rise of luxury dining at Rome. And if so, that produces another connection with the future Augustus, who personally appointed the son to replace the father as praetor when the father fell ill in 33 BCE.

Professional rhetor though he may have been, Asellius Sabinus came from a most aristocratic background: his family was senatorial and he was on intimate terms with the *domus Caesarum* of Augustus and Tiberius.

His Diet

He was not only a wit, he was an epicure in an age of gastronomy.

"[Tiberius] presented a gift of 200,000 sesterces to Asellius Sabinus for a dialogue in which he had represented the contest of a mushroom and a figpecker and an oyster and a thrush [*boleti et fideculae et ostreae et turdi certamen*]." The *Contest of the Tidbits* is unique. We can assume that each of the competing *matteae* presented its case for being the greatest delicacy at a banquet. And we should assume that their table talk was both short and witty. Surely short: most ancient dialogues were not long works, and a light and humorous debate among four *Delikatessen* would lose steam if prolonged.[25] Certainly witty: Asellius Sabinus was the wit of the age. Tiberius Caesar—highly literate, but notoriously grim and parsimonious—gave an enormous sum of money to the author of what looks to have been a jeu d'esprit. 200,000 sesterces was the annual salary of the highest paid procurator in the imperial service, in an age when possession of property worth 400,000 sesterces was the *census* required to qualify as a member of the equestrian elite of the Roman world.[26] What was Tiberius rewarding?

It is difficult to enter the thought-world of the ancient oyster: our sources have little interest in its beliefs or emotions. Very difficult, but not impossible. Thus from the third century BCE, we have the thoughts of a proud native of

Abydus on the Hellespont, a city famous for its resident molluscs. Not unexpectedly, much has been lost in translation:

> Near the earth tomb of Ethiopian Memnon, [it was not the Nile which reared me, it was the Ocean which] nursed me on the rocks of adamant (the virgin, Helle?), as I revelled in the sweet rays of Agrotera (Artemis, the moon). I am a feast without fire (uncooked) for mortal men, when Doso's bridegroom (Aphrodite's lover, Ares, the knife) cleaves me with his hide-piercing weapon.[27]

The oyster's thoughts have been set down in a six-line elegy by "a poet of the first-rank," as its first editor correctly estimated. Preserved on a fragmentary papyrus, it is a work of true Alexandrian learning, replete with hapax legomena, exotic erudition, and Homeric flourishes. Its tone is purposely ambiguous and obscure, its high value marked by the attachment to it in the second century of an astonishingly learned commentary of at least fifty lines.

Slightly later, the oysters of Italian Baiae also rose to fame, bringing us closer both to home and to the contest of the tidbits. We have a brief but succulent self-description by a Roman oyster, a molluscan Alcibiades swaggering into a banquet: "A shellfish, I have just arrived, drunk with Baian Lucrine. Luxurious, I now thirst for noble garum." A figpecker is also present, wistfully reflecting on its own puzzling name and nature: "Though the fig nourish me, yet since I feed on sweet grapes, why did not the grape rather give me my name?" Someone, perhaps a mushroom itself, remarks on the mushroom's delicate constitution and, by implication, its high value as a dinner gift: "It is easy to send silver and gold and a cloak and a gown, but sending mushrooms is difficult." And the poet intervenes with nasty wit to praise the thrush, likewise in comparison with the best: "Perhaps you may like a garland woven of roses or rich nard, but I like one made of thrushes."[28]

Animated *matteae* appealed to Roman fancies. In his *Captives*, Plautus has the old man Hegio as *imperator* organize a campaign in a *provincia* that is, in fact, the stomach of the parasite Ergasilus: his *exercitus* will be communities of food preparers and foodstuffs, including *milites* who are Turdetani and Fidiculenses—peoples clearly meant to evoke the avian tidbits, *turdi* and *fideculae* (*Capt.* 151–64). The otherwise sober Pliny the Elder imagines a potential lawsuit (*lis*) between the famous oysters from the Lucrine Lake and their recently popular rivals from distant Brundisium. Conflict is averted by a happy compromise: en route to Rome, the hungry Brundisians would be fed in the Lucrine after their long journey (*NH* 9.168). At a banquet in Lucilius' thirtieth book of Satires, figpeckers and thrushes fly about prepared and cooked (978–79 M = 1109–10 W). Along the same lines, when a Roman knight renowned for his voluptuous tastes was served a meager thrush at a banquet, he asked his host, Augustus himself, if he might let it loose. When the princeps answered, "Why not?," the man threw it out the window (Macrob. *Sat.* 2.4.42). Eventually, Claudius' notorious wife Agrippina would have a *turdus* that imitated the conversations of men, *quod numquam ante* (Plin. *NH* 10.120).

With these delicacies sharing the table, a rich culinary aroma arises from the scraps of evidence about Sabinus. The author of a dialogue among *Delikatessen*, he expressed his distaste, not coincidentally, at travelling to Rome with a tidbit, a Turdus. He also suavely digested Leonidas' laconic command to the three hundred Spartans about their meals: he would have accepted the breakfast invitation but declined for dinner. A near kinsman introduced Rome to the latest novelty in dining, young storks. Yet, ironically, Sabinus had to beg before the senate for basic sustenance, his daily food allowance in prison. He complained of hunger, pleaded for bread to keep himself alive. Never able to resist a joke, he asked facetiously to be transferred from his current prison to another nearby, the Quarries, *Lautumiae*. He wryly advised his audience not to be deceived by the name, for the place itself was not at all *lauta*, sumptuous, luxurious. The pun on *Lautumiae* and *lautitia*—elegance, luxury—is painful, but the senators were surely meant to think precisely of the prime instance of *lautitia*: that is, of luxury dining, *lautitia cenarum, lautitia epularum, lautitia mensae*—in fact, Festus' definition of the noun *lautitia* is precisely *epularum magnificentia.*[29] Sabinus' audience must have thought of his reputation as a gourmand. Fine dining was the very last thing to be expected at the Quarries: in 108 BCE, one man had eaten another there.[30]

It was the Greek Dorion who invented the dramatic Leonidean command about dining in Hades: he had spoken on the *suasoria* about the debate of the three hundred, but Seneca adds that he offered his Hades witticism not in that declamation but "on this subject" (*S.* 2.22). Unfortunately, in his haste, our author does not tell us what the actual context was: as with Sabinus' reaction to it, it may not have been offered in a declamation at all. But Seneca's impulse to throw in the laconic *sententia* is not surprising, for he had strong feelings about this Dorion, a mixture of admiration for the man's talent and dismay at his mad tendency to go over the top. In one *controversia*, a father disinherits his son for disobeying his order not to march off to battle yet again after three heroic campaigns (*C.* 1.8.16). Seneca quotes some lines from Dorion's version of the father's speech, prefacing them with mixed appraisal: he "said something rather too exalted to be tolerated by concise forensic oratory, but which excellently portrayed [*egregie exprimeret*] the stupefaction of the father." Also on the plus side, the man's *sententia* about dining in Hades was *disertissima* (*S.* 2.11). But his offering on another *controversia* was truly alarming, positing an artist who tortures a war captive in order to paint a convincing "Prometheus" (*C.* 10.5.23). Dorion spoke "insanely" (*furiose*), to justify the torture of models: how could one depict the parricidal Oedipus or Atreus without seeing their myths alive? And his contribution to the *suasoria* "Alexander debates whether to sail Ocean" (*S.* 1.12) elicits a long and passionate fulmination from Seneca: people thought Dorion's bombastic paraphrase of a passage in the *Odyssey* to be "the worst thing ever said since eloquent men [*diserti*] began to go crazy [*insanire*]." As with Leonidas dining in Hades, Dorion showed a gift for melodrama, in Seneca's view lapsing not once but twice into insanity.

Dorion was a contemporary of Seneca: hence, he flourished in the latter half of the first century BCE. We have from the same period many fragments, preserved by Athenaeus, of a book, *On Fishes*, by an author named Dorion. Close attention to those fragments reveals a diligent compilation that ranged over the ichthyological universe, offering not just the minutiae of the various names and spellings of individual fish, but also information about the differences among the species and about where they lived, as well as instructions for cooking and roasting them.[31] Occam's razor suggests that, in an age of polymaths, Dorion the writer on fish is probably Dorion the declaimer—how many contemporary Dorions can there have been?—and he leads us into a lost world.

Asellius Sabinus flourished in the Golden Age of Roman cuisine. Tacitus would be precise and damning about the era of *luxus mensae*, "which, from the end of the Actian War to the hostilities which brought Servius Galba to the acquisition of power, was practiced for a hundred years with surging expenditure."[32] The thunderous chorus of disapproval from the moralists—Tacitus, Pliny, Seneca, Columella—is too familiar to need rehearsal: Ludwig Friedländer demonstrated long ago that it must be taken with an enormous grain of salt. They were repelled by the perceived excesses of contemporary gastronomy: the luxurious and self-indulgent gluttony, the attendant debauchery, the foolish ostentation, the frivolous search for novelty, the corruption by foreigners. But to accept their disapproval as fact is to miss a universe. The history of Roman cuisine remains to be written, despite intense scholarly interest in the last few decades in "foodways," the "customs of food production, preservation, preparation, presentation, gathering, marketing, uses of food products other than for eating, and food folklore."[33] Several aspects of this culture are relevant to Asellius Sabinus, most significantly the intersection of wit, erudition, wealth, and power within the well-appointed private *triclinia* at Rome.

Ancient writing on the purchase, preparation, and serving of food survives only in fragments and testimonia, but there was a lot of it. The number and variety of known works is extraordinary, all lost now, save the bare, unrepresentative, late antique compilation of recipes ascribed to "Apicius."[34] But practical instructions for use in the kitchen were of little concern to the sophisticated diner: those were for his cooks. He himself was interested in enlightenment, entertainment, and the rational pursuit of pleasure. For guidance he turned to the extensive Greek literature devoted to gastronomy since the fourth century.[35] Its peak came early, in the mid- to late fourth century BCE, with two key works.

The acknowledged master of the genre was Archestratus of Gela, who has been called the First Gourmet. No fewer than five different titles have been transmitted for his single masterpiece, the most commonly repeated and most likely being a word coined by him, *Hedupatheia*, which has been translated as *The Life of Luxury*, or *The Experience of Pleasure*, or *La Dolce Vita*. It certainly described different foods and various aspects of cooking, although the surviving fragments, all from Athenaeus, are mainly concerned with fish: where and when to find them, how to procure them, how to prepare them. In their pursuit, Archestratus travelled far and wide around the Greek world of the Central and Eastern Mediterranean. His concerns were attacked by Hellenistic philosophers and they were largely dismissed by generations of modern classical philologists. But attitudes have changed, and in the age of *nouvelle cuisine*, slow food, and farm to table, scholars have responded with enthusiasm to a work that vigorously prescribes—indeed, demands—the finest quality, the proper season, local sourcing, and simple preparation. Moreover the form of Archestratus' work honored its content, for "It was almost certainly not a hands-on cookery book but a volume to be enjoyed at a rich man's banquet and symposium."[36] In fact, the *Hedupatheia* was a long, ingenious, and learned *poem*, and Archestratus was the "Hesiod or Theognis of epicures," as Athenaeus would call him. It was replete with witty calques and echoes of Homer, but also with echoes of the tragedians, comic poets, and others, and it would be savored by sophisticated diners as part of an evening's entertainment. The learning, the wit, and the confidently opinionated tone all rest on a foundation of wealth and leisure: "If you go to the rich land of Ambracia and happen to see the boarfish, buy it and don't leave it behind, even if it costs its weight in gold."[37] In the sixty-two surviving fragments, Archestratus names no fewer than sixty locales, from west of Sicily to north of the Black Sea, and he certainly visited most if not all of them. Indeed, his epic (as Athenaeus was to call it) opens with a hexametric memory of the opening line of the *Histories* of Herodotus. Travel was essential to the true gastronome.

The gourmand's other key text, the *Attic Banquet* of Matro of Pitane, comes from slightly later in the fourth century, and survives perhaps almost entire in 122 hexameters.[38] Where Archestratus' poem was an elegant parody of Homer, Matro's rough, rumbustious piece went beyond parody into pastiche: it is almost a Homeric cento. E. Degani neatly situated the two works in the landscape of gastronomic poetry: "We might say that while Archestratus intends to reach σπουδαῖον by means of γέλοιον, on the contrary Matro considers the

Homeric form (σπουδαῖον) nothing but a way to reach the ultimate aim of his work: γέλοιον."[39] Its Homeric format, evident in every line, inevitably guarantees that the dinner party will be presented as a battle with the food: the host is Agamemnon, the cook with his troops of frying pans and saucepans is Achilles, the parasite is Odysseus (and a seagull, and a ravening lion), another guest is Diomedes. The enemy, the various dishes, must then take on the characters of men and women, whether human or divine. Hence sea urchin, anchovy, mullet (horse-breaking), cuttlefish, conger eel, eel (white-armed), squid, tuna, razor shell and shrimp (singers of Zeus), lobster and crayfish (armored, of course), swordfish (mighty in battle), grapes, cake: Homeric personifications, they march in to be attacked and consumed. The parody of gastronomic epic demands that the food be humanized.

The influence of the masters, Archestratus and Matro, is best traced not in the Greek tradition, much of which is lost to us, but in the Latin, specifically in satire. In his *Apology* (39.2), Apuleius recalls from memory eleven lines from the *Hedyphagetica* of Ennius, a quasi-translation of Archestratus, in which the poet alludes to eleven places for the best examples of different seafoods. After which, so Apuleius informs us, he proceeded to describe the native peoples involved and the proper way to cook each dish. Lucilius devoted a poem (5.3) to a *rustica cena* of humble vegetables in which traces of Matro's mock-heroic style may be discovered.[40] One of Varro's Menippean Satires, *On Edibles*, pilloried gluttons (*helluones*) in charming senarii, describing delicacies sought out by them on land and on sea and naming some thirteen places, mainly in the Greek world—Gellius, commenting on the passage, speaks of the wandering gullet (*peragrans gula*). In the second poem of his second book of *Satires*, Horace attacks the contemporary passion for exotic dishes: peacock (which sells for gold), bass (how can you really tell where it comes from, the Tiber or the sea?), the hefty three-pound mullet, boar, turbot, sturgeon, young storks. Simple fare is much better. Then, in *Satire* 2.4, an acquaintance overwhelms him with a torrent of newly acquired wisdom, which turns out to consist not of philosophical but of culinary precepts. The long farrago of disconnected archestratan certainties includes a veritable culinary atlas of where to find the best of everything (some twenty place-names are invoked).[41] And in Satire 2.8, an anxiously uncertain would-be gourmet presides over a disastrous dinner party, especially memorable for his exquisitely pretentious description of a dish of moray eel (2.8.42–53), and for an avian course that would have been delightful, "if our host had not expatiated on their origins and natures." The themes are familiar, and with Horace we have indeed arrived at the Golden Age of luxury dining: *difficile est satiram non scribere.*

Despite the outrage and ridicule vented by satirists and philosophers about mindless self-indulgence, serious men pursued the pleasures of dining. In a pathbreaking paper, "Performing Culture: Roman Spectacle and the Banquets of the Powerful," John D'Arms sketched the deep social significance of private feasts for the rich and powerful. Banquets were indeed instruments of power, vehicles for aristocratic self-representation and interaction with others, to be admired and imitated. Settings, apparatus, entertainment, exotic foods: all could be dramatically elaborate, costly, competitive, over-the-top assaults on all of the senses, and several literary accounts are amply confirmed by material remains.[42] The sumptuous private theatrical banquets of Metellus Pius in the 70s BCE (Macrob. *Sat.* 3.13.6–13) and of the young Octavian in the 30s BCE— with his notorious Dinner of the Twelve Gods, complete with *choragus* (Suet. *Aug.* 70.1–2)—set a benchmark for the age of luxury dining.

Less flamboyant, but deeply impressive and more to the point here, is the arrestingly gastronomic flavor in Cicero's correspondence with his rich Epicurean friend in Naples, Papirius Paetus—*amandus, dulcis, iucundus*—in 46 BCE (*Fam.* 9.15–26). At his most charming, Cicero ranges over family history, obscenity, health, the life of the good citizen in trying times, and, repeatedly, fine dining, this being his mock refuge from the trying times. Paetus' half of the banter is missing, but it clearly had the same tone—that is, letter after letter of Cicero fizzes with culinary jokes and puns, all conveying stock themes. Exotic dishes are consumed, including peacock. *Lautitia* is extolled, familiar to Paetus, new to Cicero. Cicero is now both glutton (*homo edax*) and an enthusiastic late learner (*opsimathes*): he plays the *scurra*.[43] Dinner is a battle: as Paetus' *contubernalis*, he attacks his food. Declamation and dining are closely aligned: "I have Hirtius and Dollabella as my pupils in speaking, my masters in dining. As you may have heard, they declaim at my house, I dine at theirs" (*Fam.* 9.16.7). Both activities are seasoned with *sal*, wit. Paetus is a paragon of the good old Roman *sales*, saltier than the Attic variety and explicitly *urbani*, now sadly lost as the *urbs* has been overrun by *peregrinitas* (*Fam.* 9.15.2). Cicero particularly delights in the laughter and jokes at a recent banquet, and years later he deprecates Paetus' decision not to dine out: he will miss both *delectatio* and *voluptas*. Then a serious credo: joking aside, it is important for a happy life to live with good, pleasant, friendly men (*Fam.* 9.24.2), to share with them community, nourishment, and mental relaxation, the latter to be attained above all in friendly conversation, which is at its most pleasurable at dinner parties.

Cicero happily describes a recent dinner to Paetus, commenting in a general way that "I am delighted by a dinner party: there I say whatever comes to mind, and I transform a groan into shouts of laughter."[44] On this occasion, his host was Volumnius Eutrapelus, a knight close to the inmost circles of power and influence in Caesar's Rome, the friend not only of Cicero but of Atticus (who was also present at the dinner), of Dolabella, of Cassius and probably Brutus, and, above all, of Mark Antony—he would serve as Antony's *praefectus fabrum* in 43 BCE, and the mime Cytheris, his freedwoman, was Antony's mistress (likewise present at the banquet). His name was P. Volumnius; Eutrapelus, "The Witty," was a nickname. Εὐτραπελία was the Greek equivalent of *urbanitas*, with exactly the same connotation of wit as the expression of superiority, one-upmanship, aggression: Aristotle curtly defined *eutrapelia* as "cultured insolence."[45] Two letters from Cicero to Eutrapelus survive, couched in the same jokey tone as the correspondence with Paetus, and likewise clearly responding to the friend's witticisms. In one, Cicero pretends that he did not at first know which "Volumnius" had written a letter to him, but its "eutrapelous" quality gave the man away. While Cicero is in the East, Volumnius acts as the "procurator" of his "salt mines" (*possessio salinarum mearum*), and must protect Cicero against every witticism in Rome being foisted on him. In reality, Volumnius is the only one against whom he really needs to worry about defending his *urbanitatis possessionem* (*Fam.* 7.32.1–2).

Fine dining, wit, and power: a high level of culture should follow. An anonymous late antique grammarian happens to preserve a hendecasyllable attributed to a Volumnius: *stridentis dabitur patella cymae*, "a platter of sizzling young cabbage will be given." Franz Buecheler dated the line to the age of Catullus and Vergil, and suggested that Volumnius Eutrapelus was its author. This must be right, for the concern with cookery strains belief in coincidence.[46] In fact, the line is peculiar. *Stridere*—to hiss, to whistle, to rattle, and so on—is to make a terrifying noise, one overwhelmingly associated with weapons wounding and killing in battle, with monsters, and with horror. It is a much-repeated favorite of Roman epic—imparting violence some twenty-one times in the *Aeneid* alone. Here, it is applied, uniquely, to a vegetable sizzling on a platter. This sounds like the echo of another epic parody.

The Volumnian universe of dining, culture, and power continues of course into the age of one-man rule, the age of Augustus and Sabinus. Horace's patron Maecenas himself, powerful, literate and the very byword for luxury, wrote a *Symposium*. More importantly: "Maecenas set the fashion of eating donkey foals (*pullos*) at banquets, and they were much preferred to wild asses at that period; but after his time the ass lost favor as a delicacy."[47] This aligns remarkably with the contemporary fad for eating young storks (likewise *pullos*), similarly short-lived and set by the praetor who was surely a close relative of Asellius Sabinus.[48] Elite interest in gastronomy was at its peak. After listing eminent foreign authors of cookbooks, Columella adds this about "writers of our own race who, when we were free from wars [thanks, that is, to Augustus], did not disdain to contribute to human nourishment: men like M. Ambivius and Maenas Licinius, and then C. Matius, whose purpose it was by their instructions to organize the work of the baker and the cook, not to mention the butler." These are not unimportant men. Maenas Licinius, otherwise unknown, has been identified as a Licinius Mena, the son of a well-off freedman musician of the late Republic. Marcus Ambivius was certainly a knight and, as procurator, governed the turbulent province of Judaea for Augustus. And Gaius Matius was also a knight, son of Julius Caesar's close friend, himself a friend and counselor of Augustus. Dedicatee of a book on rhetoric by Apollodorus of Pergamum (the teacher of Augustus), he allegedly invented the practice of topiary around the turn of the millennium and wrote three gastronomic works, *The Cook, The Fishmonger*, and *The Pickle-Maker*, each of which instructed readers how to prepare urban feasts and sumptuous banquets (*urbanas mensas et lauta convivia*).[49] Leading the pack was the moralists' prime target, the notorious Marcus Apicius himself, "professor of popinary science" (*scientiam popinae professus*), and a magnet of abuse. On a cooler estimate, Apicius moved easily in the highest circles, among consular friends and as an intimate of Sejanus, and he was well-known to Tiberius himself and to his son Drusus Caesar. He was rich, he was creative, he held firm opinions, and he wrote about his passion. Living the life of Archestratus, he also travelled by land and by sea in search of fine comestibles.[50]

If Volumnius the Witty indeed wrote in verse, he would also fit into the tradition of clever poets who were heavily influenced by Attic comedy, writing for a sophisticated elite, deeply interested in the refinement of fine dining, and working with comic traditions of animated foodstuffs and Homeric parody. From Archestratus and Matro through the Alexandrian poet of "The Oyster," through Ennius, Lucilius, Varro, and Volumnius, through Horace and Maecenas and others now lost to us, and then on to Martial and Juvenal, one fundamental characteristic is evident: the literary tradition lies in poetry, not prose. Not a word of the dialogue of Asellius Sabinus survives, yet a hypothesis is justified: the contest among his four tidbits was a poem. The nearest known relative to the *Certamen*, as Wilhelm Teuffel pointed out long ago, is the *Iudicium coci et pistoris* of Vespa. A much later jeu d'esprit, learned, elegant, witty, and packed with gastronomic jokes, it presents a baker and a cook in contention before Vulcan, the god of fire, each asserting the superiority of his craft. Not surprisingly, it does its business in a mere ninety-nine hexameters. Sabinus' *Certamen* also aligns with a substantial body of brief fables, most of them in verse and depicting disputes about the superiority of each contestant's virtues, often specifically for the benefit of mankind, disputes between two gods or two men or two natural phenomena or, especially, two animals or two plants. The jewel in the crown, which would be known to every literate Roman, was Callimachus' fourth *Iamb*, pitting the laurel against the olive.[51]

If we accept that Sabinus' contribution was a poem working in a certain tradition, the picture snaps into focus: we can understand why Tiberius Caesar rewarded him in princely fashion, and striking parallels are at hand.

Tiberius took a true gastronome's interest in food and drink. His informed enthusiasm has been obscured for posterity by crude anecdotes about miserly feasting and heavy drinking, but it was recovered in a brilliant late paper by Ronald Syme, "Diet on Capri."[52] According to Pliny, Tiberius was "enormously pleased" by a pear named after him (*NH* 15.54). His *auctoritas* bestowed "a special glory" on African ovens for smoking grapes (*NH* 14.16). He "rebuked" his son Drusus Caesar for following the gourmand Apicius' overfastidious rejection of cabbage sprout (*NH* 19.137). He took "marvelous pleasure" in melons (*NH* 19.64), and contrived to enjoy them almost year-round, through moveable frames and greenhouses. He made famous (literally "ennobled") the parsnip, "demanding" it every year from Germany (*NH* 19.90). He "very wittily" noted that a weed growing in Upper Germany was similar to asparagus (*NH* 19.145). And he was wont to observe that doctors had conspired to "ennoble" the wine of Surrentum, which was recommended for convalescents since it was thin and healthy, but was otherwise just "well-produced vinegar" (*NH* 14.64). In short, strong opinions, vigorously expressed. Cabbage sprout was a delicacy, *laeta formosaque cyma* as Celsus describes it (*Agric.* fr. 6.1), and it takes us into a gourmets' debate: rejected by Apicius and Drusus Caesar, it was welcome at the poetic feasts of Lucilius and Volumnius Eutrapelus and well regarded by Tiberius. Lucilius' banquet had paired *viridis cyma* with *asparagi molles* (945M = 986W): Tiberius was presumably teasing asparagus connoisseurs with his common German weed. He knew his epicures. Presented with the gift of an enormous mullet, weighing some four and a half pounds, he sent it to the *macellum* for sale, confidently predicting that it would be purchased by either Apicius or P. Octavius. The two gourmets bid against each other, Octavius won, and the astute Caesar was richer by five thousand sesterces (Sen. *Ep.* 95.42).

Tiberius enjoyed a party, but he could be difficult. Suetonius tells us that he took great pleasure in his Greek dining companions, *convictores Graeculos*, yet he was hard on them, exiling one and banning another from his company (even, so we are told, driving the latter to his death), for slights real or imagined (Suet. 56). Anecdote aside, context is everything: Tiberius would propose questions for discussion with his learned guests over dinner, based on his reading that day. Seleucus the grammarian fell foul of him when Tiberius learned that the man had pumped his servants to learn what the reading was, so that he might come prepared. Lively cultural discussion at Rome veered easily into combat sport, but the free exchange of views was severely restricted when one of the combatants was an intellectual and opinionated princeps. Favorinus would raise a huge laugh among his friends a century later, under Hadrian, when he urged them to let him believe that the master of thirty legions was more learned than everyone else (*HA Had.* 15.12–13). Tiberius was surely not unaware of this. He particularly loved to torment the grammarians—"a species of men whom, as we have mentioned, he especially sought out"—with ridiculously pedantic questions about Greek mythology (Suet. *Tib.* 70.3). The grammarians were happy to oblige with answers.

Tiberius was notoriously addicted to three "Hellenistic" poets—Euphorion, Rhianus, and Parthenius—all of them prolific, erudite, and formidably ingenious, and all devout Homerists.[53] He composed Greek poems imitating them, and he stocked public libraries with their writings and their images. "Because of this, many of the learned men competed to publish a great deal about these poets for him" (Suet. 70.2), presumably texts, commentaries, and the like. This avalanche of scholarship has vanished, though distant echoes may linger behind the surviving fragments of and testimonia on the three poets. Yet chance has preserved a hint of something strikingly similar, in the opening of Diogenes Laertius' life of the third-century sceptic philosopher Timon of Phlius (9.109): "Our Apollonides of Nicaea, in the first book of his commentary on *The Silloi*, which he dedicated to Tiberius Caesar, says that Timon was the son of Timarchus and a Phlian by birth." Timon slips easily into the company of Euphorion and the others, for he was an immensely sophisticated satiric poet as well, and another devoted Homerist. His verse *Silloi* sharply mocked the battles of the various philosophical schools in strongly Homeric terms—not quite a cento, but just under 80 percent of its surviving fragments have been shown to offer clear Homeric parodies.

Perhaps there was even a gastronomic theme in Apollonides' commentary. Tiberius seems to have shared in the contemporary "craze for the surmullet": the massive mullet that he received as a gift, then sent to auction, has already been mentioned; legend had it that a fisherman climbed a cliff to present him with a mullet on Capri, with unfortunate consequences (Suet. 60);[54] and he allegedly deplored the sale of three mullets for thirty thousand sesterces (Suet. 34.1). It is likely that Timon's *Silloi* had a fishing scene, with the schools of fish representing the competing schools of philosophy, and that Plato was the leader of them all, πλατίστικος, the Big Mullet. The matter is not clear, but Tiberius would have been amused.[55]

Be that as it may, Timon's lively satire and sharp Homeric parody surely appealed to Tiberius, the sardonic devotee of Odysseus, and to a grammarian eager to win his favor. They bring us again into the world of learned Greek poetry, with a contest of words presented as a Homeric battle and perhaps a nod to gastronomy. It is a world into which Sabinus' *Certamen* likewise fits comfortably.

A highly speculative biography of a man about whom we know almost nothing might read as follows. Asellius Sabinus was born sometime in the latter half of the first century BCE and he died in the 30s CE. His family was senatorial, they and he flourished under and through the patronage of

Augustus and Tiberius, and he moved easily in aristocratic circles. He was wealthy. His culture was that of the intellectual and social elite of his day. His aristocratic wit was considered the height of sophistication by a most knowledgeable critic. He was committed to real oratory, even to the point of teaching it, but indulged as well in the contemporary craze for the imaginary that was competitive declamation. He had a sincere interest in food and its preparation, another passion of the day. And he conveyed that interest in a gastronomic poem replete with epic overtones, a clever parody that both satirized and enshrined that passion. The poem (not a word of which survives) was a serious literary creation with a long pedigree, a work both refined and erudite, and it was handsomely rewarded by another most knowledgeable critic and patron. In person, he was charming and urbane, a Noel Coward *avant la lettre*.

His Death

Asellius Sabinus could not refrain from making jokes even in dire circumstances: *nimius risus adfectator*, as was remarked of the ill-fated Cicero. Seneca was upset. Everyone knew that Sabinus should not have jested amid his troubles and dangers. How could he have done it? Our author's tone here is ominous but it is not conclusive, and his sons did not need to be told what happened to Sabinus in the end. His fate is not recorded: he may have perished in prison; he may have been executed; he may have been acquitted. Tacitus and Dio, whose histories are essentially complete for the period from 32 through 37 CE, do not include him in their bloody vignettes of the carnage of those years. In Suetonius, he is merely a passing figure in an insignificant note from Augustus and a passing item in a catalog of Tiberius' supposed transgressions. How did he die? Two scenarios might occur.

The gourmand may well have starved to death in prison. Execution by inanition was purportedly a specialty of Tiberius the gastronome. Food and starvation overwhelm the narratives. His former wife Julia he destroyed in her exile by ill-treatment and starvation, hoping that no one would notice the murder since she had been away for so long. He either executed his widowed daughter-in-law and niece Livilla or, so Dio had heard, left her to her mother, Antonia, who starved her to death. His friend Asinius Gallus, the second husband of Tiberius' first wife, survived in prison for as many as three years, kept barely alive by poor and inadequate food, and deprived of human contact, except when he was force-fed. Rumor had it that he died of starvation, whether voluntary or enforced. We are told that he dined with Tiberius on the very day of his arrest. Tiberius' mistreatment of Agrippina, his stepdaughter and widowed daughter-in-law, was even more egregiously gastronomical, if that were possible. Forewarned by Sejanus, she had declined all food at a banquet with

Tiberius. Tiberius purposely offered her an apple, knowing that she would refuse. He then complained that he was being accused of poisoning and he
stopped inviting her to dinner. Rumor had it then that her death was being
prepared. Years later, in island exile, she tried to starve herself, but he ordered
that she be force-fed. She nevertheless managed to starve herself to death—or
perhaps murder was dressed up to look like suicide. Tiberius had earlier slain
her son—his grandson, Nero—by starvation in his island exile. "They think"
an executioner had terrified him into "voluntary death." And Nero's brother
Drusus was likewise slain by starvation, but in the depths of the Palatine. Again,
"they think" that Drusus was so deprived of nourishment that he tried to eat
the stuffing of his mattress. How appropriate then that, when on his deathbed,
soon after his last banquet, Tiberius revived enough to demand food and his
surviving grandson Gaius, the brother of Nero and Drusus, refused it to him.[56]

Tiberius' alleged appetite for starvation reflects his reputation as a man
interested in food. On his deathbed, Augustus had lamented the fate of the
Roman people, to be ground by such slow jaws, and one might suspect from
the starvation anecdotes that the hostile contemporary historian took pleasure
in playing on the image of the tyrant as flesh-eating, blood-drinking monster,
the sadist who enjoyed dining with his intended victim just before he took his
life.[57] Rumor about events hidden from the public eye certainly renders suspect the accounts of the six deaths just mentioned. Yet there can be no doubt
that Tiberius was a cruel and vindictive man, and Jerzy Linderski demonstrated beyond a doubt that legal and epigraphical evidence confirms the literary picture of his treatment of Julia: whether she died of starvation or not, her
end was miserable and premeditated.[58] But the real shock is the death of Drusus. The account of it is not one of rumor and innuendo. It was confirmed by
documents read out to the senate, eyewitness records of daily beatings and
terrifying threats, verbatim transcriptions of the dying man's curses on his
grandfather, and of his final, unheeded pleas for food. Tiberius really did starve
people to death. A man who could treat his own grandson so savagely would
have no compunction about leaving a former friend to die of hunger in prison,
be he Asinius Gallus or Asellius Sabinus. He had done much worse with many
others.[59] Even if he was not responsible for the death of Sabinus, he would
surely be aware of it, and compliant senators were aware that starvation was
the order of the day.

But we can prefer to believe that the gourmet's eloquent plea to the senate
for nourishment was successful, that he won his release from prison soon
thereafter, and that he retired to live out his few remaining years in quiet luxury
on the Bay of Naples. The name Asellius is Oscan, and it is apparently attested
in *crater ille delicatus* at Puteoli, Herculaneum, and Pompeii.[60] About a kilo-
meter north of Pompeii, a sumptuous early imperial villa was excavated in the

early 1900s.[61] Spacious, comfortable, richly and tastefully decorated and appointed, it lay on the pleasant western slope of a hill facing the bay. A remarkable unity of design and remnants of Second Style wall painting date the villa's construction by a wealthy and strongminded owner to the mid-to-late first century BCE. It was very unusual. Despite being a *villa rustica* surrounded by other such villas, there is no sign of any agricultural enterprise. Perfectly oriented, it was an almost perfect square, thirty-two meters to the side. Its central garden was surrounded on three sides by harmoniously balanced groups of rooms, an exceptional number of them devoted to entertainment, their outer perimeter being a portico that could be shuttered at will. But the southern flank of the square was completely open and exposed to the sun. A bronze stamp found in one of the rooms bears the image of a wine jug and what should be the name of its owner, "Asel(lius?) Pro(culus?)."[62] It would be pleasant to imagine the charming Asellius Sabinus in quiet retirement, as he enjoyed a cup of young Pompeian wine,[63] the company of his son Proculus, his delightful villa, and the southern exposure with its stunning view of the Bay of Naples. Excavated in 1903 and 1904, the rich contents of the villa were mostly dispersed among private hands, as was the custom of the day, and the ruins were subsequently reburied. Its precise location remains unknown.

Appendix: Asellii and Aselliones

There was a family of Asellii in the senate of the late Republic. The evidence for them is elusive and confusing; it is handled tendentiously or not at all in standard works of reference; and it involves disputed readings or emendations in the texts of no fewer than three major ancient historians. None of the following appears under the rubric "Asellius" in any version of *Pauly-Wissowa*:

1) Cassius Dio (49.43.47) tells of a praetor, Λεύκιος Ἀσύλλιος, who resigned the praetorship because of long-term ill health in 33 BCE. Caesar (later Augustus) appointed his son in his place. Pighius' emendation of "Asullius" to "Asellius" is accepted in standard texts. The name "Asullius" appears very rarely on inscriptions, but it is found only once elsewhere in a literary source, viz.:

2) A fragment of Diodorus Siculus preserved by Constantine Porphyrogenitus that tells of a good governor of Sicily (probably to be assigned to a little before 92 BCE: 37.8.1–4, from Constantine's *Excerpta* 2 [1], p. 318). It introduces this man, who must have served as praetor previously, as Λεύκιος Ἀσύλλιος—that is, the same name as the praetor of 33 BCE in Dio. A few sentences later it calls him Σύλλιος.

3) At *Satires* 2.2.49–50, Horace tells us that baby storks (*ciconiae*) were safe from gourmands until an *auctor praetorius* enlightened us. The

commentator known as pseudo-Acro notes ad loc.: "A certain Asellius was the praetor, who first invented the custom of eating storks. Others want Sempronius to be the praetor, who after many things taught that even storks could be proper to eat, or their young." And Porphyrio chimes in: "Rufus the ex-praetor was said to have started the eating of young storks. And when he had been defeated for the praetorship [sic] he earned this epigram." Four verses follow, to the effect that the electorate thus avenged the death of the storks.

4) A senatorial Μᾶρκος Ἀσέλλιος Μάρκου Μαικία appears as a witness in a *senatus consultum* of April 11, 44 BCE, quoted by Josephus at *AJ* 14.220. The paradosis offers Ἀσέλλιος and Σασέλλιος, and conjectures include Gronovius' Ἀκύλιος and Niese's Γέλλιος, which he printed in his edition.

All of this confusing evidence was treated by two master prosopographers of the twentieth century, Friedrich Münzer and Ernst Badian, but in arbitrary fashion.

According to Diodorus, the proconsul of Sicily, "Lucius Asullius" (number 2 above) had a legate named Gaius Longus. Münzer enshrined the following in *Pauly-Wissowa* without argument, in his treatment of the Sempronii, *RE* no. 18, L. Sempronius Asellio: "Klein (Die Verwaltungsbeamten von Sizilien und Sardinien 59f.) quite rightly drew on this C. Longus to ascertain the corrupted name of the governor; he *should* be a L. Asellio, and both men belong to the Gens Sempronia." That would *perhaps* make him a close relative, maybe the older brother, of A. Sempronius Asellio, the urban praetor murdered in the forum in 89 BCE (*RE* 17), and the two men *might* be sons of the historian Sempronius Asellio, who had served with Scipio Aemilianus at Numantia (*RE* 16).

Badian (1968)—in a paper on the Sempronii Aselliones, in parts intricate to the verge of incomprehensibility—proposed that the name of the other "Lucius Asullius," Dio's praetor of 33 BCE (number 1 above), should likewise be emended to produce another L. (Sempronius) Asellio.

Münzer (at *RE* Sempronius 79) discussed the C. Sempronius Rufus whose complicated financial dealings are referred to in six letters of Cicero, who despised the man. He *might* be the Sempronius referred to in two other letters from the year 43 BCE and that Sempronius in turn *might* be the subject of a *Sempronianum senatus consultum* in a third letter. The praetor Sempronius of pseudo-Acro and the praetor Rufus of Porphyrio (number 3 above) are to be combined into one man and to be identified with the man in Cicero. Indeed, the *Commentator Cruquianus* gives the full name as Asinius Sempronius Rufus, hence it may be that we should emend that name in the light of what we know about the *gens Sempronia* to produce C. Sempronius Asellio Rufus: "From all these scattered notices we can obtain a unified, admittedly very hypothetical portrait of the man." Badian offered lengthy supporting argumentation, but nothing essentially new, while allowing in the end that this man could not be fitted into any stemma of the Aselliones.[64]

And finally, at *RE* Gellius 7, Münzer tacitly accepted Niese's emended reading, "Marcus Gellius" for "Marcus Asellius," in Josephus' account of the *senatus consultum* (number 4 above) and identified him with the Marcus Gellius who was subjected to a Ciceronian witticism for reading a document in a clear loud voice in the senate (Plut. *Cic.* 27.5).

Little of this is compelling:

Münzer summarily dismissed as incorrect the observation, by P. Groebe, that the M. Gellius of the Cicero anecdote was an *apparitor*: in fact there is no indication or likelihood that the man was a senator. Münzer also ignored the fact that "Gellius" in Josephus is an emendation. The texts of the *senatus consulta* in Josephus are admittedly problematic, but three assumptions are involved to produce "Gellius," none of them necessary. M. Asellius M.f. is generally accepted as a senator.[65]

The conversion of the two praetors named "Lucius Asullius" to "Lucius Asellio" is gratuitous, based on the presumption that the legate C. Longus was a Sempronius, which is mere speculation: the cognomen Longus is very common, and there were a lot of new men in the Roman senate. It also seems to be based on the tacit assumption that the man was a *gentilis* of his commanding officer, which need not be the case.

Indeed, Badian's argument should be reversed: Pighius' change of "Asullius" to "Asellius" for the praetor of 33 BCE (closer to the *paradosis* than "Asellio") can be applied to the homonymous praetor of the 90s BCE.

The *praetorius* who added storks to the cuisine (number 3 above) is problematic. "Sempronius the praetor" and "Rufus the ex-praetor" have been combined to produce "Sempronius Rufus," which may or may not be correct (the *Commentator Cruqianus* is worthless here),[66] but something has gone embarrassingly wrong: how could "Rufus the ex-praetor" who cooked storks be punished by the people's refusal to elect him to the praetorship?[67]

Above all, "Asellio" obscures the clear meaning of pseudo-Acro (see number 3 above): "[Some say that] the praetor was Asellius, others want him to be Sempronius." That is, in the scholiast's mind, rightly or wrongly, these are two different men, candidates proposed by earlier commentators. It is an unfortunate coincidence that a branch of the Sempronii bore the similar sounding cognomen Asellio, which is actually attested for only two men, the second-century historian and the praetor of 89 BCE, with whom it disappears. All else is modern speculation, "admittedly very hypothetical." Why not trust the reading in pseudo-Acro?

If we strip away modern accretions, we are left with a senatorial M. Asellius in 44 BCE and a senatorial Asellius, *praenomen* unknown, the praetor who may have introduced storks into Roman cuisine at an unknown date. The latter is presumably one of the following, their names all emended from "Asullius" in the Greek: L. Asellius, praetor before c. 92 BCE; L. Asellius, praetor in 33 BCE; or Asellius, *praenomen* unknown, praetor suffect in 33 BCE. Significantly, there is even, as so often in the late days of the Republic, a convenient legendary ancestor to certify the family as senatorial, M.(?) Asellius, allegedly tribune of the plebs in 422 BCE.[68]

8

Marcus Apicius

A SENSE OF PLACE

If we look back into past times, we find innumerable names of authors once in high reputation, read perhaps by the beautiful, quoted by the witty, and commented upon by the grave; but of whom we now know only that they once existed.

—JOHNSON, *THE RAMBLER*

The Magistrates of Minturnae

The Roman colony of Minturnae lay at the mouth of the Liris River on the marshy coast of the Gulf of Formiae, at the border between Latium and Campania. In 1931, 1932, and 1933, a young American archaeologist, Jotham Johnson, excavated the area of the Republican forum. In 1933, he published twenty-nine inscriptions that had been reused in the building of a temple near the town's theater during the early years of the principate. The texts were carved on pillars of uniform size, and comprise a list of twelve names, mostly those of slaves, with some freedmen; mostly males, with some females, each with the name of a current or former master or mistress: thus, "Sosander Pomponi Q(uinti) s(ervus)." They record the *fasti* of the *magistri* and *magistrae* of local associations: whether those associations were primarily religious or economic remains uncertain. The pillars were erected year by year in the period between the Social War and the Civil Wars (one of them is dated to 65 BCE), perhaps down to the late 30s BCE. Johnson's edition, which he produced quickly, is masterly.[1] Building on a full and careful presentation of the texts, he analyzed their format and delved into their forms, noting what he classified as epigraphical, graphic, phonetic, paradigmatic, and transcriptional "peculiarities." He then proceeded to investigate the origins of the masters (both local gentry and Roman aristocrats with local interests) and the origins of the slaves (from all over the Roman world), and he concluded with remarks on the nature of the cults involved (Ceres, Mercury Felix, Spes, Venus) and on the original location and dates of what he considered to be altars (others have thought them to be statue bases). Presenting more than 330 names, the texts are a prosopographer's paradise.

The great prosopographer of the age responded quickly to their publication. In 1935, Friedrich Münzer published a ten-page paper in the *Mitteilungen* of the German Archaeological Institute in Rome, under the title "Zu den Magistri von Minturnae."[2] Where Johnson had been concerned with investigating the geographical and ethnic origins both of the masters and mistresses and of the slaves and freedmen and freedwomen, Münzer was concerned solely with the social milieu of the masters and mistresses. The paper displayed his customary clarity, precision, learning, and imagination. Its title was modest and no conclusions were drawn, but two larger points emerge beyond question.

First, among the masters, there is an astonishingly large representation of Roman senators and knights, men who had property or commercial interests, or both, in the region (many more instances have been added since Münzer's paper). Second, and sometimes overlapping, equally well represented among the masters at Minturnae are local gentry from the surrounding area, municipal oligarchs with roots or family ties in a distinct coastal band running north through Formiae, Caieta, and Fundi up to Tarracina and south to Sinuessa. Thus, among the masters at Minturnae, Münzer observed that two named Galba, plus a C. Sulpicius and a P. Sulpicius, confirm the local roots of the Sulpicii Galbae of Tarracina. A master Lentulus and two L. Cornelii give context to Cicero's meeting with L. Cornelius Lentulus Crus at Formiae. Again, local characters in Marius' famous adventures in the swamps of Minturnae in 88 BCE are reflected among the masters on the *fasti*: his enemy Geminius of Tarracina, who pursued him (two Geminii); the C. Titinius of Minturnae, whose ex-wife took him in (nine Titinii, including two C. Titinii); perhaps even Marius himself (one C. Marius). And a Laelia C.f., who appears three times as the mistress of female magistrates, reminds us that the famous C. Laelius had a villa at Formiae and two daughters but no sons. And so on, all circumstantial but cumulatively overwhelming. By good fortune, much of Münzer's case was supported from the contemporary writings of Cicero, especially in his role as local landowner, genial neighbor, and letter writer from his *Formianum*.[3] Indeed, the period covered by the *fasti* might be defined as that of Ciceronian Rome.

A great deal of evidence has accumulated since 1935. Another magistral list has been retrieved from an eighteenth-century manuscript. Another stele, but one with nineteen names, and dedicated to the Lares in 59 BCE, was found in the area of Mantua but had assuredly migrated from Minturnae. And the rich epigraphical harvest of Minturnae has continued to grow. Münzer's initial response to the material has been amply confirmed. Not only have many more names and families representing both Roman and local elites been added—some of them famous names in Roman history—but their extensive economic interests, both local and empire-wide, are more clearly defined in light of the study of an enormous mass of *instrumenta domestica*.[4] Indeed, Münzer himself subsequently added at least one other significant example in the pages of *RE*, and more may lurk in later items among his 4,388 contributions.[5]

Seven years after Münzer's original paper, a long article devoted to "the 29 newly-discovered inscribed stelae of Minturno" appeared in *Hermes*, from the pen of one Erich Staedler. It included an elaborate reedition of the inscriptions and argued that they were put up quickly in 28 and 27 BCE, an unconvincing claim that has found little support. In his first footnote, devoted to "Literatur" (1942, 149 n. 1), Staedler cites Johnson's 1933 publication of the inscriptions, as well as ephemeral reviews of it in Italian, American, French, and British journals, a mention in a German book (of 1935, unstated), and Johnson's excellent article on Minturnae, which appeared in a *Pauly-Wissowa* Supplementband in 1940. But nowhere in forty-eight pages does Staedler mention Münzer's contribution in a major German journal. The reason is not far to seek.

The first footnote in Münzer's paper of 1935 is strikingly reticent. After giving the full reference to Johnson's publication (praised in the body of his text), he continues:

> Trotz mancher Unterstützung, für die ich dankbar bin, habe ich mich längere Zeit in Deutschland vergebens um diese Publikation bemüht. Als ich schliesslich durch freundliche Vermittlung von Herrn Professor L. Wickert und liebenswürdiges Entgegenkommen des Deutschen Archäologischen Instituts in Rom aus dessen Bibliothek für kurze Zeit erhielt, konnte ich sie infolge ungünstiger Umstände nur rasch durchsehen und war bei der Ausarbeitung deiser Bemerkungen im wesentlichen auf die daraus abgeschriebenen Texte der Inschriften angewiesen.

In July of 1935, the year in which his Minturnae paper was published despite the "unfavorable circumstances" in which it was produced, he was forced to retire, as were other professors aged sixty-five and over, to make room for Nazi sympathizers. In November of that year, he was officially classified as Jewish. In July of 1942, the year in which Staedler's paper was published, he was taken to Theresienstadt, where he died of enteritis at the age of seventy-four.

In October of 1939, the Reichs- und Preussisches Ministerium für Wissenschaft, Erziehung und Volksbildung had decreed that Jewish writers could be cited only when they were explicitly identified as Jews and only when it was absolutely essential, and that in bibliographies "Jewish" authors were to be segregated from "German."[6] It is difficult to fault Staedler for his silence, but its consequences were pernicious. Since the war, much excellent work has been done on the epigraphy, the prosopography, and the architecture of Minturnae. Yet, when it comes to discussing the history of the city and its ruling class, many good scholars refer to Staedler's paper but seem not to be aware of Münzer's contribution.[7] Familiarity with his paper would have saved unnecessary effort and added unsuspected material. At the least, his memory should be honored.

Inevitably, some of the political and economic elite of Rome were, or aspired to be, its cultural elite as well. Münzer happened in passing to weave two peripheral men of letters into his prosopographical web. One was the paradoxographer Statius Sebosus, a source for Pliny the Elder. In a formidable display of logic and erudition, Münzer overturned the man's entry in *Pauly-Wissowa*, replacing it in his paper by half a paragraph of text and a twenty-line footnote. Sebosus he backdated from the second quarter of the first century CE to emerge as a neighbor and unwanted visitor of Cicero at Formiae in 59 BCE. But then Münzer changed course, disconcertingly. He observed that chance plays a role in the coincidence of names so often that many of his suggested connections among the various characters would remain doubtful. He then announced, paradoxically, that he would conclude with an instance where a correlation of names is striking but must nevertheless actually be pure chance. The nomen Larcius appears once on an earlier inscription at Minturnae and three times in our *fasti*, one of them in the person of a Licinus, slave of Aulus and Publius Larcius. There happens to be, as Münzer reminds us, a distinguished man of letters, Larcius Licinus, who lived in the time of Vespasian (in fact, a senator of praetorian rank):

> Doch wenn in der Zeit Vespasians ein angesehener und literarisch interessierter Larcius Licinus nachweisbar ist, so hieße es die zulässigen Grenzen der Forschung überschreiten, wenn man ihn von den Minturnanischen Sklaven ableiten wollte, der im Falle seiner Freilassung auch schon so geheißen hätte.[8]

Perhaps a comment, serious or ironic, on the fundamental uncertainty of prosopography, the art of which he was the master. Perhaps a reply, ironic or despondent, to his critics, scholarly or racist. It is the last sentence of his paper.

If time and good fortune had been allowed him, he would surely have discovered to his delight another literary man connected with the magistrates of Minturnae, a far more significant figure.

Apicius: The Reputation

Marcus Apicius has an image problem. He was, notoriously, The Glutton, the slave of his gullet and of gluttony, the very incarnation of a gullet; he spent enormous sums of money on his stomach, was an extremely wealthy voluptuary, the deepest abyss of all spendthrifts; born with every talent for debauchery, he was renowned for his profligacy, a wealthy prodigal who paid a young aristocrat for sex.[9] "No one will deny that he was the *ne plus ultra* of prodigality," with "a great reputation for prodigality and extravagance and idleness of life and general depravity."[10] "He not only enjoyed but boasted of his enormous banquets, he flaunted his vices, he attracted the attention of the community to his wantonness, he enticed the young to imitate his own course"; "Apicius, who in this very city—which at one time the philosophers were ordered to leave as being 'corrupters of the youth'—defiled the age with *his* teaching, the Professor of Popinary Science."[11] "And he lived, they say, for his stomach and for those parts which are more intemperate than the stomach."[12] The horrendous abuse is standard and tralactican. It boils down simply to a completely frivolous life devoted to the repellent, obsessive pursuit of self-indulgence. Gluttony is but the tip of an iceberg of general depravity.

Two shocking anecdotes fixed this *monstrum* for eternity. Athenaeus transmits one of them in his *Deipnosophists*:

> In Tiberius' time there was an extremely wealthy pleasure-seeker named Apicius, from whom many types of cakes get the name "Apician." This fellow spent an infinite amount on his belly and lived mostly in Minturnae (a city in Campania) eating expensive shrimp, which grow very large there, larger even than the shrimp in Smyrna and the lobsters in Alexandria. When he heard that there were extraordinarily large shrimp in Libya, he sailed off without a day's delay. After much trouble at sea, he approached those regions; but before he disembarked from his ship—there had been much discussion among the Libyans about his arrival—fishermen sailed out to meet him, bringing him their best shrimp. After he saw them, he asked if they had any that were bigger; when they said that they did not grow any larger than the ones they had brought, he remembered the shrimp in Minturnae, and he ordered the helmsman to sail back to Italy by the same route, without even putting in to shore.[13]

This is the first, but not the last, connection between the gourmet and Minturnae. The same story appears in the *Suda*, with one curious alteration considered below.

The other tale concludes a ferocious tirade against Apicius by his younger contemporary Seneca, writing within a decade or two of the man's death:

> It is worth our while to learn his end. After he had squandered a hundred million sesterces upon his kitchen, after he had drunk up at every one of his revels the equivalent of many largesses of the emperors and the huge

revenue of the Capitol, then forced for the first time, overwhelmed with debt, he began to examine his accounts. He calculated that he would have ten million sesterces left, and considering that he would be living in extreme starvation if he lived on ten million sesterces, he ended his life by poison. But how great was his luxury if ten millions counted as poverty! What folly then to think that it is the amount of money and not the state of mind that matters! Ten million sesterces made one man shudder, and a sum that others seek by prayer he escaped from by poison! For a man so perverted in desire his last draught was really the most wholesome.[14]

Martial, Seneca's younger contemporary and client, offers essentially the same story in an epigram published in the late 80s CE. It may find a subsequent echo in Juvenal, a version turns up in Dio's *History*, and it is briefly repeated centuries later by Isidore of Seville and the second Vatican mythographer.[15]

In short, ancient condemnation of the man rests on a handful of brief descriptions—narrow, unoriginal, and vituperative—and on two scandalous anecdotes. With this strikingly slender résumé, he passes into the company of the heroes and villains of legend: he is recalled by a single name, he has become an adjective, he has become a proverb.[16] And yet, it is plain that something here has been dreadfully reduced, simplified, set askew. As we saw in the previous chapter, the pleasures that made Apicius' name a byword for scandal—the pleasures of the table—were the products of art and science, and were taken seriously by serious men. The foodways of Roman gastronomy reflect the shared values of an active elite. Dining was an extraordinary safety valve in a life of duty. Ideally, it offered comity, relaxation, sophisticated entertainment, education, social networking. Wit, style, and good taste (in both senses of the word) were highly valued: *urbanitas* and *lautitia* were the hallmarks of the successful feast. The highest quality of ingredients, the appropriate season, the proper source, and the suitable preparation and combination were matters of fundamental importance. Gastronomy was the passion of strongly opinionated men. Knowledge and creativity were highly valued, and they were displayed in flights of poetic fancy, in learned handbooks, in public debates as fierce as those waged by doctors and rhetoricians. At the same time, gastronomy was the avocation of the rich. Large and lavish banquets, sumptuous settings, apparatus, and entertainment, rare and costly food, elaborate preparation by ingenious master chefs—the costs could be enormous. The whole universe of Roman gastronomy is captured in the fabulous banquet of the immortal Trimalchio. That is brilliant, distorted, outrageous satire. Apicius is the reality that Trimalchio reflects. We should work a bit harder to find out who this man was.

Marcus Apicius: The Facts

The scholarship on the gourmet is extensive, thanks to the late antique cookbook ascribed to him. Readers interested in the man himself will find all that they require in three admirable recent essays: one provides a reliable account of basic facts; the second firmly distinguishes Apicius the man from "Apicius" the cookbook; and the third traces the fortunes of his posthumous reputation. And for a brilliant introduction to the man and his work nothing is better than the chapter "Ancient Rome" in Phyllis Pray Bober's magisterial *Art, Culture, and Cuisine: Ancient and Medieval Gastronomy*.[17]

A biography is impossible. The caricature of the legend is fixed for eternity, there is no hint of a public career, every meager detail preserved about his private life is in some way connected with food. Worse, many of those details are misunderstood or demonstrably false. The facts appear to be as follows.

Dates

The dates of his birth and death are unknown but we can fix his *floruit*. What evidence there is assigns his activities to the principate of Tiberius. An anecdote in the *Suda* tells us that, at one of his banquets, he entertained the consul Iunius Blaesus, whose year in office is certified as 28 CE.[18] A guest at another banquet was an ex-consul named Fabius: he is commonly assumed to be the *nobilissimus vir* (as the emperor Claudius was to call him) Paullus Fabius Persicus, scion of the Fabii Maximi and *consul ordinarius* in 34 CE.[19] Another anecdote has Tiberius sending a large mullet to the *Macellum* for auction, where Apicius is outbid by a rival. The incident may have taken place before Tiberius' final withdrawal from the capital in 26 CE, but he visited its inner suburb repeatedly up to the year of his death, so the range of possibility is 14 to 37 CE. Be that as it may, Apicius was certainly acquainted with Tiberius' son, Drusus Caesar, who was born in 15 or 14 BCE and who died in September of 23 CE.[20]

Certainly Tiberian then, but the impression may be misleading when we consider Apicius' alleged affair with Tiberius' notorious right-hand man Sejanus. Tacitus' introduction of Sejanus must be read closely: "Born at Vulsinii, his father being Seius Strabo, a Roman knight, in his early manhood he was a follower of Gaius Caesar, the grandson of the Divine Augustus, not without the rumor that he had offered the sale of illicit sex (*stuprium veno dedisse*) to the rich and prodigal Apicius."[21] His *stuprum* with Apicius is an aspect of Sejanus' *sectatio* of Gaius Caesar, which must mean that Apicius was also in some way associated with Gaius. This takes us back to the age of Augustus. Gaius Caesar was born in the late summer of 20 BCE and died early in 4 CE. We should assume that Sejanus was much of an age with his companion, perhaps even older: he was certainly mature when he is first heard of as joint praetorian prefect with his father in 14 CE. "Early manhood" (*prima iuventa*, a favorite phrase of Tacitus) is applicable anywhere up to about the age of twenty-five.[22] The alleged liaison with Sejanus (born ca. 20 BCE?) must thus be dated to the years around the turn of the millennium. Apicius was presumably the older man. We may then assign his birth very roughly to 30 BCE. That would put him in his fifties and sixties under Tiberius in the 20s and 30s CE. If so, the "ex-consul Fabius" need not be Paullus Fabius Persicus, the Tiberian consul of 34 CE. He might just as well be that man's father, Paullus Fabius Maximus, *consul ordinarius* in 11 BCE (who died 14 CE), or his uncle, Africanus Fabius Maximus, *consul ordinarius* in 10 BCE and last heard of as proconsul of Africa around 6 or 5 BCE. In short, it may very well be that Apicius flourished as much under Augustus as under Tiberius, and that the last firm date for his existence should be 28 CE, not 35 CE.

The liaison with Sejanus proves doubly useful here in that it suggests an earlier date not only for Apicius' arrival on the scene but also for his departure from it. The prefect's reputation was thoroughly and permanently blackened after his stunningly abrupt and horrific fall from power in the autumn of 31 CE and the massacre of his followers. If the alleged liaison with Apicius was part of the campaign smearing his memory, we might assume that Apicius died before him. We will not be far wrong if we assign the gourmet a lifespan of, very roughly, 30 BCE to 30 CE.

Name

He was, of course, *the* Apicius, and the familiar single name is universal, but we have it on unimpeachable authority that his *praenomen* was Marcus, which will prove useful.[23] Otherwise, his name is associated with three other *nomina*.

Two of them are to be rejected. The name "Caelius Apicius" is an unfortunate Renaissance expansion of the otherwise meaningless "API CAE" at the very beginning of the cookbook's manuscripts. It has been universally and rightly rejected by editors, though it lingers in some scholarship. It is also sometimes assumed that Apicata, the wife of the great Sejanus, was a relative. But the nomen "Apicat(i)us" is well enough attested, notably in the contemporary senator T. Apicatus Sabinus, *quaestor propraetore* of Cyprus at the turn of the millennium, and it has nothing to do with "Apicius."[24]

More appealing is the name "Marcus Gabius Apicius" in Dio. His text has (in the genitive) "Γαβ(β)ίου," a very rare nomen, but often—as probably here and as universally assumed—it is the Greek version of the much more common "Gavii." This concatenation of "Gab(b)ius / Gavius" with "Apicius" in

Dio is unique in the historical record, where the gourmet is always simply "Apicius" or "Marcus Apicius," and it has aroused no comment. Nevertheless, it appears in a passage derived from Dio's first-century source and deserves further consideration.

False Apicii

Not one but two other gourmets named Apicius are on record, one living long before our hero, the other long after. Their existence raises the unavoidable question of sources. These seem to reflect two traditions.

On the Latin side, we have notices from three younger contemporaries of our hero. Two of them, Seneca as essayist and Pliny as encyclopaedist, have nothing good to say about the man. The work of the third, a historian, is now lost but has long been known to scholars. Briefly stated, our much later major sources—Tacitus, Suetonius, and Cassius Dio—all later relied heavily for their accounts of Tiberius' times on two narratives composed in the mid-first century by Servilius Nonianus and Aufidius Bassus.[25] It is absolutely clear that Apicius' liaison with the young Sejanus in Tacitus (presented as rumor) and in Dio (presented as fact) reflect a common source in both detail and placement: the two authors introduce a biographical sketch of the sinister figure of the prefect into their respective histories in the same manner, and at the same point in their narratives, as their source had done. Be that lost source Aufidius Bassus or (more likely) Servilius Nonianus, there is no sign that he would be better disposed toward the notorious gourmet.[26] In sum, the three main Latin sources are more or less contemporary and, if we can discount the abuse, their basic facts may be true.[27]

The Greek tradition is independent, and a bewildering jumble. It is represented primarily by a handful of discrete notices and anecdotes transmitted by two authorities. One is Athenaeus, writing around 200 CE in his vast repository of gastronomic literature presented as a symposium, the *Deipnosophists*. The other is the immense tenth-century encyclopedia known as the *Suda*.[28] Two at least of the *Suda's* entries concerning Apicius are commonly presumed to be fragments from lost parts of Aelian's miscellany, *Varia Historia*, which was likewise composed around 200 CE. If that is so—and it is admittedly difficult to find justification for the common presumption—we have two texts composed in the age of the Second Sophistic more than 150 years after Apicius' death. Athenaeus and the *Suda's* source (Aelian?) clearly drew upon a common source for some of their material.

What one of them reflects of that source is bizarre. The *Suda* informs us (in entry O 720) that "When Trajan was among [the] Parthians, and was many days' journey from the sea, Apicius the gourmet (ὁ ὀψοφάγος) sent him fresh oysters packed in a clever way he devised." And at A 4660, after much random information on "small fry," the encyclopedia concludes,

> When Nicomedes the King of the Bithynians had a craving for small fry [ἀφύη] and was a long way from the sea, Apicius the gourmet [ὁ ὀψοφάγος] made an imitation of the little fish and served it to him as small fry. But this was the preparation. He took this soft turnip; cut it into small pieces so that it looked like the small fry; boiled [it] in oil; poured salt over [it]; sprinkled poppy seeds [on it]; satisfied the craving.[29]

Thus, we meet two *opsophagoi*, both named Apicius, neither of them our man. One apparently lived long after him, for Trajan campaigned in Parthia in the years 115 and 116 CE. And the other must have lived long before him, for the last King Nicomedes of Bithynia, the fourth of that name, reigned from about 94 BCE until his death in 75 or 74 BCE, when he bequeathed his kingdom to Rome. Both of these other Apicii are resourceful gourmets indeed, and each satisfies the craving for seafood of a monarch far from the sea.

Alongside these two items we can set Athenaeus' version of the same material. Surely reflecting a source shared with the *Suda*, he, in fact, made the connection between the two land-bound monarchs, Trajan and Nicomedes, a connection that has been lost in the encyclopedic organization of the *Suda*. But the deipnosophist offers a surprise:

> When the emperor Trajan was in Parthia and was very many days away from the sea, Apicius had fresh oysters sent to him packed in a clever way he devised himself. Matters were different when Nicomedes the King of the Bithynians had a craving for small fry (ἀφύη)—he too was a long way from the sea—and a cook made an imitation of the little fish and served it to him. The cook in the comic poet Euphron, at any rate, says:
>
> > (A.) I was a student of Soterides, who, when Nicomedes was twelve days' journey away from the sea once and had a craving for small fry in mid-winter, was the first to serve him some, by Zeus: he made them all cry out in amazement.
> > (B.) How is this possible?
> > (A.) He took this soft turnip; cut it into pieces so that it looked like the small fry; stewed it thoroughly; poured oil over it; salted it artfully; sprinkled 2000 black-poppy seeds on top; and satisfied the craving in Scythia.
> > (B.) And as Nicomedes chewed on turnip, he sang the praises of small fry to his friends. The cook's no different from the poet; for the genius of each consists of his technical skill.[30]

The King for whom the artificial sardine was supposedly created cannot be Nicomedes IV, and he cannot have been contemporary with an Apicius, despite what the *Suda* tells us. He must be Nicomedes I, who ruled over Bithynia from 280 to 255 or 254 BCE, since our source for the tale is, of all things, a New Comedy play by Euphron. A glance at the arrangement of the texts shows that the *Suda*'s source has transmitted Euphron's poetry all but verbatim as prose, from the king's being far from the sea and his longing for the delicacy, to his desire being fulfilled. But the fictional early third-century BCE Greek cook Soterides has become a Roman gourmet, Apicius, and the two far-from-the-sea tales of Trajan and of Nicomedes, naturally combined by Athenaeus' source, have been decoupled in the process. A real and notorious Apicius, to whom we shall come in a moment, did indeed flourish in the last century of the Republic, but this is not he. The clever gourmet with his turnip surprise is a joke based on a play. Whose fraud he is, and to what purpose, we do not know. There are too many unknowns, but the artful Nicomedean gourmet Apicius of the late Republic is a fiction.

So, too, the later imperial Apicius, the supposed contemporary of Trajan. The specificity of the information about him is impressive, with a clear context and date: Trajan, Parthia, therefore 115 or 116 CE. This Apicius flourished a century after the gourmet, and closer in time to Athenaeus, perhaps a mere two generations before him. Nevertheless, he too is fraudulent. Athenaeus and the *Suda* present the same information about him in almost exactly the same words that are clearly derived from a common source: the emperor Trajan being many days journey from the sea in Parthia, Apicius (the *opsophage*) sent him fresh oysters cleverly preserved. In similar fashion, they likewise present the same information about the earlier Apicius and a King Nicomedes in almost exactly the same words that are, again, clearly derived from a common source. Nicomedes King of the Bithynians desiring sardines and being a long way from the sea, Apicius (the *opsophage*) or a cook made an imitation of the little fish and served it to him as small fry—that is, sardines or anchovies. The tale of an Apicius and a King Nicomedes, as we saw, is a fiction, derived from Greek New Comedy: the disguised fish was prepared by a cook, and his pupil fills in the significant details of his clever invention (it was midwinter, and so on). We can see immediately that the fictitious "King Nicomedes" has dragged "Emperor Trajan" into the realm of fantasy, for the two tales are the same. A monarch is abroad fighting (in Scythia or in Parthia). He is many days journey from the sea. He is cleverly sent a seafood far from its natural habitat (an ingenious trick in one instance; an ingenious invention in the other). The story of Trajan is the secondary version, derived from the story of Nicomedes, imposing a pseudo-reality on a comic plot. Mining the same vein as Ptolemy the Quail, or Pseudo-Plutarch, or the author of the *Historia Augusta*, the fraudulent fantasist, now dateable to the second century CE, has created not one but two imaginary Apicii.[31]

True Apicii

Fortunately, there are some real Apicii who must be related to the gourmet. The first is a spectacular surprise, although he has been hiding in plain sight for more than eighty years.

MARCUS APEICIUS

The gourmet Marcus Apicius lived or at least passed his days at Minturnae. One of the stelai at Minturnae names the following among the twelve magistrates it lists: *Erophilus Apeici M(arci) s(ervus)*. The slave's master, Marcus Apeicius, must be the father or grandfather of the gourmet. He appears in distinguished company indeed, for the eleven other slave owners listed with him include a Sulpicius Galba and a Manlius Torquatus, as identified by Münzer, and almost certainly other senators and knights.[32] The Apicii must have owned property or had commercial interests, or both, in the neighborhood of Minturnae. Perhaps it was their hometown.

THE EARLIEST KNOWN APICIUS

Another flesh and blood Apicius appears briefly in Athenaeus, in two notices. First,

> It is remembered among the Romans, according to Posidonius in Book XLIX of his *Histories*, that a certain Apicius outdid all men in his profligacy. This is the Apicius who was also responsible for the exile of Rutilius, who published his *History of Rome* in Greek. We discussed another Apicius, who was also famous for his profligacy in Book I.[33]

A later passing remark must be coupled with this: "According to Rutilius, Sittius was also notorious among the Romans for his addiction to luxury and effeminacy; because [*sic*] we discussed Apicius earlier."[34] The first of these notices occurs in remarks about profligacy (ἀσωτία), a broad term particularly associated with prodigality and the "hopeless" spendthrift. The second comes in a section dealing with luxury (τρυφή). They are strikingly alike, in form as well as in subject, beginning with "among the Romans," glancing at Rutilius Rufus, and ending with reference back to an earlier Apician discussion. This and the syncopation of the second passage suggest a hasty consultation of the same note by Athenaeus. Be that as it may, it is incontrovertible that there really was another, earlier Apicius with a louche reputation, as certified by Posidonius. And we can say just how the man acquired his reputation.

It is difficult to be a prodigal if you do not have money to waste, and this earlier Apicius was rich indeed. He leads us into the legend of P. Rutilius Rufus. In the standard account of his downfall, Rutilius, who had been consul in 105 BCE, served as legate to Q. Scaevola (consul 95), the high-minded governor of the Roman province of Asia, and the two men tried to reform the corrupt administration of the province. The villains of the piece were the rapacious businessmen—merchants, tax collectors, moneylenders, above all the *publicani*—who extorted enormous profits from the empire. Their leaders were Roman knights, who controlled the criminal courts at Rome, holding the threat of prosecution over any provincial governor who opposed their interests. The situation was dangerous, for rebellion was in the air and King Mithridates waited ominously in the wings. Scaevola and Rutilius put their reforms in place, Rutilius remained behind in Asia to implement them, he returned to Rome—and in or just before 92 BCE he was prosecuted by the *publicani* in the extortion court for (of all things) oppressing the provincials. After a restrained and dignified defense, he withdrew *innocentissimus* into exile, a firm Stoic, martyred for refusing to compromise his principles and forever after the great Roman *exemplum* of virtue unjustly condemned. That, at least, is the story that was universally accepted, although other views are possible. Two aspects of it affect our tale.

Apicius was the "cause of" or "responsible for" (i.e., "to blame for") Rutilius' exile. The natural assumption has been that he led the prosecution for, as Badian insisted, "this cannot really mean anything but that Apicius was Rutilius' prosecutor."[35] The tradition is unanimous: it was the knights who brought Rutilius down, and specifically the *publicani*.[36] At a stroke then, we must assume that Apicius was a Roman knight, that he was wealthy, and that he had business interests in the province of Asia.

That he was indeed an important personage in his own right emerges from the second passage in Athenaeus. Rutilius Rufus, the Roman Socrates, wrongfully convicted, withdrew pointedly to Asia itself, the scene of his alleged crime, first to Mytilene, then to Smyrna. There, also pointedly, he adopted Greek dress and later refused Sulla's invitation to return to Rome. But he also took his revenge in an autobiography and a history (which may or may not have been the same work), wherein he indulged a "habit of attacking his personal enemies."[37] It was surely in this work that, as Athenaeus reports, he attacked Sittius for his luxury and his effeminacy and Apicius for his prodigality.[38] That is to say, the first association of the name "Apicius" with "prodigality" did not derive from some general reputation for a degenerate lifestyle "among the Romans." The source of this earlier Apicius' bad reputation was, precisely, the written revenge of a man who had been a prominent enemy and victim in a criminal court.

The legal battle must have been vicious. Witnesses and testimony from the province, honest or not, will have supported the formal charge of extortion. But beyond such evidence there will also have been the standard attacks on the character of the defendant by the prosecutor. These have been cleansed from the Rutilian martyrology, but not quite completely. Cicero lets them slip (*Font.* 38): "That most upright and moderate of men [Rutilius] listened in his trial to a lot that concerned the suspicion of sexual crimes and lustful behavior." So, when he later attacked Apicius as a prodigal, Rutilius Rufus was giving as good as he got, and Apicius had only himself to blame for the martyr's long-term revenge. In short, we have here a rich and allegedly prodigal Apicius, an Apicius who was presumably a knight with commercial interests in the East, alive some generations before our Apicius.

His nomen is not common and, with the exception of Marcus Apeicius, it does not appear on any inscription before the first century CE. Apeicius can be dated only roughly, to some time between the 90s and the 40s BCE. That is to say, he might be a son or grandson of Rutilius' prosecutor, or he might be the man himself. However he may fit into the family tree, we can appreciate that the enormous wealth of the gourmet must have accumulated by inheritance and marriage over four or five generations.[39] However much he may have added to the family fortune, our Apicius was born wealthy and, however reduced his circumstances may have been at the end, he died a wealthy man.

APINIUS TIRO

Over the centuries, the chaos of civil wars at Rome invariably provoked the emergence of local opportunism. Provincial magnates, rural landowners, urban politicians, popular reformers, religious zealots, government officials, soldiers, brigands, condottieri: all took advantage of conflict to graft their own interests onto the larger struggle for power.

The phenomenon is well captured in a confusing passage in Tacitus' *Histories* (3.57, 76–77). Vespasian's armies are advancing against Vitellius in the autumn of 69 CE. A former centurion of the fleet at Misenum tricks it into rebelling against Vitellius: "So much can be done among civil discords by the audacity even of individuals." The prefect of the fleet, Claudius Apollinaris, goes along half-heartedly but

> Apinius Tiro, who had filled the office of praetor, and who then happened to be at Minturnae, offered to head the revolt. By these men the colonies and municipal towns were drawn into the movement, and as Puteoli was

particularly zealous for Vespasian, while Capua on the other hand remained loyal to Vitellius, they introduced their municipal jealousy into the civil war. (3.57)

Against the local magnates and their mariners, Vitellius cleverly sends a former prefect of the fleet, Claudius Julianus, with an urban cohort and a troop of gladiators. Julianus and his men promptly defect to the rebels and the combined force proceeds to occupy Tarracina on its fortified hilltop. Tacitus shifts the scene elsewhere, but returns to Tarracina about a month later. It is now being besieged by Lucius Vitellius, the emperor's brother, while within its walls the two fleet commanders (Apollinaris and Julianus) abandon themselves to a life of dissipation with their gladiators and their sailors. "Apinius Tiro had quitted the place a few days before, and was now, by the harsh exaction of presents and contributions from the towns, adding to the unpopularity rather than the resources of his party."[40] The town is betrayed by a slave, a horrific massacre ensues, Lucius Vitellius has the perfidious ex-prefect Julianus scourged and executed before his eyes. In the chaos the other prefect, Apollinaris, escapes with six ships and sails out of history. Apinius Tiro is likewise never heard of again.

"Apinius" was probably not his name: it is extremely rare; the few who bear it are of no social distinction whatever; and those few are confined to an area far away in the northwest of Italy, at Aquileia and Iulium Carnicum.[41] The man in Tacitus should be not "Apinius" but "Apicius." Justification for the emendation is threefold: geographical, social, and onomastic. Apinius Tiro happens to be at Minturnae when he offers to be the *dux* of the local Flavian rebels: whereas the name Apinius is not found in the inscriptions of Latium or Campania, Apicius is well attested in the region and, as we have seen, two and possibly three earlier generations of the family held property precisely at Minturnae. There are no other Apinii of note in Roman history, while the Apicii had surely been equestrian since the age of Marius: ascent into the senate under the Julio-Claudians would be a natural progression. And there is even an Apicius Tiro of note: the *primus pilus* M. Apicius Tiro, patron and pontiff of his native Ravenna.[42] Moreover, we have another M. Apicius Tiro, owner of one or more *figlinae* that produced tiles and bricks in the area of ancient Atria and that served the towns up the Adige to Ateste and Verona, apparently in the first century CE.[43]

A plausible case can thus be made that the swaggering ex-praetor "Apinius Tiro" in Tacitus was in fact a "(Marcus) Apicius Tiro" who had inherited the social position, the local connections, and some of the still substantial fortune of his gourmandizing ancestor. He should have been rewarded by the new dynasty for his services to the Flavian cause, but he disappears from history.

MARCUS APICIUS QUADRATUS

Sometime under the principate, perhaps in the second century, the "master fishermen and leading leaseholders" of the Neilaion district dedicated a stele to the god Priapos at Parion in the Troad (*IK Parion* 5). The text is in Greek, and Priapos, who is depicted in relief, was both the main deity of Parion and the patron saint of fishermen, but Parion was a Roman colony and the flavor of the text is thoroughly Italian. It names some sixteen men. No fewer than five of them are Publii Avii (two Lysimachi, two Bithydes[?], and a Ponticus— Bithynia and Pontus were not far away), and a sixth Avius is listed without a praenomen. The secretary of the guild is a Secundus, a Menander is identified as the son of a Lucius, a Cassius (Damasippus) is named, and the local priest of Caesar (not a member of the group) is a Lucius Flavius. Most interesting of all for the Italian flavor, one member bears the relatively unusual nomen of Tongilius, while another is an apparently unique Tubellius.[44] And among their number we find a Marcus Apicius Quadratus, the only Apicius found anywhere in the eastern half of the Roman world.

What we see here is the proud governing body of a guild that leases the right to fish in one of the Hellespontine districts of Parion. It is headed by a president, five netmasters, two lookouts, two helmsmen, a cork-loosener, a daywatch, a clerk, and five *lembos*-captains, all of them "shipmates" (συνναῦται).[45] Almost all of them appear to be Roman citizens, or at least to assert their Roman ness, and it is a safe bet that Apicius Quadratus, "netmaster" though he be, was too important a man to be out in the chilly predawn actually tending to nets. Fish—above all tuna and mackerel—streamed through the Hellespont in stupendous numbers, and both Parion and its lessees grew rich off them.[46] Two simple points need hardly be made: as we might expect with an Apicius, Marcus Apicius Quadratus was a wealthy man, and his fortune was based on fish.

To recapitulate: if we strip away legendary accretions, we are left with the following certainties and probabilities, in chronological order. There was an allegedly prodigal Apicius, surely a wealthy knight, who flourished around 90 BCE; there was a slaveowner, M. Apeicius, attested at Minturnae at some time within the period between about 90 and about 40 BCE, who may or may not be the same man; and there was the gourmet M. Gavius Apicius, who resided at Minturnae and who flourished between about 30 BCE and about 30 CE. More speculatively, there was a senator Apicius(?) Tiro who appears briefly at Minturnae in the year 69 CE, and—later and farther to the east—there was a wealthy entrepreneur of the fishing industry, M. Apicius Quadratus.

Power, Money, and Dying Fish

The connoisseur's pursuit of gastronomy was a rich man's pastime, demanding not only the finest comestibles on the market but extensive travel in pursuit of them abroad, a large and varied staff of food preparers, servers, and ancillary workers, and elaborate apparatus, venues, and associated entertainments for the staging of dinners. Apicius' wealth is taken for granted throughout the legend, from the elite company at his banquets in Rome, to the instantly mounted expedition to Africa. When his noble guest Fabius accidentally breaks a large and valuable crystal cup, Apicius urges him to cheer up—surely his friend can do what his servants often do: that is, he is indifferent to the incessant smashing of expensive crystalware. He has "wine-pourers" (plural), he has not "slaves" but their metaphorical synonym "*arguronetoi*," men "bought with silver" (*Suda* M 217). In another interchange, he sets the standard when he and a fellow gourmet compete to buy a large mullet in the market. The victor boasts that he has defeated Apicius himself with a bid of five thousand sesterces for a single fish weighing four and a half pounds.[47] This in an age when a year's pay for a legionary soldier amounted to nine hundred sesterces, that of an auxiliary soldier 450.

A register of the largest private fortunes under the principate offers some twenty-nine items, ranging from four hundred million sesterces down to just under two million. Apicius comes in at number thirteen, with the sum of 110 million. Our source for this is his contemporary Seneca, who knew the value of a sesterce.[48] Even if the figure is a rough approximation, and even though there were many other enormous fortunes that have gone unrecorded, the magnitude is stunning.[49] Apicius was one of the richest men in Roman history, the ancient equivalent of today's billionaires.

Given his immense wealth, he must have been a Roman knight and, as we have seen, he surely came from a line of Roman knights. That he pursued any public career as a senator or in the service of the princeps is unlikely in the extreme. Nevertheless, he certainly moved in the highest circles at Rome. The short list of his known acquaintances speaks for itself, especially when we emphasize one common figure:

- Lucius Aelius Seianus, consul 31 CE, praetorian prefect, married or betrothed to a great-niece or great-great-niece of Augustus.[50]
- Sejanus' cousin, Q. Iunius Blaesus, consul 28 CE, husband of a great-niece of Augustus.[51]
- Paullus Fabius Maximus, consul 11 BCE, or Paullus Fabius Persicus, consul 34 CE—that is, either the husband or the son of a first cousin of Augustus.[52]

- Gaius Caesar, consul 1 CE, grandson and adopted son of Augustus.[53]
- Drusus Caesar, consul 15 and 21 CE, husband of a great-niece of Augustus and his grandson by adoption (see following).
- Tiberius Caesar—Drusus' father—consul five times, successively step-son, son-in-law, and adopted son of Augustus.

Two interactions with Tiberius himself stand on record and were noted in the previous chapter.[54] Though the princeps could be a harsh critic of public and private morals, his tolerance in both Apician anecdotes is remarkable, and the reason is not far to seek, given the delight that the emperor himself took in food and drink. The first anecdote concerns the gastronomic controversy over the merit of cabbage sprout. Pliny advises us to sow it at the autumnal equinox (*NH* 19.137):

> In the next spring after its first sowing it yields sprout-cabbage; this is a sort of small sprout from the actual cabbage stalks, of a more delicate and tender quality, though it was despised by the fastidious taste of Apicius (*Apicii luxuriae. . . . fastiditus*) and owing to him by Drusus Caesar, not without reproof from his father Tiberius.

This reproof expresses not a moralizing reprimand, but a difference of opinion. For most connoisseurs the tender sprout was a delicacy, it was welcome at the feasts described in the poetry of Lucilius and Volumnius Eutrapelus. Tiberius objects to the fastidiousness of those who would reject it. He does not disapprove of Apicius, he engages in debate.

His tone is one of amusement in the second anecdote, related by a disapproving Seneca:

> A mullet of enormous size—why don't I add its weight and provoke the gluttony of some fellows? They say it weighed four and a half pounds—was sent to Tiberius Caesar, who had it carried to the market and put up for sale. "My friends," he said, "unless I am utterly mistaken either Apicius or P. Octavius will buy that mullet." His guess succeeded beyond expectation; they bid against each other, and Octavius won and achieved immense glory among his boon companions, for buying for five thousand sesterces the fish that Caesar had sold and not even Apicius had bought.[55]

Note that Seneca presents a mini-epic: the leader's address to his companions; the contest of two powerful men arranged by a third; the immense glory among his followers of the man who defeated an Apicius and carried off the prize awarded by Caesar.[56] But the anecdote's clever form distracts us from its remarkable context.[57]

Once again, we encounter "the Roman craze for surmullets," memorably described seventy years ago by Alfred Andrews: that is, the gastronomic mania for the red mullet, a mania that lasted well into the second century but that reached the peak of its frenzy precisely in the time of the early principate.[58] The red mullet was a perfectly respectable fish in the diet of the late Republic, eaten and enjoyed but not particularly valued. The craze, a phenomenon apparently of the triumviral and Augustan period, saw rich men paying enormous sums for large mullets, the larger the better. Size, not taste, was the object. Galen, who appreciated the red mullet, was baffled by this obsession, since the flesh of the larger (and presumably older) fish was both less flavorful and tougher.[59]

The sources are consistent: large sums for large mullets. Two pounds was the minimum: red mullets rarely grew (or grow) larger, and Roman efforts to farm them proved unsuccessful, which only increased the pressure on the market. Rich men preferred three-pounders; a four-pounder supposedly sold for 1,200 sesterces, Tiberius' four-and-a-half-pounder for five thousand, a six-pounder for six thousand. Tiberius' stepson Asinius Celer (cos. 38) is variously reported to have spent six thousand or seven thousand or even eight thousand for one mullet—perhaps the precise sum was the subject of debate. But the record price must be the thirty thousand paid for three mullets, again under Tiberius, that is, an average of ten thousand per fish. Five thousand to ten thousand sesterces for a single fish: these were indeed *pretia insana*.[60]

What did the wealthy and competitive epicure want for his money? We read of two goals, both unexpected and startling to modern eyes. Seneca is our guide. In his *Natural Questions*, he discusses fish that live not in open rivers or seas but in caves far below the earth. But he is distracted:

> Are you surprised by this? How much more incredible are the achievements of luxury! How often it fakes or surpasses nature! Fish swim in a tank, and one is caught beneath the table (*sub ipsa mensa*) to be transferred into a course (*mensa*) immediately. A mullet does not seem fresh enough unless it has died in a guest's hand. They are put in glass bowls and served, and as they die people watch their color: death causes many alterations to it, as their breathing struggles. They kill other fish in fish sauce, and season them while still alive. These are the people who think it just a tall story that a fish can live under the earth and be dug up instead of caught. How incredible it would seem to them if they heard of a fish swimming in fish sauce, and being killed not *for* dinner but *at* dinner, after it had been treated like a pet for ages and assaulted the eyes before the gullet![61]

Outraged, Seneca appeals to his reader: "Permit me to set my inquiry aside and to castigate luxury." He launches into a furious excursus that has nothing to do with the subject at hand (fish in caves). Rather, it is a virtuosic expansion of the main points just made. A gourmet's mantra is repeated three times: "There is nothing more beautiful than a dying mullet." Its shifting colors are described again. It must die on the platter. To that end, couriers have rushed it alive from the sea, the road cleared before them. The gloating diner holds the glass *vivarium* in his hands, he watches the fish swim about, he praises it. It is removed from the bowl and the connoisseurs, *ut quisque peritior est*, appraise the progress of its death, the brilliant red, the bright blue, the final pallor. "I cannot stop myself from using words recklessly from time to time and crossing the boundary of propriety: in the tavern they are not satisfied with teeth, and stomach, and mouth; they are gluttons with their eyes as well. But, to return to my subject."

Seneca's contemporary, the Elder Pliny, likewise shifts into moralizing outrage when he comes to discuss the red mullet in his encyclopedia:

> The great men of the gullet (*proceres gulae*) report that a dying mullet shows a large variety of changing colors, turning pale with a complicated modification of blushing scales, at all events if it is looked at when contained in glass. Marcus Apicius, who had a natural gift for every ingenuity of luxury, thought it specially desirable for them to be killed in a fish-sauce made of their companions (*sociorum garo*)—for this thing too has found a nickname— and for fish-paste (*alecem*) to be devised from their liver.[62]

Different though their texts may look at first glance, it is clear that Seneca and Pliny drew on a single, now lost, common source. Outraged, both veer from sober scientific reports to discuss the same two offensive uses of one particular fish. The appeal of the red mullet lies not in its preparation and consumption but, perversely, in its passage from life to death actually at the dinner table. Although they focus on different details, Seneca and Pliny present the same two recherché methods of killing. In the first, death is turned into spectacular dinner theater or, rather, dinner as theater, a riveting *son et lumière* as the fish thrashes and gasps and changes colors in its death throes in a glass bowl and the sophisticated audience discusses the finer points of its demise. In the second, less flamboyant but just as shocking and more theatrical, we have the staged tableau of a fish paradoxically drowning in a sea of fish sauce. Eating and digestion are irrelevant. The offence is one of presentation, death as a show for *oculi gulosi*.

When we posit a common written source expressing indignation at a particular gastronomic fad, there is an outstanding candidate for its author, a man whose works were certainly known to Seneca and Pliny: Apion of Alexandria, learned polymath and prize-winning poet, outrageous charlatan and shameless self-promoter. Apion flourished under Tiberius and is last heard of as head of the notorious embassy to Gaius in 40 CE. Among his astonishingly varied works, we know of one entitled *On the Luxury of Apicius,* and we may even have a couple of exiguous fragments from it.[63] He was certainly a con-temporary of Apicius and he was fond of tales artfully told, some of them true.

Apion or not, what follows from the existence of this common source?

Pliny tells us that the *proceres gulae* report the mullet's colorful death. Then immediately thereafter, that Apicius thought that slaying fish in fish sauce and making a paste from their livers were excellent ideas. A series of four hypotheses may be derived from Pliny's description: that the *proceres gulae* were Pliny's sources, the *writers* who took eating and drinking seriously, M. Ambivius, Menas Licinius, C. Matius, and perhaps others;[64] that when M. Apicius expressed the opinions reported by Pliny, about *garum* and *al(l)ec,* he did so in writing; that Apicius wrote not a work just on fish but one devoted to luxury in general, which is to say that Apion's *On the Luxury of Apicius* should be understood as *On the "Luxury" of Apicius;*[65] and that a joke in that work has gone unnoticed.

The very best of fish sauces was agreed to be the one known simply as the *garum Sociorum.* Pliny elaborates elsewhere (*NH* 31.93):

> Nowadays, the most praised [*garum*] of all is made from the mackerel [*scomber*] in the fisheries of New Carthage—it is called "of the partners" [*sociorum*]—a thousand sesterces buying about two *congii.* Almost no other liquid [*liquor*] except perfumes has fetched a higher price, conferring fame on nations.

The precious liquid from Spain aroused the sermonizing wrath of Seneca and the poetic admiration of Martial: it was stunningly expensive.[66] At a thousand sesterces for about six liters, a small amphora would also cost more than the annual remuneration of a legionary soldier. The "garum of the partners" was for the super-rich. It also retained its prestige for centuries: from 79 CE, two amphorae survive at Pompeii, one large and one small, bearing the inscription *g. socciorum* [*sic*]; early in the third century, Julius Africanus observes that it was the best garum of all; Ausonius appreciates it late in the fourth century.[67]

Here we should pause to savor the joke. Pliny tells us that Marcus Apicius "thought it specially desirable for [mullets] to be killed in a fish-sauce made of their companions (*sociorum garo*)—for this thing too has found a nickname." The clever, cold-hearted wordplay is surely Apicius' own. Mullets die in a sauce made of other mullets. It is therefore a true *garum sociorum,* a sauce made of its "partners."

This elaborately theatrical culinary pun, its physical embodiment, precisely fits the taste of that other great gastronome, the former slave of Maecenas,

C. Pompeius Trimalchio.[68] It could be slipped unnoticed into the tableaux vivants conjured up by Trimalchio during his dinner party, offering foods elaborately disguised as something they are not and always with a clever point. In fact, the "partners' sauce" *has* been slipped unnoticed into Trimalchio's repertoire. A platter is brought in heaped with birds, sows' udders, and a rabbit decked out with wings to look like Pegasus. "We also noticed," Encolpius recalls, "four Marsyases around the corners of the tray. From their wineskins peppered garum flowed over fish, who swam as if in a channel."[69] These fish seem to be alive, but even better is a dead fish in fish sauce presented in the predecessor of the *Cena Trimalchionis*, Horace's *Cena Nasidieni* (*Serm.* 2.8.42–3): a moray eel is brought in, "stretched out on a platter among swimming shrimp." That the fish is dead is assured by the impossibility of it swimming on a platter, by the known connotation of *porrecta* with "stretched out dead," and by the anxious host's assurance that it was caught pregnant because its flesh would deteriorate *post partum*. The sauce consists of oil, wine, vinegar, pepper, and garum—that is, a *garum sociorum* around 30 BCE.

Fish Sauce and Beyond

A fragment of the top of a small, one-handled amphora found in Lyon was published in 1987. Like many amphorae, it bore a *titulus pictus*, one of the tens of thousands of graffiti that standardly record various details about the contents and the people involved in the manufacture, transport, and sale of those contents. In this case, we have two words, horizontal, one above the other: *Liq Apic*. To their right, and at a right angle to them vertically: *G Rufi*. This is taken to represent the genitive of the name Gaius Rufus, who may have been the manufacturer of the contents, or an agent or merchant involved in its handling, or the ultimate owner of the product. The editors note that this type of "amphorette" is common around Lyon and of local manufacture. But what it contained, *liq*(*uamen*)—the abbreviation is standard—was not local. Fish sauce came from the sea and, as happened with many products, it must have been shipped up the Rhône from the Mediterranean, decanted at Lyon from larger into smaller containers, and transshipped into the interior. Very rarely, the *liquamen* is given a maker's mark, surely one of distinction. The editors suggest, rightly, that *Apic* may be expanded as *Apicianum*. The *titulus* is unique, but it is enough.[70]

The study of the production, trade, and consumption of processed fish in antiquity has produced over the last three decades a scholarly bibliography of astonishing size, complexity, and often fascination.[71] From this, we may pick out several themes relevant here. Broadly speaking, we can discern two major and interwoven strands of research, the gastronomic and the commercial— that is, the social and the economic.

As to the gastronomic, the meanings, natures, and uses of the various fish sauces have been debated and the ancient processes for producing them have been carefully reconstructed in the light of similar modern processes. The sauces were a by-product of the enormous salted fish industry. Fish parts (innards, heads, tails) or whole small fish such as sardines or anchovies were fermented in salt over a two- or three-month period, reduced to a paste or sauce for cooking or dressing. Four names dominate our sources: garum, the generic term for the sauce; *allec*, the undissolved leftover (a paste); *muria*, the brine (a liquid); and *liquamen* (a substance whose original meaning is uncertain), which eventually replaced garum as the generic term for fish sauce. Herbs, spices, fruits, wine, vinegar, and olive oil might be added, processes were as complex and individual as those of modern vineyards, and quality and quantity varied widely to appeal to tastes mass or refined. One fundamental fact is clear: it was a staple of their diet. As commentators have noted, fish sauce is an ingredient in a startling three-quarters of the recipes in the cookbook of "Apicius," around 350 out of about 465. Or, from another angle: with 412 instances, *liquamen* is the third most common word in the cookbook, after *et* and *piper*, while garum and its compounds appear forty-three times: a diet dominated by fish sauce and pepper. Galen, drawing on previous medical writers, and reflected in all subsequent medical writings, lists in the three books of his *De alimentorum facultatibus* scores of foodstuffs to be paired with health-giving fish sauce—grains, fruits, herbs, vegetables, weeds, nuts, snails, pig's trotters, coddled eggs, seafood, and, of course, all sorts of fish—and he offers perhaps fifty recipes for their preparation.

Equally fundamental, high and low, Romans liked the flavor. Bad garum has given the sauce an undeservedly bad name. It might stink, it might taste horrible, and it might look disgusting, but reconsideration of the ancient sources in the last few decades has corrected this extreme misconception: bad sauce was simply bad sauce, and moralists and satirists found it metaphorically useful for expressing disapproval in terms of putrefaction. Even good garum might not appeal to modern Western tastes, but careful reconstruction has produced a variety of interesting and palatable sauces comparable to contemporary Eastern fish sauces.[72] Indeed, as with modern vintages, the best were highly prized, their quality proudly marked in literature and *tituli picti* as *primum, optimum, castum, vetus, excellens, praecellens*, and the like. The best was the flower, *gari flos, liquaminis flos, muriae flos* (but never *allicis flos*), even the flower of the flower, *flos floris*. Often, this was identified with a name, usually in the genitive and usually that of the manufacturer. Outstanding examples are offered by the extensive, complex, and well-documented operations of the wealthy A. Umbricius Scaurus, the leading but by no means the only wholesaler of garum at Pompeii. Not only do several amphorae survive with inscriptions advertising the flower of his garum or his *liquamen,* visitors entering one of the atria in Umbricius' mansion would see depictions in the mosaic floor of one-handled amphorae (*urcei*), proudly ranged at the four corners of the *impluvium,* each with a different *titulus pictus:* one reads g(*arum*) f(*los*) sco[*m*(*bri*)] / *ex offi*[*ci*] / *na Scau* / *ri;* another simply *liqua*(*minis*) / *flos.*[73] But the very peak of fish sauce, the best of the best, did not need to boast that it was the flower, the "garum of the partners" that we encountered above.

The *Luxury* of Apicius

In the fourth book of "Apicius," we are offered a brief recipe for a dish of small fry, *patina de apua* (4.2.11). This is followed by a dish of small fry *without* small fry, *patina de apua sine apua* (4.2.12):

> Flake the flesh of fish, either grilled or boiled, in sufficient quantity to fill the dish you choose. Pound pepper and a little rue, pour on sufficient *liquamen* and a little oil and stir the fish together in the dish with raw eggs so that a smooth emulsion is produced. Gently place sea anemones on top so that they do not mix in with the egg mixture. Place in a gentle rising heat so that they do not sink into the mixture. When they have dried out sprinkle with ground pepper and serve. At the table no one will know what they are munching on.

We are back with our friend King Nicomedes, the supposed dupe of the turnip cut into small pieces, stewed or boiled in oil, and served up convincingly as small fry, ἀφύη.[74] But here, in Latin, we have the *real* recipe for them, imitation *apua,* a much more elegant affair, slowly and carefully cooked, and involving proper ingredients. Rather than the common turnip, the deceptive edible is sea anemone (*urtica marina*). This signals the committed gastronome for, like its counterpart on land (the stinging nettle), the sea anemone could be painful to collect, and it should be harvested only in winter, as students of Aristotle would know, not in summer.[75] The preparation is thoughtful, appropriately taking an actual seafood and cooking it over but not in a fish stew, to absorb the fishy flavor. Serve the pseudo-*apuae* after drying, and no one will know they are not small fry.

The recipe fits into gastronomic tradition in another way. There is a long habit, parodied in the *Cena Trimalchionis,* of presenting theatrical versions of standard dishes, cleverly dressing up basic pork or fish, say, as something they are not.[76] They might embody an elaborate symbol or, as here, merely a clever deception. But there is a striking inversion in this recipe: sea anemones, with the complicating factors of difficult harvesting and seasonal restriction, must have been much more expensive than a common netful of real small fry, such as sardines or anchovies. What we have is a rich man's joke. The counterfeit version costs more than the real and should from its preparation alone be much tastier than the simple dish it pretends to be. But no one will know—unless you reveal it to your astonished guests, and they applaud politely. Or perhaps it will remain a secret joke, shared only with those who have read your book.

And the recipe fits into gastronomic tradition in yet another way. Archestratus himself had used the blunt language of comedy in his epic poem: "Value as shit all small fry except the Athenian kind." And that must be caught fresh in the Bay of Phaleron. Rhodian is also acceptable, but it too has to be local. And if you must eat it, buy some sea anemones, mix them with the ἀφύη, and bake them together in a frying pan.[77] In short, fresh and local would make the price of the only acceptable ἀφύη skyrocket with travel costs, unless you lived in Attica or on Rhodes, and even then, the gourmet poet continued, you must add sea anemone for flavor! Pseudo-Apicius thus places himself in a literary tradition. He plays on Archestratus, using the very ingredient the master had prescribed for mixture with ἀφύη (if you really must eat it), and cleverly turning it into small fry itself. He also surely displays his awareness of the deception in Euphron's comedy, mixing the turnip trickery of the slave cook into his own subtle response to Archestratus.

We may begin to suspect that a sophisticated and ironic work by—who else?—the real Apicius lies behind the truncated text of Pseudo-Apicius. And that that work in turn entered the gastronomic tradition itself, witness the later parodist who inserted Apicius into his own joke, substituting him for the cook as the creator of the deceptive small fry.

The surviving cookbook attributed to Apicius, its text found in two ninth-century manuscripts, is an enigma. Everyone would agree that it is, in fact, not the work of the notorious gastronome, but rather a compilation of recipes put together in late antiquity, sometime around the year 400 CE, and that it has a complex and uncertain genealogy. Beyond that, all is speculation. It was long assumed that Apicius wrote two works, one a book of general recipes, title unknown, and one devoted to sauces, something like de iuscellis or de condituris, but their existence is dubious.

In 1927, E. Brandt published his "attempt to solve the Apicius question," in which he firmly established the now canonical date of the work as the later fourth century, which is surely correct.[78] Whether and where his attempt otherwise succeeded is debatable, but many of his arguments remain valid, he offered rich comparanda, and he defined issues and possibilities clearly. The core of the work that we have is an older book of recipes, presumed to be Apicius' first-century work, but there are obvious lacunae and equally obvious additions until about the end of the second century. Brandt also argued that some of the surviving work came precisely from Apicius' book on sauces, counting some 138 recipes devoted to the creation of sauces, about one-third of the total. All of this, roughly three-fifths of the surviving work, catered to the high-end readers of Apicius, so the compiler added others that would have a more quotidian appeal from a variety of other sources, books in Latin and Greek on agriculture, a Greek book on diet, medical writings, and others. The result is a messy and not very attractive collection and arrangement of recipes, ranging from the slapdash to the precise, its title unknown (*De re coquinaria* is an invention of the fifteenth century), cobbled together by an unknown compiler who reveals almost nothing about himself, and falsely attributed to the famous Apicius who had lived three centuries earlier.

9

Seianus Augustus

But what of Remus' mob? They are followers of Fortune, as always, and hate
those who are condemned. This same crowd, if Nortia had supported her
Etruscan, if the aged emperor had been smothered off his guard, would be
hailing Sejanus as Augustus this very moment.

—JUVENAL[1]

IS THERE A MORE colorless villain in Roman history than Lucius Aelius Seianus? Demonized after his headlong fall and horrific death in the autumn of 31
CE, he is reduced by our sources to a paper-thin figure, a monster with but one
feature, his boundless, all-consuming lust for power. *Sejanus, His Fall*: such is the
title both of Ben Jonson's well-known play, first performed in 1603; it is also
the title of what is easily the best modern introduction to the whole matter of
Sejanus, A. R. Birley's paper published in 2007.[2] In the aftermath, relatives,
friends, and associates followed him to the grave, but then came the ultimate
historical indignity: he disappeared into the history books. That is, with the
single brilliant exception of the passage in this chapter's epigaph, posterity lost
interest. Sejanus did not become a general exemplum for the vanity of power, the
mutability of fortune, the inevitability of retribution, nor was any subsequent
villain compared with him.[3] Modern historical scholarship has compounded
the injury by confining itself largely to the questions that interested Tacitus,
Suetonius, and Cassius Dio: intense speculation about factional strife at
Rome, from 20 CE onward; extravagant conjecture about the nature and extent of Sejanus' conspiracy against Tiberius (if it occurred at all); and bewildering reconstruction of his kinships by blood and marriage, kinships that
were rendered particularly contentious by the publication of two precious but
frustratingly lacunose inscriptions in the last century. In all of this, it is impossible to see just what is *interesting* about the man. Were the senate, knights,
people, and armies of Rome held quiescent by fear and self-interest alone?

And what of Tiberius Caesar? The First Citizen was notoriously a man of great intelligence, deep suspicions, and formidable culture. How could he, of all people, be enthralled by such a cipher, such a man without qualities? Sejanus is a mystery.

———

The familiar story is told quickly. His equestrian father, Seius Strabo, was prefect of Augustus' *praetorium*, his mother came of a senatorial family with close consular connections, and he had "brothers" who were actually consuls. When Tiberius acceded to sole power in 14 CE, he made Sejanus joint-prefect with Strabo, and the son soon became sole prefect when his father was transferred to Egypt, presumably in the year 15 CE. We hear little about him in the first years of Tiberius' principate, when our narratives are dominated by Tiberius' tortured relations with Germanicus, his nephew and son by adoption. But Germanicus died mysteriously in 19 CE. In 20 or 23 (the year is uncertain), Sejanus is first noted as markedly increasing his power through the concentration of the praetorian guard into a single camp on the outskirts of Rome. Previously, they had been distributed in barracks throughout the city, and how actively they were employed we do not know, but this was considered a particularly sinister moment by Tacitus and later historians: at ten thousand men, the praetorian guard was the only significant military force in Italy. Also in 23 CE, Drusus Caesar, Tiberius' remaining son and no friend of Sejanus, died; long afterward, the prefect would be charged with arranging the young man's demise. It was then, in the tenth year of their association, that he allegedly began his drive to seduce and eventually to supplant the bereaved First Citizen.

The standard narrative of his drive to domination between 23 and 31 CE has three interwoven strands.

First, the corruption and destruction of Tiberius' relatives and their supporters. The initial step entails luring Drusus' wife into an affair. Drusus is done away with and then, gradually and systematically, the machiavellian Sejanus roots out opposition within Tiberius' family through the seduction, harassment, confinement, exile, and judicial murder of his nearest relatives, most notably of Agrippina, the widow of Germanicus, and of their two older sons, Nero and Drusus Caesar. And, likewise during the years after 23 CE, Sejanus' sinister agents remove the adherents of Germanicus' family through a series of trials for treason and other crimes. These stories dominate our surviving narratives, but will be considered here only in passing.[4]

Second, the accumulation and dispensation of patronage on a massive scale. As early as 23 CE, to judge by what we are told, the man acted as a princeps himself. Dio assures us that the leading men of the city, including the consuls, attended his *salutatio* at dawn in that year, both to submit private requests for transmission to Tiberius and to discuss public business; while at the end of his account of the year 28 CE, Tacitus draws a vivid, Juvenalian caricature of senators, knights, and plebs laying siege to Sejanus in Campania, whenever he and Tiberius crossed over from their stronghold on Capri. They are spurned by him as "that filth in the forecourt," but they lie in wait in fields or on the shore by night and by day, and fawn on his doorkeepers until turned away.[5] Offices and honors are the prime pursuits. Tacitus assures us that, in 23 CE, Sejanus indulged in canvassing for senatorial office (for others) and bestowed honors and provinces on his clients. This is probably anachronistic, but by 28, the only way for a man to win the consulship was said to be through Sejanus. Juvenal likewise has him assigning curule chairs and armies, and examples of Sejanus' influence in promoting his adherents are scattered throughout Tacitus' pages.[6]

But above all, third, there is the tightening grip on Tiberius himself, which gives his prefect the power to harm his enemies and to promote his supporters and his own interests. Allegedly, Sejanus is the one who persuades the sixty-six-year-old princeps to withdraw from Rome in 26 CE, never to return. And in that fateful year 26, the year of Tiberius' withdrawal, Sejanus' remarkable good fortune intervenes.

As the pair move south toward Campania, they stop at the grand and isolated imperial villa at Spelunca, on the coast about seventy-five miles south of Rome, below Terracina (Tac. 4.59). There they dine in the splendidly appointed seaside cave for which the villa was named. In the course of the banquet, a sudden rock fall crushes guests and servants to death. Soldiers rush to the rescue, to discover their prefect on his hands and knees, shielding his master with his body. From that moment on, Tiberius trusts him absolutely, and in the following year the princeps settles his headquarters on Capri.

Thereafter, men begin to treat Sejanus in Rome as if he were already First Citizen himself, dismissing the reclusive Tiberius as a mere "nesiarch," the lord of an island.[7] Tacitus believes that it was the solitude of the island that attracted Tiberius, its lack of harbors and the ease with which his guards could control the few landing places. In retreat, he could enjoy the mild climate, the beauty, and supposedly the secret vices that he had so long concealed. While he was resident in Rome, Sejanus had already worked on his suspicious nature. Now, Tacitus suggests, the distance and the solitude made Sejanus' charges against his enemies even more plausible. The man who had saved his master's life at the risk of his own now worked to destroy his master's family and their friends. And whatever his influence had been before Tiberius' withdrawal from the capital, it was surely now, from 27 CE on, as the main conduit between Capri and Rome, that his power increased enormously, in terms of both the patronage exercised and the actual honors and offices accumulated for himself.

In 23 CE, to the great annoyance of his son Drusus, Tiberius took to calling Sejanus his "assistant in command" (*adiutor imperii*). But by 30, he has become his "partner in toil" (*socius laborum*), "my Sejanus," "a part of my own body and soul."[8] He is involved with and perhaps engaged to Tiberius' niece and former daughter-in-law. His images, along with those of Tiberius are displayed, sacrificed to, and even worshipped around the empire.

On January 1 in the year 31 CE, Sejanus entered upon the consulship: henceforth, the year would be known by his name, linked forever with that of his colleague, the long absent Tiberius Caesar. Since his accession in 14, Tiberius had held that office only twice, each time as colleague with one of his sons and heirs presumptive. Indeed, in the last two or three years, Tiberius showered a vast and unprecedented array of glittering honors on his Sejanus, culminating in the grant of proconsular *imperium*, perhaps after he stepped down from the consulship on May 1. Now, in the early autumn of 31, Sejanus looked forward to sharing the ultimate prize, the tribunician power, with Tiberius, which would give him the essential authority, the legitimacy, to run the republic. With that, he would, in name as in fact, become coruler of the Roman world.

Dio's narrative of the events of October 18, 31 CE is enthralling: swift, colorful, convincingly detailed, it surely transmits an eyewitness account. Tiberius has been playing a puzzling game of cat-and-mouse with Sejanus for some months, alternating praise, rewards, and promises with puzzling checks and oblique snubs, but now the end is in sight.[9] A letter has arrived from Capri, and its bearer, Sutorius Macro, assures the anxious Sejanus at dawn that he brings the tribunician power for him. Thrilled, Sejanus rushes into the Temple of Apollo on the Palatine, where the senate now meets to confer the ultimate power on fortune's favorite. The senators cheer him wildly, and settle down to listen to the words of Tiberius. The epistle is rambling and verbose. The cheering dies down as they listen to irrelevant matters, interspersed with slight criticism of Sejanus. Increasingly puzzled, the senators grow nervous and men begin to move away from him, but he sits unconcerned by the triviality of the complaints, thinking each one no matter of great concern. The presiding consul summons him to step forward as the letter continues, but he ignores him, not out of contempt but because he is not accustomed to having orders addressed to him. The consul raises his voice, points at him, calls him a second and a third time: "Sejanus, come here." "Me? You are calling me?" He stands and the prefect of the night watch, acting on secret orders, comes to stand next to him.

The letter concludes ominously, with the request that two of his closest associates be punished and that Sejanus himself be held under guard. A firestorm of abuse erupts. Stunned, the great man is led out of the senate. A mob attacks him in the street, he is mocked and beaten and, most significantly, we are told that "they hurled down, beat down and dragged down all of his images" before his eyes. Later that same day, encouraged by the anger of the people and by the conspicuous absence of his soldiers, the senate meets to condemn him, and he is executed. "His body was cast down the Steps [of Mourning, outside the prison], where the rabble abused it for three whole days and afterwards threw it into the river."[10]

We will never be able to reassemble the prefect's *disiecta membra* into a coherent biography.[11] His Fall is everything. The narratives of Tacitus and Dio are wholly confined to the monster's misdeeds, real or alleged, the deep intrigues, the crafty machinations, the subtle manipulation of his master: it is superficial, monotonous, and thoroughly distorted by the outcome. Any talents and accomplishments are lost or subverted, goals and motivation remain controversial, personality is nonexistent. The shock of October 18 was enormous: almost everyone was taken by surprise. But how did they perceive the man on October 17, when he seemed poised to grasp a share of supreme power? "Do not think of Sejanus' last day, but of his sixteen years."[12]

————

From the beginning, he had *magna auctoritas* with Tiberius. Tiberius advanced him to *summa potentia*.[13] Not formal, sanctioned *potestas*, but naked *potentia*: the phrase *summa potentia* is found in Suetonius, but Tacitus uses the simple noun *potentia* five times in connection with Sejanus and his schemes. What was the source and significance of this *potentia*, the brute power to do good or ill?

The age was tremendously uncertain, poised between two worlds, the dying Republic and the nascent monarchy. Despite the anachronisms through which we express events, when Augustus died in 14 CE, there was no "throne" to be behind, no "dynasty," no "court," certainly no "emperor" to "succeed," no "princes of the blood" or "heirs apparent." Indeed, there was no office of "praetorian prefect," if we think of it as it developed over the following centuries, with its later array of military, legal, and financial powers. There was a princeps, surrounded by his family, the *domus Caesarum*, which enjoyed certain public honors and privileges. The reluctant First Citizen, Tiberius, who held preemptive military *imperium*, employed a private agent, Sejanus, to direct his *praetorium*. For the last five years of his career, that agent had the inestimable advantage of an absentee employer whose life he had saved, dramatically, and who trusted him implicitly. It is startling to recall that, up until the last year of his life, Sejanus held no official power at all. It was only after he had entered on the consulship on January 1, 31 CE, that it came with a rush: the consular *imperium*, followed by some form of proconsular *imperium*, and the hope for its partner, the *tribunicia potestas*, dangled before him by Tiberius Caesar.[14] Indeed, Sejanus was not even a senator before he became consul. For sixteen years and more he was a knight in charge of the *praetorium: praetorii praefectus.*[15]

Of course, before 31, the *potentia* of Sejanus lay in his proximity to—and control of access to—the *potestas* of Tiberius, but there are two important qualifications to its definition.

First, it is striking how little we hear of the Praetorian Guard in the narratives of the 20s and 30s CE. We may think of their commander as "the all-powerful praetorian prefect," and, of course, the soldiers were always a threat—the common source of Tacitus (4.2.1) and Dio (57.19.6) found their concentration into a single camp a particularly sinister step—but there is no record that Sejanus ever had *any* military career. He may have travelled with Gaius Caesar on his eastern tour between 1 BCE and 4 CE (though that is mere conjecture) and he certainly accompanied Drusus Caesar to Pannonia in 14 CE, but there is nothing about experience of either combat or command, no anecdotes, no praise, no blame. The guards are mostly absent from the tale of his machinations at Rome and, however much he cultivated them, they were remarkably quiescent at his fall. It was only after his death that they rioted, not because of their love for Sejanus but, we are told, because their loyalty had been suspected and the night watch had been preferred to them in suppressing him: if anything, this indignation suggests that they did not much care for their commander, at least in retrospect. As Lawrence Keppie observed, in these early days, the prefects were not so much prefects of the praetorian cohorts as prefects of the headquarters: "Scholars should not therefore be surprised if they were not men of high military calibre; partly, even chiefly, the job was administrative. The prefects took charge of the administration of the *praetorium*, and were responsible for the emperor's security, whether he was in Rome or on campaign. In diplomas, the close link between the emperor and the cohorts is emphasized; the prefect is not mentioned. The cohort on duty at the Palatine looked to the emperor for the nightly password."[16] There is thus no reason at all to conceive of Sejanus as the bluff military man or the idolized commander, no reason to suppose that he was anything but an efficient administrator.

On the other hand, his position at the heart of the aristocracy has surely been undervalued. This is partly because of Tacitus' sneers about the municipal adulterer, the knight polluting the nobility of the *domus Caesarum* (an attitude not shared by Tiberius Caesar), and partly because of the prosopographical tangles and uncertainties in identifying his relatives by blood and marriage, questions raised by those problematic inscriptions and by the enigmatic description of his kin by Velleius Paterculus. But it should suffice to emphasize what Velleius tells us (2.127.3): on his mother's side he "embraced"—*complexum*, a notably vague term—ancient families that were distinguished by public honors (that is, senators and *nobiles*); and he had brothers, cousins, and an uncle who had reached the consulship. All of this information can be confirmed.[17] His father, L. Seius Strabo, Velleius describes as a (or the) leader (*princeps*) of the equestrian order, an apt designation for one of Augustus' closest agents, prefect of his *praetorium* and then prefect of Egypt under Tiberius, and husband in his second marriage of a great patrician lady.[18] And Sejanus himself was married to a woman of senatorial family; he himself may have adopted a son from another senatorial family; and he himself was surely adopted, most likely by another princeps of the equestrian order, a one-time prefect of Egypt.[19] That is to say, whatever the precise identities of his kin, it is quite misconceived to assume that a municipal adulterer, a mere knight, controlled the aristocracy by fear and favor alone. In the stunned reaction to the letter from Tiberius on October 18, 31 CE, even as senators denounced Sejanus, the consul in charge was still afraid to put anything to a general vote, let alone to propose execution. There might yet be opposition and uproar, "for," says Dio (58.10.8), "he had many relatives and friends." As Ronald Syme put it succinctly, "The 'potentia' of Aelius Seianus is intertwined about the very roots of the dynasty."[20]

Where he was brilliantly innovative was in the creation and development of an image to convey his power. As was recognized some time ago, from correspondences among our surviving authors, we can conclude, "that during the twenties Sejanus cultivated an 'official image' of himself, modeled perhaps on Agrippa, the archetypal man of *labor* . . . It was the image of an indispensable state servant, just the kind that the diffident Tiberius would appreciate."[21]

Twin virtues are the heart of the image. Tacitus disparages the man's *industria ac vigilantia* (4.1.3). Velleius praises his *labor* and the fact that he is *animo exsomnis* (2.127.4): in other words, just as in Tacitus, industry and vigilance. And this pairing of industry and vigilance crops up elsewhere, in words assigned by Tacitus to the two protagonists. Sejanus' success in containing the blaze at the Theater of Pompey in 22 CE is attributed to *labor vigilantiaque*, apparently in a speech delivered by Tiberius to the senate (3.72.3). And in a letter addressed in 25 CE to Tiberius, begging for a marriage connection with him, Sejanus claims, in Tacitus' summation (4.39.2), that "he had never pleaded for the glitter of honors; he preferred lookouts and toils" (*excubias ac labores*).

A third quality is added to this constant industry and constant vigilance in the service of the state: the man's noble serenity, the grace with which he fulfils his duties. This is a virtue in Velleius but a mask in Tacitus, whose account reads almost like a parody of Velleius.[22]

Fourth, there is his becoming modesty, as incarnated in the refusal of rewards. Again, a great virtue to Velleius: others estimated his worth far higher than he did himself. But Tacitus twists the knife in the letter seeking marriage with the widow of Drusus Caesar, by having Sejanus immodestly call attention to his own modest refusal.

In short, tireless industry and constant vigilance, wrapped in noble serenity and becoming modesty. The real, supreme reward for all of his service was the two new, unofficial titles created for him by Tiberius himself, bland and imposing, and in the best Augustan tradition of presenting new wine in old bottles: *adiutor imperii*, in circulation by the year 23 CE and superseded around 30 by advancement to the much superior *socius laborum*.[23]

This extraordinary, indeed unique, position, is best appreciated not through actions but through images, not through Sejanus' alleged abuses of power, but through the progression of rewards, the honors and distinctions bestowed on him in the decade from 22 to 31 CE:

- In 22, Tiberius praised him for limiting the damage caused by fire to the Theater of Pompey. The senate responded by voting him a statue at the theater, according to Tacitus; Dio adds (under the year 23) that it was of bronze and set up by Tiberius. The historian Cremutius Cordus, witty but unwise, remarked, "Now the theater is truly dead." But many private citizens followed the senate's lead and erected statues, while the prefect was publicly praised by speakers before people and senate.[24]
- In 28, for reasons unrecorded, the senate voted to erect an Altar of Clemency and an Altar of Friendship, with statues of Tiberius and Sejanus flanking each. The programmatic implications of these two virtues for the partners in power would be hard to miss. There is no record that the altars were ever dedicated but K. K. Jeppesen has argued compellingly that the portly middle-aged figure standing in military garb to the left in the Grand Camée de France is none other Sejanus himself. The man faces right. Central to the cameo is Tiberius seated as Jupiter, with his mother Livia sitting at his side. Both face left. Standing between the princeps and "Sejanus," and physically binding the two men together, is a female figure tentatively identified by Jeppesen as Amicitia: that is, we may have precisely the concatenation of figures decreed by the senate in 28 CE, the year to which Jeppesen dates the cameo on other grounds. Be that as it may, by 28, Tiberius had settled on Capri, and the senators added to their vote a formal plea that he and Sejanus allow people to see them in Rome.[25]
- In 29, the senate voted to celebrate Sejanus' birthday as a public holiday, and it decreed yet more statues to him: so both Dio and Suetonius, the latter adding that the statues were of gold. The knights, the tribes, and leading citizens followed suit with statues beyond number. Dio continues: Tiberius and Sejanus each received separate embassies from

the senate, the knights, and the people as represented by their tribunes and plebeian aediles. People prayed and sacrificed for each, and swore by their Fortunes.[26]

- In 30, while already preparing to undermine him (so we are told), Tiberius honored Sejanus with designation to the consulship, and he continued to speak and write of him as the "partner" of his labors and "my Sejanus." In response, "people" (unspecified) set up bronze statues to both men everywhere, wrote their names together in documents, and brought gilded chairs into the theater to honor them. The senate voted that they should be consuls together every five years, and that they should be welcomed in the same manner whenever either came to Rome. "And in the end," Dio concludes, "they sacrificed to the images of Sejanus as they did to those of Tiberius" (58.4.4, 11.2). It was probably in 30, too, or possibly in 29, that the image of Sejanus was added to the *signa* of each legion.[27] In his introductory sketch of the prefect, Tacitus had noted that Tiberius allowed his images to be worshipped (*coli*) in theaters and forums and in the headquarters (*principia*) of the legions (4.2.3): surely anachronistic for 23 CE, but true in 30.
- Then, in 31, he became ordinary consul with his good friend Tiberius, *consulatus socius*, and he received proconsular *imperium* and the promise of tribuncian power. By that time, he was also betrothed, possibly even married, to a close relative of the princeps.[28]

Over this decade, the statues are a key indicator of the accumulation of honors and the growing proximity to the princeps: one in 22 CE, perhaps two more in 28, but then an explosion. Repeatedly, Tiberius praises his friend, the senate responds with statues, ordinary citizens follow suit, and Sejanus rapidly acquires the divine aura associated with the images of the *domus Caesarum*. In 29 CE: gilt statues, a sign of cult;[29] prayers and sacrifices *for* the imperial pair; and prayers to their Fortunes. In 30 CE: gilt chairs brought into the theater, another sign of cult, though ambiguous; and prayers *to* their statues, now included even among legionary *signa*. Tacitus speaks of their images in theaters, forums, and camps, and Suetonius of their inclusion among the standards. The step from sacrificing for Sejanus to sacrificing to him is of course enormous, and not only did others everywhere sacrifice both for and to his image, Dio even paints for us a bizarre picture of Sejanus sacrificing to a statue of himself in the last year of his life.[30] No wonder then that Juvenal devotes no fewer than eight brilliant lines precisely to the destruction and melting of his ubiquitous statues, with their *facies toto orbe secunda*, the number two face in the whole world, now transformed into "little jugs, basins, frying pans, and chamber pots."[31]

Other exceptional marks of distinction kept pace, all packed into the last three years, from 29 to 31 CE, and in aggregate they paint a stunning portrait.

Formal embassies from the orders in Rome; birthday as a public holiday; gilt chairs in the theater; oaths and vows; consulship every five years with his senior partner: no one but the princeps and his immediate family ever had honors like these.[32] First non-senator to be granted *ornamenta praetoria*. Consul with no previous senatorial experience. Colleague in the consulship with a princeps who had previously shared that honor twice only, with his presumptive successors. Holder of proconsular *imperium* and, at any moment now, tribunician power. Member of the *domus Caesarum* by betrothal or marriage. Statues everywhere. Prayers for and to him. Partner in Toil. My Sejanus. As Seneca, who was there, would later remark to his friend Serenus, prefect of the night watch, "You have held the highest honors, but were they as great, as unexpected, and as all-encompassing as those Sejanus had?"[33]

The evidence is overwhelming. To think of this man as the all-powerful praetorian prefect of Tiberius Caesar is to misrepresent his last years. Again, we should resist hindsight, with its conviction that no knight could dream of becoming "emperor." We should look rather to the *precedents* for Sejanus in the uncertain world of the late Republic and early principate. Knights of senatorial family like Pompey and Octavian, two of the greatest men in Roman history, who had first entered the senate as consul, as did Sejanus. And above all, the new man Agrippa, who shared supreme power and a marriage alliance with Augustus, and who would have taken over had he been the survivor. Moreover, as we have seen, unlike the utterly new man Agrippa, Sejanus had broad and deep roots in the aristocracy of Rome, and he went much, much farther in the arrogation of power and image than Agrippa had ever done as he too rose from helper to partner.[34] It is wrong to see him as the intended "regent" for a young "Julio Claudian prince" who was to "succeed" to the nonexistent "throne" of an "emperor." By January 1, 31 CE, he was the junior colleague and thus, insofar as the role existed, the heir apparent of the princeps.[35]

———

Dio sums up the situation in the final months: "Sejanus was so great a person by reason of both his excessive haughtiness and of his vast power" (58.5.1, cf. 4.1). The uniformly hostile tradition thus concentrates exclusively on the brute currency of fear and favor, but the tremendous public honors and the ubiquitous statues should prompt us to look for echoes of something else in the months and years before October 18. Roman statesmen, Augustus above all, were great traditionalists, comfortable among their peers, surpassing all others in the quantity and quality of their achievements but within the ancestral norms of competition. Can we perhaps detect in Sejanus signs of a way of life more appropriate to a Roman princeps, a life acceptable and perhaps even attractive to his fellow citizens?

In 22 CE, the noble C. Iunius Silanus, just returned from the proconsulship of Asia, was accused *repetundarum* by the provincials. Tacitus is our only source for the incident, in *Annals* 3.66–69, but he is not much interested in extortion. What engages his attention is the sycophancy of the senate. He chooses the trial to illustrate some general remarks on the subject, which he caps with Tiberius' notorious quotation, when leaving the senate house, of a line of Greek tragedy on men so ready to be slaves. So a brief half-sentence in Tacitus on the central accusation of extortion is followed by a paragraph on the supplementary charges that really interested him—that is, that the *numen* of Augustus had been violated and that the *maiestas* of Tiberius had been spurned.

Three men attached *these* charges to the original indictment: the ex-consul Mamercus Scaurus, the praetor Junius Otho, and the aedile Bruttedius Niger. Tacitus scorns all of these new accusers. Mamercus Aemilius Scaurus, citing precedents that included a famous prosecution by his great namesake, was a disgrace to his ancestors (*obprobrium maiorum*). Junius Otho, once a mere schoolmaster, had become a senator through the *potentia* of Sejanus, and, in Woodman's translation (Tac. 3.66.3–4), "he polluted his dark beginnings still further by unabashed acts of daring." "As for Bruttedius," the historian continues, with grandiloquent obscurity, "abounding in honorable attainments and—if he had proceeded along a straight path—destined to reach every brilliance, speed spurred him on, inasmuch as he had intentions of outstripping his equals, then those ahead of him, and finally his very own hopes—something which has sent to the bottom many good men too, who, spurning rewards which are late but trouble-free, hasten those which are premature but actually terminal."

After further discussion of the case, Tacitus adds a long comment on a supposedly toadying proposal made in its wake by another patrician senator.

It is all a prime example of how Tacitus shapes history to his own ends. We almost overlook his passing comment that Silanus was a savage who had indeed extorted money from the provincials, and that the man's own quaestor and his own legate joined in his prosecution. Just as interesting is something the historian leaves out. The three prosecutors are presented as types of senatorial decadence: the bad aristocrat, the bad parvenu, the man of ability ruined by excessive ambition. Junius Otho is also picked out as a creature of Sejanus. But what Tacitus knew and chose not to tell here, is that Otho's two colleagues were likewise cronies of the praetorian prefect: under the year 34 CE, he remarks in passing that it was not the friendship of Sejanus that brought Scaurus down then (as it almost had in 32), but the hatred of Macro; and his dark allusion to the grim fate of Bruttedius is confirmed by the man's agitated appearance in Juvenal's account of the aftermath of Sejanus' fall.[36] Tacitus, so prone to innuendo about Sejanus'—or anyone's—motives, was not yet ready to attack the prefect, beyond the proleptic hint with Otho. That was to come a few chapters later with the character sketch introducing the fourth book of the *Annals* and its great theme, the change for the worse in Tiberius. The target here, in the third book, is not the evil genius behind the emperor but the servile senate at his feet.

This is to introduce a second and related aspect of the Silanus affair, likewise irrelevant to Tacitus and ignored today: all three of his prosecutors on the charge of treason were rather distinguished men of letters. Scaurus, the witty and scandalously elegant patrician, was an orator of great ability, who published seven of his own speeches. A poet as well, he produced a tragedy on "Atreus," which led to his downfall, and his trenchant criticism of Ovid happens to be recorded in passing. Otho likewise is not to be dismissed as the mere former master of a *litterarum ludus*, for he was, in fact, a leading declaimer who published four books of rhetorical *colores*. And the mysterious but talented Bruttedius wrote some sort of historical work that included a description of the death of Cicero.[37] Lively company for a bland and efficient civil servant.

We do not have to look far to find men of letters paying court to the praetorian prefect. In a vicious epistle addressed to the senate, after Sejanus' fall, Tiberius attacked Junius Gallio for presuming to suggest that retired praetorian guardsmen be given seats in the first fourteen rows of the theater. What possible reason could a "satellite of Sejanus" have for interfering with the soldiers? The senate took the hint and banished Gallio. In the same letter, the princeps assailed Sextius Paconianus, an action much more to the senate's liking, says Tacitus, since the man was an audacious malefactor, a wormer out of secrets and Sejanus' assistant in undermining Gaius (Caligula). Regrettably, the scoundrel saved his skin at the last moment by turning informer.

Again, Tacitus saw no need to record that these two were also distinguished senior senators and men of letters. Gallio, who had been urban praetor as long ago as 18 CE, is the *Gallio noster* of the elder Seneca, who praised his wit and elegance, ranked him as one of the four leading declaimers of his generation, and even gave him his eldest son in adoption. More to the point: Gallio discussed literary matters with Messalla Corvinus and with Tiberius himself; he was a friend of Ovid, *Naso suus*, who sent him a poem of consolation on the death of his wife; and he left behind some writings on rhetoric.[38] Sextius Paconianus, evil henchman or not, has been revealed by an inscription to be L. Sextilius Paconianus, peregrine praetor in 26 CE. His career as informer was short-lived. In 35 CE, we find him still in prison where, Tacitus tells us, he was strangled because of poems he actually wrote there, attacking the princeps. These were not, it happens, his first foray into poetry, as four lines of verse have survived, studiously describing the four winds.[39]

Not to labor the point, the cluster of literary men around Sejanus—orators and poets—is extraordinary. Lentulus Gaetulicus, a powerful patrician, governor of Germania Superior for the last seven years of Tiberius and beyond, was also a versatile and accomplished poet in Latin and (probably) in Greek, and one whose reputation lasted for centuries; he betrothed his daughter to the son of Sejanus. Pomponius Secundus, consul under Claudius and a man praised by Tacitus, was likewise a well-known and highly respected poet and writer of tragedies: after the fall of Sejanus, in late 31 CE, he was prosecuted, as Tacitus tells us (5.8.1), "for his friendship with Aelius Gallus, who had fled to Pomponius' suburban estate as if to the surest source of support." This Gallus, it is agreed, must have been a kinsman of Sejanus, and Pomponius Secundus should be the Pomponius, otherwise unknown, who, along with Satrius Secundus, had to be courted by anyone who wanted to reach the prefect in his heyday.[40] We could add more names with literary pretensions, not least that of Pinarius Natta, the "client" of Sejanus who prosecuted Cremutius Cordus, in collaboration with the same Satrius Secundus: he is on record for a witty and perceptive criticism offered at a recitation given by Julius Montanus, who was "a tolerable poet known both for his friendship with Tiberius and for their falling-out," as the younger Seneca tells us.[41] But more names are not necessary. Mamercus Scaurus, Lentulus Gaetulicus, and Pomponius Secundus were leading *nobiles* and nothing less than the literary heavyweights of their age—for all that, their works have not survived. Junius Otho, Junius Gallio, Sextilius Paconianus, and Bruttedius Niger were high-ranking senators and serious men of letters. That is a critical mass.

Such prosopography suggests a plausible alternate history, one of a community with shared literary tastes, the memory of which was swept away by political catastrophe. At the least, the friends and followers of Sejanus are not automatically to be dismissed in hindsight as mere toadies and cowards, obscure strivers and decayed aristocrats. What is more, Sejanus enjoyed the intimate friendship of yet another passionate lover of learning (*artes liberales utriusque generis studiosissime coluit*), a lifelong student and author who makes the mass critical indeed, one who routinely discussed at the dinner table what he had read during the day, a man praised by the learned Philo of Alexandria himself as unsurpassed in his era for wisdom and erudition: Tiberius Caesar. "My Sejanus," "a part of my own body and soul": given all we know of Tiberius' reserved personality and his intense cultural enthusiasm, we might wonder what these two men could possibly have found to talk about in their long hours together in Rome or on Capri. Sejanus surely dined too at Tiberius' learned table. Was he too a lover, perhaps even a patron, of letters?[42]

―――――

Discussion of the sex life of Aelius Seianus might put us in mind of snakes in Iceland. Indeed, at first glance there is less than nothing. Sex, we are assured, was in his case simply a means to power. Having introduced the man and his boundless ambition, Tacitus sketches a sort of predecessor of Louis Mazzini in *Kind Hearts and Coronets*, the interloper and would-be heir who schemes to work his lethal way through the family tree of the Caesars, starting with Tiberius' son Drusus:

> As Sejanus tested every possibility, he decided that the readiest recourse was to the man's wife, Livia, Germanicus' sister, whose looks at the beginning of her life were unbecoming, but who later excelled in beauty. As if burning with love, he enticed her into adultery and, after he had achieved this first outrage (and, with her modesty lost, a female was unlikely to reject other things), drove her to hope for espousal, partnership in a kingdom, and her husband's execution.[43]

So Livia befouls herself with a municipal adulterer and, to lull any suspicions that his mistress might have, the callous Sejanus expels from his house his wife Apicata, the mother of his three children. Dio in epitome has essentially the same sequence of events, which must have appeared in the common source, and Tiberius himself came to believe, or profess to believe, that Sejanus and Livilla (as she was also known) had been responsible for the death of his son.[44]

So whatever mutual attraction the couple may have felt, their affair was simply a mark of Sejanus' greater lust for power. This is just the case with the other allegation against him, that he had affairs with the wives of all the leading men in order to learn what they were saying and doing, even promising to marry the women: the wife of Drusus, son of Germanicus, is cited as an example.[45] The pursuit of adultery in the service of politics is of course not unique to Sejanus, for Augustus was accused of it as well. Indeed, with the accusation, we enter the world of make-believe, for it merits an entry in Thompson's *Motif-Index* (*MI*), J 155: "King has amours with great men's wives so as to learn secrets from them."[46]

But if we again look away from the concerns of our sources, there is some curious information about Sejanus' sexuality that is interesting precisely because they make so little of it. First comes the liaison with, of all people, the rich and prodigal gourmand Marcus Gavius Apicius, the report of which again goes back to a now-lost common source of Tacitus and Dio that mentioned it in a character sketch of the prefect. In his youth, says Tacitus (4.1.2), Sejanus was a follower of Gaius Caesar, Augustus' grandson, and he was rumored to have submitted to outrage by Apicius for money. Dio asserts outright (57.19.5), with no hint of Tacitean rumor, that he was once the boyfriend of Apicius, his παιδικά, which presumably represents the Latin *deliciae*. Apicius, as it happens, is matched in Sejanus' later company by another man, Geminius, one of three knights who fell at the end of 32 CE on the charge of conspiracy. Of these men, Tacitus reports (6.14.1), Geminius was a friend of Sejanus not for any serious reason but because of the prodigality of his fortune (*prodigentia opum*), and the softness of his life (*mollitia vitae*). Extravagance and effeminacy are not the first qualities one would think of as attractive to a Sejanus.

In his *Natural History*, Pliny the Elder reports that a Sutorius Priscus purchased Paezon from among the eunuchs of Sejanus for the sum of fifty million sesterces (7.129).[47] Pliny's indignation at the astonishing sum of money—*hoc pretium belli, non hominis!*—diverts the reader's attention from the astonishing background: Sejanus—industrious, vigilant, serene, modest—maintained a stable of eunuchs, one of them named "Boytoy." Lest there be any doubt as to at least one of their employments, Tacitus explains. Sejanus selected a slow poison to carry off Drusus Caesar in 23 CE. As came out eight years later, this was administered by the eunuch Lygdus. A little after offering this nugget, Tacitus adds a rumor that he rejects at length, even though—or because—it was current in his own day: "It was said that, after corrupting Livia into crime, Sejanus by means of illicit sex [*stupro*] had constrained the heart of the eunuch Lygdus too, since, because of his age and good looks, he was dear to his master [Drusus] and among his leading servants."[48] The most telling aspect of all this is that neither Pliny nor Tacitus shows any interest in Sejanus' private life. They don't bother even to condemn it. Both pursue other themes; the eunuchs are incidental. Again, what a world we have lost here.

Eunuchs go virtually unrecorded in Roman society under the Republic, beyond a handful of references in Plautus and Terence, but under the principate there is a considerable body of information about their various tasks as servants in private households, and the phenomenon of the court eunuch is transferred from Hellenistic monarchs to Roman dynasts.[49] It is on the cusp between Republic and Principate that we first hear of sexual services among their possible duties, an employment thunderously denounced by moralists and satirists.[50] The social reality behind this literary disapproval is difficult to gauge, but one thing is clear: the world of these *Lustknaben* is small and sharply defined by a few tropes. The company of historical figures (as distinct from literary creations) who are accused or suspected of keeping eunuchs and enjoying them sexually is very small and very distinguished: Maecenas in the 30s BCE; Sejanus; Drusus Caesar (probably); the future emperor Titus; Nero and Domitian as emperors; Nymphidius Sabinus and Otho, both lovers of Sporus after Nero's demise; Vitellius and his general Fabius Valens—and that's about it.[51] Their time at Rome is pretty much confined, then, to the first century of the principate. Their masters stand accused of degeneracy but not necessarily of wickedness, witness Maecenas, Drusus Caesar, and the young Titus before his reform. And eunuchs themselves tend to travel in packs: *greges spadonum* is the common refrain, or phrases like it.[52] In sum, what we dimly perceive under Tiberius is the fashion, relatively recent in Roman households, for employing eunuchs as servants, normally slaves, sometimes freedmen; and behind that lies the fad, followed for a time by *some* very eminent men, of ostentatiously maintaining a harem of them.

Sejanus: boyfriend of Apicius, friend of Geminius because of his effeminacy, master of eunuchs for sexual pleasure, and as such in select company, from Eastern potentates to future emperors. His only known predecessor at Rome was Maecenas, up until then the most powerful knight in Roman history.

———

Thus, from different hints, Sejanus' public style of life takes on a shadowy outline, startling in its familiarity. But there is another dimension to his image, harder to detect but as important even as his public offices and honors, and one that goes to the heart of the danger to Tiberius. Under the year 29 CE, Dio records that people took oaths by the Fortunes of Tiberius and Sejanus. Again, under 31, he repeats that they swore oaths by the Fortune of Sejanus, though now, he adds, "to excess" (κατακορῶς).[53] These oaths take us into a whole new world.

First, Fortune puts Sejanus into exalted company indeed. The dedication, the oath sworn by a personal Fortune, who accompanied and protected an individual, was a cult act, one inherited from the Hellenistic kings, and before them from the Persians, and the idea of the personal Fortune, introduced by Julius Caesar to Rome (and called the "Fortuna Caesaris" by S. Weinstock), was taken up by later emperors, from Galba onward, as the *Fortuna Augusti*.[54] Sejanus is the first Roman on historical record as worshipping a personal Fortuna, and it was doubtless this particular Fortune that was worshipped by others: a powerful statement of an extraordinary, indeed a unique, position.

The "Fortune of Sejanus" was no abstract deity or mere good luck charm: she was an individual goddess with an historic mission. There are four items of evidence to be considered:

1) Dio recounts an ominous incident in the last year of Sejanus' life: "Again, there was the behavior of a statue of Fortune, which had belonged, they say, to Tullius, one of the former kings of Rome, but was at this time kept by Sejanus in his house and greatly honored by him: he himself saw this statue turn its back to him while he was sacrificing."[55] Dio's text breaks off at this point.

2) Pliny the Elder, discoursing on cloth derived from animals, mentions in passing that "the purple bordered robes [*praetextae*] of Servius Tullius, with which the statue dedicated by him to Fortune had been covered, lasted until the death of Sejanus, and it was marvelous that they had not wasted away or suffered the attacks of moths in 560 years."[56]

3) In a discussion of *phengites*, a translucent stone discovered in Cappadocia in the time of Nero, Pliny notes that "with it he [Nero] had built the Temple of Fortune, which they call Sejanus', [originally] consecrated by King Servius, encompassing it in the Golden House."[57]

To which may be added 4) the oblique light cast by Juvenal in his stunning observation of what might have been, quoted in the epigraph to this chapter: the mob follows Fortune and it hates the condemned, but if Nortia had favored the Etruscan, and the old princeps had been suppressed, the same people would right now be calling Sejanus "Augustus." Sejanus is the Etruscan, from Vulsinii; the goddess Nortia is the Etruscan version of Fortuna.

At the time of his death, then, Sejanus owned and greatly honored an unimaginably ancient statue of Fortuna, one that he and others thought, or professed to think, was originally the possession of the legendary Servius Tullius, who had ruled Rome as her sixth king some six centuries earlier. This association with Servius and his Fortune is the key to Sejanus.[58]

Let us start with Nero's temple. It has been suggested that Sejanus not only enjoyed a statue that had once belonged to Servius Tullius, but that he had somehow incorporated into his house an ancient temple of the goddess built by Servius, along with its statue.[59] This seems highly improbable: Dio speaks of the statue as being in Sejanus' house, and says nothing about the temple; Pliny has Nero build, not rebuild, the temple; and it might be wondered why Nero or anyone would ever construct a Temple commemorating the name of the reviled or forgotten Sejanus. This last point does raise a question of interpretation, for the second passage in Pliny is highly ambiguous: *hoc construxerat [sc. Nero] aedem Fortunae, quam Seiani appellant, a Servio Tullio rege sacratam, amplexus aurea domo*. Here, we must read *quam Seiani appellant* as referring to the statue itself, not to Nero's temple, and the same holds true for *a Servio rege sacratam*. That is to say, we should understand Pliny as describing "the Temple of the Fortune that they call (the Fortune) of Sejanus," not "the Temple that they call (the Temple) of the Fortune of Sejanus." In other words: Nero built a new Temple of Fortune; that temple housed an ancient statue that had belonged to King Servius Tullius; Servius had famously dedicated many temples to Fortune, at least ten of them around Rome; so this particular Fortune was distinguished, not formally, in the name given to its temple by Nero, but informally, by the people (*quam appellant*), as the one that had once been so closely identified with Sejanus. Decades after the prefect's death, in Pliny's day, as indeed in Juvenal's, however reviled or forgotten Sejanus might be, his association with this particular Fortune was still remembered.

It evokes a complex and potent image derived from the figure of Servius Tullius, a new man indeed, perhaps even the son of a slave woman—but the King of Rome.

Servius was, more than any other figure in Roman history, Fortune's Favorite. According to Plutarch, he dedicated himself and his sovereignty to the goddess, and Dionysius affirms that she seemed to favor him all of his life. Indeed, so closely bound was he to the goddess that in one version she was even his lover, and he repaid her devotion by dedicating all those shrines to her.[60] Sejanus now had one of Servius' actual Fortunes as his own. He honored her greatly, men sacrificed to her in his name, he sacrificed to her himself, she was even wrapped in a miraculous cloth: surely he was suggesting himself as Servius' heir.

Servius was, above all, a *popular* monarch. His influence with the people was said to be enormous, he courted the poor, he was famous as the man who had established and secured liberty for the citizens, he had increased their power, and after his death, the plebs had honored his memory with sacrifices on market days—and popular legends accrued around him for centuries.[61] His connection with the common citizen of Rome is emphasized by his legendary career: son of a slave, enfranchiser of slaves, founder of the Compitalia, founder of the *comitia centuriata*, creator of the local tribes, coinage, the census, taxation.

In accordance with these achievements, he was also remembered for founding at Rome the cult of the Latin goddess Diana and for building her temple on the Aventine: the day of its foundation, his birthday, August 13, was a holiday for slaves; the place, the great hill outside the pomerium, would be forever renowned as the refuge of the plebs in the Struggle of the Orders. And it was there on the Aventine, as a mysterious and mutilated inscription tells us, that Sejanus held part (at least) of the election that formally made him consul in 31 CE. This astonishing, radical departure from tradition, unreported by any literary source, was surely a bid for popularity, and the time-honored association of the Aventine with the people and with the most popular of kings strongly suggests the role Sejanus meant to play.[62]

The inscription, broken on all sides, is tantalizing. After a reference to something "of 60 years," when it first becomes decipherable, the text is attacking the "impious agitation(?) and the wicked assemblies which occurred on the Aventine when Seianus was made consul." It is immediately clear that this is a rhetorical and highly emotional speech, which carries on in the first person, thus: "And I—weak, useless, the companion of the staff that I might be a suppliant—I now propose to you with all my strength(?), good fellow-tribesmen, if I have always seemed to you a good and useful tribesman, if I was never forgetful(?) of my duty or of the republic . . ."—and the last two lines sink back into impenetrable obscurity.

The emphasis on the tribe and tribesmen in the speech is surely significant, suggesting that the consular election had been in some way conducted not, as under the Republic, by the *comitia centuriata* in the Campus Martius, nor, as currently, by the senate in its meeting place, but—absolutely without precedent—by the *comitia tributa* on the Aventine.[63] That Sejanus did indeed have a special connection with the plebs, specifically as represented by their Tribal Assembly, is confirmed by two notices in Dio. In 29 CE, not only was his birthday celebrated publicly, he received countless statues from the senate, the knights, the *tribes*, and the leading men. Moreover, the senate sent embassies both to him and to Tiberius, as did the knights, and as did the people from *among their tribunes and their (plebeian) aediles* (that is, of course, the magistrates elected by the *comitia tributa*).[64] The tribes were then somehow involved in the consular election for 31 CE on the Aventine Hill, and, whatever happened there, it was a shocking and dangerously popular innovation. Is it mere chance that a posthumous inscription damns him as a most pernicious enemy to the Roman people (*ILS* 157, *hostis perniciosissimus p[opulo] R[omano]*)?

Tradition had it that the tribes had been established by King Servius Tullius. Even better, or worse, as we know from a very learned source, Etruscan historians had disagreed with their Roman rivals on one crucial point about Servius.[65] They presented the popular monarch not as the son of a Latin slave, but as an Etruscan warrior, Mastarna, the faithful companion of a warlord of Vulci, who emigrated to Rome. Mastarna was a much more appealing image for the companion of Tiberius Caesar, a freeborn fighter, a loyal follower, and a future king, and that image too may have been part of the pageant.

In sum, the Fortune of King Servius Tullius became the Fortune of the would-be princeps Aelius Seianus, a brilliantly multifaceted image. Like Servius, he was the loyal supporter and lieutenant of his king. Like Servius, he was the champion of the people and their choice for the highest office. Like Servius, he was the favorite of the goddess Fortuna, with whom he enjoyed a mystical closeness. Conspirator or not, it was indeed a dangerous image to project.

Its power is reflected in its longevity, the one part of him that survived, still talked of as Sejanus' Fortune almost fifty years after his fall. The horrific image of the statue turning its back on him is surely part of the posthumous campaign against him, seizing on the salient item in his public persona to make a grand concluding metaphor to his life and career. And there seems to be an echo in Juvenal, when he has Nortia, the Etruscan Fortuna, withdraw her favor from Etruscan Sejanus. Sejanus' Fortune was surely Fortuna Praesens, the Present Good Fortune of the prefect bound up, through public oaths, with the good fortune of the empire. Yet it appears that Nortia of Vulsinii was portrayed not as just any Fortuna, but precisely as Fortuna Respiciens.[66] Now, Fortuna Respiciens was a more problematic figure, Fortune turning to look back over her shoulder, the apotropaic goddess akin to Fate and Nemesis, the one who reminds us of sorrow in the midst of success (the deaths of the sons of

Aemilius Paullus on the eve of his triumph), the seeds of decay sown in victory (Scipio weeping in the ruins of Carthage). It was no accident, as Filippo Coarelli pointed out, that the temple of Fortuna Respiciens at Rome loomed, as we can now be pretty sure, over the route of the triumphal procession: *Respice et te homo esse memento!* The statue of Fortuna turning her back on her favorite at his moment of triumph could not have been more devastating, when the Fortune of Servius Tullius turned into the Fortune of Vulsinii. Servius came of course to a very grisly end. A small stone *sors*, the response from an oracle—unique, probably from the fourth century BCE, and of uncertain provenance—bears an uncompromising warning in raised letters: "If you obey, I do not want to destroy [you]; if you do not obey, [remember that] Servius perished by the workings of Fortune" (*Se cedues, perdere nolo; ni ceduas, Fortuna Servios perit*).[67] Sejanus too was Fortune's favorite but, obedient to her or not, how the ambitious prefect thought that he could avoid the fate of the ancient king, we will never know.

———

Repeatedly, we have caught glimpses of a lost world, a life swept away by the cataclysm of October 18, 31 CE. We will never know for sure what prompted the First Citizen to remove Sejanus so swiftly and so savagely. History stepped in to reduce Sejanus to a two-dimensional caricature, a murderous conspirator, an automaton of ambition, and we can never draw more than the faintest sketch of the original portrait. But, however we piece together the exiguous fragments of his life, surely he was more interesting than the caricature suggests.

The real threat he posed, if threat is the correct word, is not that he was a *monstrum*, an upstart driven purely by lust for power, devoid of character, an aberration marring the reign of a nonexistent dynasty. He was rather the opposite and far more dangerous: a true insider. Despite the best efforts of Tiberius and of history to disown and to blacken him posthumously, he was by all possible standards the designated successor, a sort of Agrippa and Maecenas combined. A supremely competent administrator, connected through blood, marriage, and friendship with the aristocracy old and new, he accumulated overwhelming power, far more than any previous private citizen. We will never know if he was a man of taste and education, but circumstantial evidence suggests deep roots in the aristocratic literary culture of his age. We will never know whether he lived a princely life, but indirect evidence suggests a certain flamboyance. Above all, we can discern along with the enormous power and the appropriate lifestyle an almost Augustan finesse not merely in his gathering of the reins of power but in his manipulation of their symbolic packaging.

First, there was the public image of the hard-working and vigilant second-in-command, modest and serene. But as he became the partner of the First Citizen, and as he edged toward the divine, he seems to have developed the perfect public image in his fervent cultivation of an identification with Servius Tullius. Servius too had begun as the loyal supporter and lieutenant of his predecessor, but he had enjoyed the special favor of a goddess and he would win the eternal favor of the people of Rome, whose champion he was. Juvenal got it absolutely right: if Fortune had (truly) favored Sejanus, people would now be calling him Seianus Augustus.

NOTES

Foreword

1. For the publication history of the chapters here reprinted, see the headnotes to chapters 1–3, 5–7, and 9.

Chapter 1. Tiberius the Wise

[Ed. note: with thanks to Franz Steiner Verlag (Stuttgart) for pemission to publish here the paper that first appeared in *Historia* 57 (2008): 408–25. Copyright © 2008 Franz Steiner Verlag]

1. Suet. 60: inevitably the tale has been conflated with the charge that Tiberius had the victims of his tortures thrown into the sea below (Suet. 62.2), and it is often assumed that the poor fisherman was tossed over the cliff (reported as early as Orgitano 1858, 137–38). I am grateful to Bob Kaster and Adrienne Mayor for commenting on a first draft.

2. Slotki 1939.

3. Clouston 1887, 2:468–69.

4. Consuli 1997.

5. Retold by Isaac D'Israeli in his "Curiosities of Literature," quoted by Clouston 1887, 2:467–68.

6. *MI*, Stith Thompson's great motif-index of folk literature, was first published in six volumes from 1932 to 1936 at Helsinki in the series *FF Communications*. The now-standard "revised and enlarged edition" was issued in six volumes from 1955 to 1958 at Bloomington, Indiana. It is a classic work much in need of revision. *ATU*, in three volumes, edited by H.-J. Uther is the fourth version (2004), much revised and expanded, of Antti Aarne's likewise indispensable classification of folktale types, originally published at Helsinki in 1910 (A. Aarne, *Verzeichnis der Märchentypen*), and twice revised by Thompson in 1928 and 1961 as *The Types of the Folk-Tale* (*AaTh*). All four works appear in the *FF Communications* series, "edited for the Folklore Fellows" and published by the Academia Scientiarum Fennica.

7. Viz., French, Spanish, Catalan, Italian, Hungarian, Serbian, Rumanian, Bulgarian, Greek, Ukrainian, Turkish, Jewish, Kurdish, Tadzhik, Syrian/Lebanese/Iraqi, Palestinian, Iranian, US-American, Mexican, Brazilian, West Indian, Egyptian.

8. In Hadrian's case, compare *MI* J2415.1, "The two presents to the king: the beet and the horse," and *ATU* 1689A, "Two Presents for the King": "A man (farmer, gardener) produces a huge turnip . . . and takes it to the king as a present. The king rewards him well. His neighbor (gentleman, noble, rich man) learns about this and decides to give the king a much better present (his daughter in marriage), in the hope of an even better reward . . . The king gives him the giant turnip as his reward." See also *ATU* 928, "Planting for the Next Generation"; cf. *MI* J701.1 and Hansen 2002, 331–32.

9. As was seen long ago by G. Amali (1893, 15–16). I leave open the slight chance that the tale of the fisherman might be historical: Adrienne Mayor points out the process of "ostension," "in

which people act out what they have heard in myth or legend, thereby making a folklore motif come true" (personal communication, here and in next note). Tiberius, like other Roman dynasts, certainly acted out mythological situations (but this is neither myth nor legend), and he certainly had a grim sense of humor; on the other hand, the anecdote is so anti-Tiberian, the odds are that it was attached to him by ill-wishers, of whom there were many. For a brief recent introduction to ostension, see the opening paragraph of Kvideland 2006.

10. Plut. fr. 182. Adrienne Mayor points out that the sacred light or fire designating a new ruler "goes back to ancient Iranian kingship beliefs, in which Mithra signals his approval of a new ruler by sending an omen via his favorite animal, the horse."

11. *Aen.* 2.535–50. Turner 1943.

12. Cic. *Rep.* 3.24; Dio 77.10.7 (in 212). Discussed by La Penna 1979. Compare Jesse James' alleged comments on President Grant: "Jesse James," PBS, accessed September 10, 2023, pbs.org /wgbh/americanexperience/films/james/.

13. Petron. *Sat.* 51 (retold by Trimalchio); Plin. *NH* 36.195; Dio 57.21.5–7.

14. Lassen 1995.

15. For companions on Capri, see the impressive roster compiled at Houston 1985. No proof of the fantasy of the single companion is needed, but Tacitus elsewhere writes of two men who followed (*secuti*) Tiberius to Rhodes and Capri (6.10.2), one of whom, Vescularius Flaccus, he himself has identified as a knight (2.28.2).

16. Dio 58.28.4 (Tiberius); 71.34.1 (Marcus); Plut. *Pom.* 14 and *Mor.* 203E and 804F.

17. Tac. 6.21; Suet. 14.4; Dio 55.11.1–3 (the first from Zonaras, the second from Xiphilinus: how the two were related in Dio's original text is unknown).

18. The story is told by Plato at *Tht.* 174a. It became proverbial: in his tragedy *Iphigenia*, Ennius has Achilles remark of *astrologi: quod est ante pedes nemo spectat, caeli scrutantur plagas* (Cic. *Rep.* 1.30.3, cf. *Div.* 2.30). In their defense, the astrologers might quote Lord Darlington: "We are all in the gutter, but some of us are looking at the stars."

19. Krappe 1927 pointed out the relevance of Nectanebus to Thrasyllus but denied any connection with the seer unable to foresee his own fate: I prefer the connection described here.

20. Plut. *De def. or.* 17 (*Mor.* 419B–E. Loeb trans. Babbitt). The rationale here is, presumably, that the god's mother was mortal and therefore, yes, he could die.

21. Formerly *AaTh* 113A, "King of the Cats is Dead" [Ed. note: on the relation between *ATU* and *AaTh*, see n. 6 above.]. The whole tale is splendidly illuminated in Hansen 2002, 131–36 (Fairies Send a Message. Death of Pan), obviating much of the large and often misguided bibliography.

22. Plin. *NH* 9.9; 9.10; Phlegon 14 (on which, more below, p. 17).

23. *AJ* 18.174–76 (Loeb trans. Feldman).

24. van Dijk 1993; van Dijk 1994.

25. *Belua*: Suet. 24. *Lupus*: Suet. 25, from Ter. *Phorm.* 506, probably Greek in origin: Otto no. 987.

26. Suet. 32.2, generalizing the remark as a reply to governors who wished to raise taxes; cf. Oros. 7.4; *Suda*, s.v. Tiberius. Dio 57.10.5 is a more precise, less folkloric version: Aemilius Rectus, supposedly prefect of Egypt in 14 CE, sends more taxes than were required, to which the princeps replies that "I [not 'a good shepherd'] want my flock shorn not shaved clean." Otto no. 1354; in fable form, Babr. 51.

27. Dio 56.16.3, Bato the Pannonian to Tiberius (9 CE); cf. Otto no. 983; *MI* K206.1, "Wolf offers to act as shepherd; plan detected"; K346.2, "Fox as shepherd"; K934, "Fox in sheepskin gains admission to fold and kills sheep"; Bato combines the figures of the wise barbarian and the prisoner speaking truth to power (cf. the supposed exchange between Tiberius and the enslaved man Clemens, above).

28. Otto no. 1277; for the history of the use of the phrase, Champlin 2003a, 307–8.

29. Phaedr. 2.5.7–25 (Loeb trans. Perry).

30. On the date of Phaedrus' *Fables* (Claudian or Neronian) and their purpose, Champlin 2005, with argument that "Phaedrus" too was a Roman aristocrat with a taste for fables.

31. On the name, see p. 64.

32. Schwartz 1899, 1716–17. For all its resonance, Schwartz's theory was presented as a brief and cautious aside in a long article on Cassius Dio; for a levelheaded summary of the source problem, with bibliography, see Martin 2001, 22–26, with 6–7, the source of the phrase quoted here.

33. Again, there is no scholarly agreement as to the number and nature of the sources behind the tradition represented by Tacitus, Suetonius, and Dio. In a thorough investigation of Tacitus' Tiberian sources, Syme emphasized their multiplicity and discounted Schwartz's argument: "The theory is seductive, but not convincing. It explains too much. The historical tradition about a ruler at Rome was not formed and transmitted, during the first and second generations at least, by writers only, still less by a single man" (Syme 1958, 271–86, at 272–73). There is no doubt that at least two major annalistic histories were available, not to mention minor works, documents, and hearsay: see the summary in Sage 1990, 997–1010. But that does not affect Schwartz's central contention about the hostility of one writer and his powerful influence on the bafflingly contradictory tradition about Tiberius, which I shall pursue elsewhere. In the interim, readers might consult Townend 1962 for what I believe to be a convincing account of that author and his modus operandi. In a sense, the present chapter is an addendum to Townend, who unfortunately never pursued the subject in his groundbreaking papers on Julio-Claudian historiography.

34. Baker 1929, viii–ix. He continues, p. 8, ". . . he remained shy, a little gauche, with the fastidiousness which shows itself in apparently inconsistent ways, as a dislike of sentiment, an appreciation of poetry, an intolerance of fools, a sympathy with simplicity; he distinguished so accurately between those opposites which men habitually confuse that he puzzled his critics."

35. Suet. 58; Tac. 1.74: a quite separate charge of extortion was referred to *recuperatores*, and presumably he was convicted of that. I suspect that the changing of clothes occurs in the baths and is to be aligned with the shameful acts in latrines and brothels.

36. Philost. *Apoll.* 1.15. The charge is *asebeia*, not impiety here, but the Greek equivalent for Latin *maiestas*.

37. Philo *Leg.* 141–42, 167, 33, respectively (trans. Smallwood 1961); the text is unsure in a couple of places.

38. Phlegon 14 (trans. Hansen 1996). Compare the summons of the *philologoi* to discuss the death of Pan (above), or of the learned men to discuss the use of a non-Latin word in an edict (Dio 57.17.2–3, with Suet. *Gramm.* 22.2).

39. A shining portrait of Tiberius the Good can be painted from Dio 57.7–11 (all packed under the year 14 CE) and Suet. 26–40, both clearly derived from the same source.

40. Suet. 38–39, cf. 72.1—but see below.

41. Tac. 2.41.1 (14 CE); 3.31.3 and 47.3 (21, not 22: Bellemore 2003); Tiberius referred to the latter trip as a *peregrinatio suburbana*. This is not to say that he did not retire to the suburbs often during these years, but otherwise I know only of an undated visit to Praeneste: Gell. 16.13.5, cf. Suet. 63.1.

42. Tac. 4.58.3; 6.15.3. In 32: at the *Horti Caesaris* across the Tiber, Suet. 72.1, Tac. 6.1.1. In 33: at the fourth milestone, Tac. 6.15.1, Dio 58.21.1. In 34: at Alba and Tusculum, Dio 58.24.1. In 35: just outside the city, Tac. 6.39.2, cf. Dio 58.25.2. In 36: at Tusculum, Jos. *AJ* 18. 179, 183–204. In 37: at the seventh milestone, Suet. 72.2.

43. Suet. 38: *ut vulgo iam per iocum "Callipides" vocaretur, quem cursitare ac ne cubiti quidem mensuram progredi proverbio Graeco notatum est.*

44. Cic. *Att.* 13.12.3 (with Shackleton Bailey ad loc.): a runner? a character in a play? an entertainer renowned for running on the spot? Otto no. 305.

45. Seneca *Ep.* 95.42. In fact, as part of his general drive for austerity, and supposedly outraged by the fact that three mullets had been sold for thirty thousand sesterces, he urged the senate to control market prices annually: Suet. 34.1.

46. Hdt. 3.40–42; cf. also *MI* N211.1, "Lost ring found in fish (Polycrates)."

47. Plin. *NH* 37.2.3: *insularum et litorum tyrannus*. Nesiarch: Dio 58.5.1, contrasting Sejanus acting as emperor in Rome while Tiberius was nesiarch on Capri (see chapter 9 at n. 7). The comparison sounds like contemporary comment, rather than Dio's own observation. The word is uncommon, designating governors on a handful of Hellenistic Aegean inscriptions (a selection at *LSJ* s.v.), and obviously belittling the leader of the Roman world. It could mean something grander, as in the anecdote related at Plut. at *Demet.* 25.8, but the context there is satirical as well.

48. Plin. *NH* 37.2.4, skeptically (*si credimus*).

49. So Suetonius, at *Cal.* 11.1.

Chapter 2. Tiberius and the Heavenly Twins

[Ed. note: with thanks to Cambridge University Press for permission to publish here the paper that first appeared in the *Journal of Roman Studies* 101 (2011): 73–99. Copyright © 2011 The Society for the Promotion of Roman Studies.]

1. Suet. 72–74.

2. Gantz 1993, 318–28.

3. *ILLRP* 1271a.

4. For details and references to the temple and the cult of the twins at Rome: Steinby 1989–2012, 1:76–109 (J. Sihvola); Poulsen 1992; *LTUR* 1:242–45, "Castor, Aedes, Templum" (I. Nielsen); La Rocca 1994. R. M. Ogilvie argued (1965, 288–89, 781) that the main temple of the cult of the Castor and Pollux in Latium was at Tusculum, in the territory of which Lake Regillus lay, and that the vow of a temple to the twins at Rome rewarded not merely their assistance to the Romans but their desertion of the Latins, analogous to an *evocatio*, the ceremonial request to the enemy's deity to change sides. See further below.

5. The classic (and only) description of the parade is that of Dionysius of Halicarnassus, at 6.13.4. Cobblers, *sutores*, near the temple: Plin. *NH* 10.121–2. Bankers or moneylenders, *argentarii*, "behind the Temple of Castor" (*post aedem Castoris*): CIL 6.9177, 30748, cf. 9393 (= *ILS* 7696). A cloakmaker, *sagarius*, likewise "behind the Temple of Castor," 6.9872. Slave dealers, *mancipia ementes vendentesque, ad Castoris*: Sen. *Const.* 13.4, cf. Plaut., *Cur.* 481. Taverns: Catul. 37, cf. App. *BC* 1.54. The Severan marble plan of the city appears to show a row of shops on the far side of a small piazza at the rear of the temple: see the Stanford Digital Forma Urbis Romae Project, accessed September 9, 2023, http://formaurbis.stanford.edu/fragment.php?record=85 [T. Najbjerg, J. Trimble].

6. Briefly, Ginge, Becker, and Guldager 1989; more fully, Guldager Bilde and Poulsen 2008, 253–322. The rich commercial life around the *Aedes Castoris* and the adjacent *Basilica Iulia* and *Scalae Graecae* is vividly evoked by Neudecker 2005.

7. References at *LTUR* (see n. 4).

8. The association was first discussed by K. Scott (1930a and 1930b); brought up to date by Poulsen 1991 (an influential article: cf. the appendix, below) and La Rocca 1994. More recently, see Suspène 2004 and Sumi 2009.

9. Suet. *Claud.* 1.3, cf. Porph. ad Hor. *Carm.* 4.4.27–28 (*morbo*); Dio 55.1.4 (*nosoi*), cf. 55.2.1; Plin. *NH* 7.84 (*aegrotum*); Sen. *Marc.* 3.1 (*aegrum*); Val. Max. 5.5.3 (*gravis et periculosa valitudo*).

10. The main accounts of Drusus' death vary somewhat. Dio 55.1 has him turned back by the female apparition and dying "from some disease" on the other side of the Rhine (Strabo, a contemporary, mentions at 7.1.3 that he died across the Rhine but gives no cause). Suet. *Claud.* 1.2–3 seems to date the apparition earlier, to 11 BCE, and has Drusus die "from disease in his summer camp" at a place thereafter called "Accursed" (*Scelerata*). Liv. *Per.* 142 has him die, apparently across the Rhine, thirty days after his leg was broken by his horse falling on it. The significance of Drusus' death is emphasized by the female apparition. She represents a range of such figures

who warn conquerors and explorers that certain boundaries are set and, if those boundaries are crossed, such hubris arouses the envy of supernatural powers: Krappe 1930.

11. Val. Max. 5.5.3 (Loeb trans. Shackleton Bailey, slightly modified). Valuable analysis in Wardle 2002.

12. Various details at Liv. *Per.* 142; Val. Max. 5.5.3; Plin. *NH* 7.84; Dio 55.2.1; *Cons. Liv.* 89–94; Sen. *Polyb.* 15.5; the first four of these emphasize the haste of Tiberius' journey: beyond that, how much of the story is fact and how much is embroidery is unknown.

13. Suet. insists at 7.3 that Tiberius walked all the way with the body. But Mainz to Rome is about eight hundred miles by modern highways with bridges, viaducts, and tunnels, none of which was available in 9 BCE. Tiberius had also to reckon with an additional unknown distance across the Rhine, the heights of the Alps, and an extremely harsh winter (Tac. 3.5.1). An epic journey indeed. *Municipiorum coloniarumque primores*: Suet. *Claud.* 1.3; Dio 55.2.1; cf. Seneca *Marc.* 3.1, *Cons. Liv.* 173. At Rome, the order of the scribes received the body and brought it to the Forum where Tiberius delivered the eulogy; thence it was conveyed to the Circus Flaminius, where Augustus delivered a second eulogy. From there, the knights carried the corpse to the Campus Martius, where it was burned at the Ustrinum, and the ashes were buried in the Mausoleum. Drusus was posthumously given the name Germanicus, and awarded statues, an arch, and a cenotaph on the Rhine. On all of this, see the thorough commentary of Swan 2004, 44–47, with references.

14. References: *PIR*^{2} C 857 (Drusus), A 885 (Antonia), I 221 (Germanicus), C 942 (Claudius). Nero Claudius Drusus Germanicus Imp. appears often on the coins of his son Claudius: *RIC* Claudius 69–74, 93, 98. Livia as mother of Drusus Germanicus: named Livia Drusi f. Augusti mater Ti. Caesaris et Drusi Germanici (before 14 CE), *CIL* IX.3304 (Superaequum); and Iulia Augusta (after 14 CE), 2.2038 (Anticaria) and 11.7416 (Ferentium). In *CIL* 11.1165 (Veleia) she is, tortuously, Iulia Augusta, daughter of the divine Augustus, mother of Ti. Caesar Augustus, son of the divine Augustus, and of Nero Claudius Drusus (no mention of Germanicus).

15. *Marc.* 3.2 (Loeb trans. Basore): dated by Bellemore 1992 to the years 33 / 37, with strong arguments; in any case written no later than 41 CE.

16. Val. Max. 4.3.3; Vell. 2.97.2–3; Sen. *Marc.* 3.1, cf. *Polyb.* 15.5 (Loeb trans. Shackleton Bailey, Shipley, and Basore, respectively).

17. *Cons. Liv.*: whatever the origins of this poem, there is no reason to doubt that it is exactly what it claims to be, and that it was produced sometime between the dedication of the Temple of Castor and Pollux in 6 and Livia's death in 29; cf. *Brill's New Pauly.* Compare the poetic effusions of Clutorius Priscus, one on the death of Germanicus, for which he was rewarded by Tiberius, and one anticipating the death of Drusus Caesar, for which the senate had him executed: Tac. 3.49–51, Dio 57.20.3. Pliny's dream: Plin. *Ep.* 3.5.4, with Flower 2006, 3–5. Tacitus perhaps recalls Pliny's *Bella Germaniae* when he refers to the German deeds of "Drusus Germanicus" in his own *Germania* (34.3, on Drusus' daring) and his *Historiae* (5.19).

18. Drusus Germanicus on public inscriptions: notably *CIL* 6.40329 = *ILS* 148 (Rome, Campus Martius), 40330 (Rome: *elogium* in the Forum of Augustus), 40337, 40339 (Rome: dedication of the Temple of Castor and Pollux, on which see below), 40424 (Rome, possibly from the Ara Pietatis Augustae); *AE* 1962.37 (Saepinum); and the fragment of *fasti* at *AE* 1981.316 (Hispellum). Honors of Germanicus: the third mention of his father noted in the text above appears in the *Tabula Hebana*, recording the Lex Valeria Aurelia of 20 CE, the first two in the partially overlapping *Tabula Siarensis*, which records the decree of the senate that preceded that law. The bibliography on these and several related fragments is enormous, their reconstruction fiendishly complicated: the best place to start is Crawford 1996, 1:507–47. The memory of Drusus may also dominate the scenes on two well-known silver cups from Boscoreale: De Caprariis 2002, arguing (vs. Kuttner 1995) that they reflect well-known images generated around the dead Drusus rather than a specific (and otherwise unattested) public monument erected to commemorate Tiberius' victory. For some of the many posthumous portraits of Drusus: Boschung 1993, 51;

Rose 1997, 83, 90, 100, 108, 110, 153; Megow 1987, 180, 204, 276. Most intriguing is a veiled bust "found in Capri" and acquired by the British Museum in the nineteenth century, displaying "a certain boyishness, in spite of his obvious maturity" (Pollini 1981, 129–30, with plates 38 and 39, dating the portrait to "the later Julio-Claudian period"), clearly the same person as a togate figure from Caere (plates 37 and 38); a convincing case for Drusus is offered in Rose 1997, 63–64 with n. 75.

19. Tac. 1.33.2; Dio 55.27.3. Tacitus reverts to the theme of Drusus' popularity at 2.41.3 and 6.51.1. It bears restating that all of his posthumous honors were for a man who did not actually conquer Germany, although everyone agreed that it was inevitable: cf. Strabo 7.1.3; Porph. Hor. *Ep.* 1.3 pr. (*Drusus qui subactis Germanis Germanicus dictus est*).

20. *Cons. Liv.* 169–72; Sen. *Polyb.* 15.5. Cenotaph: Dio 55.2.3; Suet. *Claud.* 1.3. The tumulus was almost surely mentioned in the *Tabula Siarensis* a. 26–28, in which, if we accept W. D. Lebek's ingenious restoration of the Latin, we can see the compromise as the senate decreed in honor of Germanicus "that a third arch either [be built onto or be placed near that burial mound] which [the army had first begun to construct on its own initiative] for Drusus, the brother of Tiberius Caesar Augustus, and then [completed] with the consent of the Divine Augustus": Crawford 1996, 1:515. Claudius "a Germanicus": Jos. *AJ* 19.217.

21. Suet. 50.1, *Claud.* 1.3. Suetonius uses the letter to introduce a grossly unfair section of the biography of Tiberius devoted to his supposed hatred of his close relatives, suggesting that Tiberius betrayed his brother's words. But it can hardly have been a betrayal if Drusus himself made no secret of his intentions; this is the only instance given of such antipathy, against many displays of fraternal affection; and—since the incident is not dated—the republican Tiberius might well have produced the letter after the death of Augustus, as part of his own resistance to taking up the principate.

22. Suet. *Claud.* 1.5. The fragmentary inscription from the Forum Augustum, published in 1933, is now *CIL* 6.40330: [Nero] Cl[a]udiu[s] Ti(beri) f(ilius) / [Dru]sus German[i]cus / [co(n)s(ul)] pr(aetor) urb(anus) q(uaestor) aug(ur) imp(erator) / [app]ellatus in Germania. Augustus himself composed the elogia in his Forum: Plin. *NH* 22.13.

23. Memorials: inscriptions in the Mausoleum and Forum Augustum; eulogy; memoir; permission for tumulus on the Rhine (*Tabula Siarensis*). The eulogy overshadows that delivered by Tiberius: Suetonius recalls Augustus' emotional plea to the gods, but does not mention the speech of Tiberius; while in its narrative of events, the *Cons. Liv.*, whose author claims to have been there, likewise recalls Caesar's tearful laudation and his dramatic plea to the gods for a similar death (209–12, cf. 464–65), and completely ignores Tiberius' speech.

24. Busts: Tac. 3.5.1: *circumfusas lecto Claudiorum Iuliorumque imagines.* Mausoleum: von Hesberg and Panciera 1994, 74–75. None of the earlier burials in the tomb was in fact a member of the Julian family, but Agrippa was at least the biological father of Augustus' two sons by adoption, Marcellus was his nephew, and Octavia was his sister; whereas Drusus was only his stepson and the husband of his niece. *Tumulus Iuliorum:* Tac. 16.6.2, cf. Liv. *Per.* 142 (Drusus buried *in tumulo C. Iuli*), *Cons. Liv.* 161–63: Livia comforts herself, "This at least is possible—in this tomb shall we be laid together, Drusus, nor buried shalt thou go to the sires of old; I shall be mingled with thee, ashes with ashes, bone with bone" (Loeb tran. Mozley). The position of the statue in the Forum Augusti is assured by the location of the fragments of its inscription: Spannagel 1999, 288–91. Ov. *F.* 1.707: *fratres de gente deorum*; Val. Max. 5.5.3: *fraternum iugum, Claudiae prius, nunc etiam Iuliae gentis . . . decus.*

25. Dio 55.8.1–2 (Loeb trans. Cary, modified); the invaluable commentary in Swan 2004, 71–75, makes annotation superfluous. On the complex connotations of Concord at Rome, see esp. Levick 1978.

26. Dio 55.9.6, with Swan 2004 ad loc. This act of imperial brutality sits ill with Tiberius' later professed concern for the provincials, and he would be the first to recognize the irony of its

connection with "concord." However we explain it, two banal observations are valid: retired or not, he had not forgotten the Temple of Concord; and its importance to him trumped common morality.

27. Castor and Pollux: Dio 55.27.3–4 (Loeb trans. Cary, modified). Dio gives the year; the day appears in the *Fasti Praenestini* and at Ov. *F.* 1.705. Concord: Dio 56.25.1 (τὸ Ὁμονόειον). Dio and the *FP* give the year; the *FP*, the *Fasti Verulani*, and Ovid (*F.* 1.637ff.) the day.

28. Good brief introductions to the two temples at *LTUR* 1 (1993), 316–20, "Concordia, Aedes" (A. M. Ferroni), and 242–45, "Castor, Aedes, Templum" (I. Nielsen). A replacement for the standard monograph on Concordia (Gasparri 1979), announced in *LTUR* 1 as in preparation by A. Ferroni et al., has not yet appeared; the Augustan temple of Castor, on the other hand, is now thoroughly treated in Guldager Bilde and Poulsen 2008 and Nilson, Persson, Sande, and Zahle 2009. Gleaming: Ov. *F.* 1.637 (*niveum templum*). So much is known of the artwork in the Temple of Concord (mainly from Pliny) that a program has been discerned, no mere museum collection but a symbolic paean to the values proclaimed by the dynasty: Kellum 1993; Bravi 1998, approved by Hölscher 2006, 253–54. These interpretations may seem overdetermined to some readers, and curiously, neither mentions the posthumous equestrian statues in the Temple of Concord of Gaius and Lucius Caesar, of Germanicus, and probably of Drusus Caesar, which would have been hard to miss: *Tabula Siarensis* frag. b, col. 2, lines 1–12, interpreted by Heinemann 2007, 90–93. German spoils: Suet. 20, discussing Tiberius' German triumph in 12 CE, adds retroactively, "He also dedicated the Temple of Concord and that of Pollux and Castor in his own name and that of his brother, from the spoils." Ovid confirms that *munera triumphatae gentis* paid for Concord: *F.* 1.647–48.

29. On the date of the vows, see below.

30. Fires: *LTUR* 1 (1993), 317 (Concordia), 244 (Castor: correctly adding "although such a destruction is not specifically mentioned in the sources"); cf. Poulsen 1991, 121. Repeated without question in Haselberger 2002, 97, 83. The only source for these fires, and another in 12 BCE, is Dio, who gives examples of buildings damaged in each case: 14 BCE, Basilica Paulli and Temple of Vesta, burned in the same fire (54.24.2); 12 BCE, portents of the death of Agrippa, "many (buildings)" burned, including the Hut of Romulus (54.29.8); 9 BCE, portents of the death of Drusus, "many (buildings)" ruined or destroyed by a storm and lightning, and the Temple of Jupiter Capitolinus and associated deities harmed (55.1.1). How could Dio have failed to name Concord and Castor in such reports, and how could he have failed to mention such damage as the reason for Tiberius' rebuilding of them? Even more striking, *Cons. Liv.* 401–4 carefully reminds us of the damage done by lightning to Capitoline Jupiter, Juno, and Minerva (along with the *sancta domus Caesaris*, on the Palatine) as portending the death of Drusus. How could the poet, who mentions the Temples of Concord and Castor at 283–90, have ignored damage done to them in 9 BCE and repaired by Drusus' brother?

31. *CIL* VI.40339 (Rome). Brackets [] indicate portions that have been lost; parentheses () the expansion of standard epigraphic abbreviations.

32. Alföldy 1992, 39–58.

33. Nilson et al. 2009, 179–80, 183.

34. See nn. 36 and 40.

35. The following sketch is heavily dependent on Zanker 1972. For the arch of Gaius Caesar, see Rose 2005, 58–64.

36. It is inconceivable that the filiation of Tiberius ("son of Augustus" in this case) would be omitted from a public monument. That Drusus also was named as *privignus Augusti*, "stepson of Augustus" must remain a hypothesis, but is extremely probable. Alföldy 1992, 51, adduces *ILS* 148 (Rome), an exact parallel for the name and relationship restored here, and *AE* 1981.316 (Hispellum): both were highly visible public documents. The inclusion of Augustus, who loved Drusus as a son, would be a gracious gesture by Tiberius, his exclusion hard to imagine. For

what it is worth, the double appearance of Augustus in the two filiations is nicely balanced visually, and the lettering fits perfectly within Alföldy's careful and elegant reconstruction of the text.

37. Tiberius might even claim an ancestral connection with the twins, for his distant ancestor Appius Claudius Sabinus (cos. 495) had immigrated from the otherwise unknown town of Regillum, which was probably in the territory of Tusculum, the main site of the cult of Castor and Pollux in Latium, and presumably near the equally unknown site of the Battle of Lake Regillus. Note also that as princeps Tiberius had a villa at Tusculum (*CIL* 15.7814), where he certainly stayed in 34 and 36 CE, and that the imperial cult there became entwined with that of Castor and Pollux (*CIL* 14.2620, 2630).

38. Hor. *Carm.* 4.4.73–75: *nil Claudiae non perficiunt manus,* | *quas et benigno numine Iuppiter defendit;* 37–38: *quid debeas, o Roma, Neronibus,* | *testis Metaurum flumen.*

39. Suet. 20, cf. n. 28 above.

40. By sheer chance, or divine intervention, one of the six fragments used by Alföldy in the reconstruction at *CIL* 6.40339 bears the remains of two letters that seemed to confirm that the dedicatory inscription did indeed identify the building as the Temple of Pollux and Castor. Viz., frag. d (certainly from the temple), to be restored as [*aedem Pollucis e*]*t C*[*astoris*]. This was first observed by G. Tomasetti in 1890: see Alföldy 1992, 48–49, with discussion. The size of the letters assigns them to the third line of the text in his version. There is an interpunct on the stone, a small triangle marking the division between words. The first word ended with T, the second, only the top of which is preserved, began with a C or possibly G, O, or Q. From this point, the possibilities for words, combinations of words, and abbreviations on such conventional public inscriptions is severely limited (Alföldy duly cites parallels): the words *aedem, Castoris, et, Pollucis, de,* and *manubiis* are all but assured in some order, and [*r*]*ef(ecerunt)* is preserved. However, Sande (Nilson et al. 2009) sees traces of relief on the left side of the fragment (her ARC 19), two little drops that are man-made, and asserts that they represent decoration appropriate to the end of the architrave, hence that the letters belong not to the middle of the line but to its beginning. "T." will then represent not "[*e*]*t*" but "*T(emplum) C*[*astorum / is*]." As reconstructed, this is (apparently) the beginning of the dedicatory inscription. Alföldy's two shallow columns above this, his third line, are thus rejected along with the blocks on which their fragmentary letters appear. Readers need not be warned that "T. Castorum / is" cannot be. To begin the dedication of a major monument with a one-letter abbreviation would be unnecessary and inelegant, indeed grotesque, and no parallels are cited. To squeeze the proper names, let alone the inevitable titulatures of the two dedicators into what Sande assumes to be space for approximately forty-one letters between "C[astorum / is]" and "ref(ecerunt)" would be impossible however abbreviated, and no parallels are cited. The temple, commonly known as "Aedes," was indeed called "Templum" on occasion, as Sande points out, but such occasions are all literary: on inscriptions, it is invariably "Aedes." The existence and significance of Sande's traces of decoration on the stone will have to be decided by experts. For the present: *non liquet.* If the preserved letters "t.c(?)" do not represent the words "et Castoris," which we may deduce from Suetonius to have been used in the text, it is impossible to say what they signify. The historian Florus, Suetonius' contemporary, has "youths" turn up with laurelled letters announcing victory over the Cimbri in 101 BCE, which they deliver to the praetor *pro aede Pollucis et Castoris* (1.38.20). This, the only other reference to the Temple of Pollux and Castor as such, surely reflects the Tiberian inscription. Poets might invert the normal order of the pair, but it is hard to explain why the prosaic Suetonius and Florus would do so—unless they saw it on the temple.

41. Suet. *Div. Iul.* 10.1; Dio 37.8.2.

42. Hadzsits' (1931) careful assembly and analysis of the complex evidence is essential on all of this. Though not much regarded by subsequent scholarship, it nevertheless strikes me as correct, however improbable the results may first appear. Hadzsits concluded (p. 113) "that the

temple was at first and for long, Castor's; that, once Greek mythologies were widely diffused, it was possible in popular parlance to think of it and speak of it as the shrine of Castor and Pollux; that Pollux did become associated with Castor in worship—to what extent, exactly, we cannot tell, nor precisely when, though it would seem that this was an established fact in the second century BCE; that the Greeks inevitably called it the shrine of Castor *and* Pollux, regardless of dates; that it was officially rechristened by Tiberius (before he became Princeps) as 'the temple of Castor and Pollux,' or as the 'temple of the Castors.'" The crucial witness is Livy. The standard legend of the battle of Lake Regillus, as recounted above (and conveyed by such authors as Cicero, *ND* 2.6, 3.11–13; Dion. Hal. 6.13.1, Flor. 1.5.4; Plut. *Coriol.* 3.4; Val. Max. 1.8.1), is a much later invention, as all would agree. But in his account of the battle (2.20.12), Livy says only that at a critical stage the dictator vowed a temple to Castor, which was later dedicated by his son (2.42.5): no divine epiphany, no Pollux, cf. Hadzsits 1931, 101–5. (Ogilvie 1965, 289, avoids the problem.) Cults and sites dedicated to one or the other of the brothers alone: *RE* 5.1090, s.v. Dioskuren (E. Bethe); note esp. Paus. 3.13.1, 20.1. A rock near Lake Regillus was said to preserve the hoof mark of Castor's horse: Cicero, *ND* 3.11–12. Greek authors refer to *ton Dioskouron hieron, Dioskoreion*, and *naos ton Dioskouron*. These last designations are clearly anachronistic when referring to the Republic, and they uniformly mislead, since the term "Dioskouroi," so natural to the Greeks to designate the inseparable Castor-and-Pollux, does not translate any Latin equivalent: the word "Dioscuri" seems never to appear in classical Latin, whether literary or epigraphical, certainly not in an alternate name for the Temple of Castor and Pollux; cf. Hadzsits 1931, 105–6, 110–11. Note particularly Cic. *ND* 3.53, where the word is left in Greek, and Aug. *RG* 20.3, where *aedem Castoris* of the Latin original is translated in the Greek version as the "Temple of the Dioscuri," τοῦ ναοῦ τῶν Διοσκόρων. The Roman plural for the brothers, hardly equivalent to the neutral "Dioskuroi," was the unbalanced "Castores." References to the twins as such are rare in literature, the earliest being Plin. *NH* 1.2a, 7.86, 10.121 (temple), 34.23 (temple), 35.27. Their temple is called *aedes Castorum* only by Pliny (twice) and by the fourth century *Historia Augusta* (twice) and *Notitia* of the city; and although the Castores turn up in inscriptions, their temple does not. As far as I am aware, *aedes Castoris* and *aedes Castorum* refer only to the temple in Rome—that is, shrines to the twin gods elsewhere always mention Castor and Pollux.

43. For ancient references to the temple, see Hadzsits 1931 and, conveniently, *LTUR* 1 (1993), 242–45. Add, for *aedes Castoris*, the important *I. de Délos* 1511 (a senatusconsultum of 58 BCE); and for *aedes Castoris et Pollucis*, *CIL* 6.2203. For the widespread phenomenon of twins being designated by one name: Harris 1906, 58–62.

44. Prop. 3.14.17; Ov. *Am*, 2.16.13. Thereafter at Sen. *NQ* 1.1.13 and Plin. *NH* 2.101, both, like Ovid, referring to the brothers in their role as stars. And thereafter only in Suetonius and Florus (as above), referring to the temple.

45. *CIL* 9.2443 = *ILS* 147. The inscription has had a remarkably confusing history; see Bernecker 1976, Stylow 1977. The composite text presented here is that of Stylow's definitive reconstruction. Note also *AE* 1991.530, a dedication to Tiberius from a local magistrate at Saepinum in 3 / 2 BCE.

46. The fantasy of the dead Drusus engaged in public works with his living brother, thus attested on the Temple of Pollux and Castor and the gates of Saepinum, reappears on *CIL* 6.40337, the dedication of an unknown building between 4 and 14 CE: the verb is lost, but again there seems to be no indication that Drusus was not alive. It was also presumably repeated on the inscription on the Temple of Concord in 10 CE. Before Tiberius, temples vowed by one Republican nobleman, normally because of military victories, were often completed after a lapse of time and dedicated by another, usually a son or other relative: e.g., Honos et Virtus, vowed by the great Claudius Marcellus and dedicated by his son in 205 BCE (Liv. 29.11.13); or the original Temple of Castor, dedicated by the dictator's son (Liv. 2.42.5); or the Temple of the Lares

Permarini, vowed by L. Aemilius Regillus in 190 BCE and dedicated by his clansman M. Aemilius Lepidus in 170 BCE, complete with a long eulogy on a tablet over the door listing the man's deeds and his vow (Liv. 40.52.4). But I can find no instance before Drusus of a temple at Rome erected by a dead man, and no case where the dedicator's death is ignored.

47. Polydeukes / Pollux, the elder brother: Theoc. *Id.* 22.176, 183. It would be pedantic to observe that Tiberius and Drusus were not actually twins, for Tiberius was comparing, not identifying, the two pairs. On the dissimilarity of Castor and Pollux: Harris 1906, 45–48.

48. *AE* 1963.104. Bibliography reviewed and argument presented in Alföldy 1999 (whence *AE* 1999.1681), with further arguments in Alföldy 2002 and conclusions summarized in Alföldy 2005.

49. Jos. *BJ* 1.412 (Loeb trans. Thackeray), *AJ* 15.336 (Loeb trans. Marcus).

50. Jos. *BJ* 1.414, with Alföldy 1999, 96–101. Must be correct: the words "Tiberieum" on the inscription and "Druseum" in Josephus look to be unique in literature and epigraphy, both Greek and Latin; they are structures recalling two prominent and famously close brothers; they are essentially contemporary (note that Pilate's work was a refurbishment); and of all the cities in the Roman world, they come from the same one. Coincidence is unthinkable: how could the Tiberieum be anything but a pendant to the Druseum?

51. Alföldy 2002, 148, and İşkan-Işik, Eck, and Engelmann 2008, 110, citing Strabo 17.1.6 and Lucian *Quomodo* 62. Note also a ship from Alexandria named for the Dioscuri: *Acts* 28.11.

52. Work on Herod's harbor had certainly begun long before, and the pendant towers of the Druseum and the Tiberieum might be an afterthought, but 4 BCE appears to be the latest possible date. It is true that Josephus mentions only the Druseum, and the Tiberieum is only certified as existing by 26 / 36 CE, but, again, it is hard to conceive of the one being built without the other and, again, Pilate's task in 26 / 36 was to restore a previously existing structure.

53. It has been argued, and is commonly believed, that Augustus' sons Gaius and Lucius Caesar preceded Tiberius and Drusus as Castor and Pollux. There is no evidence for this: see the appendix.

54. Considered further below.

55. Ov. *F.* 1.705–8 (Penguin trans. Boyle and Woodard); *Cons. Liv.* 283–90 (Loeb trans. Mozley); Valerius Maximus 5.5.3 (Loeb trans. Shackleton Bailey).

56. Despite the forbidding reputation passed on by our three major sources, there is good evidence for Tiberius' exceptional popularity with the people of Rome, some of which is considered in chapter 1.

57. Dio 55.27.3–4 (Loeb trans. Cary, modified).

58. Germanicus and Drusus Caesar were almost the same age: Sumner 1967 convincingly argued for birthdates of May 24, 15 BCE and October 7, 14 BCE. Ov. *T.* 2.167, *Pont.* 2.81–84: *quem pia vobiscum proles comitavit euntem, | digna parente suo nominibusque datis, | fratribus adsimiles, quos proxima templa tenentis | divus ab excelsa Iulius aede videt.* The emphasis here, hard to catch in translation, falls implicitly on four generations of Caesars. A few years later, during his consulship in 15 CE, Drusus Caesar was given the nickname of Castor after he struck a distinguished member of the equestrian order, almost certainly the praetorian prefect Sejanus himself: Dio 57.14.9, 22.1; Tac. 4.3.2; on which see Scott 1930a. Who gave him that nickname and how widespread it was is not known, but it is very curious, and not immediately explicable: Pollux was the boxer, not Castor. I find no evidence that Drusus was *princeps iuventutis*, as claimed in Poulsen 1992, 128. While Germanicus and Drusus were depicted as loving brothers, there seems to be no official representation of them as Castor and Pollux: but see below. One of the most attractive portrayals of their affection is a fine coin issued after their deaths by the *koinon* of Asia, showing them sitting, togaed, in curule chairs, and calling them "Drusus and Germanicus Caesar the new gods of brotherly love" (*neoi theoi philadelphoi*). The reference is to a cult of the old Attalid dynasty of Pergamum, paid to dead kings or their dead relatives: Levy 1994, 79–89. Its application to Tiberius' dead sons is particularly neat.

59. The birth: *I. It.* 13.1.216; Tac. 2.84.1 (dating it to 19, and adding the usual nasty Tacitean comment, "for he turned everything, however chance, to glory"). The coins: *RIC* 32 (Rome). The complex of symbols—crossed *cornucopiae*, heads (the children assure the future), and caduceus (the wand of Mercury)—came to represent *felicitas temporum*, the good fortune of the age: for date, parallels, and precedents, see Meise 1966, 12–14.

60. Coins: *RPC* 946 (Cyrenaica: "Tiberius and Germanicus Caesar," with portraits on the reverse, "Drusus Caesar son of (Tiberius) Augustus," with portrait, on the obverse); *RPC* 1171 (Corinth: "Twin Caesars," with facing busts). Near Salamis: *IGRR* 3.997. Ephesus: *IK Ephesos* VII.2.4337. All of this material is presented at Poulsen 1992, 128–29; *pace* Poulsen, portraits on glass medallions from the Northwestern provinces do not appear to represent the infant twins, see Boschung 1987.

61. Death of Germanicus: Tac. 4.5.1. Tiberius' nickname of "The Twin" seems to be attested only at Jos. *AJ* 18.206 (explicitly) and on the papyrus *BGU* 156.6.

62. Plin. *NH* 10. 121–22 (Penguin trans. Healey, substantially modified). Pliny appends his usual moralizing comment, 10.123: "The Roman people considered the bird's talent a sufficiently good reason for a funeral procession and for the punishment of a Roman citizen. Yet in Rome many leading men had no funeral rites at all, while no one avenged the death of Scipio Aemilianus after he had destroyed Carthage and Numantia."

63. Compare the popular reaction to a false rumor spread at Rome in 19 CE that Germanicus had recovered from what was to prove his final illness at Antioch: "People came running to the Capitoline from every direction with torches and sacrifical victims. They almost tore the doors off the temple so that nothing would get in their way in their eagerness to fulfill the vows they had made for his safety. Tiberius was awakened by the voices of the populace everywhere as they rejoiced and shouted together: 'Safe is Rome! Safe our homeland! Germanicus is safe!'" (Suet. *Cal.* 6.1, trans. Hurley). Whether the raven incident is fact or folklore is moot. Macrobius relates two anecdotes about ravens trained to salute Augustus as *imperator*, the second of them by a poor shoemaker—indeed, Augustus has a houseful of such avian *salutatores*: *Sat.* 2.4.30. There are also echoes of our tale at Plut. *Mor.* 973B–D.

64. The standard work remains Thiersch 1909.

65. Krause 2003, 92–97. In a particularly sceptical review that draws attention to both errors and fragile speculations Wulf-Rheidt (2004, 1067) agrees with Krause's argument that the "Torre del Faro" cannot be the Pharus, but she finds the essentially unexcavated remains of the "Loggia della Marina" too exiguous to support his elaborate reconstruction of the Pharus there; in the only other serious review of the book, Gros 2004 appears to accept the identification of the "Loggia" with the Pharus. Cf. in slightly more detail the version in Krause's full-scale reconstruction of the villa: Krause 2005, 251–58.

66. Providing enough material for an entire dissertation: Jaisle 1907; cf. Harris 1906.

67. Luc. *Quomodo* 62; Strabo 17.1.6. There is a large, complex, and contentious bibliography on the construction and dedication of the Pharos in the third century BCE, well summarized by Bing 1998 (reprinted with revisions, Bing 2009, 194–216). The only matter relevant here is that it is established beyond a reasonable doubt that a statue of Zeus Soter stood atop the enormous structure (thus Bing, building on Fraser 1972, 2:47–48, et al.): that is clear from ancient representations and from epigram 11 (Gow-Page) by the contemporary Posidippus. Where then are the Theoi Soteres, the Dioskouroi? They appear only in Lucian, writing almost five hundred years after the construction of the Pharos, and the problem is compounded by the two versions of the dedicatory inscription as presented by Strabo and by Lucian. P. M. Fraser translates these as follows: "Sostratos the Cnidian, friend of the sovereigns, dedicated this for the safety of those who sail the seas, as the inscription says"; and "Sostratos, the son of Dexiphanes, the Cnidian, dedicated this to the Saviour Gods on behalf of those who sail the seas." The two texts do not fully overlap in either form or content, but they do not actually disagree with each other and, as Fraser noted, Strabo's may be read as a paraphrase. We cannot dismiss Lucian as a late source,

or as erroneously altering Dis Soter to Theoi Soteres. Such arguments are library-bound, and they stumble on the test of autopsy. Fraser (1972, 1:19), following a long scholarly tradition, reasonably remarked that "the explanation may simply be that the dedication was in fact to all the deities who protect seafarers, and that Posidippus singled out Zeus, pre-eminent among such, because his statue crowned the lighthouse." It might be noted in this regard both that the lighthouses inferred by Alföldy at Herod's harbor at Caesarea were probably dedicated "to the sailors" (Josephus), just as the Pharos was at Alexandria (Strabo and Lucian), and that they (the Druseum and the Tiberieum) would have been dominated by the great temple of Rome and Augustus, the Sebasteion or Caesareum. In that temple at Caesarea stood a colossal statue of Augustus, allegedly equal in quality to and modeled on the statue of Zeus at Olympia. That is to say, if Herod at Caesarea was indeed recalling the sailors' safe haven at Alexandria, Augustus, Tiberius, and Drusus at Caesarea would have nicely complemented Zeus and the Dioskouroi at Alexandria.

68. Luc. *Quomodo* 62 (trans. Costa 2005).

69. Readers need not be reminded of the uncertainties involved, not only those noted already, but the assumption that the inscription in Lucian's Alexandria read the same in Tiberius' day; that Strabo is paraphrasing it, not quoting; that Tiberius was responsible for constructing the Pharus on Capri; that the tower could accommodate both a statue of Zeus and a dedicatory inscription to Kastor and Polydeukes; that the Tiberieum and Druseum at Caesarea were lighthouses; and so on.

70. The link is noted by Lindsay 1995, 98, 185; Vigourt 2001, 335–38, is disappointing on the death of Tiberius. The contrary nature of the omen is noteworthy, in that a lamp going out is good for the Claudii, just as the appearance of the Dioscuri was bad for one of them. Tiberius' special relationship with fire and the sun, indeed his unique mastery of flame, is pursued in chapter 4.

71. Poulsen 1992, 122–26; cf. La Rocca 1994, Spannagel 1999, 28–34; Heinemann 2007, 45–48, 75–76; Sumi 2009, 179–81.

72. Pollini 1987, 19 (they "recall classical figures like the Dioskouroi"), 20 (they are "in a sense like the Dioskuroi").

73. Buxton and Hannah 2005.

Chapter 3. The Odyssey of Tiberius Caesar

[Ed. note: with thanks to Museum Tusculanum Press for permission to publish here the paper that first appeared in *Classica et Mediaevalia* 64 (2014): 199–246. Copyright © 2013 Museum Tusculanum Press.]

1. Homer *Odyssey* 1.1–9 (trans. Lattimore 1967).

2. Phillips 1953, 53; and passim, for a good collection and clear analysis of the evidence for "Odysseus in Italy." Cf. Malkin 1998, 178–209; Schade 1999.

3. See the account in the fine guide to the site, Cassieri 2000, 20–23; see also Cassieri 1996 for a good overview.

4. Summaries of the two main sides in the debate: Andreae 1994 and Himmelmann 1995. The collection of essays in De Grummond and Ridgway 2000 is particularly good. Anyone interested in the site and its art should begin with Ridgway 2000, a superb summary. Measurements of the site and of the sculptures as restored, whether precise or estimated, are very hard to come by, as are detailed descriptions of the excavation and of the many other artworks. E.g., the otherwise excellent Jacopi 1963, Neudecker 1988, Andreae and Parisi Presicce 1996, and Cassieri 2000. For charges of skullduggery, destruction, and suppression of evidence: Salza Prina Ricotti 2006. The villa remains essentially unpublished. [Ed. note: for scholarship on the site and sculptures published since this essay first appeared, see Bruno, Attanasio, and Prochaska 2015 (and cf. n. 8 below), Slavazzi 2015–16, Sauron 2019, Badoud 2019. Some images

are also available via the archeological museum's online photo gallery: Direzione Regionale Musei Lazio, accessed April 1, 2024, https://direzioneregionalemuseilazio.cultura.gov.it/en /luoghi/museo-archeologico-nazionale-e-area-archeologica-di-sperlonga/.]

5. Gantz 1993, 629.

6. See Smith 1991 on the dates. Weis 2000, 117–24, discusses the Pasquino group thoroughly (n. 62 cites twelve scholars for or against the identification with Odysseus). The arguments against, marshaled at p. 119 in an otherwise invaluable paper, strike me as inconclusive or misconceived (e.g., that the Pasquino warrior wears a helmet while Odysseus typically has the soft cap, the *pilos*: to which it must be replied that this Odysseus is here not the sailor or the trickster but the warrior in battle, and is often portrayed armed as such). Andreae 1994, 28–33, maintains that Menelaus and Patroclus were indeed *reworked* into Odysseus and Achilles. The dictum of Smith (2002, 90) is pertinent: "Ancient images are active, positive, structured expressions of their customers' aspirations and agendas, not neutral reflectors of reality."

7. Tac. 4.59.1–2. Suet. 39 does not mention Sejanus, and suggests merely that Tiberius took the incident as an omen not to return to Rome.

8. To pronounce on the date(s) of the creation and installation of the statuary is to dance on the edge of a scholarly volcano. Although some argue for the mid- to late first century BCE— e.g., Rice 1986, Kunze 1996 (rightly questioned by Weis 2000, 138–40)—no argument seems probative, either in support of such a dating or in denial of a later one. As will be seen, I follow La Rocca 1998. [Ed note: in an addendum to the original publication of this essay, Ted Champlin noted that the editors of *Classica et Mediaevalia* had alerted him at a late stage to Bruno, Atta nasio, and Prochaska 2012, in which the authors established that "with two minor exceptions, the Homeric sculptures are unequivocally all made of marble quarried at Docimum, in Phrygia," and that "the known history of that great quarry gives an incontrovertible chronological terminus: the sculptures could not have been carved before the last decades of the first century BC, and therefore should be a unitary group carved by one workshop and commissioned for the site by one patron with immense resources" (Champlin 2014, 241–42).]

9. Suet. 5 on his maternal grandmother as a native of Fundi. That and a statue later erected there by the senate to Felicitas persuaded some, *quidam*, to think that Tiberius himself was born at Fundi, but Suetonius preferred to follow the majority and more reliable authorities in assigning the birth to Rome. The important point is that the senate of Rome chose to celebrate Tiberian Felicitas precisely at Fundi. In a letter to the senate, Caligula accused his great-grandmother Livia of *ignobilitas*, "as if" her maternal grandfather was merely a decurion of Fundi, whereas Suetonius can assure us (*Cal.* 23.2) that public records show that Aufidius Lurco (the grandfather) held offices at Rome itself. In fact, Gaius was right and Suetonius was wrong, misled by the similarity of the names Aufidius and Alfidius. Inscriptions assure us that Livia's mother was an Alfidia (*IG* 12.6.1.371 [Samos], *CIL* 2.5.73 [Tucci], 9.3661 [Marruvium]), and the name Alfidius is attested at Fundi (*CIL* 10.6248, *AE* 1978.81). Confusion is compounded by the fact that the much more common Aufidius is also found at Fundi (Hor. *Serm.* 1.5.34–36: a magistrate). Linderski 1974 demonstrated that Aufidius Lurco was not the grandfather. Mathieu 1998 collects most of the inscriptional evidence for the Alfidii in the Roman world. It is tempting to speculate that the confusion between Alfidii and Aufidii was encouraged by Livia herself, insinuating an impressive connection that did not exist, just as her husband Augustus, or his supporters, grafted his own small-town ancestors, the Octavii of nearby Velitrae, onto the senatorial Octavii of Rome: Suet. *Aug.* 1–2. Tiberius must have inherited the estate from his grandmother or one of her relatives, not from Livia, who was still alive in 26 CE. A fragmentary bronze tablet from Fundi, dateable to the late third or first half of the second century BCE, records the *hospitium* created between the town and a Ti. C. . . . (or G. . . . or O. . . .). The patron should be a Roman senator, and for various reasons, this is most probably a Tiberius Claudius, hence an ancestor of the princeps: *CIL* 10.6231 = *ILS* 6093 = *ILLRP* 1068. If that is so, his roots in the area were deep indeed. Ancient Fundi: Di Fazio 2006.

10. Suet. 11.1. Cf. Plut. fr. 182; Quint. 3.1.7; *Suda*, s.v. Theodorus.

11. On the cultural life of Rhodes, Rossetti and Furiani 1993 is especially good.

12. La Rocca 1998, 220–28. La Rocca also argues, 212–19, that the head of a so-called Centaur found in the adjacent Horti Lamiani came from the same workshop as that of the head of Ulysses at Sperlonga. The boundary between the Horti Lamiani and the Horti Maecenatis is unsure, but Aelius Lamia died in 33 CE (Tac. 6.27) and his gardens were imperial property by the time of Caligula (Phil. *Leg.* 351; Suet. *Caligula* 59): surely bequeathed by Lamia to his great friend Tiberius.

13. *SEG* 19.623 (Sperlonga); Plin. *NH* 36.37 (Rome); *IG* 14.898 (Capri) and 1227 (Antium). Rice 1986, 239–42, collects no fewer than eight epigraphical "signatures" of Athanodorus. Of the remaining five, one comes from Trastevere in Rome, one from the theater at Ostia, one from Lindos on Rhodes, one from Rhodian territory on the mainland, and one is of unknown provenance.

14. La Rocca 1998, 203–28, drawing together several scholarly strands; at 224–25, he advances the hypothesis that the Laocoön never left the Horti Maecenatis and that it was created for Tiberius.

15. Lauter 1972; summarily rejected in Rice 1986, 245–46. Her only objection to Lauter's careful exposition seems to be that Sperlonga and other, later Roman grottoes were on a much larger and more elaborate scale. It is difficult to see the value of an argument based on difference in size when that is precisely what one would expect. Since Rice's intervention, Lauter's paper has been ignored in the Sperlonga bibliography. Rice's paper, for all of its learning, is deeply flawed in its treatment of the evidence. Among other problems, the extensive stemmata discussed are Pelions on Ossas of uncertainties and assumptions. Dates are often fudged; even on her assumption of ca. 80 BCE as the birthdate of one of the sculptors, the assertion that "Common sense argues that he did not work beyond the turning of the era" is neither persuasive nor relevant. Above all, the long argument at p. 249 rejecting Tiberius as the patron ignores the fact that he was indeed as "a young nobleman" deeply impressed by Rhodes *in 20 BCE*. In 10 BCE, the lower date allowed by Rice for Athanodorus' activity in Italy, Tiberius was one of the great men of Rome, a seasoned general and ex-consul, mature and highly educated. Another monument on Rhodes might offer a magic door into the cavern at Sperlonga. Every visitor to the acropolis of Lindos on Rhodes passes the enormous relief sculpture (5.5 meters high by 4.75 meters long), which represents in fine detail the stern of a warship, from the great curving poop (*aphlaston*) to the last oarlock, running toward the viewer's left. Ermeti 1978 identifies it as a *triemiolia*, a fast light vessel especially identified with the great naval power of Rhodes. Gabrielsen 1997, in a far superior discussion of the *triemiolia* (pp. 86–94), doubts the precise identification. Be that as it may, Ermeti (p. 196) sees an "absolute resemblance" between the ship of the Lindos relief and the vessel of Odysseus (sculpted by Rhodians) at Sperlonga, both of which offer detailed renditions of the stern half of the port side of a ship heading to the viewer's left: marvelous if true. Unfortunately, Gabrielsen, who otherwise criticizes Ermeti for lack of originality and for making a number of unsupported claims, does not comment on the resemblance.

16. Very few villas: that is, between the clusters at Tarracina and Caieta. See the maps in Lafon 2001, 73–75, 85–87, 103–5, 251–53, and especially 155. Strabo 5.3.6: Did he really know the area? Was he casually generalizing from the one great example of Sperlonga?

17. Andreae 1994, 17ff., emphasized the scale of the sculptures, over-lifesize, as suggesting imperial tastes and resources. Himmelmann (1995, 17) countered with the similarly scaled heroic figures from the Antikythera shipwreck of ca. 60 BCE, to suggest that there were private precedents. But this is the only one that he cites, and there is no sign whether these were meant for private or public display. Andreae's contention—that the Sperlonga figures were truly on a grand, normally public, scale—remains valid.

18. The Via Valeria (second century BCE) runs very near the villa on its way from Fundi and the Via Appia inland down to Formiae: Lafon 1979. Andreae 1994, 1–15 asserts (on what evidence

it is not clear: cf. Lafon) that it was no more than a mule-track inappropriate for vehicles, hence access to the villa must have been by sea. Lafon (410–13) argues for its economic importance for the local vineyards that produced the renowned Fundanum and Caecubum grapes.

19. Viscogliosi 1996; cf. Carey 2002, 61, from which the quotation is taken. The thematic similarities with these other properties were, of course, well known. They were all villas (including the "Domus Aurea"), not urban *domus*: that is, their grottoes were a mark of imperial *otium*. And, again, Augustus, who is sometimes suggested as the owner of the villa, has no known connection with the area.

20. It is indicative of the passions aroused by the Sperlonga sculptures that scholars who accept without demur thousands of unsupported "facts" thrown up by antiquity adopt an attitude of robust skepticism when asked to accept that the villa was owned by Tiberius. There is no proof that he ever lived at the so-called "Villa Jovis" on Capri either.

21. Bergmann 1999, 103–6; Bergmann 2001.

22. My estimate from various plans: as noted above, precise measurements of the site are hard to come by.

23. And dining while they watched monsters about to eat men, an irony surely not lost on the master of the house.

24. Stewart 1977, 78.

25. Andreae 1999, 185–88, citing the prophetic words of Dohrn 1977, 231; Andreae 2004, 23. Registered by Schmid 2003, 208, without comment, and going on to propose a purely hypothetical tableau with Circe (209–17). Note the warnings of Beard and Henderson (2001, 74–82) against the perils of tunnel vision at Sperlonga: that is, focusing on the four reconstructed groups while ignoring the thousands of other, unassigned fragments and the several over complete works of art from the cave and its surroundings.

26. Hyginus *Fab.* 102; Apollod. *Epit.* 5.8. In Sophocles' *Philoctetes*, he uses his companion Neoptolemus (not Diomedes) to get the bow, but the naive and upright son of Achilles repents and returns the weapons, and the situation is saved only by the intervention of Heracles as the deus ex machina.

27. The identity of her enemy varies from story to story, the best known of which is that of Ovid in *Met.* 13. Most significantly, the transformation of the beautiful girl is a Hellenistic invention, for the original Scylla was a howling monster born and bred, with twelve feet and six heads, each with three rows of teeth (*Od.* 12.85–110): on all of this, Gantz 1993, 731–33. The hybrid creature at Sperlonga is clearly not the Homeric monster. On the cave of Philoctetes, a convention introduced on the Athenian stage, see Dohrn 1977.

28. On the significance and the artifice of Roman caves, see above all Lavagne 1988 (515–56, excellent on Sperlonga) and, for a succinct analysis of caves in the mythological landscape, Buxton 1994, 104–8.

29. The phrase was coined by L'Orange 1964. By "Odyssey," we mean the adventures of Odysseus in general, including some not in the Homeric poem.

30. *Navis Argo PH*: Jacopi 1963, 47–48. Elaborate discussion of the enigmatic letters PH at Andreae 1994, 25–28, rightly doubted by Himmelmann 1995.

31. Cassieri 2000, 145–46: reconstituted from over 360 fragments. Andreae 1994, 113–20, disposes of the flimsy case for a Flavian date. For a sketch of the cave showing the relative positions of the dining platform, the Argo, and Ganymede: Andreae 1994, 208, Tafel 8 / 9.

32. Cassieri 2000, 20; recovered from the sea in the early twentieth century.

33. Cassieri 2000, 68–69. Finds at the site were first described by Jacopi 1963, 39–165; for the sculpture alone, see Neudecker 1988, 41–46, 220–33. The actual dates of creation and installation are, of course, unknown.

34. Observers may be tempted to think of the equally artificial modern theme park, but Sperlonga and Hadrian's even more elaborate villa at Tibur are, in fact, its very antithesis. A theme park is simplistic, public, and for the taste of the masses, whereas a Sperlonga is

sophisticated, private, and for the cognoscenti, however we may judge their taste. Among the pieces and fragments preserved in the museum today, all of impressive quality, note a head of Aeneas (or of his son, Ascanius); a striking relief, found near the grotto, of Venus Genetrix accompanied by a small Eros; and three charming piglets, probably the survivors of a group depicting the Laurentine sow and litter, familiar from *Aeneid* 3.388–93, 8.43–48, 81–85. That is, with these pieces, the ancestors of the Julian family, so glorified by Tiberius' adoptive father Augustus, were also represented here. Note, moreover, the archaizing heads of Dionysus and Athena (as well as that of Venus Genetrix), and the two authentic fifth-century Athenian vases found on the site, both depicting Dionysus as well. These suggest not only an antiquarian but an active collector of antiquities. Cassieri 2000, 64–66 (Aeneas / Ascanius and Venus; cf. two marble *erotes* [Eros / Cupid was likewise a Julian relative], 69–72); 63–64 (Dionysus); 74–75 (Athena); 80–81 (Dionysian vases: cf. the high quality *oscillum* with Dionysiac Sileni on both faces, 67–68). Walde 2009 for the likelihood of the Laurentine sow. On the collection of ancient vases: Cristofani 1995.

35. Stein-Hölkeskamp and Hölkeskamp 2006, 11–14 and passim for an introduction.

36. Liv. 5.52.2. Boardman 2002 on the physical recreation of the mythical past, citing some six hundred testimonia to the preserved relics of well-remembered heroes.

37. Strabo 5.3.6 (Loeb trans. Jones). From Sperlonga, the mountain does indeed look like an island. Cf. another contemporary, Dion. Hal. 4.63.1: "A towering peak like a peninsula." Strabo's "roots" refer to moly, the magic herb given by Hermes to Odysseus, to protect him against Circe's magic. Laestrygones: refs. at Wiseman 1974, 212 n. 2, starting with Cicero *Att.* 2.13.2 and Plin. *NH* 3.59.

38. Cult of Circe at Circeii: e.g., Cic. *ND* 3.48; and the restoration of "the altar of most holy Circe" by a senator, dedicated on June 15, 213 CE: *CIL* 10.6422 = *ILS* 4037 (Tarracina, probably from Circeii). A female portrait head found in the sanctuary there and dated to the first half of the first century BCE has been taken to reflect the cult statue: Andreae and Parisi Presicce 1996, 137. Elpenor's tomb, the place where myrtle first appeared in Italy: Theophrastus *HP* 5.8.7, followed by Pliny *NH* 15.119. The tale of the feckless Elpenor was familiar from *Od.* 10.552–60, 11.51–83, 12.8–15.

39. Wiseman 1995, 45–50, for a succinct summary of the tangled versions, with translations of some of the major sources at 160–68; versions 1–3 of the founding of Rome at p. 49, versions four and five at p. 50. To these might be added a sixth, the tale that Aeneas founded Rome with or after (the Greek is unclear) Odysseus himself.

40. Explicit at Hyg. *Fab.* 127.2; the tangled ancient sources are presented with customary clarity at Gantz 1993, 710–12.

41. Note also that the Argo sails out of the cliff at Sperlonga toward Monte Circeo, inevitably reminding the viewer of the Argonauts' earlier visit to Circe's island home: Ap. *Arg.* 4.659–752.

42. For Latium to the north of these regions, see above, pp. 52, 59f. Further to the south we find landfalls for two companions of Odysseus, at Laos (Lucania) and Temesa (Bruttii): Strabo 6.1.1, 4. And, of course, six other comrades were removed by Scylla, pouncing from her lair on the mainland at the straits of Messina.

43. Circeii and Sinuessa lay on the fluid borders of Latium Adiectum, between Latium Vetus and Campania: Nissen 1902, 552–54. Sinopus as the eponym of Sinuessa's predecessor, Sinope: deduced by Wikén 1937, 126–27 from a fragment of Pherecydes (144J) naming the six companions snatched by Scylla (including Sinopus), and from the report that Sinuessa was originally called Sinope (Liv. 10.21, Plin. *NH* 3.59).

44. Pithecusa: Lycophron 688–93, with Phillips 1953, 59. Tiberius died in his villa at Misenum: Suet. 72–75, *Cal.* 13; Dio 58.28.1; Tac. 6.50. Phaedrus 2.5 commemorates an earlier visit there. Misenus: Strabo 1.2.18, cf. 5.4.6. Misenus was appropriated by Vergil (*Aen.* 6.162) and by the subsequent Latin tradition to become the steersman for *his* hero, Aeneas.

45. Baius: Strabo 5.4.6. The nymphaeum, now submerged at Punta dell'Epitaffio: see the convenient summary at Carey 2002, 48–52, with bibliography. A clear and evocative description at Yegül 1996, 157–59. The palace at Baiae: D'Arms 1970, 109–11. Tiberian relics there: Suet. 6.3. At Fronto M. Caes. 1.4.3, Marcus Caesar writes *apud Baias agimus in hoc diuturno Ulixi labyrinthi* ("we are now staying at Baiae in this endless labyrinth of Ulysses"). Most likely an allusion to the hero's wanderings in the area, this enigmatic phrase has elicited a range of interpretations: van den Hout 1999, 16–17.

46. Dio 48.50. In 37 BCE, Agrippa's men cut channels from the Lucrine Lake, which lay between Misenum and Baiae, to the sea. At 48.50.4, Dio's account raises unanswered questions: "While the men were working, a statue overlooking Avernus, either of Calypso, to whom this place, whither they say Odysseus also sailed, is dedicated, or of some other heroine, was covered with sweat like a human body. Now what this imported I cannot say." Odysseus at Avernus: Strabo 5.4.5. Island off Puteoli: Philost. *Apoll.* 7.10.1–2; 7.41; 8.11. Presumably Nesis, modern Nisida. Two other locations near Italy were suggested for Calypso's Ogygia: Gozo, near Malta (Strabo 7.3.6 with 1.2.37, interpreting Callimachus), and an island ten miles off the Lacinian cape, near Croton (pseudo-Scylax 13; Plin. *NH* 3.96).

47. Pseudo-Scymnus 229 (late first century BC); Festus 16L.

48. On the homes of the Sirens in the West, see Breglia Pulci Doria 1987, 88–96; on the literary and archaeological evidence for the Athenaion, Breglia Pulci Doria 1996.

49. Suet. 43.2; Aug. 72.3.

50. The very thin evidence for any imperial connection with Capri after Tiberius is rehearsed in Booms 2010.

51. Belli et al. 1998, 145–50.

52. Belli et al. 1998, 208–16; Adamo Muscettola 1998, 263, with photographs at 261–62; Ciardiello 2010 (Gradola); Esposito 2009 (Damecuta); cf. Stewart 1977, 84. The statues have never been published: cf. De Franciscis n.d. [1964]. Further discoveries await—in 2009, divers reported the discovery of seven statue bases at a depth of 150 meters: "Roman Statues Found in Blue Grotto Cave," *NBC News*, accessed April 1, 2024, https://www.nbcnews.com/id/wbna 33058777.

53. Belli et al. 1998, 199–202.

54. Plin. *NH* 3.82; Suet. 65; Juv. 10.92.

55. Krause 1998; Krause 2003; Krause 2005.

56. Ihm 1901, 287–91.

57. Suet. 65. Deep seclusion: Dio 58.13.2 adds that he refused even to receive an embassy from the senate.

58. An unnecessary emendation in another text has produced false support for "Jovis" in Suetonius. In his precious description of Capri at 4.67, Tacitus notes *tum Tiberius duodecim villarum nominibus et molibus insederat*, a puzzling clause that Church and Brodribb translate loosely as "Tiberius had by this time filled the island with twelve country houses, each with a grand name and structure of its own" (1895, 144). The reading *numinibus* for *nominibus*, "gods" instead of "names," was suggested long ago: hence the assumption that each villa was named after one of the twelve Olympians, with the greatest naturally being Jupiter's. This unlikely double conjecture—"numinibus" in Tacitus plus "Iovis" in Suetonius—has not found much support (cf. Federico and Miranda 1998, 512), but turns up occasionally in the literature on the "Villa Jovis." Martin and Woodman 1989 have a long and thorough note on the passage at pp. 244–45, leaving it marked as corrupt; for his translation, Woodman tentatively offers *amoenitatibus et molibus*, rendering the whole clause as "now it was Tiberius who had settled there in twelve attractive and massive villas"; Bob Kaster suggests *per litteras* the appealing *moenibus et molibus*.

59. Bob Kaster also points out to me the existence of two manuscripts contemporary with the Laurentianus, not used by Ihm, that also read "Iovis": "But both are fairly extensively

contaminated, and neither has any independent authority; one of them is derived from an earlier, extant manuscript at Durham (also not used by Ihm) that reads 'Ionis.'"

60. Attempts have been made to show the importance of Io to the Julio-Claudians, however nonexistent the evidence or bizarre the interpretation. In a nutshell, the tale is that Io, a mortal beloved of Jupiter, was turned by him into a cow to escape Juno's wrath; Juno gave the cow to be watched by the many-eyed Argus, Mercury slew Argus and Juno sent a gadfly to torment Io. As a cow, she wandered the earth until she arrived in Egypt, was restored to human form by Jupiter, and gave birth to his son, Epaphus, the ancestor of Argive and Egyptian royalty. For some, Io may represent Egypt liberated from Argus / Mark Antony by Octavian (Augustus) / Mercury: Adamo Muscettola 1998, 254–56, following Ghedini 1986. Augustus was certainly portrayed as Mercury (Brendel 1935), but the rest is fantasy.

61. E.g., to take authors well-known to Tiberius, Callim. *Epigr.* 18; Prop. 2.28.17, 33A; Ov. *Met.* 1.747; cf. Hyg. *Fab.* 145; *Suda*, s.v. Isis.

62. Jos. *AJ* 18.65–80, with Suet. 36, Tac. 2.85.4.

63. According to Ihm's apparatus criticus.

64. Bernecker 1981, 109 n. 3.

65. Bernecker 1981, preferring Ion or Ino to Io, without explanation; developed at Federico and Miranda 1998, 508. [Ed. note: the conjecture *Inonis* is adopted in the 2016 Oxford Classical Texts edition of Suetonius.]

66. Kardulias 2001, emphasizing the initiatory aspect of the tale, offers extensive bibliography.

67. Plin. *NH* 3.82, 85. Her cult at Naples: *IGI* 2.94.

68. Standard reference works overlook it: the island is not in Pauly-Wissowa or *Der Neue Pauly*; nor is it to be discovered in William Smith's *Dictionary of Greek and Roman Geography* (London, 1868); nor in Talbert's magisterial *Barrington Atlas of the Greek and Roman World* (Princeton, NJ, 2000). It is listed as an ancient place name at Nissen 1902, 986, with the reference to Pliny and a question mark, but not discussed in the text. The Sirens may come to our aid. In the western tradition, which is quite distinct from that of mainland Greece, there are three of them: Parthenope, Leucosia, and Ligeia. (Breglia Pulci Doria 1987, 88–96, for the sources. The tradition seems to go back to Timaeus in the fourth century.) The geographical locations associated with them can be sorted diachronically into three successive groupings in the vicinity:

    1) the scene of their singing and the destruction of passing sailors was the Sirenes or Sirenussae islands, off the coast from Positano, visible from Capri;

    2) so upset were they when Odysseus and his crew escaped them that they threw themselves into the sea, and each washed up at a different place: Parthenope at Naples, Leucosia down near Poseidonia (Paestum), and Ligeia at Terina even further down the coast (Parthenope was famously honored by her eponymous city, later Neapolis, while Leucosia may have been worshipped at Poseidonia);

    3) all three of them enjoyed a temple together, in which (according to Timaeus) "ancient offerings" were on display, somewhere on the Sorrentine peninsula, again, probably within sight of Capri. That is, they were mortal creatures, they died by throwing themselves into the sea, and they returned as immortals: this is exactly what happened to Ino, and it was observed some time ago that the names Leucothea and Leucosia were interchangeable (Breglia Pulci Doria 1987, 88). Now, if we understand Pliny rightly, the island of Leucothea lay somewhere between the island of Capri and the island of Leucosia (which was down near Poseidonia). The only islands that appear on the map between these two are the three Sirenes (modern Li Galli), which Pliny happens to ignore. Perhaps the best guess is that each of the three Siren Islands was given a name, hence that one of them was his Leucothea, aka Leucosia.

69. Ov. *Met.* 4.525, introducing Ino's suicide.

70. In Stewart 1977, the case for Tiberius was set out briefly at pp. 78 and 82; the Odyssean coda, pp. 87–88.

71. Suet. 56: Seleucus is almost certainly the grammarian Seleucus of Alexandria, known as *Homericus*, who taught in Rome and who wrote commentaries on just about every poet (including perhaps Tiberius' three favorites, cf. below): facts and reasonable conjectures available at Brill's online *Lexicon of Greek Grammarians of Antiquity* (Selecus 1).

72. Suet. 70; Browne 1658, ch. 5.

73. Stewart 1977, 87–88.

74. Plut. *Mor.* 419B–E, duly mentioned by Stewart 1977, 88, 85. At 88 n. 109, he notes that Euphorion, one of Tiberius' favorite authors, apparently considered Odysseus himself to be Pan's father; at 85–86 he suggests a parallel between Euphorion's treatment of Odysseus and that of the Sperlonga sculptors. Roscher's *Lexikon* lists no fewer than eighteen possible unions for the parents of Pan: most of the mothers are nymphs or goddesses.

75. D. L. 9.109. Fine introductions to the *Silloi*: Long 1978; Ax 1991; and, above all, Clayman 2009.

76. So Ax 1991, discussed by Clayman 2009, 120–24.

77. *Nekuia*: it is an old debate as to whether or not the whole poem was a visit to the underworld. Long 1978, 81, is dubious. Ax 1991, 182–83, argues for it. In a judicious summary (2009, 78–116), Clayman suggests that of the three books, book 1 and least part of book 2 were set in Hades. Pyrrho as a second Odysseus, Ax 1991, 190, Clayman 2009, 100. The Homeric line is *Iliad* 3.222–23, referring to Odysseus' preeminence as a speaker, not as a warrior. Lest there be any doubt, Timon likewise linked Pyrrho with Odyssean terms in his poem *Idalmoi*. Images: Clayman 2009, 58–60 and 68–70.

78. For what is known and speculated about the grammarian Apollonides of Nicaea, consult Brill's online *Lexicon of Greek Grammarians of Antiquity*. Two of his works, *On Proverbs* and *On Fabricated Histories* might also appeal to the taste of Tiberius. It is an open question whether the grammarian of Nicaea was the Apollonides who wrote a poem about the eagle that appeared at Rhodes to foreshadow the restoration of Tiberius from exile, *Anth. Pal.* 9.287.

79. Suet. 21.6, quoting *Il.* 10. 246–47 (trans. Lattimore 1951). Diomedes' description of Odysseus: 10.242–45.

80. Combining Tac. 6.29 and Dio 58.24.3–5 with Juv. 10.81–86.

81. Champlin 2011.

82. Tac. 4.58.2; Suet. 56.

83. Stewart 1977, 87.

84. Syme 1989, 418 n. 46.

85. Overlapping sources: Suet. 10, 11.5; Dio 55.9.5–8; Tac. 1.3.1; Vell. 2.99.2. All these reasons might have come into play.

86. Vell. 2.99.4; Hom. *Od.* 7.261.

87. The five are named at Vell. 2.100.4–5; the death of Sempronius Gracchus at Tac. 1.53.

88. Gantz 1993, 713 for references, on which the following depends. In one version of the tale, Odysseus returns to Ithaca only to banish his adulterous wife, sending her back to her father: Apollod. *Epit.* 7.38; Paus. 8.12.6. Both authors report that she gave birth to Pan at Mantineia, but Pausanias does not allude to her father: not much like the exile of Julia by Augustus. More suggestive is another story that has Odysseus kill her for adultery: Apollod. 7.39. Tiberius, it was alleged, essentially starved Julia to death not long after Augustus died: Tac. 1.53; cf. Suet. 50.1. Linderski 1988 makes a convincing case for exceptional cruelty.

89. Gantz 1993, 110 for the different versions and sources.

90. Noted by Syme 1983, 243–44. The First Citizen not quite returning to Rome in his last six years is a curious pendant to the first two years of his rule, when he could not bring himself to leave the capital, to the point that people called him Callipedes, presumably after a comic actor who ran in place: Suet. 38.

91. That is, Suetonius or his source may have assumed that, on the other occasions, Tiberius did not intend to enter the city.

92. Suet. 72.2; Tac. 4.58.2. Claudius: *ILS* 206. *Apsentia pertinax*: cf. *continuus abscessus*, a description attributed to Fulcinius Trio at Tac. 6.38.2.

93. Tac. 4.58.3; compare his own description (at 3.47.3) of a *peregrinatio suburbana* in 21 CE. Woodman 1988, 186–87, building on Keitel 1984, 307–13, shows how Tacitus in the first of these, as in other passages, presents Tiberius as besieging his own city—which was not necessarily the image that the princeps had in mind.

94. Again, clearly summarized by Gantz 1993, 710–13. The oldest known and most influential of these accounts of second wanderings was the *Telegoneia* of a Eugammon of Cyrene, dating from the earlier sixth century BCE, and perhaps reflecting earlier material.

Chapter 4. The Death of the Phoenix

1. Suet. 40, 48; Tac. 4.57–59, 62–65, 67. Their accounts of Tiberius' "long-planned" retirement in 26 / 27, although broken up and set out in very different forms, strikingly follow one common, hostile source very closely. Dio's version is lost.

2. Tacitus 4.64.3. Tacitus reports the proposal in indirect discourse, rendered here as direct speech, based on Woodman's translation. On the statue of Claudia Quinta, which survived fires in 111 BCE and 3 CE, see Martin and Woodman 1989 ad loc.: the "augmentation" of the holiness of the spot is etymologically connected with the name "Augustus." Although Tiberius often allowed himself to be called "Augustus," he neither assumed the name nor permitted it to be voted to him (e.g., Suet. 26.2, Dio 57.8.1–2; Scott 1932); "Mons Augustus" would have been ambiguous at best. There is no sign that any action was taken on the proposal.

3. Suet. 14.4: *visa est* is normally translated "seemed to" or "appeared to," but "was seen to" is equally possible.

4. Suet. 21.6, quoting *Il.* 10.246–47: Diomedes chooses Odysseus as his companion on a dangerous mission; for the significance of the quotation, Champlin 2013, 234–35 = chapter 3, pp. 68–69.

5. *Odes* 4.14.24; Tiberius is called "Claudius" at line 29. At 4.14.14–32, Tiberius charges around the battlefield like a Homeric hero, devastating the enemy ranks: but his victory (over the Vindelici, not the Raeti) was in fact won on the sea, not on a battlefield—indeed, whatever he did on any campaign, he did not roam about on any charger around any battlefield, mowing down (as Horace has it) the enemy: see further below, with Thomas 2011, ad loc., noting a jumble of confusions. On the rich ancient literature about "going through fire": Tosi 2017, 1406–7, number 2055; for the phrase *medios per ignes*: cf. Hor. *Serm.* 2.3.56–57, Verg. *Aen.* 7.296–97.

6. Champlin 2011 = chapter 2, pp. 26–27.

7. Tac. 4.64.1. Tacitus' phrase *ominibus adversis* is ambiguous, perhaps intentionally: it could signify the motive for his absence (he believed, or the people believed he believed, that he would die if he returned to the city); or, as I take it here, it could reflect popular fear that he was absent despite signs that he would be needed. Tacitus can't resist commenting that it is a habit of the public to interpret chance events in terms of blame.

8. Suet. 14.3; Dio 54.9.6. If we assume some truth to the legend, it would not be lost on his thousands of soldiers that the altars and Tiberius were coevals: the battles were won in Macedonia in October of 42 BCE, Tiberius was born in Rome a month later. But we should think first of the grove of Dionysus in deepest Thrace, where unmixed wine poured on the wine god's altar (*infuso super altaria mero*) produced a flame that shot through the roof of the temple and up to heaven, when Gaius Octavius, the governor of Macedonia, inquired about the prospects of his son, the future Augustus. The priests assured him that the same portent had happened only once before, "at these same altars," when Alexander the Great had stopped by to sacrifice. Augustus and Alexander put Tiberius in elite company indeed.

9. Donkey: Plutarch fr. 182. On the King's Fire, see the references in Ogilvie 1965, 157–58, discussing Livy 1.39.1, the tale of Servius Tullius.

10. Suet. 19 (trans. Hurley 1993, modified, reading *sibi ac maioribus* for *sibi a maioribus*).

11. Dio 57.2.4. Suet. 68.2: *quod mirum esset*. Plin. *NH* 11.143: *Ferunt Ti. Caesari, nec alii genitorum mortalium, fuisse naturam ut expergefactus noctu paulisper haut alio modo quam luce clare contueretur omnia, paulatim tenebris sese obducentibus*. Sextus Empiricus *Pyr.* 1.84.

12. At *Anth. Pal.* 9.287, Apollonides refers to the prophetic occasion when an eagle, the first ever seen on Rhodes, took up residence on the house of Tiberius there (also noted at Suet. 14 and Plut. *Mor.* 340C), "when Nero held the island of the Sun"; since the poet uses the past tense, and also calls Tiberius "ruler" and "future Zeus," the date is (perhaps long) after 4 CE, when he was no longer "Nero."

13. Dio 58.28.4; Tac. 6.46.4.

14. See further Champlin 2008, 412 = chapter 1, pp. 6–7.

15. Velleius 2.99.2: the translation is that of Woodman 1977, the only accurate translation of which I am aware. The case for this being the official version is at Woodman 1977, 117–18, cf. Bellemore 2007, 434–35.

16. *Fulgor*: e.g., *fulgorem solis.... orientis* at Curt. Ruf. 4.14.24; *fulgor solis*, Hyg. 4.13.3; *solis fulgor*, Anon. *Rhet. Her.* 4.44. *Orientes iuvenes*: Vergil comes closest with *prima oriens . . . iuventa* at *Aen.* 7.51, on which R. D. Williams comments (1973 ad loc.) "*oriens* is strange, apparently in the sense of our phrase 'the rising generation,' cf. Hor. *Epist.* 2.1.130"; *orientis iuventae decus* describes Scipio Aemilianus at Val. Max. 2.10.4, written after Tiberius' statement: that is the total for "rising youth." *Pueros orientis*: Cicero *De Divinatione* 2.89.

17. Caligula as viper: the allusion should be to the tradition that young vipers kill their mother by eating their way out of her womb, Hdt. 3.109, cf. Ael. *Nat.Anim.* 1.24, Nic. *Ther.* 128–34, Plut. *Mor.* 567E–568A (my thanks for these references to Emilio Capettini, from an unpublished paper "Nero the Viper"). Here Caligula's "mother" is the *populus Romanus*.

18. Which is to say that we know of no variants to the basic details of the story that might attract the subtle, myth-obsessed princeps. Indeed, the Hesiodic version recalled by Hyginus at *Fabula* 154 made Phaethon the grandson of the Sun, as Tiberius would know.

19. Dio 58.23.4; the passage about to be cited is Suet. 62.3: both translations need to be modified, cf. below.

20. Sen. *Clem.* 2.2.2–3 (trans. Kaster in Kaster and Nussbaum 2010, 171); similarly, Suet. *Nero* 38.1 (trans. Hurley 1993): as with the Cary version of the "earth and fire" quotation in Dio above, I leave untouched here the versions as they appear in the excellent translations of Suetonius by Hurley and of Seneca by Kaster, in order to pursue a significant modification below.

21. On the history of *oderint dum metuant*, let them hate [me], provided they fear [me]: Champlin 2003a, 306–8; Tiberius' version was *oderint dum probent*, "Let them hate [me], provided they approve [my deeds]"; cf. p. 12. The name "Nero" may also have led to later confusion between Tiberius and Nero.

22. *Aen.* 2.550–56 (trans. Mandelbaum 1971, modified). Quintus of Smyrna, in *Posthomerica* 13—the only other surviving account of Priam's death—has the king wanting to die with his children and likewise already seeing his city in flames.

23. Or "let earth go up in flames" (Edwards), or "let fire devour the world" (Thomson). Seneca correctly renders the verb in Latin with *misceri*.

24. Plin. *NH* 10.3–5 (Loeb trans. Rackham).

25. The phoenix takes up over one-third of Tacitus' account of 34 CE; Dio's whole report on 36 CE is the brief paragraph quoted above. Discrepancies between Tacitus and Dio: e.g., Syme 1983 on 33 CE, or Bellemore 2003 on 21 CE. Martin 2001, 158–59 judiciously reviews the inconclusive scholarship on the problems raised by the phoenix. On what is known and speculated about Cornelius Valerianus, see *FRHist* 1.637–38 (J. W. Rich, skeptical about the speculation). Deliberate transfer by Tacitus: Syme 1958, 771–74, Keitel 1999.

26. On other versions, see below.

27. Vettius Valens 338.3–20P.

28. CCAG 8.4.100, edited by F. Cumont. The matter of sources is complicated and uncertain, but De Boor 1893 is clear and persuasive about the layers here: this particular text offers nuggets about Roman astrologers; with other late authors, it draws on a compendium of extracts about Roman emperors; that compendium was derived from an unknown work that offers details not to be found in Dio or other chroniclers. As the great Cumont observed: *Nonnulla praebet quae in illis desunt neque omni utilitate caret.*

29. The extensive fragments and echoes of his various writings are collected with very great skill by Tarrant 1993, to which we can now add *POxy.* 4941.

30. The following briefly summarizes the salient points in the exhaustive account of van den Broek 1972. Also valuable are the earlier works of Hubaux and Leroy 1939, Walla 1969, and Tammisto 1986 on the phoenix in art.

31. Our two major sources, from the early and late fourth century, are the poems of Claudian (*Carmina Minora* 27 [54]) and Lactantius, both called simply *Phoenix*: they clearly reflect much earlier traditions: see van den Broek 1972, passim.

32. Lact. 149, 155–60; Claud. 76, 80–82.

33. Ov. *Am.* 2.6.54, *Met.* 15.392; Pomp. Mel. 3.83; Mart. 5.7.2; Lact. 152; *Schol. ad Luc.* 6.680: van den Broek 1972, 356–57.

34. Nimbus: van den Broek 1972, 233–51.

35. Color palette: van den Broek 1972, 253–59: e.g., Plin. *NH* 10.3; Lact. 125–44; Claud. 17–22, cf. 86–88.

36. Suet. 68.2: *praegrandibis oculis. . . . noctu etiam et in tenebris viderent*; unique night vision (suggesting that the light shone from his eyes?) also at Plin. *NH* 11.143, quoted above. Cf. Lact. 137–38: *ingentes oculos . . . / quorum de medio lucida flamma micat*; Claud. 17, van den Broek 1972, 257.

37. The only other celebrators of triumphs alive during his principate were his sons Germanicus (triumphed 17, died 19 CE) and Drusus (triumphed 20, died 23 CE).

38. App. *Lyb.* 66; Plut. *Aem. Paul.* 34; Dion. Hal. 3.61–62.

39. Beard 2007, 228. She continues: "These colors are consistently stressed in ancient accounts of the ceremony and are so closely linked with the figure of the general that writers can describe him simply as 'purple,' 'golden,' or 'purple-and-gold,'" citing (p. 375 n. 26) Ov. *Ars* 1.214, *Tr.* 4.2 / 48; Liv. 45.39.2, 45.40.6; Sil. 17.645.

40. I state this without argument; the critical review of the sources at Beard 2007, 225–31, contains a number of errors. The red paint on the face is vouched for by Pliny, an expert on the subject of cinnabar (*NH* 35. 11–122), referring to Jupiter and the triumph at 35.111. A precise antiquarian who had witnessed triumphs, Pliny relies on Verrius Flaccus, a precise antiquarian of the age of Augustus, who quoted several sources; later, Serv. *E.* 10.27, DServ. *E.* 6.22, Isid. *Etym.* 18.2.6.

41. The Latin word *phoenix* has multiple meanings, the relationships among which are not entirely clear: the bird; the reddish-purple color; a Phoenician; and the date palm; again, exhaustive discussion in van den Broek 1972, 51–66. There are hints of these elements in the triumph of Tiberius: we do not know which among the innumerable species of palm was depicted on the triumphal tunic, but the date palm is one of the most common in the Mediterranean; late Latin glossaries remind us that the phoenix was the royal bird, *avis regia*, and therefore called "the purple one," *phoenicium*, "that is, the color of cinnabar," *miniatum* (*CGL* 4.518.15, cf. 75.11; 5.199.27). A phoenix was a symbol for astrology (Clem. Alex. *Strom.* 6.35.4: surely the bird, not a palm branch, *pace* van den Broek 1972, 56)—Tiberius, the addicted astrologer (Suet. 79), would understand.

42. Tac. 4.67.1–3, discussed by Thomas 1982, 126–30; Suet. 40–41; Plut. *Exil.* 9 (*Mor.* 602E).

43. There is a large bibliography, most notably Erkell 1952, Zieske 1972.

44. Phoenician felicity in Elysium: Sen. *HF* 743, *Tro.* 156–63; Stat. *Silv.* 2.7.112, 3.3.25, 5.1.193, 3.266, *Theb.* 8.194 (cf. Ov. *Am.* 2.6.49–54, the phoenix in a *nemus* in Elysium, with other peaceful *aves*); Serv. *A.* 5.735. Felicity on the Blessed Islands: Hor. *Epod.* 16.53; Isid. *Etym.* 14.6.8. Cf. also Arabia Felix, so called because of the spices it produced (Plin. *HN* 12.51, 84), and the island paradise of Panchaia, Diod. 5.42.4–46.7: remote, peaceful, fertile, with a temple and nearby spring that waters the plain, many trees—especially picked out is the palm tree (*phoenix*)—birds of all kinds, gardens and meadows; the clear, sweet stream is called the Water of the Sun. Panchaia was not where the phoenix lived, but it was to somewhere "near Panchaia" that, according to Plin. *NH* 10.4 (quoted above), the young bird brought the nest with the remains of its parent, to the City of the Sun, and placed them on the altar.

45. Lact. 1, 164; Claud. 101.

46. Stat. *Silv.* 2.4 (ca. 90 CE): teasing out the Phoenician clues would take too much space, but note especially the lamented ex-parrot, the leader of the birds (*dux volucrum*); its melodious voice (*canorus*, not an attribute of a parrot) is stilled; all birds mourn the passing of the King of the East (*regnator Eoae*); the parrot had been the "saluter of kings that spoke the Caesarian name," just as the phoenix was the *satelles* and acolyte of the Sun; this "glory of the airy race" is sent to the shades cremated with Assyrian *amomum*, Arabian *gramen*, and Sicanian *croca*.

47. Never fully published but well expounded by Jashemski 1967, cf. Jashemski 1979–93, 1.172–76j 2151 53, 311–76; Kruschwitz 2006; the meaning of the text (now *CIL* 4.9850) is uncertain: Solin 1968, 123–24, cf. Tammisto 1986, 177 n. 18. The expression appears on at least six other inscriptions or graffiti (including two at Pompeii: *CIL* 4.1763, 8257), and surely indicates that the speaker is happy and wants you, the viewer, to share in his or her felicity; or perhaps the line compares a customer's happiness to that of the happiest of birds: "Phoenix, you too are happy."

48. The evidence is discussed by Erkell 1952, 41–128, and elaborated rather unconvincingly by Wistrand 1987; for Augustus, see also Flory 1992. Despite the examples cited by these and other scholars, Augustus' interest in Felicity seems muted.

49. Lersch 1849. It is surely an officer's sword, now in the British Museum, carefully described by Walker and Burnett 1981, 49–50, and thoroughly discussed by Koortbojian 2013, 147–50; the Wikipedia article "Schwert des Tiberius," accessed April 1, 2024, is superb: http://de.wikipedia.org/wiki/Schwert_des_Tiberius.

50. Walker and Burnett 1981, 50–51 attempt to identify the figures as the young Tiberius presenting his victory over the Vindelici in 15 BCE to the older Augustus, but this has not disturbed the common opinion, for good reason.

51. Patron of Fundi: *ILLRP* 1068. Villa at Sperlonga: Champlin 2013 = chapter 3.

52. Vell. 2.106.3, 107.2 (both concerning the German campaign of 5 CE); Val. Max. 2 pr.; Phil. *Leg.* 33.

53. Claud. 13–16; on the phoenix's ethereal foods, van den Broek 1972, 335–56, especially 336–40 on the solar implications.

54. Lact. 11–12; Claud. 107–10.

55. 3 *Baruch* 6: trans. Gaylord 1983, with valuable commentary. On the place of Baruch in the phoenix tradition, cf. the indexes of Hubaux and Leroy 1939 and van den Broek 1972.

56. Claud. 36–37: *Iam breve decrescit lumen languetque senili / segnis stella gelu.* On the preparations for death, van den Broek 1972, 161–86 is essential. The Latin is not easy, but (*pace* van den Broek 1972, 163), I believe that Claudian here refers precisely to his earlier conjunction of shining eyes and flaming crest at lines 17–18: *lumen* is a pun, both brightness and the eye; a star, *stella*, is commonly "radiate."

57. van den Broek 1972, 179.

58. Lact. 170, eternal life; 61, age slipping away.

59. The learned Manilius cited by Pliny, quoted above, is explicit. The sources for and relevance of the Great Year are discussed exhaustively at van den Broek 1972, 67–112, summarized at 414–17.

60. Texts and discussion at Long and Sedley 1987, 1:274–79 (46: "God, fire, cosmic cycle"), 308–13 (52: "Everlasting recurrence").

61. So argued by van den Broek 1972, 113–17. The phoenix did later come to be associated with the new age and rebirth of Rome (Mart. 5.7), especially on second-century coinage, but the evidence for the Julio-Claudian era and earlier is not there.

62. De Jong 1997, 320: "The Greek and Iranian myths on Zoroaster's life only rarely coincided."

63. De Jong 1997, 322; cf. Jackson 1899, 28–29.

64. Jackson 1899, 124–27; Suet. 69.1, cf. Plin. *NH* 15.135. The Persian tradition held rather that Zoroaster died by human violence at the age of seventy-seven (Jackson 1899, 127–32). As fate would have it, Tiberius was to die at seventy-seven, and foul play was suspected, but any coincidence is beyond human understanding.

65. On Zoroastrian pseudepigrapha, see Beck 1991, a fascinating article the length of a small monograph.

66. A subject to be explored, but a good inkling is given in Syme's delightful paper of 1989, "Diet on Capri."

67. Text in Halleux and Schamp 1985. Though the letter's authenticity is less important than the tradition, this one stands out from the many forged epistolary prefaces glued onto ancient texts, betrayed by inaccurate, often anachronistic details. Not here: the title Imperator (translating the Greek Αὐτοκράτωρ) is precise and correct; the low rank of centurion is likewise restrained, not the usual tribune or general; and the centurion's name, Lucinius Fronto (Montanius Fronto in a later Greek report), looks authentic. The letter is well treated at Halleux and Schamp 216–19 and (very sceptically) 223–24.

68. Vegetarianism: De Jong 1997, 395 (from Porph. *Abstin.*); mourning: De Jong 1997, 420–24; withdrawal: De Jong 1997, 321 (Dio Chrys. *Or.* 36.41, Ammian. 23.6.33).

69. Presumably in the West, because of the founding story of Zoroaster as imparted by Dio Chrysostom, quoted above: cf. Hdt. 1.131; Xen. *Cyr.* 8.7.3; Strab. 15.3.13. But there is also the strong connection of the *khwarnah* (on which see below) with mountains in the *Avesta*: Gnoli 1999.

70. Sources for all of this at Hackl, Jacobs, and Weber 2010, 145–54; De Jong 1997, 343–50. Fundamental among them are Xen. *Cyr.* 8.3.12; Diod. 17.114.11; Isid. Char. *FGrH* F2 11; Curt. Ruf. 3.3; Ammian. 23.6.34. Strab. 15.3.15 is the earliest authority for the eternity of Zoroastrian flame.

71. Scholars universally assume that, since the fire was undying, the new flames sprang up from banked embers.

72. Quotations above from Gnoli 1999, an excellent introduction with extensive bibliography; Skjærvø 2011 offers expert translations of basic Zoroastrian texts; Shabazi 1980 discusses the striking iconography. Useful material in De Jong 1997, 299–301; Bremmer 2002, 47–50, with extensive bibliography (154 n. 54); Ellerbrock and Winkelmann 2012, 264; Meulder 2008 (stimulating but eccentric).

73. *Yast 19 of the Younger Avesta*, verse 11 (cf. 89): Skjærvø 2011, 158, "With it *they* [*sc.* the creations of Ahura Mazda] shall make the existence Perfect (*frasha*), incorruptible, indestructible, undecaying, unrotting, ever-living, ever life-giving, having command at will, so that when the dead rise again *he* will come, making alive and free from destruction, and the existence will be made Perfect in exchange value." Cf. Bremmer 2002, 48, quoting the slightly earlier translation of H. Humbach and P. Ichaporia.

74. Henning 1945, 477–80, cautiously noting that "[t]he narrator placed the story in the third century, as the reference to Sansai (line 25) shows: he was a disciple of Mani . . ."—but, of course, such folktales notoriously float in both time and space.

75. For the extensive evidence, literary and material, of Zoroastrianism in Cappadocia, see Boyce and Grenet 1991, 262–81: the kings, whether Zoroastrians or not, certainly patronized the religion. King Archelaus (*PIR²* A 1023) was a client of Tiberius, who defended him in court in the 20s BCE, and he accompanied the young man on the Armenian expedition in 20 BCE. Tiberius' avatar was the deeply learned ex-praetor Nigidius Figulus, *Pythagoricus et magus* (Jer. *Chron. ad an.* 45 BCE); on Nigidius' magism, Dickie 2001, 169–72.

76. Since 1973, it has resided in the Cabinet des Médailles in Paris: Vollenweider and Avisseau Broustet 2003, 75–76 no. 80, with plate 62; Betti and Gariboldi 2009 (bibliography at 248 n. 1). [Ed. note: an excellent image is available at Open Edition Books, accessed April 1, 2024, https:// books.openedition.org/editionsbnf/2331.] Given the careful analyses and comparanda provided by these works, Hertel's curt dismissal of the gem (2013, 222 no. 209) cannot stand.

77. Vollenweider and Avisseau-Broustet (followed by others, including Betti and Gariboldi) date Tiberius' ovation to 11 BCE and the intaglio to around 10 BCE. In fact, the ovation was held in 9 BCE, not long before the death of Drusus (Swan 2004, 47–48); and the triumphal laurel provides us with a firm *terminus post quem non* for the iconography on the gem.

78. Seyrig 1968, 175 n. 1.

79. Gariboldi, at Betti and Gariboldi 2009, 253 (the first quotation following is from Gariboldi's explanation of the inscription, the second his quotation from the Zoroastrian *Denkard*); cf. Seyrig 1968, 177.

80. "It should be noted that it is quite normal in Sassanid gem-cutting for there to be no relationship between the subject portrayed and the inscription, and therefore the owner of the seal and those who admired it were not at all upset to see the portrait of a Roman emperor associated with a Zoroastrian religious formula": Gariboldi (Betti and Gariboldi 2009). But this piece is unique. There is only one other Persian gem of similar quality, depicting a Sassanid monarch and bearing a Mithraic inscription naming a King Shapur, and it is probably much later, late third or early fourth century: Curiel and Seyrig 1974.

81. Vollenweider and Avisseau-Broustet 2003, 75.

82. The gem probably traveled from Augustan Rome to Sassanian Elam? The most likely explanation is as part of an exchange of gifts between Rome and Parthia during the long peace of the early principate: so Seyrig 1968, 177–78. The most likely occasion was the meeting of Lucius Vitellius and King Artabanus on the Euphrates in 37(?) CE during which gifts were exchanged, as recorded at Josephus *AJ* 18.101–3 (so Seyrig 1968); cf. also Suet. *Vit.* 2.4 and Dio 59.17.5; 27.2–3, but there are source problems that need not be considered here.

83. *Anth. Pal.* 7.704 = *TrGF* 2 fr. 513: Ἐμοῦ θανόντος γαῖα μιχθήτω πυρί· / οὐδὲν μέλει μοι· τἀμὰ γὰρ καλῶς ἔχει.

Chapter 5. Sex on Capri

[Ed. note: This article first appeared in *Transactions of the American Philological Association* 141, no. 2 (Autumn 2011). Published with permission by Johns Hopkins University Press. Copyright © 2011 American Philological Association.]

*This paper has profited from the comments of Donna Hurley, Bob Kaster, Joshua Katz, Tony Woodman, and the anonymous referees.

1. Tac. 6.1, in the Oxford Classical Texts edition of C. D. Fisher (1906).

2. Suet. 43, in the Teubner of M. Ihm (1908). [Ed. note: my edition of Suetonius (Oxford 2016) differs from the Teubner in reading *triplici <se> serie conexi* in the first sentence and positing a lacuna between *habitu* and *quam* in the last; neither difference affects the arguments that follow.]

3. [Ed. note: in her translation published in 2011, Hurley substituted "*sellaria*" for "holey places" and "*spintriae*" for "analists" in light of this chapter's arguments, which appear here in the form originally published, also in 2011.]

4. Yardley 2008, 184, 449. Older versions are along the same lines. J. Jackson's 1937 Loeb: "And now were coined the names, hitherto unknown, of *sellarii* and *spintriae*, one drawn from the obscenity of a place, one from the versatility of the pathic." D. Dudley's New American Library version of 1966: "It was then that new names had to be found for perversions hitherto unknown—*sellarii* and *spintriae*—descriptions suited to their obscene postures and pathic complexity." The loaded term "pathic" common to Yardley, Jackson, and Dudley is not in the Latin (Woodman is precise and correct; but Martin (below) uses the term *pathicus* in his note if not in his translation); nor is Dudley's startling "perversions hitherto unknown" in the Latin—thus are legends started: compare M. Grant's "new names for new types of perversions" in his 1986 revised Penguin. I emphasize that these are all serious translations. I ignore many others that are inaccurate, euphemistic, or intentionally ignorant. The only serious modern commentary, Koesterman's of 1965, says nothing about these words.

5. Lana 1952 ad loc.: "camere con divani"; Ailloud 1931 ad loc.: "un local garni de bancs."

6. The last four quotations derive from Hubbard 2003, 186; Lindsay 1995, 140; Wardle 1994, 168; and Hurley 1993, 53.

7. If there are any other literary references to *sellarium / us* than these four, I have not found them. Epigraphically we also have a *sellarius* at ILS 5313 (Rome), the only other reference in the rubric of the *OLD*. He appears in a list of members of a racing establishment, presumably a saddlemaker or a jockey, but certainly not a prostitute. (*Biselliarius* and *subselliarius* are irrelevant, although single variants of each do appear, with "ar" for "iar": *bisellariorum* at *CIL* 14.4136, and *supsellarius* at *ILS* 7634.)

8. Whatever his failings as an aesthete, it is hard to imagine Nero so boorish as to display his prized sculptures in the lavatory.

9. Taylor 1997, 341, 363–70.

10. Adams 1983b, 329–30, with examples rather than an exhaustive list. For the association of *foeditas* and prostitution, note Martial 9.7.2, cf. Tac. 13.25.1, and esp. Juv. 6.132 and 8.225–26; also Hor. *Serm.* 1.2.30, on the prostitute *olenti in fornice stantem*.

11. A subject not to be pursued here, the source is clearly hostile, and most likely Servilius Nonianus.

12. At first glance, *sellaria* are the places in or on which the *spintriae* performed. If *sellariorum* is tied to *foeditas loci* (place), and balanced in Tacitus by *spintriarum* and *multiplici patientia* (people), that again suggests that the word signifies a place rather than people.

13. On *prostare*, see Adams 1983b, 331–32, with examples. Tony Woodman points out to me Seneca *Ben.* 1.9.3, decrying cynical contemporary morals: *Rusticus, inhumanus ac mali moris et inter matronas abominanda condicio est, si quis coniugem in sella prostare vetuit et vulgo admissis inspectoribus vehi perspicuam undique.* This is obviously relevant, but I do not understand it.

14. *Cal.* 41.1 (Loeb trans., slightly modified): "Lupanar in Palatio constituit, . . . cellis in quibus matronae ingenuique starent" (he continues, "misit circum fora et basilicas nomenculatores ad invitandos ad libidinem iuvenes senesque"); cf. Dio 59.28.9; McGinn 1998.

15. Note also Messalina "sitting" (ἐκαθέζετο) in the palace to play the prostitute, and having other noble women join her in public sexual performances: Dio 60.31.1, 18.1. Mart. 5.70.1–4 seems to offer a fifth echo of *sellaria*: *Infusum sibi nuper a patrono | plenum, Maxime, centiens Syriscus | in sellariolis vagus popinis | circa balnea quattuor peregit.* As translated by Taylor (1997): "Syriscus pulled in the full ten million showered on him by his patron recently, Maximus, just by hanging about on cantina barstools down around the four bathhouses." *Sellariolis* is presumably a diminuitive of *sellaria*, but it should not mean "barstools" (cf. Shackleton Bailey's "stools" in the Loeb edition), and the word's relationship with *popinis* is not clear: understand "popinae which are called little *Sellaria*."

16. Acc. to Dio 64.4.2, Vitellius had been Tiberius' boytoy (παιδικά); add *HA Helio.* 33.1: *Libidinum genera quaedam invenit, ut spinthrias veterum imperatorum vinceret,* which suggests that the term was evanescent, and it does indeed seem confined to the mid-first century.

17. André 1971, 103–7. I am indebted to Joshua Katz for the essential references here and in n. 19.

18. Adams 1983b, 333–35. Neumann 1980 emends *lupatria* to *lupatris*, unconvincingly in my opinion.

19. Adams 2003: 420 and n. 15.

20. References in Forcellini, Lewis and Short, *OLD*.

21. As J. Katz points out, *lupa: lupatria :: spinter: spintria* is not perfectly proportional, since the former would have to based on **lupater*.

22. One variation on the bracelet image may be noted, the older notion, not offered lately, that the participants formed a bracelet-like chain, mouth to genital and so on round a circle. This *monstrum* is certainly possible, but such a circular tableau is completely unattested in our ancient literary and artistic sources for group sex (n. 27, below). It would seem to be a minor, and soon tedious, addition to the repertoire. Moreover, the *schema* is hard to define as involving *multiplex patientia*. Which is to say that *multiplex* would have to refer to the *patientia* of all players as a group, since each individual would be involved with two others but "patient" to only one of them.

23. *Sellaria . . . sedem*: a conscious pun by Suetonius or his source? *Arcanarum*: not only "hidden," but also with our connotation of "arcane," not for the vulgar? *Exoleti*, "mature catamites," not "male prostitutes" as in the *OLD*: see n. 32, below. *Deficientis*: "declining lusts," or "lusts of the declining (Tiberius)"?

24. Bob Kaster has sharpened the argument here. A translation of the sentence follows below.

25. Suet. *Vit.* 3.2. Curiously, the fragmentary CIL 6.37761 seems to record an *Augusti libertus* who was the brother of *nomenclator Vitelli Spintheri*: "Aug. lib.—/ nomenclatoris [in larger letters] / Vitelli. Spintheris frater."

26. *Sat.* 113.11: *Si quid ingenui sanguinis habes, non pluris illum facies quam scortum. Si vir fueris, non ibis ad spintriam.* One group of manuscripts prefaces this with [*Ancilla Tryphaenae ad Encolpium*], presuming a reference to Giton, Encolpius' boyfriend, on what authority it is not clear.

27. Clarke's excellent book of 2003 offers the full range of artistic representation; Vorberg 1928–32 has a lot of illustrations: group sex does not loom large.

28. Examples of threesomes: Clarke 2003, 38–39, 129, 144–47, 151; Johns 1982, 120, 130–31, 133; Ausonius *Epig.* 43 Green (from Strato *Anth. Pal.* 11.225, 12.210); Mart. 10.81, 11.81 (a failure); Petron. *Sat.* 140.7–10; Sen. *NQ* 1.16.5. Foursomes: Clarke 2003, 131, 139; Johns 1982, 140; Mart. 9.32.4; Sen. *NQ* 1.6.7; Gallus *Anth. Pal.* 5.491; Nicarchus 11.328.

29. Martial 12.43: Sabellus' verses discuss five and even more *symplegmata*, performed by *exoleti*, *new* "figures of Venus," *unknown* to eunuchs and the soft books of Elephantis, the sort of things that only a *perditus fututor* would dare.

30. *NQ* 1.16.5.

31. Among references to her sex manual, *Priapea* 4 and the lemma to *AP* 7.345 (cf. 450) definitely indicate heterosexuality; Tatian *ad Graecos* 34. 9, Martial 12.43, and Suetonius *Tiberius* 43.2 are not clear. Otherwise, from the only other references to her work, we can say that Elephantis certainly wrote on subjects of feminine interest: cosmetics (Galen XII. 426K) and menstrual blood as an abortifacient (Plin. *NH* 28.81). All references to the work of her much better attested predecessor, Philaenis, with whom she is often cited, suggest that it too was exclusively heterosexual.

32. *Exoleti*, commonly misunderstood as "male prostitutes," signifies rather grown-up *delicati*, ex-catamites, boy favorites beyond their sell-by date, as demonstrated by Butrica 2005, 225–31.

33. Suet. *Vit.* 3.2 (Loeb trans., modified). The father, L. Vitellius, a new man and *consul ordinarius* in 34 CE, was clearly close to Tiberius. It should be noted that Suetonius refers not to the beginning of Lucius' career (as in modern translations, but chronologically impossible) but to its advancement (that is after Tiberius' retirement to Capri in 27, which is plausible).

34. The (nonsensical) alternative reading, *impetratae*, does not affect the point here.

35. [Ed. note: or rather, "Villa of Ino": on the name, see pp. 64–66.]

36. Görler 1990 offers a convenient introduction to this naming phenomenon. Note also Gowers 2010 and the rooms or apartments on imperial property at Rome, such as the Syracusae and the Hermaeum: Suet. *Aug.* 72.2, *Claud.* 10.1. On the landscape of allusion: Bergmann 1999, 103–6; Bergmann 2001. The "Goat" enshrined on Capri presumably refers not only to the Little Pans but to the old goat himself, Tiberius: cf. Suet. 45; the "abuse" of the island's name (Goat Island) is heavily ironic but not necessarily hostile.

37. Macrob. *Sat.* 3.13.7–9, cf. Val. Max. 9.1.5; Varro *RR* 3.13.2–3; Vell. 2.83.2; Suet. *Aug.* 70.1; Tac. 11.31.2; Petron. *Sat.* 59.7. Cf. Domitian's terrifying banquet of the dead, presumably set in Hades with the emperor as Pluto: Dio 67.9.

38. Note especially the allegations about Messalina's playing the prostitute in the palace (Dio 60.31.1, 18.1) and Julia in the forum *ad Marsyam* (Sen. *Ben.* 6.32.1). On Nero's theatricals, see Champlin 2003b, 153–56. The banquet of 52 BCE: Val. Max. 9.1.8. The tribunes of that year were a racy crew, including Caelius Rufus and Sallustius Crispus. The perplexing story of Vistilia, a lady of senatorial rank who registered as a prostitute in 19 CE (Tac. 2.85.1–3) and was sent into exile for her trouble, is perhaps to be considered in this light, as is indeed the whole phenomenon of members of the upper classes yearning to perform in theater, arena, and circus.

39. Tac. 14.15, 15.37; Suet. *Nero* 27, *Cal.* 41.1. Cf. above, p. 106.

40. Suet. *Aug.* 98. 3; *desidia* at 98.4.

41. Suet. *Cal.* 11 (Loeb trans., modified); the bloodthirsty *animadversiones poenaeque* may be equally theatrical.

Chapter 6. Mallonia

[Ed. note: This paper first appeared in *Histos* 9 (2015): 220–30. Copyright © 2015 Edward Champlin.]

1. Suet. 43, 44.1. My thanks for invaluable comments from R. A. Kaster, J. T. Katz, and A. J. Woodman, and from the anonymous readers.

2. Suet. 45. The text is that of Ihm's Teubner; for *mora* as "saying," see the discussion below at n. 10. *Capreis* is commonly translated as "does," that is, female roe deer. *Capreae*, female deer, and *caprae*, she-goats, were confused in antiquity, as is demonstrated in detail by Holford-Strevens 2004. The Atellan line surely refers to intra-species (goat / goat), rather than inter-species (goat / deer), sexual intercourse. Unfortunately, "doe" is used in English not only for a female deer but for a female goat as well. For clarity, I render *capreis* here as "she-goats." "Hairy," standard in English translations, is too mild for *hirsutus*, which is usually applied to animals: hence, here, "shaggy."

3. The sense necessary for the logic of the story can be variously restored. Some manuscripts read *ne* for *nec*; less attractively, others read *et*; and Bentley conjectured *ac*. Woodman wonders (*per litteras*) about the remote possibility of the passage representing some kind of direct speech within indirect speech: "Et 'non quicquam amplius pati' constantissime recusantem," "and most persistently refusing, [to the effect that] 'she would not endure anything more.'" Kaster (citing Madvig 1873, 573–74) notes that this sort of Suetonian incoherence—inverting reality with a negative—is also found at *Iul.* 78 and *Nero* 42. If *nec* is to stand, the fault might lie with Suetonius imperfectly condensing his source. Cf. Vogt 1975, 217.

4. *Ecquid paenitet* in the context of—but not in—an imaginary trial is found in a text contemporary with Tiberius, at Sen. *C.* 7.2.2.

5. See especially Tac. 1.75.1, Suet. 33, and Dio 57.7.6 (all dependent on a single source), with Bablitz 2009.

6. That is, *capreis* can be taken as either a dative of reference or (with capital C) a locative.

7. It must be understood 1) that this is a formal trial with all the trimmings, from which the accused can withdraw into public, not a *cognitio* conducted by the princeps, and 2) that the only

possible evidence for such a trial on Capri is the fragile and inconclusive text of Tac. 6.10.2. The matter of imperial *cognitiones* is too complicated and tangential to argue here.

8. Her home is on Capri? Her audience astonished Capraeans?

9. 1) The goat's hairiness and odor are classically conjoined at Horace *Epod.* 12.5: *namque sagacius unus odoror, / polypus an gravis hirsutis cubet hircus in alis*, "for whether it's a stinking cuttlefish or a goat that lurks in your hairy armpits" (Loeb trans. Rudd). Cf. Juv. 5.155: *hirsute capella*, and Catullus' remarks on the goat-like odor of the armpits of the amorous Rufus, for which he uses both *hircus*, 69.6, and *caper*, 71.1. 2) "Odor" and "lust" are adjacent rubrics in the *TLL*, s.v. *hircus*, at 6.2821.69–80 and 2822.19–33 (*odor*), and at 6.2821.80–2822.4 (*libido*). 3) The goat's lust and hairiness occur at Martial 12.59.4–5: *Te pilosus / hircoso premit osculo colonus*, "the hairy farmer crushes you with a kiss like a billy-goat" (Loeb trans. Shackleton Bailey).

10. *Mora* makes no sense: cf. Vogt 1975, 218. Hurley neatly translates as "tag" the reading *nota* that is found in some manuscripts. But we should read *vox* for *mora*. Vogt persuasively accepts Bentley's suggestion of *vox* in the sense of *dictum*, "saying," which is often used, as here, with *excipere*, to mean "to hear with approval": cf. esp. Liv. 8.6.7: *adsensu populi excepta vox consularis*, and Curt. Ruf. 5.9.2: *adsensu excepere ceteri hanc vocem*. Ihm noted Bentley's suggestion in the apparatus of his *editio maior* of 1907, but not in his standard *editio minor* of 1908. Kaster adds that Oudendorp's *unde mira in Atellanico exodio* <*vox*> *proximis ludis* neatly accounts for the corruption of *mira* into *mora* and the loss of *vox* before *prox-* [Ed. note: Oudendorp's emendation is adopted in the Oxford Classical Texts edition of 2016.]

11. A defense of the text might be attempted: perhaps *cunnilinctio* was the "anything more" that Mallonia refused to endure, but on the Roman scale of values it would hardly be worse than *irrumatio* for her, and any confusion is the fault of the text itself. For the act, the term *cunnilinctio* (used by Adams 1982) should be preferred to the misleading *cunnilingus*.

12. A subject to be pursued elsewhere.

13. Suet. *Iul.* 22.2. The wordplay on "heads" in the two tales was observed by Holford-Strevens 2004, 73 n. 17: "Women as bearers of social and legal status, not merely as bodies." *Inludere* and *insultare* as sexual assault: discussion and references in Vogt 1975, 216; Adams 1982, 200. Cf. *capiti non parcere* at Lactantius *Div. Inst.* 6.24.

14. Vogt 1975, 217; Adams 1982, 174–75.

15. Grim examples at *TLL* 54.75–55.6, *obicio*. An anonymous reader aptly recalls Suet. *Nero* 37.2: "It is even believed that it was his wish to throw living men (*vivos homines . . . obicere*) to be torn to pieces and devoured by a monster of Egyptian birth (*polyphago cuidam Aegypti generis*), who would crunch raw flesh and anything else that was given him" (Loeb trans. Rolfe).

16. This may account for the syntactical ellipsis noted earlier. The proper way to phrase the intervention would be in the passive, *interpellata ab eo, ecquid* (as at Val. Max. 1.8 ext. 10: *interpellatus ab eo ecquid . . . mandaret*), rather than in the awkward active (as here). Examples of the verb *interpellare* signifying sexual solicitation are all third century or later (*TLL* 7.2242.73–80), but the related *appellare* (2.273.40–43) and *compellare* (3.2029.22–26) are to be found with that meaning in writers precisely of the age of Tiberius. *Interpellare* can also be the verb used for "to bring a criminal charge," and *de stupro interpellavit* can mean in the same author "brought a charge of illicit sex" and "accosted [a female] for sex": Serv. *ad Aen.* 6.445 and 286!

17. Suetonius does, however, use forms of *se proripere* no fewer than six times in just the same sense. Might the variant *se abripere* derive from his source?

18. E.g., Tac. 14.9.2, 37.3; Sil. 2.648, 13.376; Gell. 17.16.6; Aur. Vict. 5.16.

19. Examples at Adams 1982, 140–41.

20. E.g., Cic. *Div.* 2.145; Varro *R.R.* 2.7.8; 3.12.4.

21. I owe this point about Latin and Greek to the acute observation of Kaster, who also notes that Greek *phusis* likewise can mean not only "sex" but precisely "private parts," and female parts in particular.

22. Registered at Suet. 2.2. Note that in Livy's account (3.57.3), the wicked Appius Claudius is accused of imprisoning the girl's father and grandfather, "upset more by his interrupted lust than by her death." For interrupted lust, *stupro interpellato,* cf. the different meanings of *de stupro interpellare*—legal charge and sexual solicitation—in n. 16 above.

23. *Merc.* 574–76 (Loeb trans. de Melo). The old man has previously dreamed of the woman as a she-goat: 225–71.

24. Everything that needs to be said on the *morbus Campanus* can be found in a splendid essay, Adams 1983a (unknown to Knorr 2012). Aus. *Epig.* 87 (Adams' subject) begins, *Eunus Syriscus, inguinum ligurritor / Opicus magister,* "Eunus the Syrian, who is a crude and sex-crazed schoolmaster" (Loeb trans. Evelyn-White).

25. Mallonii / ae appear in Lusitania (two: *AE* 1898.1; *HEp.* 15.96); Aquitania (one: *AE* 1962.224 = *ILTG* 182); Lugdunensis (one: *CIL* 13.3123); Narbonensis (two: *CIL* 12.1983, a freedman; 2452–54a, apparently a senator); Liguria, at Albintimilium (one: *AE* 1990.381, with a Greek name); Latium, at Liternum (one: *AE* 2001.853, a freedman Augustalis) and Cumae (two: *CIL* 10.3698, 3699, a magistrate and a priest), and at Rome (two families, both with Greek names, a husband and wife at *CIL* 6.21888 and a woman with, apparently, her husband and son at 6.21889; and a later female, *ILCV* 2907). Both Kaster and Woodman tried valiantly to find a wordplay between Liguria and *ligurire,* but I remained unconvinced. That requires more knowledge about our source than we possess.

26. Respectively, again: *CIL* 10.3698, 3699 = *ILS* 4175, 4174 (Cumae); and 12.2452–54a (near Vienne: the fragments are a problematic mess). The senator is registered at *PIR²* I. 846. His elaborate polyonymity indicates a second-century date, and Mallonius is clearly not its main element. Contrast Suetonius' list of four *illustres feminae,* all supposedly seduced by Julius Caesar (*Iulius* 50.1): all senators' wives, all from senatorial families.

27. οὐδὲν μᾶλλον expresses a Pyrrhonist concept, signifying absence of determination and withholding of assent: on which, see the analysis at Bett 2000, 30–32. It was discussed by the satirist and philosopher Timon of Phlius, an author probably known to and loved by Tiberius: D. L. 9.76, with 9.109. A reader, entering into the spirit of things, wonders, "If bilingual word games are in order, perhaps the ending of Mallonia can be equally significant. ὤνια could mean a woman for sale?"

28. The fabrication might have been suggested by a real incident. In the last months of his life, Tiberius allowed the senate to delay sentencing in the treason trials, since he was supposedly tricked by Thrasyllus into believing that he would live for many years more. At 58.27. 4, in his truncated account of the year 37 CE, Dio tells us that a woman (unnamed) wounded herself (weapon unstated, presumably in an attempt at suicide); was carried into the senate (presumably for trial) and from there was taken to a prison (unspecified, presumably there to await sentencing), where she died.

Chapter 7. Asellius Sabinus: Culture, Wit, and Power in the Golden Age of Gastronomy

[Ed. note: with thanks to Peeters Publishers for permission to publish here the paper that first appeared in *Ancient Society* 47 (2017): 159–96. Copyright © 2017 Ancient Society.]

1. Syme 1986a, 354. For their comments, I am gratefuk to R. A. Kaster, J. T. Katz, M. Peachin, B. D. Shaw, and A. J. Woodman. I have profited from the good advice of many anonymous readers for journals over the years, but none has been more helpful than the referee for this paper.

2. *Scurra* is, of course, here "wit," not "buffoon." Ill-timed jokes: *C.* 9.4.17, 21, with details just below.

3. Quintilian discusses a list of nouns and adjectives conveying various aspects of humor at 6.3.17–21): *urbanitas* implies city words, tones, usage, and the assumption of tacit erudition in

the conversation of learned men; *venustus* describes something acted or spoken with grace, charm, and wit; see esp. Krostenko 2001, 40–51, 99–111, 308–9. The rare combination of *urbanitas* and *venustas* in wit has a distinctly Ciceronian flavor, as in *Dom.* 92 and *De or.* 2.228, cf. 1.17 and Catul. 22.2; but not elsewhere.

4. *C.* 9.14 is based upon this "law"—"Who shall have struck his father, let his hands be cut off"—and this fact set: "A tyrant summoned a father and his two sons to the citadel; he ordered the young men to beat the father. One threw himself down, the other performed the beating. Afterwards he was accepted into the tyrant's friendship, he slew the tyrant, and he accepted a reward. His hands are sought; his father defends."

5. The text here is Håkanson 1989; Winterbottom's graceful English translation (also 1989) is far more elegant than Seneca's Latin.

6. And they seem to suggest that two men are involved, Tullius / Iulius and Sabinus, when they obviously are not. If we were to accept "the extremely corrupt and extremely lacunose paradosis" (Watt 1991, 315) we would not only be plunged into the briar patch of a seriously faulty manuscript but flung as well into a thicket of prosopographical problems which are posed by two contemporary poets. One of those poets may or may not be "Tullius Sabinus" (the name is problematic) in the *Greek Anthology*; and he in turn might or might not be the other "Sabinus," a friend of Ovid, who died young: *PIR*[2] T 388 and S 35.

7. At *RE* Asellius 3, P. von Rhoden observed simply that the author of the dialogue might be identical with the Asillius of Augustus' letter and with the Asilius Sabinus of Seneca's *Suasoriae* (omitting the mention in the younger Seneca's *Epistulae*). A. Stein's notice at *PIR*[2] A 1213 is a masterpiece of prosopographical nuance: after introducing the man of the dialogue rewarded by Tiberius Stein allowed that "he seems to be the same as" the Asilius Sabinus of the *Controversiae* and the *Suasoriae* (duly noting that the former was an emendation), that "he seems to be not different from" the Asellius of Seneca's letter, and "also perhaps" the "Asillius (or Asellius)" of Augustus. The only other scholar to seriously consider the question of nomenclature and identity adopted a severely sceptical attitude: Orth 1973, 255–56 n. 2. For him, the amalgamation of any of these figures is a risky hypothesis because of their varied social circles (on which, see below); and there is no proof even for the generally accepted identification of the Sabinus of the *Controversiae* with the Sabinus Asilius of the *Suasoriae*.

8. Feddern 2013, 269–70, explores the situation thoroughly; more about the content of the witticism below, p. 135.

9. Mart. 13.92, cf. Petron. *Sat.* 65.1.

10. *PIR*[2] V 276, V 662. Jerome calls Varius *sublimis orator*.

11. Suet. *Cal.* 8.4. He adds that he is sending a doctor with the boy, one of his slaves, and that Germanicus may keep him if he wants, and wishes her a safe journey to her husband.

12. Cic. *Verr.* 2.5.31, 86, *Att.* 1.16.3; Catul. 2.22; see *RE* "Talarius ludus" (F. Altheim). Despite common repetition of an attractive assumption, I can see no evidence that the term ever referred to a game of dice (*tali* = ankle bones = dice).

13. As in three times out of the five instances noted here: I can find no examples in classical literature of Asil(l)ius / a other than the Asilius in Seneca's *Suasoriae* and the Asillius in Suetonius' *Augustus*; the name is extremely rare in Latin inscriptions and does not occur in Greek, Asel(l)ius is relatively common in both inscriptions and literature, East and West.

14. Orth 1973, 257 n. 15, asserts that Augustus appears in Seneca as Divus Augustus or Augustus Caesar. In fact, he is also simply Caesar, demonstrably at *C.* 10.5.21 and 22.

15. With seven generations of consular ancestors in direct succession, there was no one more "noble" than he in the Roman state under Augustus and Tiberius, nor any other remotely noble Domitius.

16. Tac. 6.19.2: the year of what he calls *immensa strages* is confirmed by the *Fasti Ostienses*. The last related prosecution seems to have occurred in 35 CE: Tac. 6.38.2.

17. How many in the mob would know that *turdus* was a delicacy served at Roman banquets—indeed, how many would understand Latin at all? We are perilously close to Blessed are the Cheesemakers.

18. The proconsul Occius Flamma is otherwise unknown, but the scanty evidence points to impressive connections. The family was senatorial since the mid-second century at least (Val. Max. 3.2.21); a contemporary Occia was a Vestal Virgin from 39 or 38 BCE to 19 CE (Tac. 2.86.1—a guardian, be it noted, of the *flammas Vestae*!); and a singular concentration of impressively aristocratic Occii in central Greece under the Julio-Claudians strongly hints at an unknown Occius as governor of Achaia in the late Republic or early principate (*IG* 2². 3280, 3364; *IvO* 453; *SEG* 29.528, 53.550).

19. P. Vinicius: *C.* 1.4.11 (steals other men's words); 7.5.11–12 (*exactissimus*; "derides" the *sententiae* of two other men); 10.4.25 (*summus amator Ovidii*). He and Varius Geminus make a ferocious pair.

20. The atmosphere seems to be one of aristocratic indifference to income and expenditure, but the witticism at 9.4.18 (like its companions) is complicated, strained, and to us extraordinarily obscure. The jester plays on two related legal terms. If one was paid for mounting a fraudulent or malicious prosecution, *calumnia*, one could be charged with *pecuniam accipere* (*Digest* 3.6.1–3, 39.6.12, 48.2.4). A hostile advocate here inquires whether the witness Sabinus had received money for prosecution, and then whether he had therefore been charged with calumny (this must be the meaning of *calumniam habere*, but it is awkward and I can find no parallel). Sabinus plays on *accipere* and *habere*. He says that he had "accepted" money but did not know whether he "had" it; he knew that he had "accepted" (a charge of) calumny, but did not know whether he "had" it. I have no idea how this was relevant to the case at hand, nor what *pars adversa* signifies.

21. Whence *SRPF*³ ii.150 frag. incert. 92, duly recorded by editors of Seneca.

22. Overlooked at *RE* Antonius 113 and *PIR*² A 884.

23. *Suda* M 989; cf. Plato *Laws* 689d. The proverb conventionally has νεῖν for swimming, but note that the *Suda* uses κολυμβᾶν in its definition, the more elegant word employed by Sabinus.

24. Considered in detail in the appendix below, pp. 146–49.

25. On the length, see further below, p. 141.

26. The literature on equestrian salaries and census is enormous. The ducenarian procurator is assured by Suet. *Claud.* 24.1.

27. Abydus: Archestratus *ap.* Athenaeus 92d; Ennius *ap.* Apuleius *Apologia* 39.2. The text in question, *P. Louvre inv.* 7733v, consisting of both the poem, titled "Oyster," and the extensive ancient commentary on it, was first published in Lasserre 1975. A conservative edition of the six lines of verse was offered in Parsons 1977; the translation here is that of Parsons. Brackets indicate reconstruction of the text based on very difficult readings; parentheses gloss the learned obscurities. I am deeply grateful to the anonymous reader for drawing my attention to this text.

28. Respectively, Mart. 13.82, 49, 48, 51 (Loeb trans. Shackleton Bailey, modified). Of the 124 gifts in Book 13, about fifteen seem to speak in the first person.

29. Cf. Paul Fest. 104 L.; Col. 12.46.1; Sen. *Ep.* 74.14, 114.9, *Brev.* 12.5; Plin. *NH* 9.119 (Fenestella *ap.* 35.162, Ateius Capito *ap.* 18.108); Mart. 11.31.20; Apul. *Met.* 5.8.1.

30. Iul. Obs. 40; from Livy, so surely known to Sabinus' auditors.

31. Fundamental here is M. Wellmann's extraordinary feat of *Quellenforschung* (1888), summarizing the work's character at p. 190; as to its author's date, we must be satisfied with the first century before Christ and perhaps more precisely its second half (p. 192–93). The ichthyological Dorion does not appear in *RE*; he receives a five-word notice, under "Cookery Books," in *Brill's New Pauly*.

32. Tac. 3.55.1. The historian proceeds to explain with great satisfaction that luxurious dining abated after 68 CE because rich families had ruined themselves; new men from municipalities, colonies, and even the provinces brought their frugality into the upper classes; and the emperor

Vespasian led a conspicuously simple, old-fashioned life pointedly different from that of his extravagant predecessors.

33. The definition is that of the 4-H Folkpatterns series (Michigan State University and its Extension 4-H Programs) quoted in J. Darnton, "Foodways: When Food Meets Culture and History," Michigan State University, accessed April 1, 2024, https://www.canr.msu.edu/news /foodways_when_food_meets_culture_and_history.

34. Cf. chapter 8.

35. Susemihl 1891, 876–83 discusses some thirty authors writing in Greek from the fourth century onward; cf. Degani 1990, 52–53.

36. Wilkins and Hill 2011, 11–32, is an excellent introduction; the quotation is from p. 32.

37. Frag. 15, cf. 34, where the reader is urged to buy the *orkus* of Samos without bargaining; 31, where the *kitharos* is pleased by big spenders; 21, stressing that if the Rhodians refuse to sell you a dogfish, you should steal it.

38. So the general opinion: what can be gleaned about its length is judiciously discussed at Olson and Sens 1999, 3–5.

39. Degani 1990, 53; Degani 1994 is a good introduction to the work, with a lively exposition of its contents at pp. 415–19.

40. Ennius: Courtney *FLP* 22–25, 501. As to Lucilius, the arguments of Shero 1929 are suggestive if not conclusive. He remarks on the mythological name Tiresias (p. 66), it can be added that Nereus also appears, another multiple personality. More pointedly, the food is humanized: *Alma Ceres; flebile cepe lacrimosaeque ordine tallae; fragmenta interficis panis.*

41. Statius piles on with his own parody of the gastronome's geographical obsession with the native habitats of the best edibles: *Silv.* 4.6.1–11.

42. D'Arms 1999, with much evidence. Serious men: there seems to be no trace of female involvement in gastronomy at Rome.

43. *Fam.* 9.20.2 might offer a brilliant gastronomic pun about Cicero's supposed new passion: *Cum homine et edaci tibi res est et qui iam aliquid intellegat;* ὀψιμαθεῖς *autem homines scis quam insolentes sint;* he is an "opsimath," but as *homo edax* surely he is also an "opsomath," learned in delicacies; the word is unattested in Greek, but cf. ὀψομανής ("mad after dainties": *LSJ* citing Chrysippus, *SVF* 3 fr. 667 = Athen. 464d).

44. *Fam.* 9.26; restrained speech and groaning are reactions to Caesar's tyranny. Syme 1961, 26–27, excellently captures Eutrapelus' career and its context.

45. *Rhet.* 1389b: πεπαιδευμένη ὕβρις; Plutarch observes (*Cic.* 5.6) that Cicero's *eutrapelia* gave him a reputation for maliciousness.

46. Courtney *FLP* 234, Hollis *FRP* 164. The poet, *RE* Volumnius 1 (H. Gundel: identity with Eutrapelus "durchaus moglich"; it is generally accepted with or without question by other scholars); Eutrapelus, *RE* Volumnius 11 + 7 (Gundel: an identification universally and rightly accepted); Cytheris, Volumnius 17.

47. Plin. *NH* 8.170 (Loeb trans. Rackham).

48. Cf. the appendix below, pp. 146–47. Storks were out of favor by the early years of Augustus' reign: Cornelius Nepos *ap.* Plin. *NH* 10.60.

49. *Col.* 12.4.2 (a vignette of practical Romans as usual imposing order and discipline on diligent but clueless foreigners for the good of humanity); Syme 1986b is essential on the identity and social stature of the three authors. For Mena, *CIL* 6.33968; Ambivius, *PIR*² A 557, with Syme 1986b; Matius, *PIR*² M 369, with Col. 12.46.1. Quint. 3.1.18.

50. Apicius is treated in depth in chapter 8.

51. Vespa: Teuffel 1871; Baldwin 1987 offers a useful introduction and commentary. Fables: conveniently collected in translation at Gibbs 2002, 93–104, with references to several others. Despite modern assumptions, there is no reason whatever to assume that Sabinus' *Certamen* was a work in prose.

52. Syme 1989.

53. Cf. chapter 3 passim on Tiberius' obsession with Odysseus.

54. Cf. chapter 1.

55. On the likelihood of the fishing scene and of Plato the mullet, see the judicious discussion at Clayman 2009, 107–12. The *platistakos* was discussed by Dorion in his *On fishes*: Athen. 18c.

56. Julia (14 CE): Tac. 1.53.2, Dio 57.18.la (both passages clearly dependent on a single source, cf. Suet. 50.1). Livilla (31 CE): Dio 58.11.7. Asinius Gallus (33 CE): Tac. 6.23.1; Dio 58.3.3–6, 23.6. Agrippina (33 CE): Suet. 53.1–2; Tac. 4.54, 6.25. Nero (31 CE): Suet. 54.2, cf. 61.1 and Dio 58.8.4. Drusus (33 CE): Suet. 54.2, Dio 58.25.4, Tac. 6.23–24. Tiberius (37 CE): Suet. 73.2, Dio. 58.28.3, cf. Tac. 6.50.4–5. Self-starvation is a theme of the age: Tac. 4.35.4, Sen. *Marc.* 22.6 (Cremutius Cordus); Tac. 6.26.1–2, Dio 58.21.2 (Cocceius Nerva); Tac. 6.48.1 (Vibius Marsus, pretended). Tiberius himself had set the pace in 6 BCE: Suet. 10.2.

57. E.g., Suet. 59.1: *Fastidit vinum, quia iam sitit iste cruorem: / tam bibit hunc avide, quam bibit ante merum.* Asinius Gallus was not the only victim deceived just before his downfall: cf. Libo Drusus (Tac. 2.28.2) and Marcus Paconius (Suet. 61.6). Tiberius reminded Matthew Arnold of a cat watching a canary: "Cruel, but composed and bland, / Dumb, inscrutable and grand, / So Tiberius might have sat, / Had Tiberius been a cat" (Matthew Arnold, "Poor Matthias," 1882, end of second stanza).

58. Linderski 1988.

59. Whatever the charges against Drusus were, and however hostile the original, now-lost source might have been, the record of Tac. 6.24, with Dio 58.25.4, cannot be explained away.

60. Oscan: *Imagines Italicae* 1350–51 (Lucania, ca. 300 BCE), cf. 821 (Pompeii: possibly G. Asillius). The *gentilicium* is "certainly of Campanian origin": Castrén 1983, 138. *CIL* 10.2109 (Puteoli); 4.7297a, 8571 (Pompeii); Camodeca 2002, 228 (Herculaneum, or possibly Nola). Brick stamps at Pompeii suggest one source of family income: Vetter 1953, 61 (nos. 37, 37a, 37b).

61. Della Corte 1921 is a detailed account, amplified and brought up to date by Stefani 1998.

62. The stamp reads THALLI / ASEL.PRO: Stefani 1998, 49, with drawing; it is commonly accepted that "Asel.Pro" represents the name of the owner, Thallus being his slave. Della Corte 1921 proposed the unlikely expansion *Thalli Asel(li) Pro(curator)*.

63. *Pompeianis summum decem annorum incrementum est, nihil senecta conferente*: Plin. *NH* 14.70.

64. Badian 1968, 3–6. D'Arms 1981, 48–55 offers a fine reconstruction of Sempronius' tangled affairs. Unfortunately, he begins his account with "C. Sempronius Rufus was certainly in the senate in 43 BCE, and apparently *praetorius* already in the preceding year": there is no evidence for this, as Badian (1968, 4–5 n. 18) showed in detail.

65. Badian 1968, 3 n. 13, cautiously allows that M. Asellius M.f., accepted by *MRR*, may be correct; the supplement *MRR* III gives a judicious summary on p. 26 (but cf. p. 99, accepting the Gellius in Cicero).

66. He has simply combined what his two predecessors wrote, and "Asinius" should be his reading of "Asellius," not (*pace* Münzer) "Asellio."

67. A question overlooked by Münzer and Badian. Desperation is in order: Did he run twice? Does *praetura* mean consulship?

68. Livy 4.42.1, a problematic text, with Ogilvie's note ad loc. One of four tribunes nobly loyal to their commander: Val. Max. 6.5.2. Not in *RE* but caught by *MRR sub anno*.

Chapter 8. Marcus Apicius: A Sense of Place

1. Johnson 1933. The preliminary report on the monuments of the forum appeared two years later: Johnson 1935.

2. Münzer 1935.

3. Senators and knights with local ties in the area whose *gentes* are represented among the masters of the *fasti* include, beyond those mentioned above, Curtilius, Sestullius (Fundi),

Eppius, Arrius, Manlius Torquatus, Aurelii Cottae, Lutatius Catulus, Vargunteius, Cosconius Calidianus, Lucilius (the satirist), Helvius (Formiae), Paccius, Statius, and Larcius.

4. The interests of an astonishing 1,700 businessmen from the Republican Era alone are meticulously cataloged in the seven hundred pages of Nonnis 2015.

5. *RE* Tuccius 6, 9 (published in 1939): Cicero's friend Tuccius Galeo, whose astonishing Mediteranean-wide economic interests have become ever more clear, as elucidated by Scardozzi 2007; see also Guidobaldi and Pesando 1989, and for an up-to-date onomasticon of Minturnan gentes in the late Republic, see Gregori and Nonnis 2014, with scattered notices in Nonnis 2015. Scores of Roman senators and knights enjoyed social ties and economic interests centered on Minturnae.

6. Kneppe and Wiesehöfer 1983, 124. Add to their excellent biography the six upsetting documents at Birley 2016, 159–61.

7. E.g., Guidobaldi and Pesando 1989 (I should emphasize the value of their contribution). Badian (1980, 474 n. 12) observes, "Münzer's article and his suggestion on P. Curtilius seem to have been known to the editor of *CIL* I² 3, published in Berlin in 1943, . . . but—not surprisingly, perhaps—there is no actual reference to Münzer." Degrassi noted Münzer's paper in 1963, at *ILLRP* 2:152.

8. Münzer 1935, 330.

9. Respectively, *Schol. ad Querol.* p. 22 ed. Peiper; Isid. *Etym.* 20.1.1; *Schol ad Iuv.* 4.23; *Suda* A3207 (cf. K387, K 1649); Athen. 7c; Plin. *NH* 10.133; Plin. *NH* 9. 66; Athen. 168e; Tac. 4.1.2, cf. Dio 57.19.5.

10. *Suda* M 217 and A 3213 (trans. Suda On Line [SOL]).

11. Sen. *Helv.* 10.10, 10.9 (Loeb trans. Basore, modified).

12. *Suda* M 217 (trans. *Suda* online, modified).

13. Athen. 7a–c; translations of Athenaeus are from the excellent Loeb Classical Library version by S. D. Olson, occasionally modified, as here.

14. *Helv.* 10.8–9 (Loeb trans. Basore).

15. Mart. 3.22, with, perhaps, Juv. 11.2–3: *Quid enim maiore cachinno / excipitur volgi quam pauper Apicius?* (cf. 4.23 *miser et frugi: . . . Apicius*); Dio 57.19.5; Isid. *Etym.* 20.1.1; Vat. Myth. 2.225.

16. Hence "Apicianus" and Otto no. 126. Also generalized as the plural "Apicii."

17. Lindsay 1997 (covering also text and contents); Grainger 2007 (writing for a nonspecialist audience); Gutsfeld 2014; and Bober 1999, especially 149–59. Good editions of the cookbook and much useful material are available in André 2002, written by a master of Roman flora and fauna, and in Grocock and Grainger 2006, from the pens of a mediaeval scholar and a food historian.

18. *Suda* A 3213, the consuls (Q.) Iunius Blaesus (*PIR*² I 739) and L. (Antistius Vetus); their year was formerly thought to be 26 CE, which is now excluded by *AE* 1987, no. 163, and 28 CE is the only possible alternative.

19. *Suda* M 217, Persicus *PIR*² F 51, mentioning the Apicius connection.

20. Mullet: Sen. *Ep.* 95.42. Drusus: Plin. *NH* 19.137.

21. Tac. 4.1.2 (trans. Woodman modified).

22. And it is so used of Julius Caesar at Val. Max. 6.9.15.

23. Plin. *NH* 8.209, 9.66 (a contemporary); Dio 57 19 5 (reflecting the now lost contemporary historian); and *Suda* A 3213 (cf. B 326, E 3945, I 630).

24. Apicata: Tac. 4.3, 11; Dio 58.11.6. Sabinus: *AE* 1994, no. 1756, improving on *AE* 1961, no. 9.

25. E.g., Syme 1958, 274–77, 287–90.

26. Tac. 4.1.2 (quoted above). Dio 57.19.5 shares the father Strabo, the Apicius affair, and the emphasis on prodigality. He adds the anecdote about Apicius' suicide in fear of poverty, which is also part of the Latin tradition, derived by him either from the common source or from Seneca.

27. Main sources: Sen. *Ep.* 95.42, 120.19, *Vit. Beat*; 11.4; *Helv.* 10.8–9; Plin. *NH* 8.209, 9.66, 10.133, 19.137, 143; Mart. 2.69, 89, 3.22, 10.73; Juv. 4.22–3, 11.2; Tac. 4.1.3 (with Dio 57.19.50). Later

authors deal solely with reputation, not fact: e.g., Tert. *Apol.* 3.6, *Anim.* 33.4, *Ieiun.* 12, *Pall* 5.7; *HA Ael. Ver.* 5.9, *Helio*, 184, 20. 5, 24.4; Jer. *Ep.* 29.1, 333, *Iov.* 1.40; and cf. nn. 9 and 15 above.

28. Athen. 7a–c, 294f, 647c are the only three passages that concern our hero. Confusingly, 7d, 168e, and 543a–b all concern other Apicii, who will be considered below. The relevant passages in the *Suda* that treat our hero reduce to three: A 3207 (the lemmata at K 387 and K 1649 simply refer to this article), A 3213 (with cross-references at A 4184, B 326, E 3945, I 630, and S 352), and M 217. The Apicii at A 4660 (cross-reference A 3214) and O 720 are other men, likewise to be considered below.

29. I have translated ἀφύη as "small fry" for reasons that will become clear: something like anchovy or sardine or sprat is meant.

30. 1.7d–f (Loeb trans. Olson, modified).

31. A third item derives from this fantasist as well: Athenaeus' life-defining anecdote, placing Apicius at Minturnae, was quoted above at n. 13, and the same disreputable tale is told in the *Suda* at A 3207, where again the Greek text is an all-but-verbatim version of Athenaeus or his source, with the baffling substitution of Kintouri in Galatia—a city otherwise unknown to history—for Minturnae in Italy.

32. *CIL* I² 2697 (unfortunately not included in Degrassi's *ILLRP*). Hiding in plain sight: that is, at Minturnae, unknown to the bibliography on the gourmet; except for a notice at Nicolet 1974, 779, and a fine treatment at Mratschek-Halfmann 1993, 192–93, he seems to have evaded the notice of historians.

33. Athen. 168d–e (Loeb trans. Olson, modified); the reference to "Book One" corresponds to 7a–c, quoted above.

34. Athen. 543a–b (Loeb trans. Olson, modified).

35. Badian 1964, 108, 111 n. 14 (whence the quotation in the text); similarly, Gruen 1966, 53; Nicolet 1974, 779.

36. Vell. 2.13; Liv. *Per.* 70 (*publicani*); Dio fr. 97. 1; Val. Max. 2.10.5 (*publicani*). Cf. Cic. *Fam.* 1.9.26 (*publicani*); Diod. 37.5.1–4 (*publicani*); [Ascon.] 202 ed. Stangl (*publicani*).

37. Life and works are admirably discussed by C. J. Smith at *FRHist* 1:278–81. He mentions the habit at 3:288 and notes examples of ad hominem attacks at 1:279 n. 11.

38. Despite the faulty phrasing, there can be no doubt that, when taken with the first passage, Apicius is presented here as an enemy.

39. We know moreover that P. Rutilius Rufus owned an estate at Formiae. His nomen is borne by a P. Rutilius P.f. Ter. Veratianus, a native of nearby Minturnae: *CIL* X. 6049. If Minturnae was the base of the Apicii, the contest between Apicius and Rutilius Rufus may reflect a local feud.

40. *Hist.* 3.76 (trans. Church and Brodribb 1905).

41. A search for "Apini" in the *Epigraphik-Datenbase Clauss / Slaby* produces a scant fifteen inscriptions. Of these, seven or eight are versions of the nomen, along with a single Apinianus. Aquileia and Iulium Carnicum account for seven of the fifteen. The only distinguished member of the family is much later, a *curator rei publicae* of Carnicum in 373 CE. The name does not appear in Latium or Campania, and only once at Rome; it does not appear in Greek epigraphy, nor in ancient literature (with the possible exception of P. Apinius at Cic. *Mil.* 75, who is more likely to be a Papinius).

42. *CIL* 11.19 = *ILS* 2664: presumably the descendant of a dependent of the Apicii, given their commercial interests in the northeast.

43. Zerbinati 1986, 264–65, with catalog entries at 289–91. His presentation is very confusing and, like tens of thousands of inscriptions on *instrumenta domestica*, this material remains generally unnoticed (not in *CEIPAC* or *RTAR*). Zerbinati concludes vaguely of the stamp (p. 265), "puo forse essere al I sec. d.C." Three versions of it, each in multiple copies, appear to refer to the same person, viz.: M Apic Tiron; M A T; and Apic. A fourth stamp exists in three broken copies (not four, as at Zerbinati 1986, 264) with the common text, it seems, as follows: Apic

Apiciorum SFT. The great gain here is the plural Apiciorum: the factory was a family business, with an Apicius (a freedman, perhaps, or one of the family) acting as an agent. The letters SFT correspond to no known epigraphical abbreviation: the best guess is that they represent the *cognomina* of three Apicii, with Tiro being the "T" (so Bollini 2001).

44. The surviving harvest of other inscriptions from Parion tells a similarly colonial tale, presenting not only the usual variety of widespread Roman gentes but also some very rare Italian names indeed: e.g., the priest L. Calea L.f. Arn. Rufus—*IK Parion* 1014 (Latin); cf. *IK Sestos* 69 (likewise Latin) a priest Lu. Calea Lu. f. Arn., apparently the same man; or Sebi(u)s, father of Sebia Theophila (*IK Parion* 1100, 1174; otherwise only *CIL* VI. 20928); or Tufidius, late husband of Catulla Lucilla (*IK Parion* 1085), all nomina unique, or almost unique, in the Roman world.

45. Cf. *IK Parion* 6, concerning another fishing district ("Phrou . . ."), dated by another priest of Caesar, and displaying both Roman names and similar titles ("leading lessees," "lookouts"): both inscriptions were thoroughly elucidated in Robert and Robert 1950.

46. Robert and Robert 1950, 91–92; *IK Parion*, p. 85.

47. Sen. *Ep.* 95.42, quoted more fully below.

48. Duncan-Jones 1982, 343–44. Mart. 3.22 gives seventy million as the size of Apicius' fortune: that would merely slip him down to number fifteen. Even with his remaining ten million, he ties with Vergil at number twenty-three (note also that number eight is certainly fictitious and number twenty a generalization).

49. "For rough computational purposes" Scheidel and Friesen carefully calculate a "total elite wealth" (that of the senatorial, equestrian, and decurional orders) of three to five billion sesterces shared among some 150,000 families under the principate: Scheidel and Friesen 2009, 75–82. With his fortune of 70 or 110 million, Apicius was indeed one of the richest men of the era.

50. See Champlin 2012, 372–73 (= pp. 183–84) for details.

51. *Suda* A 3213 (the descent of his wife is deduced from Tacitus *Hist.* 3.38.3, with theories as to his identity, at Syme 1986a, 163, 302). Again, wealth is the subtext of the *Suda*'s anecdote, concerning a banquet to which Blaesus brought an uninvited companion, "for it was permitted to invite additionally certain extra guests like shadows of oneself. And so Apicius had to spend his substance both for friends and strangers" (trans. Suda On Line [SOL]).

52. See pp. 156–57.

53. See at n. 21.

54. See p. 142, on the cabbage-sprout question and the outsize mullet.

55. Sen. *Ep.* 95.42 (Penguin trans. E. Fantham).

56. Powerful men: the *praenomen* Publius being rare among elite Octavii, P. Octavius is very likely to have been one of two contemporary P. Octavii, likewise without *cognomina*, a proconsul of Crete and Cyrene under Tiberius, between 14 and 29 CE (*PIR*[2] O 19), or (his father?) a prefect of Egypt under Augustus, ca. 1 BCE to 3 CE (O 20, cf. 21). The latter will have hosted Gaius Caesar during his visit to Egypt: perhaps an occasion to discuss cuisine with Marcus Apicius?

57. It would be good to know the circumstances of the auction. Was it part of the normal rhythm of the market, or a special occasion needing an announcement? Probably the latter. Octavius and Apicius may indeed have bid in person, since the gastronomic tradition imposes an ideal, at least, of the gourmet's personal attendance at the market.

58. Andrews 1949; cf. p. 143 above.

59. *De alimentorum facultatibus* 3. 26 (K 6. 715–17).

60. I simply report the sources gathered by Andrews: 2 lbs., Plin. *NH* 9.64; Mart. 3.45.5, 11.49.9, 14.97 (*libras debet habere duas*); farming unsuccessful, Plin. *NH* 9.64, Col. 8.17.7; 3 lbs., Hor. *Serm.* 2.333–35, Mart. 10. 37.8; 4 lbs., Marti.10.31.3; 6 lbs., Juv. 4.15–33; Asinius Celer, Plin. *NH* 9.67, Tert. *Pall.* 5, Macrob. *Sat.* 3.16.9 (referring to *pretia haec insana*); the three mullets,

Suet. 34. With Tiberius, the craze passes into folklore, in the notorious anecdote of the fisherman who scaled the cliffs of Capri (Suet. 60, with pp. 3–5 above).

61. *NQ* 3.17.2–3, with the quotation from 3.18.1–191 in the next paragraph (trans. Hine 2010, modified).

62. *NH* 9.66 (Loeb trans. Rackham, modified).

63. Apion's extensive fragments are now well and conveniently edited by P. T. Keyser as *BNJ* 616 (2015). *On the Luxury of Apicius* is named at Athen. 294e (*BNJ* F 24), with possible fragments at Plin. *NH* 32.19 (*BNJ* F 31) and Athen. 642e (*BNJ* F 32): all three items concern fish. Apion's reputation was blackened by Josephus in his *Contra Apionem*, and many contemporaries clearly disliked the man with good reason, but the publication in 2014 of *POxy.* 5202 (with up-to-date bibliography) has cast astonishing new light on his career.

64. On these three, see the preceding chapter, pp. 140–41.

65. Cf. the third-century forgery attributed to Aristippus of Cyrene (who died in the mid-fourth century), *On the Luxury of the Ancients* (Περὶ παλαιᾶς τρυφῆς), which ran to at least four books: all the fragments and references to it occur in Diogenes Laertius (1.96, 2.23, 48, 3.29, 4.19, 5.4, 39, cf. 8.60) and concern sex.

66. Sen. *Ep.* 95. 25: *Quid? Illud sociorum garum, pretiosam malorum piscium saniem, non credis urere salsa tabe praecordia? Quid? Illa purulenta* (and so on); cf. Mart.13.102 (*fastosum garum from a dying mackerel as munera cara*), Manil. 5.671–72 (*sanies pretiosa* produced as the dismembered fish liquefies).

67. Étienne 1970 offers an elaborate account. Pompeii: *CIL* 4.5659 and *EE* 1.189 = *ILS* 8600a; Iul. Afr. *Cesti* 7.19 (overlooked by Étienne); Auson. *Ep.* 19a.4–9 Green.

68. Trimalchio and Apicius offer two extremes of self-awareness: otherwise, the dish could be served in the *Cena Trimalchionis* without readers noticing. When and where Apicius made his joke will be considered below.

69. Petr. *Sat.* 36. Garum with pepper at Apicius 7.15.1; *piperogaron* at Alex. Trall. 1.15.

70. Desbats, Lequément, and Liou 1987, 154–56, with photograph and drawing. *AE* 1988, no. 874j: *Liq(uamen) | Apic(ianum?) | G(aii) Rufi*. For the often-complex structure of *tituli picti*, see the useful chart at Martin-Kilcher 2003, 78.

71. The watershed is splendidly marked by Curtis 1991, which incorporates several of his earlier articles. Curtis 2005 synthesizes the history of research and the current understanding of both production and trade; cf. the convenient summary of Curtis 2009a. For an overview of advances in the study of food technology over three decades, and the reasons for them, see Curtis 2009b.

72. Pride of place here goes to Grainger 2012, Grainger 2013, and Grainger 2014, all with striking illustrations.

73. Curtis 1984, summarized briefly in Curtis 1991. Scaurus' business will be considered below.

74. See above, p. 159.

75. Dalby 2003, 296.

76. References in André 2002.

77. Wilkins and Hill 2011, 44–45, translation of and commentary on Athen. 285B

78. Brandt 1927. The author of the *Testamentum Porcelli* was surely familiar with the cookbook of "Apicius" (see the commentary of Nesterov 2011); and St. Jerome refers to the *Testamentum* in the first book of his *Contra Rufinum* (1.17), dated to 401 CE.

Chapter 9. Seianus Augustus

[Ed. note: with thanks to the Deutsches Archäologisches Institut for permission to publish here the paper that first appeared in *Chiron* 42 (2012): 361–88. Copyright © 2012 Deutsches Archäologisches Institut. Available online at https://doi.org/10.34780/0cf9-2d61.]

1. Juv. 10.72–77 (Loeb trans. Braund, modified).

2. The material in this chapter was first presented at a symposium held in December 2007, to honor the retirement of Professor T. D. Barnes from the University of Toronto. I am grateful for the invaluable remarks of Tony Birley, Bob Kaster, Tony Woodman, and my teacher Tim Barnes. Soon after delivering the paper mentioned above, I received a copy of Professor Birley's essay, which I cite below, passim. Readers will note that while covering much of the same ground, this paper is concerned to explain more Sejanus' rise than his fall. Jonson's play includes several long translations of passages from Tacitus into good English blank verse.

3. Recounting Sejanus' demise, Dio asserts in passing (58.14.1) that he had more power than any other prefect before or after him, save Plautianus, but he notably forgoes any comparison of the two men. He does reflect on the change of fortune, but it is the mutability of the crowd that concerns him (58.11.1–3). La Penna 1980 makes the attractive but unprovable suggestion that Seneca's portrait of the usurper Lycus in the *Hercules Furens* is modeled on Sejanus.

4. Hennig 1975, 41–67 neatly deflates Sejanus' role in the treason trials and as an enemy of Agrippina and her family before 26 CE.

5. Dio 57.21.4; Tac. 4.74.3–4 (with the notes of Martin and Woodman 1989), cf. 6.8.5. The flattery and attention lavished on Sejanus is a commonplace of the era, e.g., Col. 1 pr. 9–10, Plut. *Mor.* 814D.

6. Tac. 4.2.3, 68.2; Juv. 10.91–92. For examples: Martin and Woodman 1989, 90, cf. Dio 58.4.1 on benefits bestowed, Hennig 1975, 101–21, on his followers.

7. Dio 58.5.1, with 58.4.1 (Xiphilinus). As Dio's source presumably knew, the reference may recall the flatterers of Demetrius Poliorcetes, who disparaged his rival monarchs with demeaning titles, among them "nesiarch" for Agathocles of Syracuse: Plut. *Demet.* 25, *Mor.* 823C–D. There were also Ptolemaic officials called "nesiarchs" in the Aegean islands in the third century BCE; in the unlikely event that Tiberius' detractors knew of them, Tarn's (1911, 151) summary is striking: "The nesiarch . . . had no military authority and very little power; he was the Ptolemaic Resident."

8. Tac. 4.7.1, 4.2.3; Dio 58.4.3, 9.

9. Cat-and-mouse details in Dio 58.6–8, e.g., conflicting health bulletins, praise and blame of Sejanus, honor and disgrace for his friends, priesthoods for Sejanus and his son along with Gaius (Caligula) but no summons to Campania and instructions to remain in Rome and expect Tiberius momentarily; then, the final trick of Tiberius' letter.

10. Dio 58.11.5. Abuse of the corpse: cf. Juv. 10.85–86; Val. Max. 9.11. ext. 4; Sen. *Tranq.* 11.11.

11. The best introduction is Birley 2007, Hennig 1975 is sound and cautious: see next note.

12. So Sejanus' friend Terentius, defending himself in 32 CE, Tac. 6.8.5. I deliberately avoid here the nature and extent of his "conspiracy," and the bloodbath of family, friends, and followers. Modern scholarship on the conspiracy is well summarized at Birley 2007, 129–34; Hennig 1975, 144–56 rightly concludes that there is no good evidence for any conspiracy. Syme's oft-repeated dictum (1958, 406) stands up well after sixty years: "The only plot that can safely be assumed and narrated is the plot devised and executed by Tiberius Caesar." The official treatment of Sejanus' memory is a puzzle. *Pace* Varner 2004, 92–93, there was no *damnatio memoriae*, indeed the only "memory sanction" (the more accurate term) was the forbidding of mourning, part of a much longer senatorial decree (Dio 58.12.4–5, 7–8); the meager evidence is correctly gathered and discussed at Flower 2006, 172–74.

13. Tac. 1.24.2; Suet. 55; other references to his authority and his power at *PIR*² A 255.

14. For the consulship, to the references in *PIR*, add *AE* 1953.88 = 1969 / 1970.233, (Juromenha, Lusitania), dated January 21, 31 CE, with Sejanus' name as consul intact. The coins from Bilbilis naming Tiberius and him as consuls, many of them with his name carefully chiseled off, are now conveniently available as *RPC* 1.398–99. (Mr. J. Geranio of Oakdale, California, informs me that a careful survey of sale catalogs over the last twenty-five years has turned up some fifteen to twenty examples of these coins for sale, about half with the name intact and half erased.) *Imperium proconsulare*: Dio 58.7.4. *Spes tribuniciae potestatis*: Suet. 65.1, Dio 58.9.2, 4, 10.3.

15. The *ornamenta praetoria* granted in 20 CE (see below) did not confer senatorial rank. At some point in 31 CE, Sejanus, his son, and Tiberius' grandson Gaius were made priests: Dio 58.7.4, 5; cf. Suet. *Cal.* 12.1. Prefect: Tac. 1.24.2; cf. 6.8.2 and Dio 57.19.6.

16. Keppie 1996, 120. Sejanus and the praetorians: Dio 57.19.6 and Tac. 4.2.1–3, single camp; 58.4.2, Tiberius fears his hold over the praetorians, in 30 CE; 58.9.2, 5, Macro secretly appointed commander, shows praetorians letter from Tiberius giving him command and promising them rewards, and sends them back to camp; 58.11.4, emboldened by mob and by guards' absence, senators condemn Sejanus to death; 58.12.2, soldiers riot because suspected of good will to Sejanus and because they were upset the night watch preferred to them; 58.18.26, in 32 CE, Tiberius honors them with words and money; Suet. 48.2, a thousand sesterces per man for not siding with Sejanus. Note that at Dio 57.24.5, Tiberius seems to be ordering the guard directly rather than through Sejanus. Sejanus was a follower of Gaius Caesar (Tac. 4.1.2), and the two were probably contemporaries, but the common assumption that he was with him in the East is pure speculation (Tacitus does not mention it), and even if he was with him, there is no need to assume that his role was military. In 14 CE, he escorted Drusus Caesar to deal with the mutiny in Pannonia (Tac. 1.24.2); praetorian cavalry accompanied them, but Sejanus' role was that of "mentor" (*rector*) for the young man, no fighting was involved, and, indeed, he plays no part at all in Tacitus' narrative. At *Marc.* 22.5, Seneca calls him *perfidus miles*, but that is to make the rhetorical contrast with Pompey, the *maximus imperator*, whose theater Sejanus polluted with his own statue.

17. Syme 1986a, 300–312, with Table XXIII, is masterly; see also Birley 2007, 123–26; some of Hennig's conclusions (1975, 5–18) are debatable. The following seems a plausible minimum. 1) The distinguished families, ancient and notable for their honors, which Sejanus "embraced" through his maternal line, included Aelii Tuberones and Cassii Longini. 2) The consular brothers included half-brothers, Q. Aelius Tubero (cos. 11 BCE) and Sex. Aelius Catus (cos. 4), and a brother (by adoption?), L. Seius Tubero (cos. 18). 3) The consular maternal uncle is Q. Iunius Blaesus (cos. 10), and one of the consular cousins is that man's son, also Q. Iunius Blaesus (cos. 28). Velleius is studiously vague, not claiming actual descent from senatorial families, merely relationship with them.

18. *PIR*² S 322. Again, the following seems plausible. 1) Strabo came from Vulsinii: his son was born there (Tac. 4.1.2, 6.8.3; Juv. 10.74), he himself received a dedication there (*CIL* 11.2707), and two brothers, A. and L. Seius, A. f., are now attested as *curatores aquae* at Vulsinii under Augustus (Corbier 1983, whence *AE* 1983.395, to be added to *PIR*²). 2) As all would now agree, Strabo must be the prefect of Egypt whose name lost on the fragmentary inscription from Vulsinii (*CIL* 11.7285 = *ILS* 8896) that has aroused so much speculation: that prefect dedicated a bath along with his mother Terentia A. f. and his wife Cosconia Gallitta, daughter of a Lentulus Maluginensis. 3) This Cosconia should be Sejanus' stepmother, and was presumably the sister of Ser. Cornelius Lentulus Maluginensis (cos. 10), from a grand patrician family. 4) Terentia A. f., who should be Sejanus' grandmother, *may* be a member of the old senatorial family of the Terentii Varrones and a sister of the wife of Maecenas (the conjecture of Cichorius 1904, commonly accepted); but if that were so, how could Velleius have overlooked such lofty and direct connections which were so pertinent to his theme? *PIR*² A 102 is rightly dubious. 5) Nonetheless, there is a strong case to be made for Strabo's father marrying another time, into the lesser senatorial family of the Teidii, based on the compelling restoration of *CIL* 1².1328 by Wiseman 1963. In sum, no direct senatorial connections on the paternal side (hence the silence of Velleius Paterculus), but still useful step-connections, taking in the patrician Cornelii and Sex. Teidius Valerius Catullus (cos. 31), not to mention all of their unknown relatives.

19. Again, plausibilities. 1) Sejanus' wife Apicata was a close relative, presumably a sister, of T. Apicatus Sabinus, *quaestor pro praetore* of Cyprus around the turn of the millennium (*AE* 1961.9, 1994.1756). The partial homonymity with Sejanus' acquaintance, the gourmand Apicius (on whom see chapter 8), is fortuitous. 2) Sejanus' son, Capito Aelianus, known only from the record of his execution in 31 CE in the *Fasti Ostienses*, is usually presumed to have been adopted

by a senatorial Capito, but there is no certainty. 3) Sejanus himself, born the son of Seius Strabo, was adopted by a Lucius Aelius, hence becoming L. Aelius Seianus: the most likely candidate for the adoptive father is Aelius Gallus (*praenomen* unknown), prefect of Egypt in 24 BCE, especially when we remember the mysterious Aelius Gallus who fled for his life after the execution of Sejanus, Tac. 5.8.

20. Syme 1958, 384. Cf. Jos. *AJ* 18.181: many of the senators and the (imperial) freedmen supported Sejanus, and the army had been suborned.

21. Woodman 1977, 252–53.

22. Vell. 2.127.4: *vultu vitaque tranquillum*; Tac. 4.1.3: *palam compositus pudor.*

23. See at n. 8 above. The chronology is muddled by Tacitus' great character sketch of Sejanus at 4.1–3. For the historian, 23 CE was to be the year of the momentous change in the reign, with Sejanus as the central villain. Therefore, everything is packed into these chapters, looking both backward and forward, although Sejanus had been a powerful figure at least since 14 CE and had been mentioned in the *Annals* earlier. Tacitus ends his sketch in 23 CE with Sejanus' image being worshipped throughout the empire—something that Dio suggests happened much later—and with Tiberius calling him *socius laborum.*

The distinction between *adiutor imperii* and *socius laborum* is significant, the gulf between "helper" and "partner." From the start, Tiberius was eager to share the burden of power (cf. Tac. 1.11.1, *sociatis laboribus*), and Germanicus and Drusus Caesar, however unsatisfactory, were duly groomed for the role. Sejanus was certainly *adiutor* in 23 CE: Drusus, who died in 23, called him that, and Velleius expounds at length upon his role as *singularis principalium onerum adiutor.* But he was not yet *socius*: Velleius, writing in 29 or 30 CE, does not call him that. Dio first mentions Tiberius' use of the phrase as one of his weapons to soothe suspicions in the year 30 CE; above all, Tacitus himself tells us that Drusus Caesar, speaking as the outraged son, complained of Sejanus that someone else was called *adiutor imperii* and that it would not be long before that person was called *collega.* From which we should conclude that Sejanus was *not* called *socius* (surely *collega* is a Tacitean synonym for *socius*) in 23 CE: Tacitus is purposely anachronistic in naming him as such. In sum, Sejanus was powerful for decades, but it was only in the last three years, 29–31 CE, that he became a true political marvel, just as it was only in 31 that he ceased to be a knight. Cf., briefly, Bellemore 1995, 258–59.

24. Tac. 3.72.3; Dio 57.21.4; Sen. 22.4. Sejanus' honors are treated at Hennig 1975, 122–38, to be used with some skepticism.

25. Tac. 4.74.2, Jeppesen 1993. [Ed. note: an enlarged image of the Grand Camée can be viewed at Library of Congress, "Great Cameo of France," accessed April 1, 2024, https://www.loc.gov/item/2021669238/.] Approving the identification, Birley notes (2007, 137–38) that it has been overlooked in recent scholarship; the scholars he mentions are classicists. Curiously, there seems to be little reaction to Jeppesen's paper among art historians: it is apparently ignored by the standard monographs of Giard 1998 and Giuliani 2010 (whose identification of the figure is not possible). Varner 2004, 92–93, at n. 82, finds the identification "entirely unconvincing" and concludes that "the gem must be Claudian . . . as proposed by Jucker": needless to say, not all art historians would agree.

26. Dio 58.2.7, cf. 6.2; Suet. 65.1. Suetonius adds that the statues were worshipped (*coli*) presumably conflating the actions of the years 29 and 30 CE; see following.

27. Sejanus among the *signa*: Suet. 48.2 reports in passing that after Sejanus' fall, Tiberius rewarded the Syrian legions because they alone had not placed his bust among their standards, a move perhaps connected with the fact that the governor of Syria throughout the years of Sejanus' ascendancy was Tiberius' old friend L. Aelius Lamia, who remained in Rome and governed the province *in absentia* (Tac. 6.27; *PIR*² A 200).

28. A desperately obscure problem: betrothed, or married? And to Julia, daughter of Drusus Caesar, granddaughter of Tiberius, or to her mother, Livia / Livilla, widow of Drusus Caesar and Tiberius' niece? For a clear discussion, see Bellemore 1995, making a strong case that Livia's

is the name lost on the *Fasti Ostienses*, where they record that the wife (?) of Sejanus committed suicide on October 25, 31 CE. Birley 2007, 141 allows that "the case seems very plausible," but some items of evidence remain stubbornly irreconcilable.

29. Scott 1931, 112–14 and passim.

30. Dio 58.7.2; see further below.

31. 10.58–64, at 63 (Loeb trans. Braund). Statues toppled and abused on the day of his downfall: Dio 58.11.3.

32. Weinstock 1971 offers convenient context for the cultic aspect of these honors: birthdays as public celebrations, 206–12; golden chairs in public, 281–84; oaths and vows, 212–14, 217–20.

33. Sen. *Tranq.* 11.11; on Sejanus' honors, cf. Juv. 10.74–77, discussed below.

34. Agrippa's *novitas*, a standard subject, is brilliantly characterized by his younger contemporary Seneca at *C.* 2.4.13.

35. So Birley 2007, concluding at 148.

36. Tac. 6.29.3 (34), cf. 6.9.3–4 (32); Juv. 10.83.

37. Scaurus as orator: Sen. *C.* 10.pr.2–3. His *Atreus*: Dio 58.24.3–4, Tac. 6.29. On Ovid: Sen. *C.* 9.5.17, cf. 1.2.22. Otho's *colores*: Sen. *C.* 2.1.33. Bruttedius *historicus*: Sen. *S.* 6.20–21. Otho and Niger also acted together for the defense in a case of adultery: Sen. *C.* 2.34–35. Seneca's memories here of Otho happen to conclude with a tart criticism of the man's talent by none other than Aemilius Scaurus, *C.* 2.39.

38. Tac. 6.3.1–4, Dio 58.18.3–4. Gallio; urban praetor, *AE* 1991.307; praised by Seneca, *C.* 2.1.33, 9.3.4; *noster* at *C.* 2.5.11, 13, 3.pr.2, 7.pr.5, *S.* 3.6.; son, *PIR*² I 757. Messalla, Tiberius, *Naso suus*: Sen. *S.* 3.5–7; Ov. *Pont.* 4.11. Rhetoric: Quint 3.1.21.

39. Peregrine praetor: *AE* 1987.163, a fragment from the Arval fasti; therefore, *PIR*² S 675 = S 656: both articles rightly suggest the identification, but overlook the new fragment confirming it. *Carmina*: Tac. 6.39.1; Courtney, *FLP* 343–44. Now that his true name seems to be revealed as Sextilius, not Sextius, one wonders whether there might be some relationship with another fragmentary poet, Sextilius Ena of Corduba, an acquaintance of Valerius Messalla, Asinius Pollio, and Cornelius Severus: Courtney, *FLP* 329, from Sen. *S.* 6.27. A relationship might also be inferred with M. Paconius, the legate of C. Iunius Silanus, who joined in his prosecution in 22 CE (see above), was later held to be a martyr to Tiberius (Suet. 61.6; Tac. 16.28.1, 29.2), and was presumably the father of the senator-philosopher Q. Paconius Agrippinus (*PIR*² P 27).

40. Gaetulicus: *PIR*² C 1390. Latin verse: Courtney, *FLP* 345–46; and later reputation at Mart. 1 pr.; Pliny *Ep.* 5.3.5; Sidon. *Carm.* 9.259, *Ep.* 2.10.6. Greek verse: Page, *FGE* 49–60. Betrothal: Tac. 6.30.2. Secundus: *PIR*² P 754, with references to his literary influence; and especially Swan 1976. Praised by Tacitus: 5.8.2, 12.28.1. Prosecution: Tac. 5.8.1–2. Gallus: Syme 1986a, 308–9. Sejanus' Pomponius: Tac. 6.8.5. I see no reason to identify this man as low-born (despite *PIR*² P 687, which misleadingly suggests that Tacitus calls him Sejanus' *cliens*), and it is wrong automatically to assume that a friend of Sejanus could not be noble in either birth or character.

41. *Ep.* 122.11. Again, it is quite wrong to assume, as at *PIR*² P 410, that he was not connected with the Pinarii Nattae, obscure patricians by the time of the late republic: Sejanus, after all, came from the heart of the aristocracy. Ovid seems to have shared the opinion of Montanus' talent with Seneca and Pinarius (*Pont.* 4.16.11), but Seneca's father thought him *egregius* (*C.* 7.1.27). Other literary connections: 1) Apicius (on whom see chapter 8) wrote on cooking, even if the cookbook surviving today under his name is a later compilation: Tac. 4.1.2. 2) Sejanus' cousin, Q. Iunius Blaesus (cos. 26 CE) was a friend of the historian and critic Asconius Pedianus, whom he brought to a dinner hosted by Apicius: *Suda* A 3213. 3) C. Cassius Longinus (cos. 30), probably Sejanus' nephew and one of the great jurists of the age, wrote at least ten books on civil law. 4) The future emperor Claudius, whose son was betrothed to the daughter of Sejanus, was a voluminous author who was already writing history under Augustus. 5) And perhaps Q. Curtius Rufus is to be added, the author of the surviving *Histories* of Alexander the Great. The standard assumption, unprovable but eminently plausible, identifies him with Q.

Curtius Rufus (cos. 43) and with the contemporary Q. Curtius Rufus, a professional rhetor discussed in a now-lost part of Suetonius' work on rhetors (cf. the senator-rhetor Otho). In an influential paper, Sumner (1961) argued from Tac. 11.21.2 that Rufus was a follower of Sejanus and suffered a setback in his career after his patron fell.

42. Suet. 56, 70.1; Philo *Leg.* 141–42, cf. 167, 33. Love of Sejanus: Dio 58.4.3, 9. On Tiberius the intellectual, Syme 1986a, 346–66, and chapters 1–4 in this volume. I am very tempted to identify Sejanus with "that Tuscus" (*homo quam improbi animi tam infelicis ingenii*) the man who "had made [Aemilius Scaurus] a defendant on the charge of *maiestas*," but that would require an elaborate and inconclusive interpretation of Sen. *S.* 2.22. The point is that Seneca's *Tuscus ille* could be read as "that Etruscan" rather than "that (man named) Tuscus": cf. *Tuscus*, "the Etruscan" (= Sejanus) at Juv. 10.74.

43. Tac. 4.3.3. Hennig 1975, 33–40, mounts a good case for seeing the "murder" of Drusus as a later fabrication against Sejanus.

44. Dio 57.22.2, cf. 58.11.6; Suet. 62.1.

45. Dio 58.3.8. This marriage of Drusus to Aemilia Lepida was mentioned in a lost part of the *Annals*, as were her frequent charges (*crebris criminibus*) against him: Tac. 6.40.3, where in 36 CE, she is accused of adultery with a slave and commits suicide.

46. Suet. *Aug.* 69.1: *Adulteria non libidine sed ratione commissa*. Cf. Alexander the Great: Plut. *Alex.* 48–49, *Mor.* 339D.

47. The transmitted sum of fifty million has not been seriously challenged, but "Sutorius" is routinely emended to "Clutorius." If that is correct, the execution of Clutorius Priscus in 21 CE (Tac. 3.49–51; Dio 57.20.3) would give us a *terminus post quem non*, and the two most likely dates for the purchase would then be the periods of public mourning after the deaths of Augustus in 14 CE and of Germanicus in 19. But Birley 2007, 148–49, briefly suggested that we accept the transmitted *Sutorio*, and that the man could have been a freedman of Sutorius Macro. *Per litteras* he makes the case more expansively, "that the buyer was indeed Sutorius [*not* Clutorius] Priscus, that he was probably a freedman of Sutorius Macro acting on Macro's behalf, and that the sale was *after* Sejanus' death—I imagined an auction of Sejanus' property (cf *Ann.* 6, 2, 1). A 'time of national grief,' *in luctu civitatis*, could surely perfectly well refer to the state of things in the period after October 31, cf. *Ann.* 6.7; 6.19; 6.25.1 on the *dolor* two years later at deaths of Drusus III & then Agrippina; or 6.26.2, *mala rei publicae*, and especially 6.27.1, *tot luctibus funesta civitate pars maeroris fuit*." That scenario is certainly persuasive: *Sutorio* should stand.

48. Tac. 4.8.1, 10.1–3 (with the valuable commentary of Martin and Woodman).

49. Guyot 1980 for details. His prosopography of court eunuchs runs to some 118 entries.

50. Guyot 1980, 59–60, with references.

51. Maecenas: Sen. *Ep.* 114.6, cf. Porph. Hor. *Serm.* 1.1.105; Titus: Suet. *Tit.* 7.1; Dio 67.2.3; Vitellius and Fabius Valens: Tac. *Hist.* 2.71, 3.40.

52. Vitellius' followers are *greges spadonum*. The unchastity of the young Titus is marked by his *exoletorum et spadonum greges*. Curtius Rufus, writing earlier in the century, tells us that Darius' palace held *spadonum greges*, "practiced in playing the woman's role" (6.6.8). The declaimer T. Labienus referred, under Augustus, to wealthy *principes viri* who possess *castratorum greges*: Sen. *C.* 10.4.17. These "flocks" hark back to the corrupt East, symbolized by Cleopatra and her *contaminato grege turpium morbo virorum* in Horace (*Carm.* 1.37.9–10, cf. *Epod.* 9.13–14), which the scholiast Porphyrio dutifully glosses *cum grege spadonum*. During the civil war, Maecenas was accompanied around Rome by two eunuchs; his namesake Trimalchio Maecenatianus played ball with two eunuch attendants (Petron. *Sat.* 27. 3); King Herod had three, all of whom were corrupted by his son Alexander (Jos. *AJ* 16.230–31). Cf. Marulla with her Coresus and Dindymus at Mart. 6.39.21. Ammianus refers much later to a *multitudo spadonum*, following their master through the streets of Rome, *mutilorum hominum agmina* (14.6.17), and to a *coetus spadonum* plotting with the *cohors Palatina* (18.5.4).

53. Dio 58.2.8 (in epitome), 6.2.

54. Weinstock 1971, 112–27. Note also that desertion by a patron deity is a mark of the highest status: Hekster 2010.

55. Dio 58.7.2–3: Immediately before this, Dio has recounted another terrifying omen involving a statue, one of Sejanus himself.

56. *NH* 8.197: The figure 560 is roughly right, calculating from Servius' death in (notionally) 535 BCE to Sejanus' death in 31 CE. Syme 1956, 261, suggested that since the robes seem to have perished with Sejanus, the mob assailed and looted his mansion.

57. *NH* 36.163, discussed below.

58. This section is deeply indebted to Syme 1956, a classic that is as fresh today as it was several scholarly generations ago. I regret that this discussion was written long before I became aware of Pistellato 2007, an excellent essay that anticipates several arguments in this section, especially its fundamental point that the relationship between Sejanus and Servius was "il nodo centrale della propaganda ideologica dell'*eques* di *Volsinii* negli anni del massimo prestigio, precisamente indirizzata all'elemento populare dell'*Vrbs*, a cui la figura del re era particolaramente cara." Hence the brevity of this section.

59. On the temple: *LTUR* 2.278, s.v. Fortuna Seiani, Aedes (L. Anselmino and M. J. Strazulla); cf. Coarelli 1988, 265–68 (253–77 is invaluable on the many Fortunes of Servius Tullius). Coarelli contended, as others have done, that the temple lay within Sejanus' house, and that it is to be identified with the Temple of Fortuna Virgo on the Esquiline. In an important paper of 2001, he argued that the remains of a sixth-century BCE *sacellum* and a first-century CE house under San Pietro in Vincoli were precisely the temple (along with the tomb) of Servius Tullius and the house of Sejanus itself; rightly doubted at Pistellato 2007, 495–97.

60. The major sources are Plut. *Fort. Rom.* 10 (*Mor.* 322E–323D), *Quaest. Rom.* 36, 74, 281 (*Mor.* 273B–C, 281D–E, 287E–F); Dion. Hal. *Ant.* 4.27.7.

61. Beyond the passages just cited, note Dion. Hal. *Ant.* 3 and 4, passim; Cic. *Rep.* 2.7–42; Val. Max. 3.4.3; Florus 1.1.6; Ov. *Fast.* 6. 71–84; Macrob. *Sat.* 1.13.18, 16.33. Vernole 2002 covers all of the ancient material and modern bibliography; of the latter, Ridley 1975 is particularly good on the development of Servius' reputation.

62. The Aventine inscription: *CIL* 6.10213 = *ILS* 6044; G. Camodeca's edition at *ILMN* 1.159 supersedes all previous versions. Essential bibliography on the "Aventine election" includes: Syme 1956; Hennig 1975, 72–76, 140 (bafflingly eccentric); Yavetz 1998; Torelli 2006, 268–69, cf. Torelli 2011; Pistellato 2007; Birley 2007, 138–41. The restoration of the first word in line 3, [- 2 / 3-]*itatio*, remains unresolved, despite many suggestions; I follow here Torelli's [*ag*]*itatio*, for which he neatly cites Cic. *Mur.* 29 [35], discoursing on the *agitationes commutationesque fluctuum* of the *comitia* (*centuriata*).

63. And, of course, we suspect but cannot prove that the outraged old man who addresses his fellow tribesmen is none other than Tiberius himself; cf. Birley 2007, 139 n. 65, for doubts. So far as I am aware, the point made here about Sejanus' ties with the tribes in Dio has not been noticed before; and only Pistellato seems to have contemplated the possibility that the *comitia* referred to was the *tributa*, not the *centuriata*. According to Dio 58.8.2, he felt that that the people had been on his side until Tiberius started showing favor in 31 CE to Gaius (Caligula), the son of their idol Germanicus.

64. Dio 58.2.7–8 (τό τε πλῆθος ἔκ τε τῶν δημάρχων καὶ ἐκ τῶν ἀγορανόμων τῶν σπετέρων).

65. As was noted in a speech by the emperor Claudius himself: *ILS* 212.

66. This and most of what follows is based on Strazzulla 1993; on the significance of *Respiciens*, pp. 331–35.

67. *ILLRP* 1070. Essential are Guarducci 1949–51 and Guarducci 1973. I follow her Italian translation of the text in the latter paper, published after *ILLRP*. In that paper, she also argued that the stone may have come, appropriately, from Fanum Fortunae.

BIBLIOGRAPHY

Adamo Muscettola, S. 1998. "L'arredo delle ville imperiali: Tra storia e mito." In *Capri antica: Dalla preistoria alla fine dell'età romana*, ed. E. Federico and E. Miranda, 241–74. Capri.

Adams, J. N. 1982. *The Latin Sexual Vocabulary*. Baltimore.

Adams, J. N. 1983a. "An Epigram of Ausonius (87, p. 344 Peiper)." *Latomus* 42: 95–109.

Adams, J. N. 1983b. "Words for 'Prostitute' in Latin." *Rheinisches Museum* 126: 321–58.

Adams, J. N. 2003. *Bilingualism and the Latin Language*. Oxford.

Ailloud, H. 1931. *Suétone: Vies des douze Césars*. Paris.

Alföldy, G. 1992. *Studi sull'epigrafia augustea e tiberiana di Roma*. Rome.

Alföldy, G. 1999. "Pontius Pilatus und das Tiberieum von Caesarea Maritima." *Scripta Classica Israelica* 18: 85–108 [*AE* 1999.1681].

Alföldy, G. 2002. "Nochmals: Pontius Pilatus und das Tiberieum von Caesarea Maritima." *Scripta Classica Israelica* 21: 133–48 [*AE* 2002.1556].

Alföldy, G. 2005. "Zwei römische Statthalter im Evangelium: Die epigraphischen Quellen." In *Il contributo delle scienze storiche allo studio del Nuovo Testamento*, ed. E. dal Covolo and R. Fusco, 226–36. Vatican City. [*AE* 2005.1583.]

Amali, G. 1893. *Tiberio a Capri secondo la tradizione popolare*. Trani. [Originally in *Rassegna pugliese* 10 [1893]: 3–20.]

Andrè, J. 1971. *Emprunts et suffixes nominaux en latin*. Geneva.

André, J. 2002. *Apicius: L'Art Culinaire*. Paris.

Andreae, B. 1994. *Praetorium Speluncae: Tiberius und Ovid in Sperlonga*. Mainz.

Andreae, B. 1999. *Odysseus. Mythos und Erinnerung*. Mainz.

Andreae, B. 2004. "Tre questioni conclusive a proposito del programma iconologico di Sperlonga." In *Studi di Archeologia in onore di Gustavo Traversari*, ed. M. Fano Santi, 1–10. *Archeologica* 141. Rome.

Andreae, B., and Parisi Presicce, C. eds. 1996. *Ulisse: Il mito e la memoria*. Rome.

Andrews, A. C. 1949. "The Roman Craze for Surmullets." *Classical Weekly* 42: 186–88.

Ax, W. 1991. "Timons Gang in die Unterwelt: Ein Beitrag zur Geschichte der antiken Literaturparodie." *Hermes* 119: 176–93.

Bablitz, L. 2009. "Three Passages on Tiberius and the Courts." *Memoirs of the American Acaedmy in Rome* 54: 121–33.

Badian, E. 1964. "Mam. Scaurus Cites Precedent." *Classical Review* 8: 216–20 (= *Studies in Greek and Roman History*, 105–11. Oxford, 1964).

Badian, E. 1968. "The Sempronii Aselliones." *Proceedings of the African Classical Association* 11: 1–6.

Badian, E. 1980. "A *Fundus* at Fundi." *American Journal of Philology* 101: 470–82.

Badoud, N. 2019. "Le Laocoon et les sculptures de Sperlonga: Chronologie et signification." *Antike Kunst* 62: 71–95.

Baker, G. P. 1929. *Tiberius Caesar: Emperor of Rome*. London.

Baldwin, B. 1987. "The *Iudicium Coci et Pistoris* of Vespa." In *Filologia e forme letterarie: Studi offerti a Francesco Della Corte*, ed. S. Boldrini et al, 135–49. Vol. 4. Urbino.

Beard, M. 2007. *The Roman Triumph*. Cambridge, MA.

Beard, M., and Henderson, J. 2001. *Classical Art: From Greece to Rome*. Oxford.

Beck, R. 1991. "Thus Spake Not Zarathustra: Zoroastrian Pseudepigrapha of the Greco-Roman World." In *A History of Zoroastrianism*. Vol. 3, *Zoroastrianism under Macedonian and Roman Rule*, by M. Boyce and F. Grenet, 491–565. Leiden.

Bellemore, J. 1992. "The Dating of Seneca's *Ad Marciam de consolatione*." *Classical Quarterly* 42: 219–34.

Bellemore, J. 1995. "The Wife of Sejanus." *Zeitschrift für Papyrologie und Epigraphik* 109: 255–66.

Bellemore, J. 2003. "Cassius Dio and the Chronology of A.D. 21." *Classical Quarterly*, n.s., 53: 268–85.

Bellemore, J. 2007. "Tiberius and Rhodes." *Klio* 89: 417–53.

Belli, R., Carsana, V., de Crescenzo, M. V., and Pelosi, A. 1998. "Il territorio dell'isola di Capri: le evidenze." In *Capri antica: Dalla preistoria alla fine dell'età romana*, ed. E. Federico and E. Miranda, 129–223. Capri.

Bergmann, B. 1999. "Rhythms of Recognition: Mythological Encounters in Roman Landscape Painting." In *Im Spiegel des Mythos: Bilderwelt und Lebenswelt; Lo Specchio del Mito: Immaginario e Realità*, ed. A. de Angelis and S. Muth, 81–107. Wiesbaden.

Bergmann, B. 2001. "Meanwhile, Back in Italy . . . Creating Landscapes of Allusion." In *Pausanias: Travel and Memory in Roman Greece*, ed. S. E. Alcock, J. F. Cherry, and J. Elsner, 154–66. Oxford.

Bernecker, A. 1976. "Zur Tiberius-Inschrift von Saepinum." *Chiron* 6: 185–92.

Bernecker, A. 1981. *Zur Tiberius-Überlieferung der Jahre 26–37 n. Chr.* Bonn.

Bett, R. 2000. *Pyrrho, His Antecedents and His Legacy*. Oxford.

Betti, F., and Gariboldi, A. 2009. "Una gemma con ritratto di Tiberio alla corte dei Sasanidi." In *Aquileia e la glittica di età ellenistica e romana: Atti del convegno "Il fulgore delle gemme, Aquileia e la glittica di età ellenistica e romana," Aquileia, 19–20 giugno 2008*, ed. G. Sena Chiesa and E. Gagetti, 247–57. Trieste.

Bing, P. 1998. "Between Literature and the Monuments." In *Genre in Hellenistic Poetry*, ed. M. A. Harder, R. F. Regtuit, and G. C. Walker. Groningen, 21–43.

Bing, P. 2009. *The Scroll and the Marble: Studies in Reading and Reception in Hellenistic Poetry*. Ann Arbor, MI.

Birley, A. 2007. "Sejanus: His Fall." In *Corolla Cosmo Rodewald*, ed. N. V. Sekunda, 121–50. Monograph Series Akanthina 2. Gdańsk.

Birley, A. 2016. "A Letter from Momigliano to Syme, May 1967." *Politica Antica* 6: 151–64.

Boardman, J. 2002. *The Archaeology of Nostalgia: How the Greeks Re-Created Their Mythical Past*. London.

Bober, P. P. 1999. *Art, Culture, and Cuisine: Ancient and Medieval Gastronomy*. Chicago.

Bollini, M. 2001. "Gli affari di *M. Apicius Tiro*, militare e imprenditore." *Commerci e produzione in età antica nella fascia costiera fra Ravenna e Adria*, ed. C. Vernesi, 107–18. Ferrara.

Booms, D. 2010. "The *Vernae Caprenses*: Traces of Capri's Imperial History after Tiberius." *Papers of the British School at Rome* 78: 133–43.

Boschung, D. 1987. "Römische Glasphalerae mit Porträtbüsten." *Bonner Jahrbücher* 187: 193–258.

Boschung, D. 1993. "Die Bildnistypen der iulisch-claudische Kaiserfamilie." *Journal of Roman Archaeology* 6: 39–79.

Bowersock, G. W. 1965. "Some Persons in Plutarch's *Moralia*." *Classical Quarterly*, n.s., 15: 267–70.

Boyce, M., and Grenet, F. 1991. *A History of Zoroastrianism*. Vol. 3, *Zoroastrianism under Macedonian and Roman Rule*. Leiden.

Brandt, E. 1927. *Untersuchungen zum römischen Kochbuche: Versuch einer Lösung der Apicius-Frage.* Leipzig.

Bravi, A. 1998. "Tiberio e la collezione di opere d'arte dell'*Aedes Concordiae Augustae*." *Xenia Antiqua* 7: 41–82.

Breglia Pulci Doria, L. 1987. "Le Sirene: il canto, la morte, la polis." *AION (archeol)* 9: 65–98.

Breglia Pulci Doria, L. 1996. "Atene e il mare: Problemi e ipotesi sull'Athenaion di Punta della Campanella." In *Dalla Magna Grecia a Cos: Richerche di storia antica*, 37–54. Naples.

Bremmer, J. N. 2002. *The Rise and Fall of the Afterlife.* London.

Brendel, O. 1935. "Novus Mercurius." *Mitteilungen des Deutschen Archäologischen Instituts (Rom)* 50: 231–59 [German.] (= *The Visible Idea: Interpretations of Classical Art*, 26–47. Washington, DC. 1980. [English]).

Browne, T. *Urn Burial.* London, 1658.

Bruno, M., Attanasio, D., and Prochaska, W. 2012. "I marmi docimeni dei gruppi scultorei dell'antro di Tiberio a Sperlonga." *Lazio e Sabina* 8: 403–17.

Bruno, M., Attanasio, D., and Prochaska, W. 2015. "Docimium Marble Sculptures of the Grotto of Tiberius at Sperlonga." *American Journal of Archaeology* 119: 343–73.

Butrica, J. L. 2005. "Some Myths and Anomalies in the Study of Roman Sexuality." *Journal of Homosexuality* 49: 206–69.

Buxton, B. A., and Hannah, R. 2005. "*OGIS* 458, the Augustan Calendar, and the Succession." In *Studies in Latin Literature and Roman History* 12, ed. C. Deroux, 290–306. Brussels.

Buxton, R. 1994. *Imaginary Greece: The Contexts of Mythology.* Cambridge, UK.

Cameron, A. 1980. "The *Garland* of Philip." *Greek, Roman, and Byzantine Studies* 21: 43–62.

Camodeca, G. 2002. "I consoli del 43 e gli Antistii Veteres d'età claudia dalla riedizione delle Tabulae Herculanenses." *Zeitschrift für Papyrologie und Epigraphik* 140: 227–36.

Capdeville, G. 1999. "Voltumna ed altri culti del territorio volsiniese." In *Volsinii e il suo territorio: Atti del VI convegno (1998)*, 109–35. Annali della Fondazione per il Museo Claudio Faina 6. Rome.

Carey, S. 2002. "A Tradition of Adventures in the Imperial Grotto." *Greece & Rome* 49: 44–61.

Cassieri, N. 1996. "Il complesso archeologico della villa di Tiberio a Sperlonga." In *Ulisse: Il mito e la memoria*, ed. B. Andreae and C. Parisi Presicce, 270–79. Rome.

Cassieri, N. 2000. *La Grotta di Tiberio e il Museo Archeologico Nazionale Sperlonga.* Rome.

Castrén, P. 1983. *Ordo Populusque Pompeianus: Polity and Society in Roman Pompeii.* 2nd ed. Rome.

Champlin, E. 2003a. "Agamemnon at Rome: Roman Dynasts and Greek Heroes." In *Myth, History and Culture in Republican Rome: Studies in Honour of T. P. Wiseman*, ed. D. Braund and C. Gill, 295–319. Exeter.

Champlin, E. 2003b. *Nero.* Cambridge, MA.

Champlin, E. 2005. "Phaedrus the Fabulous." *Journal of Roman Studies* 95: 97–123.

Champlin, E. 2008. "Tiberius the Wise." *Historia* 57: 408–25.

Champlin, E. 2011. "Tiberius and the Heavenly Twins." *Journal of Roman Studies* 101: 73–99.

Champlin, E. 2012. "Seianus Augustus." *Chiron* 42: 361–88.

Champlin, E. 2013. "The Odyssey of Tiberius Caesar." *Classica et Mediaevalia* 64: 199–246.

Church, A. J., and W. J. Brodribb, trans. 1895. *The Annals of Tacitus.* London.

Church, A. J., and W. J., Brodribb, trans. 1905. *The History of Tacitus.* London.

Ciardiello, R. 2010. "Abitare a Capri in età romana: Il complesso residenziale di Gradola." *Università degli Studi Suor Orsola Benincasa, Annali*: 447–68.

Cichorius, C. 1904. "Zur Familiengeschichte Seians." *Hermes* 39: 461–71.

Cima, M., and La Rocca, E. 1998. *Horti Romani.* Rome.

Clarke, J. 2003. *Roman Sex: 100 BCE to AD 250.* New York.

Clayman, D. L. 2009. *Timon of Phlius: Pyrrhonism into Poetry.* Berlin.

Clouston, W. A. 1887. *Popular Tales and Fictions: Their Migrations and Transformations*. 2 vols. London.

Coarelli, F. 1988. *Il Foro Boario: Dalle origini alla fine della Repubblica*. Rome.

Coarelli, F. 2001. "Il sepolcro e la casa di Servio Tullio." *Eutopia* 1: 7–43.

Consuli, J. P., ed. and trans. 1997. *The Novellino, or One Hundred Ancient Tales*. New York.

Corbier, M. 1983. "La famille de Sejan a Volsinii: La dédicace des *Seii curatores aquae*." *Mélanges de l'École française de Rome—Antiquité* 95: 719–56.

Corbier, M. 1991. "Du nouveau sur l'*avunculus* de Sénèque?" In *Mélanges Etienne Bernand*, ed. N. Fick and J.-C. Carrière, 165–91. Paris.

Costa, C.D.N., trans. 2005. *Lucian: Selected Dialogues*. Oxford.

Crawford, M. H., ed. 1996. *Roman Statutes*. 2 vols. London.

Cristofani, M. 1995. "Dalla 'collezione' della grotta di Sperlonga." *Mitteilungen des Deutschen Archäologischen Instituts (Rom)* 102: 311–15.

Curiel, R., and Seyrig, H. 1974. "Une intaille iranienne." In *Near Eastern Numismatics, Iconography, Epigraphy, and History: Studies in Honor of George C. Miles*, ed. D. Kouymjan, 55–59. Beirut.

Curtis, R. I. 1984. "The Salted Fish Industry of Pompeii." *Archaeology* 37, no. 6: 58–59, 74–75.

Curtis, R. I. 1991. *Garum and Salsamenta: Production and Commerce in Materia Medica*. Leiden.

Curtis, R. I. 2005. "Sources for Production and Trade of Greek and Roman Processed Fish." In *Ancient Fish and Fish Production in the Black Sea Region*, ed. T. Bekker-Nielsen, 31–46. Aarhus.

Curtis, R. I. 2009a. "Umami and the Foods of Classical Antiquity." Supplement, *The American Journal of Clinical Nutrition* 90: 712S–718S.

Curtis, R. I. 2009b. "Food Processing and Preparation." In *The Oxford Handbook of Engineering and Technology in the Classical World*, ed. J. P. Oleson, 369–92. Oxford.

Dalby, A. 2003. *Food in the Ancient World from A to Z*. London.

D'Arms, J. H. 1970. *Romans on the Bay of Naples: A Social and Cultural Study of the Villas and Their Owners from 150 BCE to AD 400*. Cambridge, MA.

D'Arms, J. H. 1981. *Commerce and Social Standing in Ancient Rome*. Cambridge, MA.

D'Arms, J. H. 1999. "Performing Culture: Roman Spectacle and the Banquets of the Powerful." In *The Art of Ancient Spectacle*, ed. B. Bergmann and C. Kondoleon, 301–19. Studies in the History of Art 56, Center for Advanced Study in the Visual Arts, Symposium Papers XXXIV. Washington, DC.

De Boor, C. 1893. "Römische Kaisergeschichte in byzantinischer Fassung." *Byzantinische Zeitschrift*: 195–211.

De Caprariis, F. 2002. "Druso, Giove Feretrio e le coppe 'imperiale' di Boscoreale." *Mélanges de l'École française de Rome—Antiquité* 114: 713–37.

De Franciscis, A. n.d. [1964]. *Le statue della Grotta Azzurra nell'Isola di Capri*. Capri.

De Grummond, N., and Ridgway, B. S., eds. 2000. *From Pergamon to Sperlonga: Sculpture and Context*. Berkeley, CA.

De Jong, A. 1997. *Traditions of the Magi: Zoroastrianism in Greek and Latin Literature*. Leiden.

Degani, E. 1990. "On Greek Gastronomic Poetry I." *Alma Mater Studiorum* 3: 51–63.

Degani, E. 1994. "Problems in Greek Gastronomic Poetry: On Matro' s ΑΤΤΙΚΩΝ ΔΕΙΠΝΩΝ." In *Food in Antiquity*, ed. J. Wilkins et al., 413–28. Exeter.

Della Corte, M. 1921. "La 'villa rustica Aselli.'" *NdS* s.n.: 426–35.

Desbats, A., Lequément, R., and Liou, B. 1987. "Inscriptions peints sur amphores: Lyon et Saint-Romain-en-Gal." *Archaeonautica* 7: 141–66.

Dickie, M. 2001. *Magic and Magicians in the Greco-Roman World*. London.

Di Fazio, M. 2006. *Fondi e il suo terrritorio in eta romana: Profilo di storia economica e sociale*. Oxford.

Dohrn, T. 1977. "Helden und die Höhle." *Mitteilungen des Deutschen Archäologischen Instituts (Rom)* 84: 211–34.

Duncan-Jones, R. 1982. *The Economy of the Roman Empire: Quantitative Studies*. 2nd ed. Cambridge, UK.

Echavarren, A. 2007. *Nombres y personas en Seneca el Viejo*. Pamplona.

Ellerbrock, U., and Winkelmann, S. 2012. *Die Parther: Die Vergessene Grossmacht*. Darmstadt.

Erkell, H. 1952. *Augustus, Felicitas, Fortuna*. Göteborg.

Ermeti, A. L. 1978. "Il rilievo navale di Lindos: Definizione di hemiolia e trihemiolia." *Atti della Accademia Nazionale dei Lincei, Classe di Scienze Morali, Storiche e Filologiche: Rendiconti* 33: 175–97.

Esposito, A. 2009. "La Villa di Damecuta a Capri: Annalisi dei resti e ricostruzione dei livelli dell'edificio." *Oebalus* 4: 323–39.

Étienne, R. 1970. "A propos du 'garum sociorum.'" *Latomus* 29: 297–313.

Feddern, S. 2013. *Die Suasorien des älteren Seneca: Einleitung, Text und Kommentar*. Berlin.

Federico, E., and Miranda, E., eds. 1998. *Capri antica: Dalla preistoria alla fine dell'età romana*. Capri.

Flory, M. B. 1992. "A Note on Octavian's Felicitas." *Rheinisches Museum* 135: 283–89.

Flower, H. I. 2006. *The Art of Forgetting: Disgrace and Oblivion in Roman Political Culture*. Chapel Hill, NC.

Fraser, P. M. 1972. *Ptolemaic Alexandria*. 3 vols. Oxford.

Gabrielsen, V. 1997. *The Naval Aristocracy of Hellenistic Rhodes*. Aarhus.

Gantz, T. 1993. *Early Greek Myth. A Guide to the Literary and Artistic Sources*. Baltimore, MD.

Gasparri, C. 1979. *Aedes Concordiae Augustae*. Rome.

Gaylord, H. E. 1983. "3 (Greek Apocalypse of) Baruch." In *The Old Testament Pseudepigrapha*. Vol. 1, *Apocalyptic Literature and Testaments*, ed. J. H. Charlesworth, 653–79. Garden City, NY.

Ghedini, F. 1986. "Una pasta vitrea aquileiese e il mito d'Io nella propaganda Giulio-Claudia." *Aquileia Nostra* 57: 665–76.

Giard, J.-B. 1998. *Le Grand camée de France*. Paris.

Gibbs, L. 2002. *Aesop's Fables*. Oxford.

Ginge, B., Becker, M., and Guldager, P. 1989. "Of Roman Extraction." *Archaeology* 42, no. 4: 34–37.

Giuliani, L. 2010. *Ein Geschenk für den Kaiser: Das Geheimnis des grossen Kameo*. Munich.

Gnoli, G. 1999. "Farr(ah)." *Encyclopaedia Iranica*. Online edition. Accessed April 1, 2024. http://www.iranicaonline.org/articles/farrah.

Görler, W. 1990. "Syracusae auf dem Palatin; Syracuse, New York: Sentimentale Namengabung in Rom und später." In *Pratum Saraviense: Festgabe für Peter Steinmetz*, ed. W. Görler, and S. Kloster, 169–88. Stuttgart.

Gowers, E. 2010. "Augustus and 'Syracuse.'" *Journal of Roman Studies* 100: 69–87.

Grainger, S. 2007. "The Myth of *Apicius*." *Gastronomica* 7: 71–77.

Grainger, S. 2012. "What's in an Experiment? Roman Fish Sauce: An Experiment in Archaeology." *EXARC* 1. Accessed April 1, 2024. http://exarc.net/issue-2012-1/ea/whats-experiment-roman-fish-sauce-experiment-archaeology.

Grainger, S. 2013. "Roman Fish Sauce: Fish Bone Residues and the Practicalities of Supply." *Archaeofauna* 22: 13–28.

Grainger, S. 2014. "*Garum, Liquamen*, and *Muria*: A New Approach to the Problem of Definition." In *Fish and Ships*, ed. E. Botte and V. Leitch, 37–45. Arles.

Gregori, G. L., and Nonnis, D. 2014. "Il porto di Minturnae in età repubblicana: Il contributo delle fonti epigraphiche." In *L'Epigrafia dei Porti*, ed. C. Zaccaria, 81–122. Trieste.

Grocock, C., and Grainger, S. 2006. *Apicius: A Critical Edition with an Introduction and an English Translation of the Latin Recipe Text 'Apicius'*. Totnes.

Gros, P. 2004. Review of *Villa Jovis: Die Residenz des Tiberius auf Capri*, by C. Krause. *Journal of Roman Archaeology* 17: 593–98.

Gruen, E. 1966. "Political Prosecutions in the 90's B.C." *Historia* 15: 32–64.

Guarducci, M. 1949–51. "La Fortuna di Servio Tullio in un antichissima *sors*." *Atti della Pontificia Accademia Romana di Archeologia. Serie III, Rendiconti* 25–26: 23–32 (= *Scritti scelti sulla religione greca e romana e sul cristianesimo*, 121–30. Leiden, 1983).

Guarducci, M. 1973, "Ancora sull'antica *sors* della Fortuna e di Servio Tullio." *Atti della Accademia Nazionale dei Lincei, Classe di Scienze Morali, Storiche e Filologiche: Rendiconti* 27: 183–89 (= *Scritti scelti sulla religione greca e romana e sul cristianesimo*, 131–37. Leiden, 1983).

Guidobaldi, M. P., and Pesando, F. 1989. "Note di prosopografia minturnense." In *Minturnae*, ed. F. Coarelli and P. Arthur, 67–81. Rome.

Guldager Bilde, P., and Poulsen, B. 2008. *The Temple of Castor and Pollux*. Vol. 2, *The Finds*. Rome.

Gutsfeld, A. 2014. "L'*Histoire Auguste* et Apicius." In *Historiae Augustae Colloquium Nancinense*, ed. C. Bertrand-Dagenbach and F. Chausson, 265–77. Bari.

Guyot, P. 1980. *Eunuchen als Sklaven und Freigelassene in der griechisch-römischen Antike*. Stuttgart.

Hackl, U., Jacobs, B., and Weber, D. 2010. *Quellen zur Geschichte des Partherreiches: Textsammlung mit Übersetzungen und Konmentaren*. Vol. 1, *Prolegomena, Abkürzungen, Bibliographie, Einleitung, Indices, Karten, Tafeln*. Göttingen.

Hadzsits, G. D. 1931 "History of the Name of the Temple of Castor in the Forum." In *Classical Studies in Honor of John. C. Rolfe*, ed. G. D. Hadzsits, 101–14. Philadelphia, PA.

Håkanson, L., ed. 1989. *L. Annaeus Seneca Maior: Oratorum et Rhetorum Sententiae, Divisiones, Colores*. Leipzig.

Halleux, R., and Schamp, J. 1985. *Les Lapidaires Grecs*. Paris.

Hansen, W., trans. 1996. *Phlegon of Tralles' Book of Marvels*. Exeter.

Hansen, W. 2002. *Ariadne's Thread: A Guide to International Tales Found in Classical Literature*. Ithaca, NY.

Harris, J. R. 1906. *The Cult of the Heavenly Twins*. Cambridge, UK.

Haselberger, L., ed. 2002. *Mapping Augustan Rome*. Portsmouth, RI.

Heinemann, A. 2007. "Eine Archäologie des Störfalls: Die toten Söhne des Kaisers in der Öffentlichkeit des frühen Prinzipats." In *Römische Bilderwelten: Von der Wirklichkeit zum Bild und zurück*, ed. F. Hölscher and T. Hölscher, 41–109. Heidelberg.

Hekster, O. 2010. "Reversed Epiphanies: Roman Emperors Deserted by Gods." *Mnemosyne* 63: 601–15.

Hennig, D. 1975. *L. Aelius Seianus: Untersuchungen zur Regierung des Tiberius*. Munich.

Henning, W. B. 1945. "Sogdian Tales." *Bulletin of the School of Oriental and African Studies* 11: 465–87 (= *Selected Papers II*, 169–91. Leiden, 1977).

Hertel, D. 2013. *Das römische Herrscherbild*. Vol. 1, *Die Bildnisse des Tiberius*. Wiesbaden.

Himmelmann, N. 1995. *Sperlonga: Die homerischen Gruppen und ihre Bildquellen*. Opladen.

Hine, H. M. 2010. *Seneca, Natural Questions*. Chicago.

Holford-Strevens, L. 2004. "Capreae." *Exemplaria Classica* 8: 69–74.

Hölscher, T. 2006. "Greek Styles and Greek Art in Augustan Rome: Issues of the Present versus Records of the Past." In *Classical Pasts: The Classical Traditions of Greece and Rome*, ed. J. I. Porter, 237–69. Princeton, NJ.

Houston, G. W. 1985. "Tiberius on Capri." *Greece & Rome* 32: 179–96.

Hubaux, J., and Leroy, M. 1939. *Le Mythe du Phénix dans les littératures grecque et latine*. Liège.

Hubbard, T. K. 2003. *Homosexuality in Greece and Rome: A Sourcebook of Basic Documents*. Berkeley, CA.

Hurley, D. W. 1993. *An Historical and Historiographical Commentary on Suetonius' Life of C. Caligula*. Atlanta.

Ihm, M. 1901. "Die sogenannte Villa Jovis auf Capri und andere Suetoniana." *Hermes* 36: 287–304.

Ihm, M., ed. 1907. *C. Suetoni Tranquilli opera.* Vol.1, *De vita Caesarum libri VIII.* Editio maior. Leipzig.

Ihm, M., ed. 1908. *C. Suetoni Tranquilli opera.* Vol.1, *De vita Caesarum libri VIII.* Leipzig.

İşkan-Işik, H., Eck, W., and Engelmann, H. 2008. "Der Leuchtturm von Patara und Sex. Marcius Priscus als Statthalter der Provinz Lycia von Nero bis Vespasian." *Zeitschrift für Papyrologie und Epigraphik* 164: 91–121.

Jackson, A.V.W. 1899. *Zoroaster: The Prophet of Ancient Iran.* New York.

Jacopi, G. 1963. *L'antro di Tiberio a Sperlonga.* Rome.

Jaisle, K. 1907. *Die Dioskuren als Retter zur See bei Griechen und Römern und ihr Fortleben in christlichen Legenden.* Tübingen.

Jashemski, W. 1967. "The Caupona of Euxinus at Pompeii." *Archaeology* 20: 36–44.

Jashemski, W. 1979–93. *The Gardens of Pompeii, Herculaneum, and the Villas Destroyed by Vesuvius.* 2 vols. New Rochelle, NY.

Jeppesen, K. K. 1993. "Grand Camee de France: Sejanus Reconsidered and Confirmed." *Mitteilungen des Deutschen Archäologischen Instituts (Rom)* 100: 141–75.

Johns, C. 1982. *Sex or Symbol? Erotic Images of Greece and Rome.* London.

Johnson, J. 1933. *Excavations at Minturnae.* Vol. 2, *Inscriptions.* Part 1, *Republican Magistri.* Rome.

Johnson, J. 1935. *Excavations at Minturnae.* Vol. 1, *Monuments of the Republican Forum.* Philadelphia.

Johnson, S. 1750. *The Rambler* 21.

Kardulias, D. R. 2001. "Odysseus in Ino's Veil: Feminine Headdress and the Hero in Odyssey 5." *Transactions of the American Philological Association* 131: 23–51.

Kaster, R. A., and M. C. Nussbaum, trans. 2010. *Seneca: Anger, Mercy, Revenge.* Chicago.

Keitel, E. 1984. "Principate and Civil War in the *Annals* of Tacitus." *American Journal of Philology* 105: 306–25.

Keitel, E. 1999. "The Non-Appearance of the Phoenix at Tacitus *Annals* 6. 28." *American Journal of Philology* 120: 429–42.

Kellum, B. 1993. "The City Adorned: Programmatic Display at the *Aedes Concordiae Augustae.*" In *Between Republic and Empire: Interpretations of Augustus and his Principate,* ed. K. A. Raaflaub and M. Toher, 276–307. Berkeley, CA.

Keppie, L. 1996. "The Praetorian Guard before Sejanus." *Athenaeum* 84: 101–24.

Kneppe, A., and Wiesehöfer, J. 1983. *Friedrich Münzer: Ein Althistoriker zwischen Kaiserrreich und Nazionalsozialismus.* Bonn.

Knorr, O. 2012. "*Morbus Campanus* in Horace *Satires* 1.5.62." *Classical Quarterly* 6: 869–73.

Koortbojian, M. 2013. *The Divinization of Caesar and Augustus: Precedents, Consequences, Implications.* New York.

Krappe, A. H. 1927. "Tiberius and Thrasyllus." *American Journal of Philology* 48: 359–66.

Krappe, A. H. 1930. "Der Tod des Drusus." *Zeitschrift für deutsches Altertum und deutsche Literatur* 75: 290–96.

Krause, C. 1998. "L'edificio residenziale di Villa Iovis." In *Capri antica: Dalla preistoria alla fine dell'età romana,* ed. E. Federico and E. Miranda, 225–40. Capri.

Krause, C. 2003. *Villa Jovis: Die Residenz des Tiberius auf Capri.* Mainz.

Krause, C. 2005. *Villa Jovis: L'edificio residenziale.* Naples.

Krostenko, B. A. 2001. *Cicero, Catullus, and the Language of Social Performance.* 2001.

Kruschwitz, P. 2006. "Die Bedeutung der Caupona des *Euxinus* für die epigraphische Poesie Pompejis (und darüber hinaus)." *Rivista di Studi Pompeiani* 17: 7–13.

Kunze, C. 1996. "Zur Datierung des Laokoon und der Skylla-Gruppe aus Sperlonga." *Jahrbuch des Deutschen Archäologischen Instituts* 111: 139–223.

Kuttner, A. L. 1995. *Dynasty and Empire in the Age of Augustus: The Case of the Boscoreale Cups.* Berkeley, CA.

Kvideland, R. 2006. "Legends Translated into Behaviour." *Fabula* 47: 255–63.

L'Orange, H. P. 1964. "Odysseen I marmor: De store nye funn av hellenistisk og romersk originalskulptur i Tiberiusgrotten i Sperlonga." *Kunst og Kultur* 47: 193–228.

La Penna, A. 1979. "Il bandito e il re." *Maia* 31: 29–31.

La Penna, A. 1980. "Seiano in una tragedia di Seneca." *Orpheus* 1: 26–31 (= *Da Lucrezio a Persio: Saggi, studi, note*, 272–78. Milan, 1995).

La Rocca, E. 1994. "'Memorie di Castore': Principi come Dioscuri." In *Castores: L'immagine dei Dioscuri a Roma*, ed. L. Nista, 73–90. Rome.

La Rocca, E. 1998. "Artisti rodii negli *horti* Romani." In *Horti Romani*, by M. Cima and E. La Rocca, 203–74. Rome.

Lafon, X. 1979. "La voie littorale *Sperlonga-Gaeta-Formiae*." *MEFR* 91: 399–429.

Lafon, X. 2001. *Villa maritima: Recherches sur les villas littorales de l'Italie romaine (III⁰ siècle av. J.-C. / III⁰ siècle ap. J.-C.).* Bibliothèque des Écoles Françaises d'Athènes et de Rome 307. Rome.

Lana, I. 1952. *Vite dei Cesari.* Turin.

Lassen, H. 1995. "'The Improved Product': A Philological Investigation of a Contemporary Legend." *Contemporary Legend* 5: 1–37.

Lasserre, F. 1975. "L'élégie de l'huitre (P. Louvre inv. 7733 v⁰ inéd.)." *Quaderni Urbinati di Cultura Classica* 19: 145–76.

Lattimore, R. 1951. *The Iliad.* Chicago.

Lattimore, R. 1967. *The Odyssey of Homer.* New York.

Lauter, H. 1972. "Kunst und Landschaft—Ein Beitrag zum Rhodischen Hellenismus." *Antike Kunst* 15: 49–59.

Lavagne, H. 1988. *Operosa antra: Recherches sur la grotte à Rome de Sylla à Hadrien.* Rome.

Lersch, L. 1849. *Das sogenannte Schwert des Tiberius.* Bonn.

Levick, B. 1978. "Concordia at Rome." In *Scripta Nummaria Romana: Essays Presented to Humphrey Sutherland*, ed. R.A.G. Carson and C. M. Kraay, 217–33. London.

Levy, B. 1994. "The Date of Asinius Pollio's Proconsulship." *Jahrbuch für Numismatik und Geldgeschichte* 44: 79–89.

Linderski, J. 1974. "The Mother of Livia Augusta and the Aufidii Lurcones of the Republic." *Historia* 23: 463–80.

Linderski, J. 1988. "Julia in Regium." *Zeitschrift für Papyrologie und Epigraphik* 72: 181–200.

Lindsay, H. 1995. *Suetonius: Tiberius.* London.

Lindsay, H. 1997. "Who Was Apicius?" *Symbolae Osloenses* 72: 144–54.

Long, A. A. 1978. "Timon of Phlius: Pyrrhonist and Satirist." *Proceedings of the Cambridge Philological Society* 204: 68–91.

Long, A. A., and Sedley, D. N. 1987. *The Hellenistic Philosophers.* Vol. 1, *Translations of the Principal Sources with Philosophical Commentary.* Cambridge, UK.

Madvig, J. N. 1873. *Adversaria critica.* Vol. 2. Copenhagen.

Malkin, I. 1998. *The Returns of Odysseus: Colonization and Ethnicity.* Berkeley, CA.

Mandelbaum, A., trans. 1971. *The Aeneid of Virgil.* Berkeley, CA.

Martin-Kilcher, S. 2003. "Fish-Sauce Amphorae from the Iberian Peninsula: The Forms and Observations on Trade with the North-West Provinces." *Journal of Roman Pottery Studies* 10: 69–84.

Martin, R. H. 2001. *Tacitus: Annals V and VI.* Warminster.

Martin, R. H., and Woodman, A. J. 1989. *Tacitus: Annals Book IV.* Cambridge, UK.

Massa-Pairault, F.-H. 1999. "Mito e miti nel territorio volsiniese." In *Volsinii e il suo territorio: Atti del VI convegno (1998), Annali della Fondazione per il Museo "Claudio Faina"*, 77–108. Rome.

Mathieu, N. 1998. "Les Alfidii dans le monde romain: Étude d'un nom." *Annales de Bretagne et des pays de l'Ouest* 105: 7–33.

McGinn, T.A.J. 1998. "Caligula's Brothel on the Palatine." *Échos du monde classique* 17: 95–107.

McGinn, T.A.J. 2004. *The Economy of Prostitution in the Roman World: A Study of the Social History of the Brothel.* Ann Arbor, MI.

Megow, W .R. 1987. *Kammeen von Augustus bis Alexander Severus.* Berlin.

Meise, E. 1966. "Der Sesterz des Drusus mit den Zwillingen und die Nachfolgepläne des Tiberius." *Jahrbuch für Numismatik und Geldgeschichte* 16: 7–21.

Meulder, M, 2008. "Le future empereur Tibère et le XᵛARəNAH." *Les Etudes Classiques* 76: 175–96.

Mratschek-Halfmann, S. 1993. *Divites et Praepotentes: Reichtum und soziale Stellung in der Literatur der Prinzipatszeit.* Stuttgart.

Münzer, F. 1935. "Zu den Magistri von Minturnae." *Mitteilungen des Deutschen Archäologischen Instituts (Rom)* 50: 321–30 (= *Kleine Schriften*, ed. M. Haake and A.-C. Harders, 111–20. Stuttgart, 2012).

Nesterov, M. 2011. "Testamentum Porcelli: O smislu i svrsi jedne posnoanticke parodije." *Lucida Intervalla* 40: 103–36.

Neudecker, R. 1988. *Die Skulpturenausstattung römischer Villen in Italien.* Mainz.

Neudecker, R. 2005. "Ein göttliches Vergnügen: Zum Einkauf an sakralen Stätten im kaiserzeitlichen Rom." In *Lebenswelten: Bilder und Räumer in der römischen Stadt der Kaiserzeit,* ed. R. Neudecker and P. Zanker, 81–100. Wiesbaden.

Neumann, G. 1980. "*Lupatria* in Petron c. 37, 6 und das Problem der hybriden Bildungen." *Würzburger Jahrbücher für die Altertumswissenschaft* 6a: 173–80.

Nicolet, C. 1974. *L'Ordre équestre à l'époque républicaine (312–43 av. J.C.).* Paris.

Nilson, K. A., Persson, C. B., Sande, S., and Zahle, J. 2009. *The Temple of Castor and Pollux.* Vol. 3, *The Augustan Temple.* Rome.

Nissen, H. 1902. *Italische Landeskunde.* Vol. 2, *Die Staedte.* Berlin.

Nonnis, D. 2015. *Produzione e distribuzione nell'Italia repubblicana: Uno studio prosopografico.* Rome.

Ogilvie, R. M. 1965. *A Commentary on Livy Books 1–5.* Oxford.

Olson, S. D., and Sens, A. 1999. *Matro of Pitane and the Tradition of Epic Parody in the Fourth Century BCE.* Atlanta.

Orgitano, G. 1858. "Massa e Capri." In *Usi e costumi di Napoli e contorni,* ed F. de Bourcard, vol 2, 129–45. Naples.

Orth, W. 1973. "Ein vernachlässigtes Zeugnis zur Geschichte der romischen Provinz Creta und Cyrene." *Chiron* 3: 255–63.

Parsons, P. J. 1977. "The Oyster." *Zeitschrift für Papyrologie und Epigraphik* 24: 1–12.

Phillips, E. D. 1953. "Odysseus in Italy." *Journal of Hellenic Studies* 73: 53–67.

Pistellato, A. 2007. "Seiano, Servio Tullio e la Fortuna: Note a CIL VI 10213." In *Studi in ricordo di Fulviomario Broilo: Atti del convegno, Venezia, 14–15 ottobre 2005,* ed. G. Cresci Marrone and A. Pistellato, 487–512. Padua.

Pollini, J. 1981. "Gnaeus Domitius Ahenobarbus and the Ravenna Relief." *Mitteilungen des Deutschen Archäologischen Instituts (Rom)* 88: 117–40.

Pollini, J. 1987. *The Portraiture of Gaius and Lucius Caesar.* New York.

Poulsen, B. 1991. "The Dioscuri and Ruler Ideology." *Symbolae Osloenses* 66: 119–46.

Poulsen, B. 1992. "Cult, Myth and Politics." In *The Temple of Castor and Pollux: The Pre-Augustan Temple Phases with Related Decorative Elements,* ed. I. Nielsen and B. Poulsen, 46–53. Rome.

Rice, E. E. 1986. "Prosopographika Rhodiaka." *Annual of the British School at Athens* 81: 209–50.

Ridgway, B. S. 2000. "The Sperlonga Sculptures: The Current State of Research." In *From Pergamon to Sperlonga: Sculpture and Context,* ed. N. de Grummond and B. S. Ridgway, 78–91. Berkeley, CA.

Ridley, R. T. 1975. "The Enigma of Servius Tullius." *Klio* 57: 147–77.

Robert, J., and Robert, L. 1950. "Inscriptions de l'Hellespont et de la Propontide." *Hellenica* 9: 78–97.

Rose, C. B. 1997. *Dynastic Commemoration and Imperial Portraiture in the Julio-Claudian Period.* Cambridge, UK.

Rose, C. B. 2005. "The Parthians in Augustan Rome." *American Journal of Archaeology* 109: 21–75.

Rossetti, L., and Furiani, P. L. 1993. "Rodi." In *Lo spazio letterario della Grecia antica.* Vol. 1, *La produzione e la circolazione del testo.* Part 2, *L'ellenismo,* ed. G. Cambiano, L. Canfora, and D. Lanza, 657–715. Rome.

Sage, M. 1990. "Tacitus' Historical Works: A Survey and Appraisal." *Aufstieg und Niedergang der römischen Welt,* part II, 33, no. 2: 851–1030, 1629–47.

Salza Prina Ricotti, E. 2006. "Le grotte di Polifemo." *Palladio* 19: 5–22.

Sauron, G. 2019. "The Architectural Representation of the 'Kosmos' from Varro to Hadrian." In *Cosmos in the Ancient World,* ed. P. S. Horky, 232–46. Cambridge, UK.

Scardozzi, G. 2007. "Le anfore di *M. Tuccius Galeo* dalla valle del Liris." In *Spigolature aquinati: Studi storico-archeologici su Aquino e il suo territorio,* ed. A. Nicosia and G. Ceraudo, 59–76. Aquino.

Schade, G. 1999. *Lykophrons "Odyssee": "Alexandra" 648–819.* Berlin.

Scheidel, W., and Friesen, S. J. 2009. "The Size of the Economy and the Distribution of Income in the Roman Empire." *Journal of Roman Studies* 99: 61–91.

Schmid, S. 2003. "Wieder einmal Sperlonga: Trink- und andere Geschichten in Latium." *Numismatica e Antichità Classiche* 32: 199–225.

Schwartz, E. 1899. "Cassius Dio." *RE* 3: 1684–722 (= *Griechische Geschichtschreiber,* 394–450. Leipzig, 1959).

Scott, K. 1930a. "Drusus, Nicknamed 'Castor.'" *Classical Philology* 25: 155–61.

Scott, K. 1930b. "The Dioscuri and the Imperial Cult." *Classical Philology* 25: 379–80.

Scott, K. 1931. "The Significance of Statues in Precious Metals in Emperor Worship." *Transactions and Proceedings of the American Philological Association* 62: 101–23.

Scott, K. 1932. "Tiberius' Refusal of the Title 'Augustus.'" *Classical Philology* 27: 43–50.

Seyrig, H. 1968. "Un portrait de Tibère." *Review numismatique* 10: 175–78.

Shabazi, A. 1980. "An Achaemenid Symbol II: Farnah 'God Given Fortune' Symbolised." *Archaeologische Mitteilungen aus Iran* 13: 119–47.

Shero, L. R. 1929. "Lucilius's *Cena Rustica.*" *American Journal of Philology* 50: 64–70.

Skjærvø, P. O. 2011. *The Spirit of Zoroastrianism.* New Haven, CT.

Slavazzi, F. 2015–16. "La villa della Grotta a Sperlonga: Nuove indagini." *Atti della Pontificia Accademia Romana di Archeologia: Serie III, Rendiconti,* 88: 203–20.

Slotki, J. J., trans. 1939. *Midrash Rabbah: Leviticus.* London.

Smallwood, E. M., ed. and trans. 1961. *Philonis Alexandrini "Legatio ad Gaium".* Leiden.

Smith, R.R.R. 1991. Review of *Laokoon und die Gründung Roms,* by B. Andreae. *Gnomon* 63: 351–58.

Smith, R.R.R. 2002. "The Use of Images: Visual History and Ancient History." In *Classics in Progress: Essays on Ancient Greece and Rome,* ed. T. P. Wiseman, 59–102. London.

Solin, H. 1968. "Pompeiana." *Epigraphica* 30: 104–25.

Spannagel, M. 1999. *Exemplaria Principis: Untersuchungen zu Enstehung und Ausstattung des Augustusforums.* Heidelberg.

Staedler, E. 1942. "Zu den 29 neu aufgefundenen Inschriftstelen von Minturno." *Hermes* 77: 149–96.

Stefani, G. 1998. "Boscoreale: La villa di *Asellius* e le sue pitture." *Rivista di Studi Pompeiani* 9: 41–62.

Stein-Hölkeskamp, E., and Hölkeskamp, K.-J., eds. 2006. *Erinnerungsorte der Antike: Die römische Welt.* Munich.

Steinby, E. M., ed. 1989–2012. *Lacus Iuturnae*. 2 vols. Rome.

Stewart, A. F. 1977. "To Entertain an Emperor: Sperlonga, Laokoon and Tiberius at the Dinner-Table." *Journal of Roman Studies* 67: 76–90.

Strazzulla, M. J. 1993. "Fortuna etrusca o Fortuna romana: Due cicli figurativi a confronto (Roma, via S. Gregorio e Bolsena)." *Ostraka* 2, no. 2: 317–49.

Stylow, A. U. 1977. "Noch einmal zu der Tiberius-Inschrift von Saepinum." *Chiron* 7: 487–91.

Sumi, G. S. 2009. "Monuments and Memory: The Aedes Castoris in the Formation of Augustan Ideology." *Classical Quarterly* 59: 167–89.

Sumner, G. V. 1961. "Curtius Rufus and the *Historiae Alexandri*." *Journal of the Australasian Universities Language and Literature Association* 15: 30–39.

Sumner, G. V. 1967. "Germanicus and Drusus Caesar." *Latomus* 26: 413–35.

Susemihl, F. 1891. *Geschichte der griechischen Literatur in der Alexandrinerzeit*. Vol. 1. Leipzig.

Suspène, A. 2004. "Tiberius Claudianus contre Agrippa Postumus: Autour de la dédicace du temple des Dioscures." *Revue de Philologie* 75: 99–124.

Swan, P. M. 1976. "A Consular Epicurean under the Early Principate." *Phoenix* 30: 54–60.

Swan, P. M. 2004. *The Augustan Succession: An Historical Commentary on Cassius Dio's Roman History, Books 55–56 (9 BCE–A.D. 14)*. Oxford.

Syme, R. 1956. "Seianus on the Aventine." *Hermes* 84: 257–66 (= *Roman Papers*, vol. 1, 305–14. Oxford, 1979).

Syme, R. 1958. *Tacitus*. 2 vols. Oxford.

Syme, R. 1961. "Who was Vedius Pollio?" *Journal of Roman Studies* 51: 23–30 (= *Roman Papers*, vol. 2, 518–29. Oxford, 1979).

Syme, R. 1983. "The Year 33 in Tacitus and Dio." *Athenaeum* 61: 3–23 (= *Roman Papers*, vol. 4, 223–44).

Syme, R. 1986a. *The Augustan Aristocracy*. Oxford.

Syme, R. 1986b. "Three Ambivii." *Classical Quarterly* 36: 271–76 (= *Roman Papers*, vol. 5, 622–29. Oxford, 1988).

Syme, R. 1989. "Diet on Capri." *Athenaeum* 77: 261–72 (= *Roman Papers*, vol. 6, 409–20. Oxford, 1991).

Tammisto, A. 1986. "Phoenix Felix et Tu: Remarks on the Representation of the Phoenix in Roman Art." *Arctos* 20: 171–225.

Tarn, W. W. 1911. "Navarch and Nesiarch." *Journal of Hellenic Studies* 31: 151–59.

Tarrant, H. 1993. *Thrasyllan Platonism*. Ithaca, NY.

Taylor, R. 1997. "Two Pathic Subcultures in Ancient Rome." *Journal of the History of Sexuality* 7: 319–71.

Teuffel, W. 1871. "Vespae iudicium coci et pistoris iudice Vulcano." *Rheinisches Museum* 26: 341–42.

Thiersch, H. 1909. *Pharos: Antike Islam und Occident; Ein Beitrag zur Architekturgeschichte*. Berlin.

Thomas, R. F. 1982. *Lands and Peoples in Roman Poetry: The Ethnographical Tradition*. Cambridge Philological Society, supplementary vol. 7. Cambridge.

Thomas, R. F., ed. 2011. *Horace: Odes, Book IV, and Carmen Saeculare*. Cambridge, UK.

Thompson, S. 1955–58. *Motif-Index of Folk-Literature: A Classification of Narrative Elements in Folktales, Ballads, Myths, Fables, Mediaeval Romances, Exempla, Fabliaux, Jest-Books, and Local Legends*. 6 vols. Bloomington, IN.

Torelli, M. 2006. "Tarquitius Priscus *haruspex* di Tiberio e il *laudabilis puer* Aurelius: Due nuovi personaggi della storia di Tarquinia." In *Archeologia in Etruria meridionale. Atti delle giornate di studio in ricordo di Mario Moretti, Civita Castellana, 14–15 novembre 2003*, ed. M. Pandolfini Angeletti, 249–86. Rome.

Torelli, M. 2011. "The *Haruspices* of the Emperor: Tarquitius Priscus and Sejanus' Conspiracy." In *Priests and the State in the Roman World*, ed. J. H. Richardson and F. Santangelo, 137–59. Stuttgart.

Tosi, R. 2017. *Dizionario delle sentenze latine e greche*. Milan.

Townend, G. 1962. "The Trial of Aemilia Lepida in A.D. 20." *Latomus* 21: 484–93.

Turner, A. 1943. "A Vergilian Anecdote in Suetonius and Dio." *Classica Philology* 38: 261.

van den Broek, R. 1972. *The Myth of the Phoenix according to Classical and Early Christian Traditions*. Leiden.

van den Hout, M.P.J. 1999. *A Commentary on the Letters of M. Cornelius Fronto*. Leiden.

van Dijk, J.G.M. 1993. "Fables in Ancient Historiography." *Bestia* 5: 27–41.

van Dijk, J.G.M. 1994. "*Addenda ad Aesopica*: Unnoticed and Neglected Themes and Variations of Greek and Latin Fables." *Bestia* 6: 95–135.

Varner, E. 2004. *Mutilation and Transformation: Damnatio Memoriae and Roman Imperial Portraiture*. Leiden.

Vernole, V. E. 2002. *Servius Tullius*. Rome.

Vetter, E. 1953. *Handbuch der italischen Dialekte*. Vol. 1, *Texte mit Erklärung, Glossen, Wörterverzeichnis*. Heidelberg.

Vigourt, A. 2001. *Les Présages impériaux d'Auguste à Domitien*. Paris.

Viscogliosi, A. 1996. "*Antra Cyclopis*: Osservazioni su una tipologia di *coenatio*." In *Ulisse: Il mito e la memoria*, ed. B. Andreae and C. Parisi Presicce, 252–69. Rome.

Vogt, W. 1975. *C. Suetonius Tranquillus: Vita Tiberii Kommentar*. Würzburg.

Vollenweider, M.-L., and Avisseau-Broustet, M. 2003. *Camées et intailles*. Vol. 2. *Les portraits romains du Cabinet des médailles: Catalogue raisonné*. Paris.

von Hesberg, H., and Panciera, S. 1994. *Das Mausoleum von Augustus: Der Bau und seine Inschriften*. Munich.

Vorberg, G. 1928–32. *Glossarium eroticum*. Stuttgart.

Walde, E. 2009. "Eine laurentische Sau in Sperlonga?" In *AIAKEION Beiträge zur klassischen Altertumswissenschaft zu Ehren von Florens Felten*, ed. C. Reinholdt, P. Schreiber, and W. Wohlmayr, 171–77. Vienna.

Walker, S., and Burnett, A. 1981. "Augustus and Tiberius on the 'Sword of Tiberius.'" In *Augustus: Handlist of the Exhibition and Supplementary Studies*, by S. Walker and A. Burnett, 49–55. London.

Walla, M. 1969. *De Vogel Phoenix in der antiken Literatur und der Dichtung des Laktanz*. Vienna.

Wardle, D. 1994. *Suetonius' Life of Caligula*. Brussels.

Wardle, D. 2002. "The Heroism and Heroisation of Tiberius: Valerius Maximus and his Emperor." In *Hommages à Carl Deroux*, ed. P. Defosse, 433–40. Vol. 2. Brussels.

Watt, W. S. 1991. Review of *L. Annaeus Seneca Maior: Oratorum et Rhetorum Sententiae, Divisiones, Colores*, by L. Håkanson 1989. *Gnomon* 63: 314–17.

Weinstock, S. 1971. *Divus Julius*. Oxford.

Weis, H. A. 2000. "Odysseus at Sperlonga: Hellenistic Hero or Roman Heroic Foil?" In *From Pergamon to Sperlonga: Sculpture and Context*, ed. N. de Grummond and B. S. Ridgway, 111–65. Berkeley, CA.

Wellmann, M. 1888. "Dorion." *Hermes* 23: 179–93.

Wikén, E. 1937. *Die Kunde der Hellenen von dem Lande und den Völkern der Apenninhalbinsel bis 300 v. Chr*. Lund.

Wilkins, J., and Hill, S., eds. 2011. *Archestratus: Fragments from the Life of Luxury*. 2nd ed. Totnes.

Williams R. D., ed. 1973. *Virgil: Aeneid Books VII–XII*. London.

Winterbottom, M., ed. 1974. *Seneca the Elder: Controversiae, Suasoriae*. 2 vols. Cambridge, MA.

Wiseman, T. P. 1963. "Teidia's Husband." *Latomus* 22: 87–90 (= *Roman Studies: Literary and Historical*, 1–5 [with addenda p. 373]. Liverpool, 1987).

Wiseman, T. P. 1974. "Legendary Genealogies in Late-Republican Rome." *Greece & Rome* 21: 153–64.

Wiseman, T. P. 1995. *Remus: A Roman Myth*. Cambridge, UK.

Wistrand, E. 1987. *Felicitas Imperatoria*. Göteborg.

Woodman, A. J. 1977. *Velleius Paterculus*. Vol. 1, *The Tiberian Narrative (2.94–131)*. Cambridge, UK.

Woodman, A. J. 1988. "History and Alternative Histories." In *Rhetoric in Classical Historiography*, 160–96. London.

Wulf-Rheidt, U. 2004. Review of *Villa Jovis: Die Residenz des Tiberius auf Capri*, by C. Krause. *Göttinger Forum für Altertumswissenschaft* 7: 1063–69.

Yardley, J. C., trans. 2008. *The Annals: The Reigns of Tiberius, Claudius, and Nero*. Oxford.

Yavetz, Z. 1998. "Seianus and the Plebs: A Note." *Chiron* 28: 187–91.

Yegül, F. 1996. "The Thermo-Mineral Complex at Baiae and *De Balneis Puteolanis*." *Art Bulletin* 78: 137–61.

Zanker, P. 1972. *Forum Romanum: Die Neugestaltung unter Augustus*. Tübingen.

Zerbinati, E. 1986. "Produzione laterizia e sua diffusione nel territorio polesano ad occidente di Adria in età romana." In *L'antico polesine: Testimonianze archeologiche e paleoambientali: Catalogo delle esposizioni di Adria e di Rovigo, Febbraio-Novembre 1986*, ed. S. Bonomi, 259–310. Adria.

Zieske, L. 1972. *Felicitas: Eine Wortuntersuchung*. Hamburg.

INDEX

This index lists Roman males according to the names used in this book, not their formal nomenclature or titles, with brief additions in parentheses to distinguish homonyms: thus "Tiberius (emperor)" (not "Claudius Nero, Tiberius" or "Iulius Caesar Augustus, Tiberius") and "Drusus (brother of the emperor Tiberius)" (not "Claudius Drusus, Decimus" or "Claudius Drusus, Nero").

A NOTE ON THE TYPE

This book has been composed in Arno, an Old-style serif typeface in the classic Venetian tradition, designed by Robert Slimbach at Adobe.